A Philosophy of Hope

Moral Philosophy and Moral Theology Series
Romanus Cessario, O.P., and Joseph Koterski, S.J., series editors

1. Martin Rhonheimer, *Natural Law and Practical Reason: A Thomist View of Moral Autonomy.* Trans. by Gerald Marlsbary.
2. Anton Losinger, *The Anthropological Turn: The Human Orientation of the Theology of Karl Rahner.* Trans. with a foreword by Daniel O. Dahlstrom.
3. Thomas S. Hibbs, *Virtue's Splendor: Wisdom, Prudence, and the Human Good.*

A Philosophy of Hope

JOSEF PIEPER
AND THE CONTEMPORARY
DEBATE ON HOPE

BERNARD N. SCHUMACHER

Translated by D. C. Schindler

FORDHAM UNIVERSITY PRESS
New York
2003

Moral Philosophy and Moral Theology Series, No. 4
ISSN 1527-523X

Library of Congress Cataloging-in-Publication Data

Schumacher, Bernard N.
    [Philosophie de l'espérance. English]
    A philosophy of hope : Josef Pieper and the contemporary debate on
hope/Bernard N. Schumacher ; translated by D.C. Schindler.—1st
English language ed.
        p. cm.—(Moral philosophy and moral theology series, ISSN
1527–523X ; no. 4)
Includes bibliographical references (p. 259) and index.
    ISBN 0-8232-2281-0
    1. Pieper, Josef, 1904– 2. Hope. I. Title. II. Moral philosophy and
moral theology ; no. 4.
B3323.P434S3813 2003
128–dc21   2003011112

Printed in the United States of America
07 06 05 04 03   5 4 3 2 1
First English language edition

Translated from the French:
*Une philosophie de l'espérance: La pensée de Josef Pieper dans le contexte du
débat contemporain sur l'espérance.* Paris/Fribourg: Cerf/Editions Universitaires
Fribourg Suisse, 2000.

To my parents and Myriam

CONTENTS

CONTENTS

ACKNOWLEDGMENTS

No man is an island, and no work is the fruit of a solitary effort. If I live in hope and if I have been able to write on the subject, it is due largely to the support and collaboration of a number of people and institutions. To them I owe my profound gratitude.

I am first of all deeply thankful to my wife, Michele Marie, whose excellent comments, numerous and incisive criticisms and arguments, and close reading of the text were an enormous help in the revision of the work. The long and stimulating discussions we had in Tübingen greatly shaped this book. To her I owe much gratitude, not only for her loving and encouraging support, but also and especially for our three beautiful girls, Myriam, Sophia, and Teresa.

Secondly, I thank Evandro Agazzi for his encouragement, suggestions, and comments on the present study, as well as for his generosity during my assistantship under his direction. I thank Ruedi Imbach for his valuable comments and advice and for his generous availability. To Romanus Cessario and Joseph Koterski I extend my special thanks for their invitation to publish this study in their series.

Josef Pieper remains a luminous presence in my memory. The discussions I shared with him on several occasions in Münster helped me clarify certain key points of his thought. I also express my appreciation to Berthold Wald, the editor of Pieper's *Werke,* as well as to the Josef Pieper archives (Marbach am Neckar) and the Ernst Bloch archives (Ludwigshafen).

This work was made possible through the financial aid of a grant from the Swiss National Scientific Research fund, which financed my stay as a visiting scholar in 1993–94 at the Catholic University of America (Washington, D.C.) and the University of Notre Dame (Indiana), where much of this work was written. I am grateful to Alasdair MacIntyre, John Jenkins, Ralph McInerny, Robert Sokolowski, and Jude Dougherty for the welcome they extended and for their comments on particular points and chapters from this book. I am particularly grateful to Gregory Reichberg, Kenneth Schmitz, Josef Godfrey, Jean-Yves Lacoste, and Thomas De Koninck for their patient reading of the manuscript and for their judicious and precise suggestions, criticisms, and comments. I am extremely grateful to D. C. Schindler for his excellent translation and for the outstanding kindness he has shown me throughout the months that we worked together. I thank also Juan Francesco Franck who spent long hours in the library looking up the English translations of references for the footnotes and the quotations, and who prepared the index. Finally, I owe a large debt of gratitude to my parents, and most especially to my mother who provided constant support throughout the long period of my study. This book is dedicated to them and to my first child, Myriam.

INTRODUCTION

The theme of human hope has been put to a severe test at the end of the millennium, a period characterized by a certain pessimism and accompanied by a growing uncertainty about the future of human progress and the dignity of the human person. We need think only of the tragedies scattered throughout the twentieth century: Auschwitz, Hiroshima, Rwanda, the former Yugoslavia, and so on. In an age of nuclear weaponry, we find it difficult to imagine how those in the past could seriously affirm that mankind was making steady and confident progress toward a better state, and how they did not even consider the possibility that the opposite could be the case. Indeed, Lady Hope enjoyed a certain success once she donned the optimistic garb of the eighteenth- and nineteenth-century philosophers of progress. In particular, she was viewed as the fundamental impetus of the historical dynamism of mankind in its march toward what Kant calls the "ethical community," or what Bloch calls the "New Jerusalem." Toward the end of the nineteenth century, this hope—that is, optimism about progress toward improvement, which Turgot, Condorcet, Kant, Marx, and Comte all predicted—began to give way to the rise of the nihilism expressed by Nietzsche, and later to the contemporary current of nihilistic existentialism. Hope was treated as an illusion, a vice, a poisoned gift, a curse that the gods had inflicted upon the human being. It was described as a promise that could not be kept, a beautiful idea bereft of any concrete reality, a folly, an opiate, and even as the greatest enemy, the worst of evils. Certain thinkers have even gone so far as to affirm that Nietzschean nihilism is the epoch-defining event of the beginning of the millennium, which marks the culmination of a universal movement.[1]

This rise of despair has provoked, in turn, a reaction in defense of the primacy of hope, which occupies a decisive place at the dawning of the third millennium. This defense focuses not only, as the philosophers of progress did, on the relation between hope and the historical development of the human species with a view to the end of this development, but also on the concrete human individual in relation to his future, which is the aspect the ancients considered in their treatment. Indeed, the majority of contemporary philosophers who deal with this subject maintain that the act and the object of hope are not only collective, but also personal.

Nevertheless, the theme of hope is not a uniquely modern concern; it has been the focus of many studies over the course of Western history. Already in ancient Greece, one finds various attempts to define it in different historical periods, distinguishing it, for example, from expectation and from desire, and integrating trust into its meaning.[2] The Fathers of the Church and the Scholastics approach it from a theological perspective,[3] while some also analyze hope (*espoir*) as a passion. Though Descartes, Spinoza, Leibniz, Hobbes, and Locke devote little attention to the subject, hope reemerges once again as a theme in modern thought in the writings of Kant, for whom it constitutes one of the four principal questions to which the philosopher has an obligation to respond, and also represents a concern for Hume, Mill, and Kierkegaard.

Nevertheless, Bloch was not altogether incorrect in asserting that the theme of hope was "as unexplored as the Antarctic"[4] before the 1956 publication of his *The Principle of Hope*. Indeed, in the history of philosophy, hope has never been a dominant theme; it was generally treated, if at all, "incidentally," just as it continues to be treated today among the majority of philosophers. And yet, given the urgency of the contemporary historical situation, which manages too often to drive people to despair, it is surprising that such a topic would not have provoked more reflection in philosophy, which has for its part too often and too quickly abandoned the theme to sociology, psychology, or theology. But hope is philosophically significant by virtue of the fact that it constitutes a fundamental and central mode of human existence; it is the principal driving force of the historical-temporal human being *in via*. A human being without hope is like a walking corpse, which is both physiologically and metaphysically absurd.

In fact, there are a number of different twentieth-century philosophical analyses of human hope that appeared long before Bloch's remarkable encyclopedic reflection. The subject of human hope has been approached from various perspectives: ethics, anthropology, phenomenology, politics, and metaphysics. Some develop an ontology of *not-yet-being* as the foundation undergirding the act of hope; some work out a more clearly defined understanding of the nature of hope by distinguishing it from desire and expectation; some discuss its status as a passion and as a virtue, interpreting it both at the personal and at the communal level. The contemporary philosophical discussion of hope stretches out over several decades and involves various cultures: in Germany, we have the studies by Zimara (1933), Pieper (1935, 1968), Middendorf (1937), Grentrup (1948), Bollnow (1955), Bloch (1956), Fahrenbach (1956), and Edmaier (1968); in France, we have the writings of Landsberg (1937), Le Senne (1942), Marcel (1944), and Minkowski (1959); in Spain, the work of Lain Entralgo (1956); and in the English-speaking world, there are the most recent studies by Fitzgerald (1979), Muyskens (1979), Dauenhauer (1986), Godfrey (1987), Sutherland (1989), Fendt (1990), and Day (1991).

The purpose of the present study is, on the one hand, to come to an understanding of the German philosopher Josef Pieper's view of hope, and, on the other hand, to set this view into dialogue with other contemporary understandings. To achieve this purpose, I did not restrict myself to the works Pieper explicitly devoted to hope alone; instead, I took a more general approach, and considered his oeuvre as a whole. This has allowed me better to situate Pieper's understanding of hope within the broader context of his thought and to bring out certain points or underlying ontological and anthropological foundations, which the philosopher himself did not work out in detail in the works specifically devoted to hope. Indeed, an adequate grasp of his position requires a deep and comprehensive reading of all of his writings. Moreover, on occasion I had to read between the lines, which was in many cases the last resort for grasping the most profound dimension of his thinking. "What is self-evident is not discussed"[5] is Pieper's watchword; we can complement this observation with Heidegger's affirmation that the doctrine of any particular philosopher lies in the "unsaid in what is said."[6] An interpretation of a text ought also to bring out what the author sought to express without saying it explicitly; it ought to lay bare the fundamental intuitions that underlie his thought and run through everything he does in fact say.

In order to illuminate both the originality and the controversial aspects of Pieper's position on the various issues concerning hope, I have set it in dialogue with those contemporary philosophers who have treated the topic since the beginning of the twentieth century. I did not limit myself to the authors whom Pieper himself discussed and from whom he drew inspiration—for example, Gabriel Marcel and Ernst Bloch—but I also included authors to whom he did not refer, and who belong to various philosophical schools spanning several decades. In addition to the existentialist–neo-Marxist debate, I also took account of phenomenological, analytic, and Anglo-Saxon analyses, as well as different psychological, medical, or psychiatric studies insofar as it was possible. This method not only allowed me better to situate Pieper's thought within the heart of the philosophy of the twentieth century—emphasizing not only his unique contribution, but also his inadequacies and omissions—but also better to understand the nature of human hope in a systematic way.

With Marcel and Bloch, Pieper contributed to the rediscovery of the ontological foundation of human hope; he articulated an ontology of *not-yet-being,* which is accompanied by an eschatological dimension expressing the internal structure of human nature ordered toward a future. He thus represents in a certain way one of the pioneers among the twentieth-century philosophers of hope in the rediscovery, not only of the importance of the ontological concept of human existence *in via* (for which he draws inspiration as much from Thomas Aquinas and Przywara as from Heidegger) for understanding hope, but also of the way to approach it. To be sure, several books and articles on hope were already in existence before the appearance of his first work devoted to the theme, published in 1935 and showing signs of his youth. But these were either theological, or they did not show the intrinsic connection between an ontology of *not-yet-being* and hope.

It is thus historically false to claim that Bloch and Marcel were alone responsible for reinstating hope as a philosophical problem, or to maintain that, to date, the philosophical problem of hope has not yet been dealt with, as Bloch does with some presumption in the preface to his *The Principle of Hope,* ignoring all of the philosophies of hope that open up with transcendence toward the transcendent. Nevertheless, it is true that Pieper, inspired by Marcel and provoked by Bloch, completes and deepens his philosophy of hope only after the Second World War, when he enters into a fruitful discussion with contemporary philosophers of hope and of the absurd.

In the world of philosophy, Pieper also represents something of a pioneer in the way he understands the virtues and their importance for the total fulfillment of the person, an approach that became fashionable only in the 1980s, with the appearance of MacIntyre's celebrated book, *After Virtue*. Just after the war, Pieper also developed a theory of leisure and celebration, which for him is intrinsically connected to the distinction between the attitude of *theoria* and that of *praxis*. His notion of *theoria* also provides the foundation for his understanding of human hope, insofar as hope is unable to achieve its object simply on the basis of the individual's own resources, but also requires a gift from the other.

Disturbed by the shadows of history and the existential shocks of Auschwitz and Hiroshima, in which the human being became, for the first time in history, as Anders remarks, "the master of the apocalypse,"[7] Pieper looks for a foundation for a philosophy of hope. He adopts a position that is not only opposed to the nihilists who proclaim that the Nothing is better than being and that existence is an imperfection and absurdity, but also to the social religions that in the name of science or of *praxis* promise perfect and endless happiness, the construction of the "New Jerusalem" on earth.

> This is one of the reasons why today [in 1950], at a time of temptations to despair, it may appear necessary to bring into view a notion of the End in which an utterly realistic freedom from illusion not only does not contradict hope but in which the one serves to confirm and corroborate the other.[8]

Hope thus constitutes one of the cornerstones of Pieper's philosophy; and yet, of the many works that have been published on his philosophy, not one of them has yet taken up this theme as its central focus. One finds studies on goodness and reality,[9] on leisure and celebration,[10] on the university,[11] on the virtues in general,[12] on philosophy and poetry,[13] on truth,[14] or even on anthropology.[15] Moreover, there have not been any works to date that have tried to take account of and synthesize the various currents of contemporary thought on the theme of hope. The great majority of studies focus on one or two authors (Bloch or Marcel, to mention only the two most important), or else they treat only the studies published in a particular language, or remain within a particular school of thought (existentialism, neo-Marxism, phenomenology, neo-Thomism, or analytic philosophy).

The first chapter of the present study analyzes the ontological foundations of a philosophy of hope; chapters two through five treat the nature, the characteristics, the object, the content, the reason, and the justification of human hope, as well as contrasting attitudes; finally, the sixth chapter explores the relationship between hope and history in light of the ultimate end of history.

Chapter one lays out the ontological and anthropological foundations undergirding a philosophy of hope. On the basis of the distinction between *res naturalis* and *res artificialis,* on the one hand, and between a metaphysics of *theoria* and a metaphysics of *praxis,* on the other, it is possible to inquire into the origin of human nature, as Sartre and Pieper have done, and more particularly, to ask whether this nature is characterized by a fully autonomous and a priori freedom or whether by a freedom inscribed within a natural inclination toward the complete (determinable) fulfillment of the individual. The two authors share an anthropology in which the human being is essentially projected, either freely (according to Sartre) or in a manner that is both free and determinate (according to Pieper), toward the *future,* the place wherein the human being realizes his possibilities. The human being is fundamentally possibility or project. He hopes to become or to possess what he has himself freely projected into the future, or that toward which he has been projected. This inclination and openness toward the future of possibilities, which form the basis of a philosophy of hope, have their roots in an ontology of *not-yet-being* (Heidegger, Bloch, Pieper), which is in turn rooted in Heidegger's notion of the *existentiell* temporality of Dasein. According to Pieper and Bloch, the human being hopes to be able to pass from the state of *not-yet-being,* that is, of *minimal-being* to the state of *being-more* or *being-fulfilled.* Human hope is intrinsically linked to the itinerant condition of human existence, which thus always implies existential uncertainty.

Once the anthropological and ontological foundations of an analysis of human hope have been outlined, I offer in the second chapter a definition of the act of hope by indicating its constitutive properties, as well as by integrating the diverse perspectives of contemporary philosophers of hope. Here I raise the question, to what extent is human hope—which is an intentional movement toward a good, difficult, possible, and future object—distinct from desire and expectation, and to what extent does it necessarily presuppose an act of belief accompanied by an act of trust? Next, I ask whether uncertainty regarding the obtainment of the object hoped for is an essential component of the act of hope. In addition to the analysis of the elements of fear and love that accompany hope, and the distinction drawn between hope and optimism, I show that the structure of hope is inherent both to the philosophical act and to reason.

The distinction between hope as *espoir,* or ordinary hope, and hope as *espérance,* or fundamental hope, which is affirmed by the great majority of authors, forms the theme of chapter three. Taking my bearings from limit-situations, such as terminal illness, suicide, martyrdom, and being condemned to death, which can be the occasion for the manifestation of fundamental hope, I suggest that the object of hope as *espoir* is interchangeable, that is, it changes constantly according to circumstances, while the object of fundamental hope is by nature unique and identical. While the majority of authors (whether philosophers, doctors, psychologists, or psychiatrists) qualify the object of fundamental hope in different ways, it can be defined as the actualization and complete fulfillment of the person. Hope as *espoir* is articulated through an analysis of the relation between it and the passions (Thomas Aquinas, Hume, and Bloch), which can be accompanied by moral virtues, such as magnanimity and humility. Fundamental hope can be considered either as one of Dasein's first principles, or as a virtue. It is appropriate to raise the question at this point whether the virtue of hope must be understood only as a theological virtue, or, by contrast, whether there also exists a natural virtue of fundamental hope. The discussion of this controversial question debated among the philosophers of hope will be followed by a description of the relationship between ordinary hope and fundamental hope as one of dependence and anteriority.

An exploration of human hope entails, moreover, a discussion of attitudes that form a contrast with it: namely, presumption and despair. Chapter four will focus its discussion primarily on the attitude of despair, that is, the expectation of nonfulfillment, which is commonly described as anticipated death, or a rupture with existence and coming-to-be. Despair has its roots in the boredom of the Moderns and in the *acedia* of the Ancients, attitudes that are captured well in the notions of *verbositas* and *curiositas,* which Heidegger vividly described in his analysis of average-everydayness. In this chapter, despair is then related to the totalitarian state of work and to leisure. The attitude of despair raises the delicate problem of the existence of a total and absolute despair with respect to the fundamental hope that is constitutive of human Dasein.

I will then turn my attention in the fifth chapter to one of the essential problems of a philosophy of hope: death, the "anti-utopia," as Bloch describes it, which brutally interrupts the projection of possibilities into the *future*. Is human Dasein a *being-toward-death* or a *being-toward-hope?* In order to answer this question, we will have to examine the reason for the fundamental hope that sustains those people who find themselves in limit-situations. In this context, I will primarily set the positions of Pieper and Bloch into dialogue with one another with respect to the arguments they set forth in their attempt to overcome the anti-utopia of death. In doing so, I will bring out both their common points and their basic divergence, at the same time taking into account once again the position of contemporary philosophers of hope in today's world.

The sixth and final chapter is devoted to the relationship between human hope and history or, more specifically, the end of time. A philosophy of hope is not concerned solely with the future of the personal destiny of the historical-temporal individual, but it must at the same time—particularly after Hiroshima—formulate a position with respect to the possibility of the self-destruction of the human race. This collective death represents a correlate to personal death. While it is possible to affirm, as Bloch does, a transcendence of personal death, insofar as man's historical progress continues essentially on its march toward the "new, earthly Jerusalem," and thus in a certain way to safeguard the principle of hope, the possibility of global self-destruction raises the question of the anti-utopia of death in a new way. There is no consciousness greater than that of the human race as a whole that would enable us to transcend this "second death." Thus, what position do we take with respect to the uncertain future of history? This is one of the most important questions facing us today. Does the irreducible anti-utopia that finds its symbol in Hiroshima, that is, the death of humanity, simply wipe out the principle of hope? Does it necessarily give way to nihilistic despair? Or is transcendence possible in spite of everything? Will humanity ever attain Bloch's "homeland," Kant's "ethical community," or even Teilhard's "Omega point"? The question that is raised once again in this context, just as it was before with respect to personal death, is the question of the *reason* that founds fundamental hope in light of the end of history: What reason do the philosophies of progress or of nihilism offer for affirming that everything will turn out well in the end, or that everything will turn out for the worst? Is it reasonable to hope, or ought we rather to hand the laurels to the metaphysics of the Nothing and of despair? Will human history end in bitter defeat or nothingness? If so, wouldn't it make more sense to commit suicide immediately rather than wait for the end and suffer needlessly? Or, by contrast, could we say that the creeds of the various currents of the philosophy of progress of the last two centuries are correct to advocate an optimism, which holds that humanity will reach its homeland in spite of personal death, by means of the transformation of the world achieved through science and reason? Or again, is there a middle position that would accept the possibility of catastrophe within history, and at the same time offer a justification for hope? What, when all is said and done, is the ultimate reason that would provide the foundation for hope, and even for despair, with respect to both personal and collective death?

NOTES

1. Kopf, *Der Weg des Nihilismus von Friedrich Nietzsche bis zur Atombombe,* 13. Edmaier, *Horizonte der Hoffnung,* 11–13. Ellul, *L'espérance oubliée,* 10. Leist, *Existenz im Nichts,* 166. Jannoud, *Au rendez-vous du nihilisme,* 25, 127. Smith, *Hope and History,* 1–31.

2. Menxel, *Elpis. Espoir. Espérance.* Woschitz, *Elpis. Hoffnung.*

3. Ballay, *Der Hoffnungsbegriff bei Augustinus.* Bernard, *Théologie de l'espérance selon Saint Thomas d'Aquin.* Bougerol, *La théologie de l'espérance aux XIIème siècle.* Glenn, *A Comparison of the Thomistic and the Scotistic Concepts of Hope.*

4. Bloch, *The Principle of Hope,* 6 [5].

5. Pieper, *The Silence of St. Thomas,* 45 [*Werke,* Vol. 2, 13].

6. Heidegger, *Platons Lehre von der Wahrheit,* 5.

7. Anders, *Die Antiquierheit des Menschen,* Vol. 1, 239.

8. Pieper, *The End of Time,* 79. [*Werke,* Vol. 6, 330f.]. See also "Die Verborgenheit von Hoffnung und Verzweiflung," 165, and *Faith Hope Love,* 112 [*Werke,* Vol. 4, 274].

9. See Haas, *The Holy and the Good.*

10. See Akwali Okafor, *Pieper's Theory of Festivity.* Matsuda, *On 'Yutori': Symposium on Joseph Pieper's Philosophy of Leisure.* Inagaki, "Pieper's Philosophy of Culture." Maier, "Das Heilige und das Denken. Zum Werk Josef Pieper." Wald, "Vollendete Negativität oder theologisch gegründete Weltlichkeit? Die Kulturphilosophie Josef Piepers als eine Antwort auf das Nein zur Welt."

11. See Lauand, *O que e una universidade?*

12. See Meilaender, "Josef Pieper: Explorations in the Thought of a Philosopher of Virtue." Wald, "Moralische Verbindlichkeit und menschliches Richtigsein. Zur Rehabilitierung der Tugend."

13. See Kranz, "Der Philosoph und der Dichter. Zum Werk von Josef Pieper." Müller, "Über das rechte Verhältnis von Philosophie und Theologie. Josef Pieper im Kontext einer neu entfachten Debatte." Schumacher, "'Quelle ressemblance y a-t-il entre un disciple de la Grèce et un disciple du ciel?' Le rapport entre philosophie et théologie chez Josef Pieper." Wisser, "Philosophieren und Philosophie. Das Denken Josef Piepers und Helmut Kuhns."

14. See Pellegrino, "Verità e antropologia in Josef Pieper." Wald, "Wahrheit und Sinn."

15. See Dessauer, "Was ist der Mensch." Pellegrino, "Crisi dell'uomo e metafisica in Josef Pieper" and "Antropologia naturale e supranaturale in Josef Pieper." Sturm, "Das Menschenbild. Zum Werk Josef Piepers." Vernekohl, "Deuter des christlichen Menschenbildes." Wald, "Wende zum Menschen." See also Dominici, *La filosofia di Josef Pieper in relazione alle correnti filosofiche e culturale contemporane.* Fechtrupp, Schulze, and Sternberg, eds., *Dokumentation der Josef Pieper Stiftung.* Rodheudt, *Die Anwesenheit des Verborgenen. Zugänge zur Philosophie Josef Piepers.* Schumacher, ed., *La filosofia cristiana del novecento (I). Josef Pieper.*

1

The Anthropological and Ontological Foundations of Human Hope

1. THE ORIGIN OF HUMAN NATURE ACCORDING TO JOSEF PIEPER AND JEAN-PAUL SARTRE

The question of human nature and its origin is linked to the problem of the distinction and the relation between essence and existence, a problem that runs through and has dominated the history of Western thought. Without explaining how they relate or which comes first, Aristotle draws a clear distinction between knowing *what* a human being is and knowing *that* he is.[1] While existence answers the question *an est*—that is, existence is the act that holds a being above the threshold of the nothingness from whence it comes—essence responds to the question *quid est.* In the present context, I will not enter into the controversy surrounding this issue, important though it is; instead, I will limit myself to elaborating Pieper's approach to the topic and his disagreements with Sartre's interpretation. In order to avoid any misunderstanding, let me make clear from the outset that the two philosophers share, at least formally, the same understanding of the concepts of essence and existence. Moreover, it is crucial to underscore the fact that, though Pieper devotes only a few pages explicitly to the problem of essence and existence and their relationship,[2] he frequently touches upon it indirectly in his philosophical writings.

The essential question at the heart of the debate surrounding the origin of human nature and what it implies for our understanding of that nature is to know whether, for the human being in particular, essence precedes existence or, to the contrary, existence precedes essence. In the first case, which is Pieper's position, the divine Being forms the archetype or essence of human nature in his intellect and then breathes existence into that essence through an act of the will. In the second case, which corresponds to Sartre's position, the sole origin of human nature is an absolutely autonomous freedom, which is founded on an a priori atheism.

1.1 The distinction between res artificialis and res naturalis

The reasoning behind Pieper's discussion of which of the two, essence or existence, holds priority is based on the distinction between the two sorts of *res* that make up reality: *res naturales,* which are independent of the human being with respect to both their nature and their existence, and *res artificiales,* which owe the origin of both their nature and their existence to the intellect and will of the human being.[3] This distinction, which we find in both Ancient thought and in Sartre's, has nevertheless been disputed by certain people who reduce the whole of the world, including human beings, to *res artificiales.*

But is it possible to affirm that all of reality has its initial origin in the human intellect, which fashions the archetype of reality and projects it into existence through an act of the will? If this were the case, the human being would become the creator of all things, including himself (that is, his own nature). Reality would then ultimately be a creation of the human intellect. Nothing would be able to exist independently; the world would be constituted, from top to bottom, by my own representations.

If we push this view of reality still further, wouldn't it be possible to conclude that, if there were no human beings, the world would not exist? This is the line of thinking lying behind the statement of the German novelist Hacks, who describes the world a priori as "social dispositions and objects produced by the human being."[4] For the quantitative mentality that reduces the existence and the structure of thought to that which can be measured, it is indeed "awkward to distinguish between the natural and the artificial."[5] Along these same lines, in a play that portrays several characters discussing Plato's *Gorgias,* Pieper has a well-known writer say that there is no such difference between the natural and the artificial:

> The difference between the natural and the artificial has been grossly overrated. The truth is, it is secondary. In fact, it doesn't even exist. The artificial, that is, everything that the human being makes, fabricates, produces, manufactures (automobiles, refrigerators, physical and philosophical theories, poetry)—all of that is just as "natural" as anything the human being finds in the world, such as "nature" itself, and even human nature.[6]

Throughout his writings, Pieper repeatedly criticizes this tendency to reduce the real to the artificial, to a creation of the human intellect. His view, by contrast, is that reality exists in itself independently of the human intellect. *Homo theoreticus,* as Pieper calls him, is one who silently contemplates reality as it is in itself, allowing himself to be imbued by it so he may subsequently act in accordance with the laws inherent in it.

> Knowledge presupposes the subject's total surrender to the thing. The moment that the content of knowledge is defined, or co-defined, by something other than the object, it becomes impossible to speak of knowledge in a general manner, precisely to the extent that these extrinsic elements are operative. If the subject is thus not capable of keeping silent and disappearing before the object of knowledge, he is to that extent incapable of knowing. But, objectivity means nothing other than the subject's will and capacity to gaze solely upon the *object* in knowledge, to refrain from trying to determine or co-determine the content of knowledge arbitrarily.[7]

The act of contemplation *(theoria)* expresses the fact that existing things were not produced by human subjectivity. It is an attitude of openness and receptivity in relation to reality, which affirms the unfathomable mystery of the world. Pieper links this act to a *metaphysics of being and gift.* According to him, the "theoretical" disposition expresses itself in an intuitive and contemplative knowledge of reality, which constitutes the perfect form of knowledge, in contrast to *ratio,* which is carried out by a discursive movement of the intellect, that is, through the exertion of an effort.

In the context of his philosophical reflection on authentic leisure, Pieper raises the question of how intellectual knowledge occurs. In the first place, he recalls the ordinary experience of daily life in focusing, for example, on the way a traveler gazes at the passing landscape through the train window. There are two different ways he can look at this landscape: either peacefully, in a relaxed manner, simply observing reality without scrutinizing it, without exerting an effort or putting up a resistance, without work; or, with a tensed mind, analyzing, measuring, and examining the reality from a certain perspective, with a precise intention. Looking at something can either be contemplative or observant:[8] Can something similar be said with regard to intellectual knowledge?

Opinions differ on this point; or rather, according to Pieper, we can see a shift of perspective that begins at the end of the eighteenth century. There are certain thinkers who say human knowledge consists in an *activity*, it comes about through an effort that is expressed through acts of comparison, abstraction, and demonstration. Thought is composed entirely of such acts, and any other way of knowing is excluded as non-rational. Pieper first draws our attention to this issue in the inaugural course he offered in the summer of 1946 at the University of Münster, "Defending Leisure: On Philosophical Education and Intellectual Work,"[9] then in *Leisure as the Basis of Culture (Musse und Kult)* (1948), as well as in several articles devoted to the philosophy of leisure. Moreover, he refers to the position set forth by Kant, who, in his essay "Of a Gentle Tone Lately Assumed in Philosophy"[10] rejects the so-called contemplative philosophy as a "pseudo-philosophy," since "one need not *work*, but only hearken to the oracle in *one's self* and enjoy it, in order to bring thoroughly into his possession all wisdom, by which is meant philosophy."[11] In this article, Kant understands philosophical knowledge as essentially governed by the law of reason, according to which we acquire knowledge only through work, through a "herculean labour."[12] Effort is a *sine qua non* for genuine knowledge, and to the extent that effort is lacking, we are entitled to judge the knowledge as false or worthless. The law of reason states commands to "acquire a possession for one's self by labour."[13] There is only one source of intellectual knowledge, namely, mental effort. Kant denies that the contemplative attitude can be a source of knowledge insofar as it implies that knowing has an intrinsic gift-dimension. Without work, there is no knowledge. Effort becomes the criterion of the truth of knowledge, in the sense that, if one obtains knowledge without effort, that knowledge cannot be true.

Pieper takes the opposite position. He affirms that, beyond this activistic reduction, there exists another dimension of knowledge that holds value. To support this claim, he appeals to the distinction between two sorts of intellectual knowledge: on the one hand, the discursive knowledge the Ancients called *ratio*, and on the other hand, contemplative knowledge, which lies open to receive the "gratuitously" offered object. This knowledge is called *intellectus*, and it is the capacity for a *simplex intuitus*, for a simple, receptive, and nondiscursive apprehension of the real. Human knowledge results from both *intellectus* and *ratio*, insofar as receptivity and activity, release and tension, enjoy a symbiotic relationship. Each of these two acts has its own place in the philosophical act, which does not allow itself to be wholly reduced to a critical and discursive grasp but rather possesses at its heart an attitude of silence and contemplative listening to the reality that offers itself to the *intellectus.* Nevertheless, it is not sufficient to content oneself with intuition, with this listening to the oracle that unveils being. Rather, this intuition must be integrated with *ratio.*[14]

Pieper never tires of insisting that the intuitive knowledge of reality (knowledge that is of the order of a metaphysics of gift) is the constitutive element, indeed, the most important part of the philosophical act. According to him, intuition is not nonrational; full knowledge of reality can be had only through the conjunction of intuition and *ratio.* In this respect, Pieper is critical of both intuitionism, a certain idealism that tends toward subjectivism, and philosophical intellectualism, which reduces the philosophical act to *ratio* and thus excludes any other way of knowing as nonrational. The essence of philosophical thought therefore does not lie solely in the fact of intellectual effort, of working discursively on a precise problem, but it is present wherever reality shows itself as it is, wherever it reveals itself gratuitously to the intellect that welcomes it in silence as a gift.

Theoria, in Pieper's eyes, is thus the core attitude of the philosopher, who takes for granted that there exist *res* that do not depend on the human being for their existence, and who, in contemplating these things, is struck with wonder and overwhelmed by their *Unaustrinkbares Licht* (their inexhaustible radiance). By contrast, the person who is characterized purely by *praxis* is no longer one who contemplates; he is convinced the essential and even existential origin of reality can be found within himself. The one who knows is no longer filled with wonder. Péguy remarks—a little too radically in my opinion—that, in contrast to the philosopher of antiquity, "modern man *does not wonder* . . . ; it is never the other he encounters, but always and everywhere merely his own knowledge."[15] For the person of absolute *praxis,* who turns up repeatedly throughout the history of thought, nature is no longer something welcomed, listened to, and contemplated; rather, it is summoned to respond to the questions posed to it. It must at every turn mold itself to the norms of reason. This absence of wonder not only affects the very nature of philosophy, but also deprives the philosophical act of the dynamism of hope.

In the eyes of the pure activist, a worldview centered on the act of *theoria* is indefensible and ought to be systematically eliminated. Pieper describes the war that *homo practicus* has declared upon *homo theoreticus* throughout human history: the former is becoming increasingly important, according to Pieper, and seeks to govern one day as absolute ruler over a "totalitarian work-a-day world," in which contemplative and free activities will be wiped out (at least as much as they can be), or else they will continue to exist only to the extent that they serve *praxis*. There will no longer exist any genuine poetry, music, leisure, celebration, or, of course, philosophy. *Homo theoreticus* will have to be eliminated, insofar as his presence reminds us that the totality of the real cannot be reduced to having and doing, that there exists an openness that transcends *praxis*. The totalitarian workaday world, which instrumentalizes the person for the sake of production, would affirm that the "human being is a functional entity," that "any free activity that does not possess a social utility is condemnable and ought to be suppressed."[16] The existence of the human being would no longer flow from its being, but rather from the degree to which it can be put to work.

Pieper describes this mortal conflict between *praxis* and *theoria*—which is like the conflict that takes place between the executioner and his victim—as one-sided with respect to forces and available resources: while *praxis* seems to have various institutional powers at its disposal, the only "weapon" *theoria* possesses is the truth that it beholds and seeks to defend. *Homo practicus,* as exemplified by Callicles, has no interest in the truth of things, because for him *res* have value only to the extent that they can serve as instruments for a precise goal. He rejects *artes liberales* in the name of *artes serviles,* or worse still, he reduces the former to the latter. He fails to see that the intuitive cognitive act called *intellectus,* at the heart of which lies the spirit of gift, of gratuitous receptivity, and of leisure, represents a genuine intellectual act. He prizes *ratio* alone, which achieves its results through intense activities, after a strenuous intellectual effort. The attitude of *homo practicus* taken to its extreme is ultimately the rejection of a metaphysics of gift, of an authentic openness to the other, of genuine love and fundamental hope. Indeed, this mania of work for work's sake, this need for constant activity, in which each activity passes the baton to the next without any moment of respite that would allow the subject to take rest in contemplation—"all activity, even criminal activity, has a positive value, while passivity is always senseless"[17]—in the end expresses, according to Pieper, an attitude of despair. This attitude is tied to presumption and to the absolute autonomy of the person, who refuses in principle to receive anything at all from the other, an attitude we find in the reduction of rational knowledge to the sole dimension of *ratio*. "They are the revealing marks of the intellectual sclerosis that comes with not being able to receive or accept, of that hardening of the heart that refuses to suffer anything."[18] The exclamation, "I don't want to receive anything as a gift!" captures in a nutshell the attitude that refuses any dependence on an other, an attitude that rejects the dimension of gift.

Ancient philosophy offers two beautiful examples of the disdain and even desire to kill that *praxis* has for *theoria*, in its seeking the "triumph of the hand over the eye."[19] Thales, absorbed in contemplating the heavens and filled with wonder and admiration, did not look where he was going and thus fell into a well. A slave-girl who witnessed this spectacle laughed at the poor philosopher. In her opinion, he would have been better off spending his time on productive and useful activities rather than gazing at the heavens, which has no practical goal. This contemplation of reality, namely, philosophy, was in her eyes nothing but a pure waste of time, the product of an infantile imagination. By jeering at him, she was expressing the uselessness she believed characterizes all of philosophy. If philosophy nevertheless has to exist, it ought to do so only in a way that serves *praxis*.[20]

In the *Gorgias*, Callicles says repeatedly that philosophy, like any theoretical activity, is educational if it is practiced in one's youth, on the condition, however, that one indulges in it only in moderation. If, however, a person continues to philosophize even as he grows older, "the thing gets ridiculous," because in this case he withdraws from work and the life of the city. "My own reaction to men who philosophize is very much like that to men who speak haltingly and play like children. . . . I think such a man by this time needs a flogging. . . . Listen to me, my good man, and stop this refuting. 'Practice the sweet music of an active life.'"[21]

This overturning of the primacy of *theoria* over *praxis* is found not only in certain Greek authors, however. It is also given concise and radical expression, according to Pieper, in Marx's famous eleventh thesis on Feuerbach, which states that, while philosophy has hitherto interpreted the world in various ways, the point henceforward is to change it. Human activity thus becomes, for *homo practicus*, the determining

factor of the development of the world. The human being himself is
the cause of all transformation of the real: he has become the master
of history and of time, the "master and possessor of nature."[22]

Given that the world, in Pieper's opinion, is becoming increasingly
technical, that is, the things with which one works are becoming more
and more artificial, the modern human being, driven by his will to
transform things, runs the risk of thinking there is no essential difference between the rose on his work table and the chair produced by
the carpenter, both being things that owe their origin to the creative
human intellect. All of reality is ultimately something artificial, that is,
a pure product of technological ingenuity.[23] The human being himself
would fall under the same category, becoming a thing, a tool one could
use at will.[24] Another German philosopher, Anders, concludes in his
Die Antiquiertheit des Menschen that such a "reified" and artificial vision
of the world results from assuming an identity between world and
apparatus, such that existence is accorded only to that which is suited
to become a part of an apparatus.[25] We see this tendency to reduce all
things to *res artificiales* in the conviction that the human being can
know all things down to their most minute details, just as they are able
to know the artificial things whose archetypes lie in the human intellect.[26] Pieper sees a connection between this reduction and the
absolute primacy accorded to *praxis*. Indeed, for there to be a contemplative act at all, there must exist *res*, the archetypes for which do not
lie in the human mind.[27]

The relationship between reality and the human being leads to a
new question: Is the nature of the real independent of the human intellect, or is it the human being who fashions its archetype in his mind?
In order to resolve the question of the distinction between *res artificialis* and *res naturalis,* Pieper refers both to the methods by which
things are produced and the way a human being experiences his
mind's apprehension of reality. We observe that the human mind does
not know the essences of *res* directly, that is, it does not normally know
them in an infused way, through a "vision," to use Kant's expression,
without exerting an effort. If this was the only possibility, the *res*
grasped by intuition would be the result of a supervening gift, which
the subject could either accept or reject. In order to grasp essences, the
human being must abstract from sense-perception and think through
these abstractions, through acts that are sometimes considerable.

Because of the natural limitation of the human mind, which can indeed know things but never comprehend them completely (*"rerum essentiae sunt nobis ignotae"*),[28] we can say that the archetypes of *res naturales* must originate in and through an intellect other than the human intellect. If this were not the case, the human being would know things directly and would comprehend them completely, without needing to make use of abstraction and reasoning, for he would possess in his own mind the very ideas of the *res* in question.

This argument—which Pieper himself does not make explicitly, but which I extrapolate from what he does say—rests on the intrinsic and logical necessity that every essence or nature of any entity whatever always originates in an intellect as an archetype before it is projected into existence through a free and voluntary act of the will.

> [W]e are dealing with the fundamental and unalterable difference between things made by man and things not made by man, between *res artificiales* and *res naturales,* that is: between those things that have received their identity from human ingenuity and are therefore totally knowable, and those things that have received their identity from a divine thought and are for this reason forever beyond our full comprehension; for no finite power will ever penetrate so deep as to reach the archetypes that dwell in the mind of God.[29]

This distinction between two types of *res* presupposes, as we shall see, a strict relation between the being and the creative intellect and will (which forms the thing down to its innermost depths). What is at stake in this distinction is no less than the way we understand human nature and its origin.

1.2 The production of a res artificialis

For both Pieper and Sartre, the way the artist creates a *res artificialis* helps us to engage the question of the origin of human nature. The word "artist" is used here in the broad sense of the term, indicating the one who makes or produces something. This definition needs to be specified further in relation to the human act, which can be understood in two different ways: either as *agere,* in which the object is the human being himself, that is, his act; or as *facere,* in which the object is the *res* the human being produces. It is in this latter sense that I understand the artist's activity. Moreover, I should point out that, following the Ancients, I am not using the notion of creation in the precise sense of

creatio ex nihilo, but rather in the analogous sense of the act of creation
that presupposes a minimum of matter—with its own proper nature and
with the qualities that belong to it and exist independently of the
thought and will of the one who is creating—as a substrate necessary to
the carrying out of the production. Since existence in the sense that we
experience it every day is not something the human being possesses by
nature, he cannot project an entity into existence out of nothing.
Nevertheless, we may compare the human being to the demiurge who
creates through work.

Before beginning to work on wood, the carpenter starts out by fashioning an idea of the form or essence of the concrete object—for example, of the chair—which he intends to produce. Pieper refers to this idea
as the "archetype" (*Vor-Form*).[30] The idea of the chair nevertheless at
this point is found potentially in the matter, though its form remains
invisible to the eyes of others. The creative intellect alone perceives the
form, and so it remains until the form is either externalized in matter
or communicated to another intellect. The idea of the chair does not,
by itself, imply its material existence. In order to achieve existence, it
must be actualized through an act of the artist's will, which is carried
out in coordination with instrumental causes such as the carpenter's
hands and his tools. Thus, the human mind is the source of the nature
of the *res artificialis*.

We find the same idea in Sartre: "Let us consider some object that
is manufactured, for example a book or a paper-cutter: here is an
object which has been made by an artisan whose inspiration came
from a concept. He referred to the concept of what a paper-cutter is
and likewise to a known method of production, which is a part of the
concept, something which is, by and large, a routine."[31] Sartre concludes that, for all *res artificiales*, essence precedes existence. For him,
as for Pieper, the human intellect is the source of the nature of the *res
artificialis*. The human being provides its measure. It is important to
stress, however, that the measure (the archetype lying within the intellect) and that which is measured (the *res artificialis*) are always identical with respect to their nature. The essence of every *res artificialis*
originates in an idea produced by the intellect of the artist, who must
still, in order to bring it about in reality, project it into existence
through an act of will.

1.3 The origin of res naturales

After having described the internal mechanism at work in the actualization of a *res artificialis* and having emphasized the dependence of the nature of the man-made object on the human intellect, Pieper turns his attention to the origin of *res naturales* and, in particular, to the origin of human nature. To do so, he draws on an analogy based on the structural similarity between the actualization of *res artificiales* and *res naturales,* even though he remains aware of the limitations of this analogy. Now, every being—with respect to its nature, that is, its form or essence—originates in an intellect before it is projected into existence through an act of the will. Every creative intellect, whether it be that of the artist or the intellect that forms *res naturales,* creates in its "inner depths" an original form, an idea, or an archetype that contains the particular essence of the thing to be created, and which thus determines what it is going to be. The notion that a being is "thought up," that it receives its essence from an intellect, is not meant to be understood figuratively; rather, as Pieper says, we should take it quite literally. The creative will, in turn, determines freely that a thing is, that it exists.[32] Thus, Pieper sees that the nature of a *res artificialis* is dependent on the human intellect, and so, by analogy, he inquires into the intellect that lies at the origin of the nature of *res naturales,* and, in particular, human nature.

Though Pieper does not say so explicitly, the source of this analogy is Aristotle's *Physics,* in which Aristotle affirms that "if a house, e.g., had been a thing made by nature, it would have been made in the same way as it is now by art; and if things made by nature were made also by art, they would come to be in the same way as by nature."[33] On the basis of the principle that art imitates the activity of nature, it is possible to infer that nature must proceed in a manner analogous to that of art. We find this idea not only in Aristotle and Thomas Aquinas, but also in Goethe—who, in 1782, describes Lady Nature as "the sole artist"[34]—and in the French physiologist Bernard.[35] In light of this analogy, Pieper's argument could be summarized by the Thomistic affirmation that "all created things . . . stand in relation to God as products of art to the artist."[36]

Pieper points out that Sartre himself draws on the analogy between art and nature with respect to their operation. He praises Sartre's philosophy for its radicality and the clarity of its thinking on the theme of the origin of human nature, which leads Sartre to deepen the intrinsic relation between nature and what it means to be created. Sartre says, in effect, that it is impossible to affirm the notion of nature, understood here in the broadest sense, while simultaneously denying the notion of creation, given that these two concepts are logically inseparable. They are fundamentally interdependent;[37] that is, on the one hand, every essence originates in an intellect, and, on the other hand, every intellect implies an intentionality, that is, a consciousness of something, of which it grasps the essence. Sartre appeals to an analogy between God's and the human being's productive activity in order to describe the relation between the nature of a *res* and the creative intellect.

> Thus, the concept of man in the mind of God is comparable to the concept of paper-cutter in the mind of the manufacturer, and, following certain techniques and a conception, God produces man, just as the artisan, following a definition and a technique, makes a paper-cutter. Thus, the individual man is the realization of a certain concept in the divine intelligence.[38]

The fundamental thesis articulated by both Pieper and Sartre can thus be summarized in the affirmation that, if there is no intellect to form a conception of a *res,* the entity will possess no essence or nature. Sartre would thus unhesitatingly agree with Pieper when the latter affirms that "things possess an essence insofar as they are thought,"[39] or that "human nature would not exist if there were not a creator conceiving and positing it."[40]

Drawing on the same analogy, Sartre excludes the possibility that the human intellect could be the source of the nature of nonartificial things. The human being is not capable of comprehending and explaining *res naturales,* which implies that he did not form their essence in his intellect, and thus that he is not their creator: "this root [of a tree], on the other hand, existed in such a way that I could not explain it."[41] If the human being had formed the essence of the root within his own intellect, he would have been able to comprehend and explain it, just as the carpenter is able to explain the chair he has produced. Thus, Sartre concludes, "man does not create the world, man can only observe it."[42] Having excluded both the human intellect and the divine intellect as sources, he remains silent on the subject of the origin of *res naturales.*

The analogy Sartre uses here considers only one of the two faculties constitutive of human nature, namely, the intellect. He attaches hardly any importance either to the second faculty, the will, or to its activity in the production of a thing. I had noted in the analysis of *res artificiales* that in order for the idea of any nature formed in an intellect to be actualized and thus to pass from its material non-existence—that is, from a merely intentional existence—to its historical and real existence, an act of the will must be superadded. In light of this will-existence relation, which is similar to the intellect-essence relation, we can raise the question of the origin of *res naturales* with respect to their material existence.

1.4 The origin of human nature: Pieper and Sartre

Because there is an intrinsic relation between the intellect and the nature of a *res*, Pieper affirms that there is an intellect behind *res naturales*, and in particular, behind human nature—namely, the intellect of God.[43] He agrees with the Thomistic analogy cited above, according to which "every created entity is related to God as a work of art is related to an artist." Following Augustine and Thomas Aquinas, Pieper calls the archetypes that contain the essences of *res naturales* divine ideas.[44] The human being is one of God's thoughts. Pieper comes to this conclusion in his writings that focus primarily on human nature, without however seeking to explain why it is impossible for the human intellect itself to be the source of its own nature. Nevertheless, reading between the lines in his other works, it is possible to work out the following argument, based on the theory of knowledge elaborated above, which implies not only the discursive method proper to the human intellect[45] that allows it to grasp a *res*, but also a natural limit to the possibility of knowing created things. The intellect that forms the archetype of human nature cannot be a human intellect, otherwise the human being would have a perfect understanding both of his own nature and of *res naturales*, insofar as he would be the source of their essence. This intellect must therefore be other than a human intellect. We find a similar argument in Pieper's *Habilitationsschrift*, which treats the notion of the truth of things.[46]

Drawing on the same intellect-nature analogy, Sartre comes to the opposite conclusion regarding human nature. He is severely, and justly, critical of the eighteenth-century atheists, who, though they claim they do not believe in God, still cling to the traditional conception of human nature, according to which the human being remains in "possession of a human nature," which he himself nevertheless did not create.[47] Like Pieper, these atheists insist that essence precedes existence. Sartre, who has no interest in going only halfway, seeks clearly to draw "all the consequences of a coherent atheistic position,"[48] a position that necessarily entails certain implications for how we understand human nature and its origin. Because the notions of essence and creative intellect are inextricably bound up with each other, he concludes, contrary to the eighteenth-century atheistic philosophers, that "there is no human nature, since there is no God to conceive it."[49] Sartre does not, strictly speaking, deny the existence of human nature altogether; however, he insists that, insofar as its archetype was formed and projected by an intellect other than that of the human being himself, human nature will always be fixed and determined from the first moment of its existence. The French philosopher thus rejects any nature that would be "imposed" on the human being, and to which he would be subordinate, because this would suppress his freedom. In his talk, *Existentialism and Human Emotions,* Sartre says, alluding to his atheism, that, if God did not exist, then "there is at least one being in whom existence precedes essence . . . and . . . this being is man."[50] Though, here, he makes use of the phrase "at least," thus leaving open the possibility that there may be other things in which existence precedes essence, Sartre later rejects this possibility. In an explanation of his talk, he makes clear that "it is in man—and man alone—that existence precedes essence."[51] Such an affirmation is crucial for his defense of human freedom.

It seems to me that Sartre is here evading the real issue. To be sure, he asserts that it is the human being who is the source of his own nature, but not by forming the archetype in his intellect, which he would have to affirm to stay true to the intellect-nature analogy employed above. Instead, the human being makes himself insofar as he acts, insofar as he finds himself in a situation, insofar as he commits himself, thus engaging his freedom, which is absolutely autonomous and anterior to all determination and prior to any other actualization of the various human faculties. In this respect, according to Sartre it is freedom that is the source of human nature: freedom constitutes the essence of the human being. As the human being exists, he fashions his own image, his nature. Sartre maintains that, if he is self-creating, he produces his own nature. This means that "at first he is nothing. Only afterward will he be something, and he himself will have made what he will be. . . . Not only is man what he conceives himself to be, but he is also only what he wills himself to be after this thrust toward existence. Man is nothing else but what he makes of himself. . . . Man is at the start a plan . . . ; nothing exists prior to this plan; . . . man will be what he will have planned to be."[52] We could raise the question in this context, as I did in relation to the origin of *res naturales* with reference to the existence-will analogy, about what the source of man's existence is. Sartre recognizes that the human being "did not create himself,"[53] that is, that he did not give himself his own existence. "I'm rather . . . amazed before this life which is given to me—given for nothing."[54] If this life is given to the subject, we could ask whence it comes, or in other words, where is the will that brought it into existence? If we begin a priori from the fact that God does not exist, it is chance[55] that takes the place of the divine will as initiator of existence. But chance does not possess a will. Sartre maintains that the human being was projected into the world.[56] But if he was projected, then what will projected him? Sartre refuses to answer this question.

If he had taken his bearings, not only from the connection he highlights so well between the intellect and the nature of a *res,* but also from the connection between the will and existence, he would have been compelled in a certain sense to enter more deeply into the problem of the existential origin of the human being. Pieper, for his part, although he is aware of the will-existence connection and applies it both to God and to the human being, accords it less importance than the intellect-essence connection. Nevertheless, we should point out that the German philosopher does refer to the will-existence connection in order to affirm both that every *res* is essentially good and that everything is willed by God.[57]

Sartre's thesis concerning the self-production of human nature and atheism have their foundation in his conception of freedom, the central notion of his thought. He rejects the conception that freedom is inscribed in a pregiven human nature, which is how Pieper understands it,[58] a notion that roots freedom in the natural inclinations of the human faculties of the will (toward the good) and the intellect (toward the true), insofar as this understanding subjects freedom to determination. For Sartre, freedom must by contrast be something altogether

autonomous and indeterminate with respect to every natural determination[59] and, for this reason, it is prior not only to the exercise of the
will, the intellect, and any other faculty, but also and above all to the
actualization of human nature. It is freedom that "makes possible" the
existence of this nature and that is at the origin of every essence, in
other words, it *is* "the being of man,"[60] "man is freedom,"[61] he does
not only *possess* freedom. "Human freedom precedes essence in
man";[62] it is the foundation of his being. Since it is absolutely first,
choice, in Sartre's view of freedom, does not presuppose any act of the
intellect or of the will. This choice, to the contrary, is utterly indeterminate, "deprived of motives,"[63] beyond the deliberation of the will.

Being and Nothingness[64] is above all else an ontology of freedom,
and Sartre's atheistic humanism belongs in the category of ethics. He
desires to liberate himself from any sort of heterodetermination by
determining himself to act, a tendency that ends with the ego's decla-
ration of absolute autonomy in the encounter with his rival, who is
none other than God. Commenting on the concept of freedom in
Descartes, for example, he concludes that this latter "had given to God
what properly belongs to us."[65] Sartre wants to return the human being
to the position God had stolen from him, a program that, in the final
analysis, follows the same lines as the project of Nietzsche and the atheistic thinkers of the nineteenth century;[66] after countless centuries spent
in alienation and servitude to God, the human being has finally managed to break his chains and recover the place that is his by right.

Unable to imagine that the human being could be fundamentally
free if God indeed exists, insofar as this would imply the human
being's dependence on God and would thus limit his freedom, con-
demning him to a state of alienation, Sartre feels obliged to make a radical choice between two alternatives: if God exists, the human being
cannot be free; if he is free, then God cannot exist.[67] Thus, if the
human being wants to be absolutely free and responsible, he must
"'kill" God. There is no other choice, even if this leads to absurdity.
Sartre, who takes up Hegel's master-slave dialectic and thus rejects any
dependence on another, draws the final conclusions from the new
humanism that Zarathustra has revealed: "God is dead . . . I teach you
the overman."[68] The slaves' revolt from the master who refuses to recognize his identity leads to his authentic autonomy, and ultimately to
his self-creation. After the long birth pangs that free him from the

"'original sin" of the mythical representation of a transcendent God, a new day finally dawns.

Now that his adversary is dead, the human being comes into possession of a freedom that is absolutely prior to essences and is thus what creates them. He is indeterminate with respect to all possible ends, he chooses freely not only his own nature, which he continues to fashion throughout the whole of his existence, but also his future goal, his morality, and his finality. He prescribes for himself all intermediate finalities and decides the content of happiness, for there is nothing that is determined in advance. "Life has no a priori meaning."[69] One rejects God because one does not want to be determined from the moment of one's birth to pursue an ultimate *telos:* "I cannot bear the idea that I was produced one day in a moment of boredom and that the path was already traced out for me to follow, on pain of going to hell. Thus, I eliminated God,"[70] exclaims Dostoevski. "The first principle of play is man himself; through it he escapes his natural nature; he himself sets the values and rules for his acts."[71]

This conception of the primacy of freedom has important ethical implications. Sartre criticizes the position of the French professors of 1880 who, in eliminating God, wanted nevertheless to hold onto a priori values, so society could function with as little friction as possible. Wanting to be logical in his atheism, Sartre affirms, "if I've discarded God the Father, there has to be someone to invent values."[72] This someone is none other than the human being himself, who chooses himself and who, out of his primal, autonomous, and indeterminate freedom, creates his moral values without reference to a pre-existent and a priori moral law written somewhere in heaven. He thus takes the place of God who, for the Ancients, freely established not only every moral value, but also the final destination of the human being's voyage through history. "[I]t [is] very distressing that God does not exist, because all possibilities of finding values in a heaven of ideas disappears along with Him; there can no longer be an *a priori* Good, since there is no infinite and perfect consciousness to think it. Nowhere is it written that the Good exists, that we must be honest, that we must not lie; because the fact is we are on a plane where there are only men."[73]

Once God has been wiped out, human freedom has to become the source of moral values; in other words, the human being is his own legislator, he invents his own law. Sartre agrees with the ideas of Camus and

Dostoevski, who say that "if God didn't exist, everything would be possible"[74] to the free human being. What this position implies is that, on
the one hand, the human being is placed in his own hands, no longer
knowing where to turn for guidance in moral activity—his freedom experiences the dread of "being the groundless foundation of values"[75]—and,
on the other hand, he is faced with a moral relativism, according to
which there is no longer any moral value good or bad in itself.[76] The
morality of the human act receives its source and measure in the sheer
indeterminate freedom that lies at the origin of every essence.

1.5 The antagonism between nature and freedom as the interpretive key to Sartre

The question of the origin of human nature in Sartre can be understood not only in the light of the intellect-nature analogy, but also in the
light of the master-slave dialectic, of his atheism, and even of his obses-
sion to keep freedom at any price from having any connection at all
with a deterministic and mechanistic conception of the human being
and of history. The sole possibility he sees for escaping from determinism is to grant freedom a primacy and anteriority with respect to
human nature. "The being which is what it is," that is, the being that
possesses a nature it has received, which would precede freedom, "can
not be free."[77] It would obey whatever its nature would dictate to it. In
order to safeguard freedom, Sartre refuses "to give the human being
an eternally fixed nature."[78] He denounces not only Mauriac's project,
which transforms persons into things by bestowing on them an a priori
essence,[79] but also that of Proust, whom he reproaches for having contributed to "the spreading of the myth of human nature."[80] Sartre
brings out the incompatibility between human nature and freedom in
a magnificent passage from *Being and Nothingness,* in which he
explores, with Leibniz, the question whether Adam was truly free
either to take the apple or abstain from taking it. He rejects Leibniz's
solution, for if human nature arises out of a divine idea, the human act
could not be free, and thus could not be responsible, by the "rigorous
necessity of the very essence of Adam":

> But Adam's essence is for Adam himself a *given;* Adam has not chosen
> it; he could not choose to be Adam. Consequently he does not support
> the responsibility for his being. . . . For us, on the contrary, Adam is
> not defined by an essence since for human reality essence comes after

existence. Adam is defined by the choice of his ends. . . . The problem
of freedom is placed on the level of Adam's choice of himself—that is,
on the determination of essence by existence.[81]

The only being that can be truly free is the one that is entirely indeterminate with respect to its nature—that is, the one that does not
receive its nature from another. By identifying determinism and possessing a received human nature, Sartre implies that the human being
must either be completely free or completely determined. He excludes
any other alternative: "Man cannot be sometimes slave and sometimes
free; he is wholly and forever free or he is not free at all."[82]

The fact that these are the only two possible alternatives arises from
a false understanding of the concept of determinism, an understanding
that identifies it with the concept of fatalism. For the well-known physiologist and father of the experimental method in medicine, Claude
Bernard, the human being is subject, like other organisms, to (neurophysiological) determination. "Every manifestation in the living being,
we say, is a physiological phenomenon and is associated with definite
physicochemical conditions, which permit it when they are present and
prevent it when they are absent."[83] This observation, which is the fruit
of experimental research, rests on the principle of the existence of a
finalizing and "intelligent" process inscribed in the nature of the organism, which orders the development of its diverse forms and functions
from the very first moment of its existence to the actualization of its
being. The biological event manifests itself as a series of acts or phenomena that are grouped together, that occur in concert, and are har-
monized in such a way that they achieve a determinate result. Life is
not reducible to chemical and physical processes alone, but there exists
a *guiding idea*, a *vital plan*, a *vis formativa*, that is rooted in the inmost
depths of the being, constituting its center, and by virtue of which it
progresses toward a *telos*. But since it is accessible to the intelligence
alone, this *eidos* escapes the grasp of the senses. "In every living germ
is a creative idea which develops itself and exhibits itself through
organization. As long as a living being persists, it remains under the
influence of this same creative vital force, and death comes when it can
no longer express itself; here as everywhere, everything is derived from
the idea which alone creates and guides."[84]

Bernard agrees with Aristotle[85] who, drawing on the art-nature analogy, sees an intentionality at work in nature, an intrinsic principle in

the organism, an "intelligent" organizing and creative force that orders the organism with a constant regularity toward a precise determinate end, that is, the ultimate development of its nature. Organisms are determinate with respect to a precise future, which is death, and also with respect to the unfolding of the actualization of their physiological being from the moment of their birth until the moment of their death. The human being is ordered in a determinate way to its natural end, just like the plant is ordered to the form of plant or, to take Sartre's example,[86] like the peas that actualize themselves in conformity to their respective guiding idea. Observing reality, we notice that, if certain minimal requirements are met, a particular seed is always and systematically ordered to the actualization of its being, it aims at obtaining what is best for itself. The development of organisms is not due to chance, but has its source in the seeds that possess pregiven formative properties, the results of which are already determined.

Thomas Aquinas,[87] who also abides by Aristotle's intuition, likewise saw that there must necessarily be a guiding idea in an organism. We again encounter in Aquinas the principle that every agent acts in view of an end, that is, its activity is ordered toward a predetermined end, for otherwise it would remain in a permanent state of indeterminacy, never passing over into concrete action. If there were no guiding idea, we would be led to the absurd possibility that the seed of a pea plant could in principle grow into a plant of some other type. Granted that the minimal requirements are met, the pea-plant seed is capable of developing itself only by virtue of, and in conformity to, a guiding idea that "intelligently" organizes the various materials in accordance with itself and in view of a precise end, the actualization of the seed. Every organism is thus subject to a natural and physiological determinism, which orders it toward a *telos* established in advance in conformity with its nature, and which is the actualization of its faculties.

The human being is also determined with respect to some of its actions. He is not in a position, for example, to choose freely to abstain from doing what his nature prescribes for him to do in order to continue living: eating, drinking, or breathing. Of course, he always has the possibility of choosing no longer to nourish himself, but he would in this case have to accept the consequences that such a choice would entail, namely, certain death. Nor is he able to choose that his intellect not take the truth for its object or his will the good; as we will see, he

is also not capable of choosing that his being not be ordered to an ultimate end inscribed in his nature.

Sartre rejects the existence of a final cause—that is, actualization by
means of a preconceived form inscribed in the creature in a way that
is independent of human freedom—for this would entail determination.
For the same reason, he refuses to attribute an individual substance to
things,[88] or a substantial form. The organism is a series of interconnect-
ed phenomena, and it exists only in the mode of actuality. Sartre
denies that it possesses any possibility of existing in potential.

As he strolls through a public garden, the protagonist of the novel
Nausea, Roquentin, who is none other than Sartre himself,[89] remarks, as
he looks at the things around him, that "all was fullness and all was
active, there was no weakness in time. . . . Suddenly, they existed, then
suddenly they existed no longer."[90] Roquentin denies all coming-to-be.
He is moreover struck by the fact that things had no desire to exist. To
prove what he was saying, he provides the reader with a description of
trees that are drying out, in the final stage of their existence. One wonders, how would he have understood reality if he had seen a young tree
blossoming in the springtime, lit up by the sun? In the garden, he discovers the contingency of reality, which is shot through with absurdity
and by a profound non-sense, and this is what brings about his feeling
of nausea. He cannot keep himself from crying out that "it is absurd that
we are born; it is absurd that we die."[91] Every existing thing is uncreat-
ed. Existence does not imply necessity. It is simply there. It comes about
for no reason, and there is no way that one could deduce existing things
from other existing things. Since existence is nothing but an imperfection, Sartre concludes that it is superfluous, that being, all being, including human being, is "too much" for eternity.[92]

In these few crucial pages, the author does not offer any rational reasons to prove what he is saying, but he relies instead on feelings and
impressions. His vision arises out of an existential experience. We can
clearly see the vehemence of his desire to demonstrate the nonexistence
of a final cause or a guiding idea rooted in living things, as well as the
absurdity of reality that would follow from this. This absurdity constitutes "the key to Existence, the key to my Nauseas, to my own life."[93]
It seems that Roquentin was nevertheless a hair's breadth away from
admitting the existence of a certain finality, a guiding idea inherent in
organisms, which would have allowed him to transcend absurdity.

Leaving the public garden, he turns to look at it one last time. Though he was not in any way expecting it, a tiny fact shakes him and seems to call his conception of reality into question. He sees the garden smiling at him, as if "it *wanted to say* something; that was the real secret of its existence." Unfortunately, it was impossible for him to understand this smile, which expressed the existence of a meaning. "This little sense annoyed me: I *could not* understand it, even if I could have stayed leaning against the gate for a century."[94]

It seems that, in the passage we are discussing, Sartre had the experience, for an instant, through an intuitive grasp, that a living thing may indeed possess a reason inscribed in its nature, that there exists in reality a *glimmer of meaning,* difficult to grasp to be sure, but nevertheless accessible to human understanding. But since it seemed to him impossible to understand the final meaning, the ultimate meaning, in short, the final cause emanating from living things, Roquentin denies its existence altogether and returns to his hotel discouraged. He despairs of ever understanding it. This experience, a sort of happy ecstasy, a profound intuition that he rejects, could have been the beginning of a discovery of the meaning of reality. This discovery would have been able to help him free himself from the absurdity of the world.[95]

As I emphasized above, the trouble Sartre has in reconciling freedom and human nature is due not only to his atheism, but primarily to the fact that he does not distinguish sufficiently between neurophysiological determinism, to which the human being is subject, and "spiritual" determinism. Although the human being is conditioned by the physiological laws rooted in his nature, he, unlike plants and animals,[96] is able to transcend them by virtue of his intellectual capacity and his will, which allows his activity to be free. Because his intellect is open to the infinite, and because he is able to grasp the entire universe conceptually and in a certain sense to become it, the human being is able in some respect to transcend biological determination. Moreover, we see here that there is a certain indeterminacy intrinsic to the human being that has its roots in freedom and that escapes the fixity of matter. Physiological laws are not the cause of free acts, but they make them possible. Freedom, like various physical causes, actualizes itself in conformity to laws that belong intrinsically to its nature. It does not exist prior to human nature, but it is the result of the constitution of the will, which is naturally determined. The will necessarily wills the universal essence of the good. There exists, of course, a dialectical opposition between determinism and freedom, but in a certain respect it is impossible to think of one without the other; they are never mutually exclusive. Physiological determinism is the necessary precondition for the actualization of freedom.

Although Sartre denies that the will is determined, he nevertheless admits that the human person is "naturally" a free creature, that is, he is necessarily free. He recognizes that freedom is not a reality that the human being is able either to accept or reject, but that he is "condemned to be free . . . we are not free to cease being free."[97] If the human being were indeed possessed of absolute freedom, how would Sartre explain the fact that every human being has a common form and matter, which is precisely what allows us to call them all human beings? He is at least obliged to admit that the human being is determinate to a certain extent with respect to his corporeality and to the functioning of his faculties, or even to the proper object of certain of his faculties. Given that it is not possible for him to eliminate a determinate human nature altogether, Sartre cannot avoid affirming that, at a given moment of human existence, essence precedes existence in a certain way.[98] The ideal of the absolute primacy of freedom, the ideal of a completely indeterminate and a priori freedom, can be compared to the platonic ideas that exist nowhere else but as theoretical ideas in heaven.

If, in contrast to Sartre, we posited the existence of a determinate freedom, wouldn't we fall into the paradox of wanting to maintain that freedom is free without, for all that, being completely free, that it includes a certain determinate indeterminacy or, in other words, that the natural will is ordered to a precise good but is nevertheless free? To what extent is freedom still genuinely free?

On one hand, freedom can be influenced to some degree as much by hereditary, psychological, sociological, historical, economic, and other factors—which in certain cases can determine the activity of the human being quite particularly—as by instinctive impulses and passions. On the other hand, the faculties of the mind and will, upon which freedom depends, are determined with respect to their functioning.[99]

Regarding the act of the will, one can distinguish between the final end and the proximate ends, the means. The human being is determined, as Pieper stresses, independently of his free will, as much with respect to the desire for happiness, which is the universal good, as to the finalities inscribed in his nature. He nevertheless is free to choose both proximate ends and the means to attain the end or ends, both those that are freely chosen and those that are determined.[100] With Simon, one could also distinguish between a natural will and a free will.[101] The natural will is a natural inclination of the will according to its proper being toward that which corresponds to it, and it remains faithful to the metaphysical principle according to which all potentiality possesses a necessary ordination to its proper object, which is the common Good or happiness. The free will allows one to accept or reject the inclinations that proceed from the natural will.

The human will is both natural and free, that is to say, it can be understood as an (ethically and psychologically) indeterminate metaphysical "determination." The human being acts freely within the determinate framework of his nature, which establishes both the internal functioning of the faculty of freedom and the fact that it is ordered to the good and the true.

2. THE QUESTION OF HAPPINESS

Pieper maintains, contrary to Sartre, that human nature is ordered in a determinate way to a goal. Following the Greeks, he does not ask what the human being is obliged to do, but rather what he "naturally" wants to do.[102] In posing the question thus, he presupposes the Thomistic analysis of the transcendentals,[103] as well as the definition of the good as that which every living thing desires. The proper object of the appetitive faculty of the will is the good, which according to Thomas Aquinas is identified with being qua appetible, that is, it is the object of desire. Every being, qua being, is in act and, therefore, for Thomas, every being represents a certain form of perfection. To the extent that being is perfect to some degree, it is desirable for the faculties of the appetite, and thus it is good. This is the point of departure of Aristotle's *Nichomachean Ethics* and Thomas Aquinas takes it up himself: *bonum est id quod omnia appetunt.*[104]

Observing the concrete action of human beings and assuming the soundness of his conception of a human nature that is simultaneously determined and free, Pieper concludes that the human being is ordered by nature to happiness,[105] which he identifies with the completion of the human being, his total fulfillment.[106] Pieper's notion that every human being strives "naturally" for happiness, like an arrow aimed at a target, is rooted in the Thomistic conception of appetite, of natural desire,[107] which Aquinas calls either *appetitus naturalis, amor naturalis,* or even *potentia passiva naturalis.* Pieper however does not devote any study specifically to the concept of natural desire and the various ways it is interpreted. This natural appetite, which is distinct from the elective appetite of the will and which has a metaphysical, rather than physical, psychical, or psychological significance, expresses an organism's being ordered to an end that is proper to it and so must be achieved, an end that represents the fulfillment of its nature, its flourishing, its proper perfection. Appetite is meant to be understood in this context as a determinate ordering toward the ontological good, the good in general, which constitutes the formal object of the will.

The human being, in Pieper's view, seeks in all of his actions and throughout the whole of his life to possess the good that will make him happy in a profound sense, the good that will allow his life to turn out well. It is impossible that the will not be ordered not only to the good in general, but to the ultimate good, which is identical with the complete actualization of the person. The human being cannot not desire happiness, or, as Pascal put it, in spite of his wretchedness, he "wants to be happy, only wants to be happy, and cannot help wanting to be happy."[108] It is impossible for the will to desire evil for evil's sake; it can pursue evil only *per accidens.* Pieper stresses that no one wants happiness for the sake of happiness, that no one is able to rejoice for the sake of rejoicing, but that the human being always needs a reason for rejoicing. And it is this reason—the fact that the human being has acquired something good that is loved and desired—that forms the object of the will. Happiness and joy are the logical consequence of possessing a good.[109]

This affirmation is quite common in Greek thought. For the Greeks, the *telos* toward which human nature is ordered is the *eudaimonia* in which he achieves the fullness of his being, in which his principal aspirations find their perfection. On the basis of the common experience of human beings, and also in reference to Eudoxis, Aristotle affirms that every living thing and every human action always aim at some good. The good that the rational animal desires most intensely is the supreme good.[110] In the *Philebus,* as Socrates and company endeavor to define together what the good is, Plato has Protarchus say that "everything that has any notion of it hunts for it [the good] and desires to get hold of it and secure it."[111] While the Greek philosophical texts most often use the terms happiness and the happy life to designate the goal toward which the human being is naturally ordered, Christian writings use the word "beatitude."[112]

Pieper's affirmation of happiness as the goal toward which human nature strives does not necessarily imply an awareness of what happiness is. The question concerning the nature of happiness was raised well before the modern age by Aristotle, who observes in the second chapter of the first book of the *Nichomachean Ethics,* that human beings agree with respect to the designation of the object toward which their desires aim (happiness), but their opinions about its contents diverge rather quickly. Along the same lines, in the *City of God,*[113] Augustine, in light of a book by Varron that lays out a table of theories concerning the contents of the good (according to his calculations, there are 288 theories), affirms that the human being has much difficulty in specifying the essence of the good. This attempt to define happiness and the end of the many goods constitutes one of the central problems in ancient thought. Nevertheless, in spite of this multiplicity of goods, the philosophers prior to Augustine posit the existence of *a single* final end. The human being thus finds himself in a paradoxical situation: he is stuck between, on the one hand, his natural orientation toward happiness and the impossibility of evading the question of happiness, and on the other, the divergence of answers concerning the content of the good that will bring him supreme happiness. For some, happiness is physical or intellectual pleasure, or well-being; for others, it is bodily or external goods, glory, honor, rule, power, posterity; and for others still, it is the possession of the virtues.

In an effort to analyze the diversity of meanings collected under the single word "happiness," Pieper introduces an interesting distinction between the small happiness that expresses the brief experiences of happiness one has every day and that are not capable of giving complete fulfillment to human existence nor of answering the ultimate desire for happiness, and happiness *simpliciter,* taken in its singularity, which expresses the absolute and universal good.[114] If one looks through his writings on hope, one is surprised to see that he did not correlate the distinction between hope [*espoir*] and fundamental hope [*espérance*] with that between the two kinds of happiness. The small experiences of happiness and hopes are ordinary, impermanent, and change with the seasons. They are not able to satisfy the natural human desire with plenitude or happiness, which is the object of fundamental hope.

After having quickly reviewed the various goods (minor experiences of happiness) that human beings have taken to be the supreme good, Pieper concludes by taking up the traditional argument of certain ancient thinkers, that none of these particular and finite goods, even if they were joined together, suffice to satisfy the human heart; as Gide says, "the terrible thing is that one can never get sufficiently drunk."[115] What then is the good toward which the human being strives with all of his being? According to Pieper, it has to be complete, absolute, eternal, constant, and unchanging, and in a state of perfect harmony. It must be a perfect good capable of completely fulfilling desire, without which there would be no final end, and there would always remain something to be desired. In effect, complete happiness, for Pieper, which occurs when this good has been secured, is a state that does not imply movement or becoming, but a rest.

Pieper calls this good the *bonum universale*, which can also be designated by the concepts *summum bonum, beatitudo,* or *ultimus finis*.[116] The possession of the supreme good, which Augustine defines as "that for the sake of which other things are to be desired, while it is to be desired for its own sake,"[117] brings human beings happiness in a profound sense. Observing that the goods desired by human beings are organized in an architectonic structure, Aristotle tries to discover the existence of a good that would be desired for its own sake and that would be at the same time the root of the goodness of other goods. What, in the end, is this *summum bonum,* which is capable of slaking the thirst of the natural human desire? To respond to this question, Pieper does not work out a series of arguments, but refers to a quotation from Thomas Aquinas, according to which the universal good cannot be found anywhere in the world, but solely in God, who is the good *par excellence*.[118]

Beatitude, from Pieper's perspective, is the final destination of the human being's journey toward fulfillment with respect to the actualization and complete satisfaction of his being, a goal that he did not choose but toward which he is ordered by nature. For Aristotle, this ultimate *telos,* this *eudaimonia,* the object of which is virtuous human being, can be achieved by human effort by bringing to maturity his innate dispositions; that is, this end is natural and proportionate to human nature. Christian thought distances itself from this immanent conception of the end by denying the indissoluble unity between the three notions of *physis, dynamis,* and *telos,* which defines the Greek teleological approach and according to which the end is inscribed *in potentia* in the reality of the *physis* of the human being. Augustine distances himself from the Greek conception of the human being *in via* toward complete fulfillment as much with respect to the means of this actualization as to the object of the ultimate good: for him, the human being is not capable of reaching his ultimate *telos,* which is God, except through God's help.[119] Thomas Aquinas, for his part, grants human nature an obediential potential, which is a capacity to open oneself positively to the supernatural level, which is the second state of perfection. If he draws a distinction, within the natural desire for happiness, between two beatitudes, this does not imply the existence of two ultimate ends, but rather of two degrees of the same end.

Though he does not devote a particular study to this topic, Pieper takes up the distinction between these two currents of thought, the Greek and the Christian: on the one hand, imperfect beatitude by itself, which is divided into two types of happiness, the *vita contemplativa* and the *vita activa,* and, on the other hand, the perfect beatitude, which does not for all that eliminate imperfect beatitude.[120]

He denies that the human being is able to come into possession of perfect beatitude through his own efforts, or through technical knowledge alone, which entails a mechanistic conception of happiness. Ultimate happiness cannot be produced, it cannot be bought like merchandise. One can receive it only as a gift, which is also true for fundamental hope.[121]

This distinction between the two degrees of beatitude corresponds to two orders of human perfection, that of nature and that of supernature. This latter, which is not opposed to nature, could be situated within the polemic Pieper engages against the totalitarian state of work permeated by a metaphysics of *praxis,* even if he himself does not draw the connection explicitly. This state prohibits not only any contemplative act that has its end in itself, but any perfect beatitude which is of the order of gift. The world of pure *praxis* maintains that science and the technical power that is tied to work are capable of bringing the human being complete happiness. It rejects any happiness that would be the result of a gift. The object of the principle of hope is reduced to the dimension of that which the human being is capable of achieving through his own efforts. This restriction of happiness, and subsequently of the object of human hope, to a metaphysics of making or doing is inscribed within the current of thought ubiquitous in our century, which politicizes not only happiness, but hope as well.[122]

3. THE HUMAN BEING *IN VIA*

3.1 Human hope is founded on an ontology of not-yet-being

Hope cannot exist and flourish unless its subject is ontologically constituted by a *not-yet* that expresses the *temporality* into which he is projected. This ontological openness that Dasein has to the future, in which various possible goods lie, is constitutive of the act of hope. Without it, the human being would be static; he would cease to be *"in via."* Another element essential to hope is the category of possibility, which is inscribed within the process of becoming that is inherent to the organism. The free projection of Dasein toward the possibilities of his ability-to-be is what makes hope possible. Like temporal being, Dasein is caught between the past and the future, between his origin and his goal, whether this be an already-determined goal inherent to his nature, or a freely-chosen goal.

Pieper views the future and time from the perspective of an ontology of *not-yet-being* and sees in this the indispensable foundation for a renewed understanding of the eminently existential attitude of Dasein that constitutes hope. Although he did not, strictly speaking, devote a thorough study to the temporality of human existence, as Heidegger did so impressively, it remains the case that Pieper's *ontology of not-yet-being* and his philosophy of hope are deeply marked by a philosophy of time that moreover accepts an openness to a nontemporal dimension. This distinction and interpenetration between temporality and non-temporality, in which "the temporal is inwardly sustained, saturated, pervaded by the untemporal,"[123] presupposes a metaphysics of transcendence with transcendence.

3.2 The ontology of not-yet-being: *Pieper, Heidegger, and Bloch*

Pieper rejects the unfounded reproach that, according to a certain contemporary discourse about hope and the future, traditional metaphysical philosophy is trapped within a purely static conception of being, and, from Plato all the way to Hegel, has privileged the past, considering being (*Wesenheit*) to be that which has been (*Gewesenheit*),[124] and thereby rendering any genuine philosophy of hope illusory. It is of course true to say that, for traditional philosophy, reality is more important than the category of possibility, but this fact teaches that Dasein possesses an ontological dynamism, and is ordered by its intrinsic temporal structure to a future.

Pieper works out his philosophy of hope from within an ontology of *not-yet-being*,[125] which is characterized by a static-dynamic dialectic that is played out between the categories of *minimal-being* and *full-being*. He devotes the same attention to the organism's origin (in his discussion of Sartre's thought) as to its future (in his discussion with Bloch), underscoring that, without an origin, the future is futile. He maintains that the Aristotelian concepts of possibility (*dynamis*) and substance (*ousia*) are intrinsically related, that is to say that the category of possibility accorded to an organism presupposes above all a metaphysical foundation: namely, the substance that defines the being of a particular organism. Pieper thus distinguishes, on the one hand, a substantial form present from the very first instant of human existence, that is, an actual minimal being, a *not-yet-being* that is more than a *not-being*, and, on the other hand, the human being's act, which orders it in a manner that is both determinate and indeterminate, that is, free, toward an ultimate end inscribed in the depths of its nature, and which implies the free actualization of the totality of the human being's *ability-to-be*. The human being journeys toward the actualization—as much by nature as by free acts and by gift—of the potentialities inherent in and extrinsic to its nature, toward a *full-being*, or toward a *full-possession*.[126] As Pindar and Nietzsche said, the human being must become what he is, he must actualize his nature, in all of its dimensions.[127] This striving can, nevertheless, end in imperfection, the *forever-out-of-reach*. The human being is thus a traveler projected into temporality, between the past and the future, between his origin and his ultimate end, toward the realization of possibilities. He can attain the plenitude of his person only if he unfolds what he is, actualizing and bringing about his definition, his project.[128] He does so, Pieper says, by practicing the human virtues that make such an actualization of potentialities possible. The virtues constitute "the attempt to realize" and to sustain that which the human being is and wants to be by nature.[129]

Pieper appeals to the concept of the *status viatoris,* which is not a simple sentimental or religious notion, in order to designate the intrinsic structure of the historicotemporal human condition. The human being begins at a precise moment in the unfolding of time, in which he has been projected, and advances toward the future by virtue of a "natural" striving toward the actualization of his project for being. Because of this ontological structure, as long as the human being is alive, he cannot but find himself "on the way."[130] He is not capable of avoiding the dynamic, temporal ontology of *not-yet-being* that directs him toward the future in which he hopes to attain the fullness of possible being.[131]

Pieper draws his inspiration from Heidegger's ontology,[132] making use of some of his categories, but he distances himself from Heidegger insofar as he maintains that the end inscribed in the structure of Dasein transcends temporal finitude. Pieper thus enters into dialogue with Bloch, who says, in his ontology of *not-yet-being,* that the essence does not yet exist in the present, but that it belongs to the future.

Heidegger rejects any static ontology that would trap Dasein in the present moment. He says repeatedly in *Being and Time*—which is an attempt at an ontology that poses the question: To what extent time belongs to the meaning of Being—that the ultimate ontological foundation of Dasein is temporality. This latter is composed of three *Extasen:* Dasein is projected from a *past* into the *present* toward the *future,* wherein lies the possible realization of Dasein's possibilities. The future constitutes the original sense of existentiality, as well as the ontological end of Dasein. Dasein moves within the tripartite dimension of temporality, which not only allows it to exist historically, but also to realize the authentic fullness of its being. Time forms not only that in which (*das Worinnen*) phenomena bring themselves about, but also and especially that by which (*das Wodurch*) everything that is is able to be. Heidegger "identifies" human essence and existence in the sense that the essence of the human being is at the same time its existence, its temporal mode of "being there." Existence is included in the human essence; its essence consists in its existence. The human being exists to the extent that it is under way toward the future, a historical journey that is made possible by its insertion in temporality, in the mode of being of the project.

Heidegger introduces into his analysis of the temporality of existence the concept of *possibility,* which ought to be understood in an existential, rather than in a logical or contingent sense. This category is the ultimate and the most primordial determination of the human being, which is not a being to which one subsequently attributes *powers,* but which, because of the "already" structured into Dasein, enabling it to "be able," is turned toward the future in which it actualizes its *ability-to-be.* Since it is always itself its own possibility, the human being transcends itself; in other words, it is fundamentally transcendence. Projected into the temporal world, knowing neither where it is going nor whence it comes, but only its being "there" (*Da*), the human being is open to an infinite spectrum of possibilities of existing. It is fundamentally an *ability-to-be,* which expresses the anticipatory character of Dasein, which is ontologically a projection toward its possibilities. Dasein is therefore not a static being that would already have reached its fullness, but a dynamic being striving toward its future fulfillment, remaining by nature concretely open to transformation. The future toward which Dasein strives by its temporality does not here designate "a 'now' which has *not yet* become 'actual' and which sometime *will be* for the first time. We have in view the coming [*Kunft*] in which Dasein in its ownmost potentiality-for-Being, comes toward itself."[133]

Heidegger's notion of ontological becoming contains a "lack" inherent within the process-character of being as it projects itself continuously toward possibilities: the *not-yet-being.* Heidegger here introduces the reality of death, which he does not understand ontically (literal death), but ontologically.[134] This *not-yet-being,* with respect to the end, does not express the anticipation of a completion, something that would come about in the future and which does not belong to the present formally. The *not-yet-being* is instead already present in the temporality of the present in the sense of an anticipation and insofar as it forms "something constitutive" of Dasein, which is "*already its not-yet.*"[135] To the extent to which the *ability-to-be* forms the essence of Dasein, this latter must, insofar as it exists, "*not yet be* something."[136]

Dasein, being fundamentally a *not-yet,* is nevertheless projected toward a future that is posited a priori as an end. Its various possibilities spring into reality from the impossibility of all possibility, which is death, and which constitutes the ontological end of Dasein. Dasein's projection into open temporality is what makes possible the principle of hope.

Pieper and Bloch both teach an ontology of becoming, of *not-yet-being*, which they apply to the human being, who is defined by a dynamic state of striving toward the *Totum* or the *summum bonum*, toward full realization. Insofar as he is alive, the human being is constantly moving forward; his condition is that of the *homo viator*. The two German thinkers nevertheless differ from one another with respect to that which concerns the endpoint and the content of this coming-to-be, the means of attaining it, and finally in the way they conceive human nature.

Bloch's position has its basis in a dialectical materialism, and more precisely, in an interpretation of the left-wing Aristotelianism affirmed by Avicenna and especially Averroes. Matter is not understood as rigid and unchangeable, which are qualities that, according to Bloch, both a certain current of Marxism and the traditional ontology attribute to it. Instead, it is understood as being according to possibility (*kata to dynaton*) or as being-in-possibility (*dynamei on*), which can give rise to all sorts of forms of the real,[137] in correlation with the category of the really possible. *Dynamis* is an inherent property of matter, possessing in itself a multitude of possible determinations that have not yet been realized. Matter constitutes the first and absolute cause of all ulterior production, the basis of utopia, the land of real anticipation, of the perpetual coming-to-be of the various possibilities lying deep within. This interpretive conception of matter and the possible, which is the essential category of Bloch's philosophy, is what makes the unfolding of history possible. This unfolding is permeated by the principle of hope:

> The Authentic or essence is that *which is not yet, which in the core of things drives towards itself, which awaits its genesis in the tendency-latency of process;* it is itself only now founded, objective-real—hope. And its name ultimately borders on 'What-is-in-possibility' in the Aristotelian sense and in a sense which goes far beyond Aristotle, on what is ostensibly the most certain thing there is: matter.[138]

Bloch argues against divine creation *ex nihilo* and replaces it with the category of matter understood within the context of real possibility, the sole foundation: "God and matter become identical."[139] Denying the initial *Perfectum*, he posits the existence of a *potentia subjectiva activa*, which is neither accidental nor constitutive *ens quo*, but which is the contrary of the *actus purus* and which we could call a *potentia pura,* which gives itself a meaning. He replaces the Aristotelian unmoved mover with the *natura naturans,* the self-creating potential matter that Bruno had called the *mater formarum.* Matter is a pure real-being, bereft of any determinate form, a pure *Dass* (*quod*) without any *Was* (*quid*). It is productive of all forms, that is to say, of the concretely real, of the historical process. Its finality is the *materia ultima.*

Bloch's ontology, which maintains that being cannot exist except in the mode of *not-yet-being,* is characterized not only by the fundamental categories of becoming and possibility, which I will address in a moment, but also by four concepts in particular: *Not, Not-yet, Nothing,* and *Everything.* The *Dass* of the human being's present, which it does not manage yet to live and which therefore remains in the "darkness of the lived moment,"[140] is not yet determined; it is empty, it is a *Not* that is at the same time necessary for the possibility of a being; that is, for the plenitude of the as-yet indeterminate *Dass.* This *Not,* understood as *Not-yet,* is not simply a bare nothing, but, as a *Not-having,* it is characterized by a lack. An entity strives after what it lacks, and it hopes to be able one day to come into possession of it. This striving is set in motion through the instinct of hunger. While the *Not* in the *Da des Jetzt* lies at the basis of the striving that drives the being of the empty to fullness, the *Nothing* is the negation of something; that is, it is the contrary of the *Everything.*[141] The human being, which we could define as a being that lacks, a being that hungers, is journeying between the *Everything,* which expresses fulfillment, and the *Nothing,* which signifies failure. The human being, like any other entity, is not yet identical to itself; rather, it is inserted in a dynamic process that begins with the *Nothing* and moves toward a state that has not yet come to be, a *Novum* that rises up from the obscurity of the lived moment. This fact of striving toward the *Novum* is possible insofar as there is such a thing as the category of real possibility. The moment the *Novum* is transformed into an *Ultimum,* the dynamic process comes to a stop, and the possibilities vanish.

This ontology of becoming, of *not-yet-being,* which accords absolute primacy to the category of possibility—understood as possibility in conformity to the object ("das sachhaft-objektgemäss Mögliche") or as real possibility ("das objektiv-real Mögliche")[142]—with respect to the category of the real, can be summarized in a logical formula that expresses the Archimedean point. Reversing Hegel's formula, which affirms that the subject must develop itself according to the idea inherent in it, Bloch affirms that the essence of the subject does not develop except within a dynamic and utopian historico-temporal process: "*S is not yet P,* the subject is not yet the predicate,"[143] that is, there exists a fixed and static subject (S) to which a concrete predicate (P) is attributed. Applied to the human being, this formula means that its potential humanity is not yet realized, that the world in its totality and nature itself have not yet found their true essence. "Essential being is not Beenness; on the contrary: the essential being of the world lies itself on the Front."[144] The human being is thus not human at the very first moment of its existence, it does not yet possess that which characterizes it and what makes it precisely a human being, but rather it develops progressively into itself. This *not-yet* implies a negation (*not*) that is at the same time provisional (*yet*); that is, the nature of the human being, though not the fulfillment of this nature with respect to inherent potentialities, is no longer found at the origin but in the future, at the end of its development: S is not yet P, but it will become P. It must become P if it wants truly to be S. Thus, to the extent that S is not P, it is not yet truly itself. Hope, the motive force of this process, is inserted within the heart of S's inherent dynamic toward P.

Here we have an open system, the foundation of which is the category of the *possible,* as we have seen in Heidegger, and also in Sartre and Hartmann[145] (though this essential concept acquires a particular meaning according to the author and his ontology). Nothing is definitive in the world, which exists in an experimental state. Everything real is marked by an open process of incompletion, of continual gestation, of infinite possibility. Bloch belongs to the current of the ontological reversal, in which the primacy of being, such as it has been conceived by tradition, has given way to the primacy of movement.

According to Bloch, existing things are essentially turned toward the future. This orientation is expressed by the mode of *future-possibility* [*Möglichkeit-nach-vorwärts*]. The fact that it is inherent to being offers a good explanation of the "anticipatory consciousness" to which Bloch devotes the second part of the first volume of the *Principle of Hope,* and which he explains by referring to his theory of daydreams. Observing that the human being is an organism that lives in part on its dreams, he draws a distinction between the daydream, which looks to the future and which lacks any mythological or symbolic meaning, on the one hand, and, on the other, the night-dream, which is tied to the past and the present, the type of dream that psychoanalysis (especially that of Freud, Jung, and Adler, which Bloch discusses) has privileged in its analysis.[146] Both types of dream express, through the imagination, the fulfillment of a wish or a possibility. The daydream, which is important for an analysis of hope and which is ordered by its essence toward the future, expresses, for Bloch, not an escape from reality, as Freud believes, but rather an anticipation of a state that has not yet come about, a concrete utopia (as opposed to the various illusory utopias); a conscious hope that is guided by the *not-yet,* and whose concrete goal is the betterment of the world and the human condition; a progressive dynamic toward the fatherland in which all antagonisms will disappear, a fatherland that is brought about uniquely through *praxis,* and which Bloch describes as the absolute identity between the human being and nature, "the naturalization of man and the humanization of nature."[147] This anticipatory consciousness expressed in dreams must, according to Bloch, get beyond its *not-yet-conscious* state in order to anticipate consciously a concrete future, thus allowing hope, which is an "affect" of expectation, to be transformed into an instrument of utopia, into a *docta spes.*

3.3 The existential uncertainty of the human being

We have seen that Pieper affirms both a determinate and an indeterminate principle as constitutive of the human being. Although Pieper believes, in contrast to Sartre, that the human being is naturally ordered to a final goal that constitutes his realization and total fulfillment, the good *par excellence,* he nevertheless remains free not to attain this goal in reality. An inclination ordered to a goal, which is described here as happiness, does not necessarily imply its accomplishment. Indeed, if the subject is not in a position to choose freely not to want to obtain this good, he may nevertheless freely undertake actions that do not concretely lead to the ultimate good, or even ones that lead away from it.

We can explain this capacity to fail to attain the end, in Pieper's opinion, with the help of a comparison, admittedly imperfect, between human existence and artistic activity. The artist is capable of not achieving an established aim, just as an archer could fail to hit a target, or could practice an art poorly by not following the minimal norms or rules required by the art. Aristotle uses the same analogy in saying that

> it is possible to fail in many ways . . . while to succeed is possible only in one way (for which reason also one is easy and the other difficult—to miss the mark is easy, to hit it is difficult); for these reasons also, then, excess and defect are characteristic of vice, and the mean of virtue.[148]

Pieper remarks that there is nevertheless a difference here: while an artist is capable of practicing his art poorly and remaining all the same in possession of it (and thus remaining a good artist), the human being is not capable of living viciously and continuing to possess the virtues, that is, continuing to be a "good" person, to practice the "art" of good living, and even of fulfilling himself personally.[149]

While *in via*, the human being is characterized by an existential uncertainty,[150] that is to say, he remains in a state of uncertainty with respect to the realization of his proper flourishing, understood by Pieper as a virtuous life. In effect, in spite of the fact that the frequent exercise of a virtue implies an increasing probability that the subject will not lose it, the subject never holds the virtue in his possession in an irrevocable and definitive way. He could in fact lose it gradually by performing a certain number of acts that run contrary to the virtue and could thus fall into indifference or into vice, replacing the first *habitus* by the second.[151]

This insecurity with regard to the human being's complete fulfillment acquires a new dimension in the context of Pieper's notion that the theological virtues contribute to the ultimate end, which he describes as a supernatural beatitude, even though this beatitude does not deny the natural fulfillment of the human subject through the natural moral virtues.[152] Uncertainty in this context concerns, on the one hand, the individual's lack of trust in the wholly Other who gives himself to the individual and who is the source of the theological virtues, and, on the other hand, the possibility for the individual to reject the gift of these virtues, which dispose him to receive the gift of God himself.

Uncertainty can also arise at the natural level, insofar as the subject is not capable of obtaining by his own efforts the end toward which he has decided to strive; that is to say, that end whose possession depends radically on the other. In the case in which the individual is able to attain a good by his own means, uncertainty comes either from a lack of confidence in own's own capacities, or from external events.

The historicotemporal human being exists in the constitutive form of uncertainty, of becoming, of the *not-yet*, of hope. The uncertainty of the human condition cannot be eliminated; it can only be overcome through the principle of hope.[153]

NOTES

1. See Aristotle, *Posterior Analytics*, II, 7, 92b10.

2. See Pieper, *Faith Hope Love*, 96 [*Werke*, Vol. 4, 261]. "Kreatürlichkeit und menschliche Natur," [*Werke*, Vol. 3, 174ff.]. *Guide to Thomas Aquinas*, 134ff. [*Werke*, Vol. 2, 273ff.]. I follow Pieper in taking the concepts of essence and nature as identical ("Kreatürlichkeit," 42).

3. See, for example, Pieper, *In Defense of Philosophy*, 66f., 77 [*Werke*, Vol. 3, 117, 123f.]. "Kreatürlichkeit," 40ff. *The Silence of St. Thomas*, 53ff. [*Werke*, Vol. 2, 118ff.].

4. See Hacks, *Das Poetische*, 118.

5. Ronze, *L'homme de quantité*, 134. See also 146. Scheler, *Tod und Fortleben*, 29.

6. Pieper, *Kümmert euch nicht um Sokrates*, 17–18. Pieper speaks of a "progressive invasion of natural reality by the artificial" in "Auf dem Wege sein," 71.

7. Pieper, "Sachlichkeit und Klugheit," 72ff. See *Living the Truth*, 135ff. [*Werke*, Vol. 5, 65ff.]; *Happiness and Contemplation*, 76–77, 99 [*Werke*, Vol. 6, 194, 208]; *Was heisst Akademisch?* [*Werke*, Vol. 6, 76f., 82f., 102ff., 121]; *Leisure the Basis of Culture*, 101ff. [*Werke*, Vol. 3, 25ff.]; *In Defense of Philosophy*, 45f., 53, 60f. [*Werke*, Vol. 3, 101f., 107, 111f.]; "Kreatürlichkeit," 62. "Philosophie und Gemeinwohl," 75. *Weistum. Dichtum. Sakrament*, 101f.

8. See Pieper, *Arbeit, Freizeit, Musse*, 12. *Arbeit, Freizeit, Musse—Was ist eine Universität?*, 12f.

9. See Pieper, "Verteidigung der Musse. Über philosophische Bildung und geistige Arbeit," [*Werke*, Vol. 3, 1–14].

10. In this article, published in 1796 in the *Berlinischen Monatsschrift*, Kant discusses the question of intellectual activity, on the one hand, with respect to the German Romantic philosophy of Jacobi, Schlosser, and Stolberg—who hold that it is possible to receive a knowledge that would disclose to the philosopher the totality of wisdom through an oracle, without intellectual work and through pure intellectual contemplation—and, on the other hand, with respect to the philosophy of Plato, whom he calls "the father of all fanaticism *with philosophy*" (Kant, "Of a Gentle Tone Lately Assumed in Philosophy," 175 [A.B., VIII, 398]).

11. Ibid., 163 [390].

12. Ibid., 164 [390].

13. Ibid., 168 [393].

14. See Pieper, *Happiness and Contemplation*, 74 [*Werke*, Vol. 6, 195]; see also "Musse und menschliche Existenz" in: *Mensch und Freizeit*, 26. "Verteidigung der Musse," 293. *Prudence*, 20ff. [*Werke*, Vol. 4, 7f.]; *In Defense of Philosophy*, 50f. [*Werke*, Vol. 3, 105f.]. For a more in-depth study of the acts of *ratio* and *intellectus*, see Hufnagel, *Intuition und Erkenntnis nach Thomas von Aquin;* Jolivet, *L'intuition intellectuelle et le problème de la métaphysique;* Peghaire, *Intellectus et ratio selon S. Thomas d'Aquin;* Rousselot, *The intellectualism of Saint Thomas;* Cottier, "Intellectus et ratio."

15. Quoted by Finkielkraut, *Le mécontemporain*, 70f.; see also 56f.

16. Pieper, "Vie humaine et loisirs." Arendt also describes this glorification of work for the sake of work in her *The Human Condition*, 294ff. [332ff.]. See Pieper, *In Defense of Philosophy*, 23, 28–31 [*Werke*, Vol. 3, 86, 90–93]. "Der Mensch ohne Wahrheitsverhältnis," 261.

17. A comment from Hitler, as reported by Rauschning (*Gespräche mit Hitler*, 211), which Pieper describes as pure madness (*Arbeit, Freizeit, Musse*, 13).

18. Pieper, *Leisure the Basis of Culture*, 36 [*Werke*, Vol. 6, 11].

19. Ronze, *L'homme de quantité*, 34.

20. See Plato, *Theaetetus*, 174a–b. Pieper, *Was heisst Akademisch?*, 53ff., 57.

21. Plato, *Gorgias*, 485b–486c.

22. Descartes, *Discourse on the Method*, I, 119 [VI, 61–62]. We find this thought also in Bacon (*Novum Organum*, I, 81, 117), for whom science has no other purpose than to change reality for the sake of humanity, the goal is "that human life be endowed with new discoveries and powers."

23. See Pieper, *The Silence of St. Thomas*, 53f. [*Werke*, Vol. 2, 118f.].

24. This reduction of the human being to a thing or tool can be viewed in relation to the world of *praxis*, in which the principle of work is valued simply for its own sake.

25. See Anders, *Die Antiquiertheit des Menschen*, Vol. 2, 21ff. *Die atomare Drohung*, 194ff.

26. It is worthwhile making clear at this point that, for Pieper, the creative human being certainly knows the essence of the things he has produced, but that he does not know it down to its most minuscule details insofar as he is not, properly speaking, its creator *ex nihilo*. The artisan always works on materials whose essence he himself did not produce. I will return to this idea in Pieper, to which he devoted a talk (*The Silence of St. Thomas*, 57–67 [*Werke*, Vol. 2, 112–29]), the point of which was to show that it is impossible for the human being to comprehend anything at all completely, even though he is at least potentially capable of knowing all things.

27. See Pieper, "Diskussion," 132. See *Leisure the Basis of Culture*, 102ff. [*Werke*, Vol. 3, 26ff.]. One of the consequences of this marginalization of all

theoria, however subtle it may be, is a rejection of the fundamental hope that is essentially characterized by gift. The sole hope that can germinate in such circumstances is the sort whose fulfillment depends entirely on human means, on *praxis.* We find a certain parallel to this in a text from Thomas Aquinas (*Summa Theologiae,* I–IIae, 40, 2, 1) which distinguishes the passion of hope as two types: on the one hand, the type whose object is something the human being is capable of attaining through his own efforts and which we could relate to the type of hope that *homo practicus* defends, and, on the other hand, the hope whose object is such that the human being must have recourse to the aid of another in order to attain it, and which constitutes the root of fundamental hope. This second passion of hope implies that, in order to actualize the hoped-for object, the subject is not only dependent on the other, whether this other be the contingent thou or, in the context of a metaphysics of a transcendence with transcendence, the absolute Thou, but also that the subject is open to the gratuitous reception of a gift. The attitude of *homo practicus* expresses in a nutshell Bloch's position, which I will address in the second part of this study.

28. Thomas Aquinas, *Quaestiones disputatae de veritatae,* 10, 1. I will return later to fact that the human intellect is incapable of comprehending a single entity.

29. Pieper, *In Defense of Philosophy,* 78 [*Werke,* Vol. 3, 124]; see "Kreatürlichkeit," 44f.

30. See Pieper, *Living the Truth,* 121ff. [*Werke,* Vol. 5, 55ff.]; *Prudence,* 17ff. [*Werke,* Vol. 4, 5f.]; *Living the Truth,* 39f. [*Werke,* Vol. 5, 126ff.]; "Wahrheit der Dinge—ein verschollener Begriff," 421f.

31. Sartre, *Existentialism and Human Emotions,* 13 [17–18]; see *Nausea,* 122 [163]; *Situations,* vol. 3, 289–305.

32. See Pieper, "Kreatürlichkeit," 56. *Living the Truth,* 121–22 [*Werke,* Vol. 5, 54–55]; *Living the Truth,* 39f. [*Werke,* Vol. 5, 126]; *The Silence of St. Thomas,* 50f., 61 [*Werke,* Vol. 2, 116f., 123].

33. Aristotle, *Physics,* II, 199a13; see also II, 8, 199a16, 194a21. *The Parts of Animals,* 65a. Aristotle compares nature to an architect (645a9), to a sculptor (*On the generation of animals,* 654b31), and to an administrator (744b16). On the notion that "art imitates nature," see the studies by Flasch, "Ars imitatur naturam: Platonischer Naturbegriff und mittelalterliche Philosophie der Kunst" and Meyer, *Natur und Kunst bei Aristoteles.*

34. Goethe, "Die Natur," in *Naturwissenschaftliche Schriften,* 922.

35. See Bernard, *The* Cahier Rouge *of Claude Bernard,* 82 [141]. *La science expérimentale,* 326.

36. Thomas Aquinas, *Summa contra gentiles,* II, 24 (p. 72); see also III, 40, 100. *Summa Theologiae,* I, 117, 1.

37. See Sartre, *Existentialism and Human Emotions,* 13ff. [17ff.]. Pieper, "Kreatürlichkeit und menschliche Natur," [*Werke,* Vol. 3, 179]; *The Silence of St. Thomas,* 52ff. [*Werke,* Vol. 2, 117ff.].

38. Sartre, *Existentialism and Human Emotions,* 14 [19–20]. See "Notes. A propos de l'existentialisme," 84.

39. Pieper, *The Silence of St. Thomas,* 51, 52, 69 [*Werke,* Vol. 2, 116, 117f., 128].

40. Pieper, "Kreatürlichkeit und menschliche Natur," [*Werke,* Vol. 3, 180]; see "Kreatürlichkeit," 42.

41. Sartre, *Nausea,* 129 [169].

42. Sartre, *Situations,* vol. 9, 53.

43. According to Pieper, the existence of God forms the object neither of a proof of *ratio* nor of a pure act of faith, but rather of *intuitio.*

44. See Pieper, *Prudence,* 17ff. [*Werke,* Vol. 4, 5f.]; *The Silence of St. Thomas,* 66–67 [129]; *Living the Truth,* 43–46 [*Werke,* Vol. 5, 129–32]. *Living the Truth,* 122–23 [*Werke,* Vol. 5, 55–56]; "Wahrheit der Dinge—ein verschollener Begriff," 424.

45. The human being must be willing to make considerable efforts in order to grasp the essence of a *res naturalis.*

46. See Pieper, *The Truth of All Things,* in *Living the Truth.*

47. See Sartre, *Existentialism and Human Emotions,* 14ff., 21 [20ff., 34]. "Notes. A propos de l'existentialisme," 84.

48. Sartre, *Existentialism and Human Emotions,* 51 [94]; see also 13, 15, 21 [17, 21, 33f.]. Sartre describes this atheistic project as a "cruel and lengthy undertaking," which he believes he has "carried . . . through" (*The Words,* 253 [210–11]). He is in agreement with Gide, regarding whom he says "he *lived* his ideas; and one, above all—the death of God. . . . What Gide gives us that is most precious is his decision to live to the finish the agony and death of God. . . . He lived *for us* a life which we have only to relive by reading" (*Situations,* 66–67 [IV, 88–89]). Sartre's atheism has its psychological source in his childhood experiences. Commenting on Naville's atheism, he recognizes that this position is not the result "of a gradual discovery. It is the sheer, *a priori* adoption of a position on a problem that infinitely surpasses our experience. This position is one I share" (*Situations,* Vol. 3, 139). "For my part, I start from the opposite hypothesis: I do not need God and have nothing to do with him. I assert at the outset: God does not exist, man suffices unto himself. Beyond that, there is nothing." This affirmation, which Sartre makes in the famous talk he gave in 1943 (see *Existentialism and Human Emotions*) is cited by Descoqs, "L'athéisme est un humanisme," 56–57. Sartre will nevertheless attempt to demonstrate the nonexistence of God on the basis of the two ontological notions of the *in-itself* (which is characterized by contingency) and the *for-*

itself (which is characterized by its freedom and consciousness), as well as on a false understanding of God as *Ens causa sui.* In order to exist, God, in this case, would have to be *in-himself* and *for-himself* at the same time. But an identity between these two ontological notions is precisely impossible.

49. Sartre, *Existentialism and Human Emotions,* 15 [22]; see also "Notes," 85; "Introduction," 35f.; "A propos de l'existentialisme."

50. Sartre *Existentialism and Human Emotions,* 15 [21–22]; see *Situations,* Vol. 9, 53.

51. Sartre, "Notes," 84; see *Being and Nothingness,* 60, 603f. [61, 547].

52. Sartre, *Existentialism and Human Emotions,* 15–16 [22–23]; see also 16ff., 32, 43 [25ff., 55, 78]. *Being and Nothingness,* 702 [634]. "Notes," 84. In the last interview he gave shortly before being hospitalized and dying, Sartre affirmed once again very clearly that "there is no a priori essence, and therefore it is not yet determined what a man is," Sartre and Lévy, *L'espoir maintenant,* 36.

53. Sartre, *Existentialism and Human Emotions,* 23 [37].

54. Sartre, *Nausea,* 151 [196].

55. Ibid., 84 [114].

56. See Sartre, *Existentialism and Human Emotions,* 23 [37].

57. See Pieper, "Kreatürlichkeit," 51ff. On the issue of the will-existence connection, see Welte, "Das Gute als Einheit des Unterschiedenen," 138ff.

58. Pieper's sense of freedom is rooted in human nature, which is prior to it, and by virtue of which it is able to exist and to act. With respect to its actualization, freedom always presupposes the presence of an intellect and a will. At the root of freedom there is a choice, and thus a voluntary act that presupposes a comparison, that is, a judgment, which is an act of intelligence. Freedom is an attribute of the will to the extent that the will is a rational appetite.

59. See Sartre, *Being and Nothingness,* 363 [330]. "Introduction," 21.

60. Sartre, *Being and Nothingness,* 60 [61].

61. Sartre, *Existentialism and Human Emotions,* 23 [37]; see also 46 [83f.]; *Being and Nothingness,* 566f., 568f., 581, 606f. [514, 516, 527, 550]. "Introduction," 18, 21, 50, 52.

62. Sartre, *Being and Nothingness,* 60 [61].

63. Ibid., 605 [559].

64. For a close reading of *Being and Nothingness,* see Schumacher, ed., *Jean-Paul Sartre. Das Sein und das Nichts.*

65. Sartre, "Introduction," 51.

66. On the question of modern atheism, see Buckley, *At the Origins of Modern Atheism;* Cottier, *Horizons de l'athéisme;* Girardi and Six, eds., *L'athéisme dans la philosophie contemporaine;* de Lubac, *The Drama of Atheist Humanism;* Paul, *Dieu est mort en Allemagne.*

67. We see this crucial choice in Goetz, who affirms that, "if God exists, man is nothing; if man exists . . ." and he leaves the sentence in suspense. See Sartre, *The Devil and the Good Lord,* Act III, Scene X, 141 [267]. For Bakunin (*Philosophie der Tat,* 120), the acceptance of the idea of God means "the decisive negation of human freedom and necessarily leads to the enslavement of the human being, both in theory and in practice. . . . If God exists, the human being is a slave; but the human being can and must be free: therefore, God does not exist."

68. Nietzsche, *Thus Spoke Zarathustra,* 124 [Vol. 4, 14]; see also 197–98 [Vol. 4, 109–10]; *The Gay Science,* bk. 3, no. 125, 181–82 [Vol. 3, 480–81].

69. Sartre, *Existentialism and Human Emotions,* 49 [89].

70. Cited by Verneaux, *Leçons sur l'athéisme contemporain,* 27.

71. Sartre, *Being and Nothingness,* 741 [669]. See idem, *Situations,* Vol. 1, 330; *The Flies,* 159 [135].

72. Sartre, *Existentialism and Human Emotions,* 49 [89]; see also 16, 21, 23, 43, 51 [23, 34, 38, 78, 93]; *Being and Nothingness,* 76, 613f. [76, 556f.].

73. Sartre, *Existentialism and Human Emotions,* 22 [35–36].

74. Ibid.

75. "That my freedom is the unique foundation of values and that *nothing,* absolutely nothing, justifies me in adopting this or that particular value, this or that particular scale of values. . . . My freedom is anguished at being the foundation of values. . . . I do not have nor can I have recourse to any value against the fact that it is I who sustain values in being. . . . I have to realize the meaning of the world and of my essence; I make my decision concerning them—without justification and without excuse," Sartre, *Being and Nothingness,* 76–78 [76–77]; see *Existentialism and Human Emotions,* 22.

76. See Sartre, *Existentialism and Human Emotions,* 20, 21, 23, 26ff. [31, 33, 38, 44ff.]; *The Devil & the Good Lord,* Act III, Scene X, 141 [267].

77. Sartre, *Being and Nothingness,* 568 [516].

78. Sartre, "Notes, A propos de l'existentialisme," 85.

79. See Sartre, *Situations,* Vol. 1, 47f.

80. See Sartre, *Situations* [French edition], Vol. 2, 20.

81. Sartre, *Being and Nothingness,* 603 [546–47].

82. Sartre, *Being and Nothingness,* 569 [516]; see *Existentialism and Human Emotions,* 22f. [36f.]. Sartre is in agreement with Lachelier, for whom it would be a contradiction to posit a real freedom that was an integral part of human nature. Indeed, the opposition between freedom and nature is for him "the fundamental opposition of philosophy," in: Lachelier, *Oeuvres de Jules Lachelier,* Vol. 2, 197; see also 123. Bloch (*Experimentum Mundi* [*Werke,* Vol. 5, 181–82]) also maintains that the human being "has not yet been determined. . . . In every case, 'naturally' means that the human being is obedient, from birth to death, to unchangeable characteristics."

83. Bernard, *Lectures on the Phenomena of Life Common to Animals and Plants*, 42 [61]; see also 39f. [56].

84. Bernard, *An Introduction to the Study of Experimental Medicine*, 93 [147–48]; see *La science expérimentale*, 326; *The* Cahier Rouge *of Claude Bernard*, 24f., 32f., 82, 84 [58f. 69, 141, 144]; *Lectures on the Phenomena of Life common to Animals and Plants*, 268 [13, 370]; *De la physiologie générale*, 326f. See also Jonas, *The Phenomenon of Life*. Spaemann and Löw, *Die Frage wozu?*

85. See, for example, Aristotle, *Physics*, 200a34.

86. See Sartre, "Notes, A propos de l'existentialisme," 84.

87. See Thomas Aquinas, *Summa theologiae*, I, 19, 103, 1 ad 1; I–II, 1, 1 and 2; II–II, 23, 2; *Summa contra gentiles*, III, 2; *Quaestiones disputatae de Potentia Dei*, 5, 1.

88. See Sartre, *Nausea*, 129f. [168f.]; *Existentialism and Human Emotions*, 22 [33]; *Situations*, 184f. [Vol. 4, 355].

89. See *The Words*, 251 [210].

90. Sartre, *Nausea*, 132f. [173].

91. Sartre, *Being and Nothingness*, 699 [631]; see also 25ff. [31ff.].

92. See Sartre, *Nausea*, 84, 122, 127f., 131 [114, 160, 166ff., 171].

93. Ibid., 129 [168].

94. Ibid., 135 [176].

95. One could argue from the order in the garden to the existence of someone who arranged it into that order. When an artist creates a work, he possesses in his intellect a representative idea of the object, before he actualizes the object in matter. This initial idea which contains the object as yet *in potentia*, will play the role of cause with respect to its actualization, because without it, nothing would happen. The artist inscribes an intention into this idea, so that the thing he creates is ordered to a precise purpose: for example, the chair is made primarily for sitting. Of course, it can be put to other uses, but these are not strictly speaking the proper finality for which it was made. When the artist creates an object, he refers to an *eidos*, which organizes its determinate actualization in an intelligent manner and which expresses the why, the goal, the usefulness of the created object. The artist thus acts with an intention. Using an analogy, which is of course imperfect, and drawing on the connection between the intelligence and the *eidos*, we could say that an intellect has inscribed an *eidos* in *res naturales* (for *res artificiales* it is the human intellect), an analogy to which Bernard himself alludes (*The* Cahier Rouge *of Claude Bernard*, 25 [59]). With respect to organisms, we observe that it is not the human being who has inscribed this finality into nature, but to the contrary it existed already before the human being, for his intelligence discovers it, just as the scientist discovers not only the internal structure but also the laws governing the organism. What intellect is it, then, that lies at the origin of *res*? On the relation between nature, end, and intellect, see Aertsen, *Nature and Creature*, 347ff.

96. Inanimate and animate bodies, possessing a vegetative life, function in view of an end in a completely different manner. Without being conscious of it, they perform the movement that is inscribed in their nature. The organisms that belong to the realm of creatures that are sentient but lack reason also act for an end, and even possess a certain "knowledge" of this end through their senses and natural instinct.

97. Sartre, *Being and Nothingness*, 567 [515]; see also 623f., 625f., 706f. [565, 567, 639]; *Existentialism and Human Emotions*, 23 [37].

98. See Sartre, *Being and Nothingness*, 625f. [566f.]; *Anti-Semite and Jew*, 63 [76].

99. The intellect is ordered in a determinate way to the true, the will to the good.

100. See Pieper, *Alles Glück ist Liebesglück*, 12ff.; *Happiness and Contemplation*, 20f. [*Werke*, Vol. 6, 159]; *The Concept of Sin*, 23ff., 29f., 36 [*Werke*, Vol. 5, 224f., 228f., 233]. "Kreatürlichkeit," 58f. Pieper agrees with the teaching of Thomas Aquinas who maintains that, while being free, "the rational creature, furthermore, naturally desires to be happy; hence it cannot wish to be happy" (*Summa contra gentiles*, IV, 92, 339). See *Summa Theologiae*, I, 19, 10; 82, 1; 94, 1; I–II, 13, 6. Schockenhoff (*Bonum hominis*), discussing this Thomastic doctrine, observes that "the will is bound and set only in relation to that good which presents itself universally as the unlimited good" (143); "the fact that the will is exercised in conformity with the goal that is given as part of its nature does not in any way mean for Thomas that the human being is no longer free with respect to the *concrete choice* of ways to live and in the determination of his own personal 'final goal'; such an interpretation would have failed to grasp the existential seriousness of the Thomistic conception of freedom" (144). "What is always already given to freedom is merely the formal structure of being ordered to the *finis ultimis;* the realm of the *ea quae sunt ad finem*, which is open to a free determination, contains everything that substantializes this ordering to a final end, an ordering that is in itself still free of content, in relation to a concrete plan of life, and everything that enables its fulfillment through the multifaceted means and modes of activity" (170).

101. See Simon, *Freedom of Choice*, 113, 138 (84, 101f.). Thomas Aquinas distinguishes between the will *ut natura* and the will *ut ratio*. See *Summa Theologiae*, I–II, 12, 4 and III, 18, 4. On this distinction, see Alvira, *Naturaleza y libertad;* Millan Puelles, *La sintesis humana de naturaleza y libertad;* Montanari, "La distinzione tra 'voluntas ut natura' e 'voluntas ut ratio' nella doctrina tomistica della libertà."

102. See Pieper, *Glaube, Hoffen, Lieben*, 14. Spaemann (*Basic Moral Concepts*, 14 [25]) observes that the Greeks did not inquire into "'what should we do?,' but 'what do we fundamentally and truly want?' . . . The Greeks

thought that if we could arrive at a precise understanding of the object of our basic and fundamental wants, then we would also know what we ought to do and what right living would consist of. The Greeks called this object of our most fundamental wants, the underlying reason for all our other desires and the reason for all our actions, the Good, or the highest good." Tugendhat ("Antike und moderne Ethik," 43–44) remarks that "the ancient question of the 'agathon,' or the 'bonum' concerned that which is always good for the individual, his well-being, that which can truly fulfill his desire, his 'eudaimonia.'. . .The way ancient ethics put the question was: what is it that I truly want for myself."

103. See Aquinas, *Quaestiones disputatae de veritate*, 1, 1.

104. See Aquinas, *Summa theologiae*, I–II, 1.

105. See Pieper, "Was heisst Glück?," 133f.; *Happiness and Contemplation*, 16f., 17f., 21f. [*Werke*, Vol. 6, 156f., 158, 160].

106. Ibid., 63f. [188].

107. See Aertsen, *Nature and Creature*, 342ff. Cauchy, *Désir naturel et béatitude chez St. Thomas*, 23ff. Laporta, *La destinée de la nature humaine chez Thomas d'Aquin* and "Pour trouver le sens exact. . . ." Walgrave, "Quelques remarkques sur le désir naturel chez Saint Thomas."

108. Pascal, *Pensées*, no. 134, 66 [no. 169, 119]. Pieper's affirmation that every human being necessarily strives after happiness, as well as his reflection on human destiny, is part of the renewal of interest that philosophical thinking and the various human sciences have increasingly shown in the ancient question of human happiness. Pieper responds to this question by referring for the most part to Aristotle and Thomas Aquinas, for whom the theme of happiness constitutes the underlying problematic of their work, a theme that has inspired in this century many profound studies. See Eickelschulte, "Beatitudo als Prozess." Kleber, *Glück als Lebensziel*. Guindon, *Béatitude et théologie morale chez saint Thomas d'Aquin*. Kluxen, *Philosophische Ethik bei Thomas von Aquin*. Wittmann, *Die Ethik des Hl. Thomas von Aquin*.

109. See Pieper, *Happiness and Contemplation*, 44ff. [*Werke*, Vol. 6, 175f.]; "Was heisst Glück?," 135; *Alles Glück ist Liebesglück*, 6. On the question of the relationship between happiness and joy, see Delesalle, "Le plaisir, le bonheur et la joie." Kleber, *Glück als Lebensziel*, 5f. Frankl, *La psychothérapie et son image de l'homme*, 146f. and *The Will to Meaning*, 34 (20).

110. See Aristotle, *Nichomachean Ethics*, I, 1 (1094a2); *Topics*, III, 1 (116a19–20); *Rhetoric*, I, 6 (1362a21ff.); and X, 2 (1172b10–15). Pohlenz, *Die Stoa*, Vol. 1, 111ff.

111. Plato, *Philebus*, 20d; *Gorgias*, 467b, 499e.

112. See Holte, *Béatitude et sagesse*, 13f.

113. See Augustine, *The City of God*, XIX, 1 and X, 1, 1; *On Christian Doctrine*, XVI, 24–25.

114. See Pieper, "Was heisst Glück?," 135.

115. Gide, *Journals*, I, 73 [89]. "We live it [i.e., Happiness] in them, they [i.e., the minor experiences of happiness] bring Happiness about in themselves, but only partially, like constantly inadequate approximations, signifiers surpassed by what they signify. Nor are they able to equal it, just as we are unable to reach the horizon that runs away from us and unceasingly reforms itself always a bit further on the very moment we think we've reached it. Does this mean that the horizon is an illusion? No, not if it is true that it is against the background of the horizon that the objects of our vision organize and hierarchize themselves. The same can be said for Happiness." Delesalle, "Le plaisir, le bonheur et la joie," 12.

116. See Pieper, "Was heisst Glück?," 138. On the various names given to this supreme good, see Eickelschulte, "Beatitudo als Prozess," 158ff.

117. Augustine, *The City of God*, XIX, 1.

118. See the text to which Pieper is referring (*Happiness and Contemplation*, 41 [*Werke*, Vol. 6, 173] and "Was heisst Glück?," 138): "For man to rest content with any created good is not possible, for he can be happy only with complete good which satisfies his desire altogether: he would not have reached his ultimate end were there something still remaining to be desired. The object of the will, that is the human appetite, is the Good without reserve, just as the object of the mind is the True without reserve. Clearly, then, nothing can satisfy man's will except such goodness, which is found, not in anything created, but in God alone. Everything created is a derivative good. He alone, *who fills with all good things thy desire*, can satisfy our will, and therefore in him alone our happiness lies." Thomas Aquinas, *Summa Theologiae*, I–II, 2, 8.

119. See Holte, *Béatitude et sagesse*, 16ff., 90, 94, 199.

120. See Pieper, "Irdische Kontemplation" and *Happiness and Contemplation*, 76ff. [*Werke*, Vol. 6, 196ff.]; "Kann der Zeitgenosse ein kontemplativer Mensch sein?," 404f. On the distinction between imperfect and perfect beatitude, see Adam, "Aquinas on Aristotle on Happiness"; Aertsen, *Nature and Creature*, 361ff.; Cauchy, *Désir naturel et béatitude chez St.-Thomas*, 87–120; Eickelschulte, "Beatitudo als Prozess," 158–85; Hamain, "Morale chrétienne et réalités terrestres. Une réponse de saint Thomas d'Aquin: La 'béatitude imparfaite'"; Kluxen, *Philosophische Ethik bei Thomas von Aquin*, 124–44; MacInerny, *Aquinas on Human Action*, 25–50; Schockenhoff, *Bonum hominis*, 103–28.

121. See Pieper, *Happiness and Contemplation*, 25f. [*Werke*, Vol. 6, 162]; "Hoffnung–auf was?," 162.

122. See Matz, "Zur Problematik der heute wirksamen Staatszielvorstellungen," 94f.

123. Pieper, *The End of Time*, 69f. [*Werke*, Vol. 6, 323f.].

124. See Bloch, *Subjekt–Objekt*, 485; *The Principle of Hope*, 6 [4]. Bloch's criticism is aimed at a scholastic metaphysics permeated by an Enlightenment spirit or a Wolfian pseudo-scholastic spirit. For Pieper, it is to be taken seriously that for Bloch "whole areas of the great Western ontological and anthropological tradition, in which a 'closed and static concept of being' never enjoyed any validity, have remained unknown to him," *Hope and History*, 80 (fn. 36) [*Werke*, Vol. 6, 418, fn. 137]. See Pieper, "Herkunftlose Zukunft und Hoffnung ohne Grund?," 181ff. Hollenbach, *Sein und Gewissen*, 44. Beck, "Materialistische Dialektik und thomasischer Seinsakt."

125. Pieper not only contributed to the rediscovery of this ontology of *not-yet-being*, but he is one of the first to make it the foundation of a philosophy of hope. He explains in a discussion with Moltmann that "I myself have not been uninvolved in bringing about this way of thinking and speaking; I too, for example, have called the future that which alone truly belongs to us, and hope man's authentic answer to the reality of his existence as not-yet-being," in Pieper, "Herkunftslose Zukunft und Hoffnung ohne Grund?," 178. It is false to maintain that the working out of this ontology of becoming, of *not-yet-being*, as the foundation for a philosophy of hope would have remained unknown had Bloch not introduced it. See Schulz, "Der Tod, als die stärkste Nicht-Utopie," 67. Hempel, "Das Sein—und Zeit—Verständnis Ernst Blochs," 19. Braun, "Possibilité et non-encore-être," 157ff. This latter observes, indeed with justification, that for traditional philosophy reality is more important than possibility, while Bloch reverses this order of priority (161). Although Bloch, a neo-Marxist philosopher, depends on the notion of open possibility, his ontology, just like that of the so-called traditional ontology, is ordered in a determinate way toward the "fatherland of freedom," even though the possibility always remains that the human being may never reach it.

126. In the light of several texts that describe this ontology of becoming, it seems that Pieper teaches that the human being does indeed possess a nature, but that he still has to actualize it, to bring it about, in order "truly" to become a human being. (See "Die Aktualität der Kardinaltugenden," 111f.; *Auskunft über die Tugenden*, 11.) In these texts, Pieper makes use of the same concept (human being or nature) to designate two distinct realities: human nature, understood as species, which is unchangeable in its essence, and the goal toward which human nature is ordered. Rhonheimer has brought out the weakness of this point in Pieper, reproaching him—on the basis of a single passage from his writings—for not having distinguished these two concepts of human nature (*Natural Law and Practical Reason*, 18ff. [39f.]; he refers to Pieper, *Living the Truth*, 159f. [*Werke*, Vol. 5, 83f.]). Although his criticism does not bear directly on the question we are discussing, but rather on that of nature as the foundation of morality, he nevertheless wrongly concludes that

Pieper distances himself from the teaching of Thomas Aquinas who distinguishes between *actus primus* and *actus secundus,* that is, between a plenitude of human nature proper to its species and a plenitude that the human being achieves through his action. In his treatment of happiness and contemplation, Pieper, who is more precise in his language, clearly subscribes to this Thomistic distinction, distinguishing, on the one hand, the substantial form that is present from the beginning of human existence, that is, a minimal being that is already actualized and, on the other hand, the action of the human being, which orders it toward an ultimate end inscribed in the depths of the human being's nature and which implies the free actualization of the totality of his *ability-to-be.* The nature of the human being is not found in the future, as it is in Bloch, but in the past and in the present. See Pieper, *Happiness and Contemplation,* ch. VI, fn. 11, p. 118 [*Werke,* Vol. 6, 182, fn. 87]; *The Concept of Sin,* 36ff. [*Werke,* Vol. 5, 233ff.]; *Death and Immortality,* 76f. [*Werke,* Vol. 5, 355f.]; "Die Aktualität der Kardinaltugenden," 119f.; *Das Viergespann,* 10; *Living the Truth,* 160f. [*Werke,* Vol. 5. 84f.].

127. We find this understanding also notably in Gehlen, *Der Mensch,* 24 (33), Lain Entralgo (*L'atteinte et l'espérance,* 545f.); Marcel (*Man Against Mass Society,* 57 [55]); Ortega y Gasset, Przywara, Revers (*Über die Hoffnung,* 7); Scherer, Wust (*Der Mensch und die Philosophie,* vol. 4, 315); Luyten (*Mensch-Sein als Aufgabe*).

128. Pieper's ontology of *not-yet-being* is nevertheless opposed, as we have seen, to Sartre's ontology, which replaces being with the project of being. Sartre maintains that the human being does not possess a precise essence from the first moment of his existence, which in this case would already be determined, but he creates it himself by forming his own nature to the extent that he acts, to the extent that he engages himself through the use of his freedom. The human being is nothing but project, he is nothing until he throws himself into the future. He journeys toward the state of coinciding with himself, toward the unity of the *for-itself* and the *in-itself,* which is nevertheless doomed from the beginning to failure. The human being, "this useless passion," projects his future in freedom, that is to say, without any constraint or determination; he continually invents it. Sartre's ontology of *not-yet-being* in fact turns out to be a philosophy of despair and of the absurd.

129. See Pieper, "Die Aktualität der Kardinaltugenden," 118; see also 117, 120; *On Hope,* 25 [*Werke,* Vol. 4, 263]; *Menschliches Richtigsein,* 1; *Auskunft über die Tugenden,* 10, 12; "Tugendlehre als Aussage über den Menschen," 156f; *Happiness and Contemplation,* 91f. [*Werke,* Vol. 6, 206]. *Das Viergespann,* 10; "Nachdenkliches über die Klugheit," 93; *Über das christliches Menschenbild,* 19f. Schockenhoff, *Bonum hominis,* 34, 117. Meiländer, *The Theory and Practice of Virtue,* 6f. We find this thought already in the Greeks,

for whom the human being needs only to develop his own being in order to reach the best state, *arete*, wherein lies *his eudaimonia.*

130. See Pieper, *On Hope*, 12, 17f. [*Werke*, Vol. 4, 258, 261]; "Herkunftlose Zukunft und Hoffnung ohne Grund?," 181; "Tod und Unsterblichkeit," *Universitas*, 1275; *Menschliches Richtigsein*, 1; *Hope and History*, 106f. [*Werke*, Vol. 6, 436]; *Glauben, Hoffen, Lieben*, 20.

131. This orientation of the human being toward full realization can also be inserted into the framework of the theological affirmation that defines the human being as having been created in the image of God, an affirmation that constitutes the heart of Thomistic moral theology. It is interesting to note that the first sentences of *Über das christliche Menschenbild*, in which Pieper presents a quick overview of the cardinal and theological virtues, begins by expounding the prologue of the prima-secundae of Aquinas's *Summa Theologiae* ("Because, according to St. John Damascene, the human being was created in the image of God . . . ," I, 93, 5, obj.2). Although the human being was created in the image of God, one nevertheless must actualize this image over the course of one's life, in order that it may shine forth in all of its fullness. "The human being was created or produced *in order* to be the image of God" (Geiger, "L'homme, image de Dieu," 515. See Ibid., 518f., 529). This "in order to" expresses the state of striving toward *full-being.* Such an anthropological conception implies an ontology of becoming, of *not-yet-being*, of the *status viatoris:* the human being is not yet perfectly that which he is in the depths of his being, but he has to become it, he has to fulfill the nature he has received. For Pieper, this orientation toward actualization is the result of the fact that every being is ordered to and raised up toward pure act, toward God. Every creature that aims to realize itself thereby strives in an intrinsic way to resemble God. The human being is thus ordered on the basis of this *minimal-being* toward the actualization "of the divine plan incarnated in the creature" (Pieper, *Menschliches Richtigsein*, 2; see *Auskunft über die Tugenden*, 11; *Belief and Faith*, 61 [*Werke*, Vol. 4, 236]; *Living the Truth*, 112 [*Werke*, Vol. 5, 50]).

132. Pieper draws inspiration no doubt also from Przywara's ontology. See Pieper, "Kreatürliche Metaphysik."

133. Heidegger, *Being and Time*, 373 [325]. He distinguishes between two futures (ibid., 385f. [336f.]): on the one hand, the future in which Dasein comports itself toward its proper future (the authentic future) and, on the other hand, the future in which Dasein comports itself toward that which answers its concerns (the inauthentic future).

134. On Heidegger's understanding of death, see Schumacher, "La mort comme la possibilité de l'impossibilité de l'être. Une analyse critique de Heidegger."

135. Heidegger, *Being and Time*, 288 [244].

136. Ibid., 276 [233].

137. See Bloch, *Tübinger Einleitung in die Philosophie*, 233–34; *The Principle of Hope*, 206ff. [237ff.]; *Das Materialismusproblem, seine Geschichte und Substanz*, 140ff. and 479–546; *Tendenz-Latenz-Utopie*, 409–13.

138. Bloch, *The Principle of Hope*, 1373 [1625–26]; see also 235ff. [271ff.]; *Tübinger Einleitung in die Philosophie*, 227.

139. Bloch, *The Principle of Hope*, 236 [272].

140. Ibid., 290 [338].

141. Ibid., 306f. [357]. Bloch's ontology of *not-yet-being*, which is composed of these four fundamental concepts (*Nicht, Noch-Nicht, Nichts*, and *Alles*), has three basic parts: "In such a way however that the *Not*, unable to bear the presence of itself, characterizes the intensive, ultimately interest-based *origin* (the That-based Realizing element [das *Daßhaft-Realisierende*]) of everything. The *Not-Yet* characterizes the *tendency* in material process, of the origin which is processing itself out, tending towards the manifestation of its content. The *Nothing*, or conversely the *All*, characterizes the *latency* in this tendency, negative or positive towards us, chiefly on the foremost Front-field of material process." Bloch, *The Principle of Hope*, 307 [357–58].

142. Bloch, *The Principle of Hope*, 229f. [264f.], 235 [271ff.]. On the distinction of the possibility category into four distinct parts, see Holz, "Kategorie Möglichkeit und Moduslehre."

143. Bloch, "'*S ist noch nicht P*, Subjekt ist noch nicht Prädikat.' Das noch nicht erlangte P des S, Prädikat des Subjekts ist noch ausstehendes Quid pro Quod, das ist: ausstehendes Was der Essenz fürs Dass der Existenz. So viel hier von Bin und Ist, das sich noch nicht hat; die ganze Reihe dieser angeführten Verdichtungen markiert in einem Schlag die ontologische Einheit: Nicht = Nullpunkt, Noch-Nicht = Utopie, Nichts oder Alles = Kern" ["*S is not yet P*, the Subject is not yet the Predicate." The as-yet-unachieved P of the S, the predicate of the subject, is the yet-to-be-realized Quid pro Quo; in other words, the yet-to-be-achieved "what" of the essence for the "that" of existence. The same goes for "an" and "is," which is not yet in possession of itself; the entire series of the considerations here presented delineate in a single breath the unity of being: Not = Nullpoint; Not-Yet = Utopia, Nothing or Everything = the Core], Bloch, *Tübinger Einleitung in die Philosophie*, 219f.

144. Bloch, *The Principle of Hope*, 18 [18]; see also 235 [271], 300 [349]; *Experimentum Mundi*, 172; *Tübinger Einleitung in die Philosophie*, 216–17; "Der Mensch als Möglichkeit," 361.

145. See Sartre, *Being and Nothingness*. Hartmann, *Möglichkeit und Wirklichkeit*. This latter rejects the concept of possibility as it is understood in Aristotle's hylomorphism and opts for the Megaric theory of possibility, which affirms that the possible is what is real. Edmaier (*Horizonte der Hoffnung*,

147–48) summarizes the difference in thinking between Heidegger and Hartmann by emphasizing that "while Nikolai Hartmann begins with the positively given being and understands reality always only as the present moment in the actual context, and therefore completely absorbs possibility into reality as necessity, Heidegger goes to the other extreme. He views all worldly being exclusively from the perspective of the aspect of the possible unfolding of existence for the individual human being, as ordered, therefore, to human freedom, which is the key to his interpretation of the world. What is in fact decisive for Heidegger is only that which is carried out to promote the enabling of true human being in freedom. This is why, for him, possibility is higher than actuality."

146. See Bloch, *The Principle of Hope*, 77ff. [86ff.]. On Bloch's relation to psychiatry, see Schnoor, *Psychoanalyse der Hoffnung.*

147. See Bloch, *The Principle of Hope*, 313 [364]; see also 209 [241], 235 [271], 240 [277], 247 [285], 1175 [1382]; *Experimentum Mundi*, 264. See also Raulet, *Humanisation de la nature. Naturalisation de l'homme*, 155ff. In Bloch's philosophy, we find two sorts of antagonism (that of the human being and that of nature, of the *quod* and of the *quid*, of the *Dass* and of the *Was*) which strive toward their elimination through the union of their terms, a union that Bloch calls the absolute identity of oneself and nature, the Fatherland of Freedom. Drawing on a philosophy that accords an absolute primacy to *praxis*, he states that the human being must free itself in order to become what it truly is in the future. Bloch makes clear (*The Principle of Hope*, 1375f. [1628]) that, before the human being achieves complete fulfillment, "man everywhere is still living in prehistory, indeed all and everything still stands before the creation of the world, of a right world. *True genesis is not at the beginning but at the end,* and it starts to begin only when society and existence become radical, i.e., grasp their roots. But the root of history is the working, creating human being who reshapes and overhauls the given facts. Once he has grasped himself and established what is his, without expropriation and alienation, in real democracy, there arises in the world something which shines into the childhood of all and in which no one has yet seen: homeland (*Heimat*)."

148. Aristotle, *Nichomachean Ethics*, II, 5 (1106b28ff.).

149. Aristotle repeatedly affirms that the good of the human being, its happiness, consists in leading a virtuous life for the whole of one's life; see also I, 6 (1098a15f.; 1099b15; 1100b10; 1101a14f.).

150. On the theme of uncertainty, see the analysis of Wust, *Incertitude et risque.* Bollnow, *Neue Geborgenheit*, 20, 160, 188f. Edmaier, *Horizonte der Hoffnung*, 42ff. Fahrenbach, *Wesen und Sinn der Hoffnung*, 69, 115. Laín Entralgo, *L'attente et l'espérance*, 503f., 520, 526f. Marcel, *Problematic Man*, 140, 144 [182, 187]. *Homo viator*, 52, 54f. [70, 73]. Plügge, "Über die Hoffnung," 65.

151. On this topic, see also chapter five, sections 5.2 and 5.3.

152. Pieper devotes several works and articles to the virtues that lead the human being to the utmost accomplishment of what he is by nature, to the complete flourishing of his person (see *Werke,* Vol. 4). He enumerates these as the four cardinal virtues and the three theological virtues. The actualization of the intellectual virtues (which are divided into two groups according to whether they refer to the speculative intellect [the virtues of understanding, knowledge, and wisdom] or the practical intellect [art and prudence, this latter being at the same time a moral virtue]) and the natural moral virtues (which reside in the appetitive powers of the human being and can be reduced back to the four cardinal virtues: prudence, justice, courage, and temperance), which one can achieve through one's own efforts alone, leads the subject to natural beatitude. Nevertheless, according to Pieper, there are other virtues—the infused moral virtues and the three theological virtues—that the human being acquires by accepting to receive them as gifts, and as things leading to supernatural beatitude. "Insofar as the cardinal virtues are rooted in the theological virtues, the ethos of the Christian is distinguished from the ethos of the 'gentleman,' the naturally noble human being." (*Über das christliches Menschenbild,* 61. See *Menschliches Richtigsein, 2. Das Viergespann,* 10. *Auskunft über die Tugenden,* 12). This view of the fulfillment of human nature by means of the virtues comes from the thought of Thomas Aquinas, for whom the actualization of the virtues represents, among other things, the human being on his way toward God, as well as the progressive realization of the divine image engraved in the inmost heart of the human being (see Schockenhoff, *Bonum hominis,* 88f., 126).

153. See Pieper, *On Hope,* 20f., 72 [*Werke,* Vol. 4, 262, 287].

2

Characteristics of Human Hope

Pieper's endeavor to work out the features of human hope begins in the second half of the 1950s,[1] with his conception of language and, in particular, of the ordinary, or nonspecialized, language of the man in the street as the bearer of a message concerning the nature of reality. He thus joins Plato, Aristotle, Augustine, Thomas Aquinas, Kierkegaard, and Newman, who all teach that we must go back to the living language in order to discover the essence of reality. Without such an orientation, without this openness to reality, Pieper says, thought would become "ethereal, insubstantial, fantastic."[2]

The moment the human being comes to know something, he gives it a name, expressing by means of a sign the essence of what is perceived: the objective reality of the world is disclosed as such in the name.[3] Such an affirmation rests on an understanding of language as a sign of something for someone. The reality comes first, the knowledge comes second. By means of ordinary language, the human being expresses certain profound aspects of a precise reality, even if he is not able to articulate the essence of this object. It is the philosopher's task to bring it out.

In order to grasp something true concerning reality, and to define a fundamental concept, it is necessary, explains Pieper, "as always,"[4] to take our bearings from ordinary language. He rejects not only the definitions of hope that have no direct relationship to the concrete world—such as that of Spinoza[5] and of Jaspers[6]—but also of any reduction of philosophical language to a jargon or artificial terminology. He, like several other contemporary philosophers of hope, opts for the vernacular language, which he believes has a better grasp of reality than "artificial language."[7] He does not withdraw into his philosophical cell in

order to work out a definition of hope with the tools of an artificial terminology; instead, he takes the concrete and lived reality of the everyday world as his point of departure, the world that expresses itself in
ordinary language. The analysis of ordinary language, which is more
than just a simple linguistic analysis, helps to bring out the essence of
the object conceptualized in words.

Nevertheless, Pieper does not linger over the enumeration and discussion of the features of human hope. He contents himself with indicating six of these features, which, moreover, he treats fairly briefly.[8] In
what follows, I will first present his enumeration, before entering into a
deeper analysis of a few of these features, as well as other specific characteristics of human hope.

Hope is accompanied by (1) a minimum of *certitude* and *assurance*
with respect to the possible possession of the thing hoped for, the thing
for which the subject aims. If this minimum is lacking, we are no longer
speaking of hope, but of simple desire. The object hoped for is (2) a
good, understood not in the moral but in the ontological sense. The
thing must be good in a certain respect, something desirable for the
subject. In order to be able to speak of hope, there must be an inclination toward the object, there must be a desire on the part of the individual for the object, a hunger or thirst for the object, which falls under
the aspect of goodness. The object hoped for must be (3) *difficult to
obtain.* We do not hope for something that demands no effort on the
part of the individual. This applies as much to the things the subject is
able to realize through his own efforts as to the things that do not
depend on him, things offered to him as a gift. The difficulty that
attends these latter can also become evident in an individual's reserva-
tions about receiving the good gratuitously—for example, the reception
may require a certain humility. A thing that can be possessed through
a simple act of will, by contrast, does not form an object of hope. An
object of hope (4) *is not something that is necessarily realized.* It escapes
all planning. We cannot, strictly speaking, hope night will fall or day will
break, for these are events that occur naturally—unless, of course, something were to disrupt this natural sequence, which has never happened
before. We know or we expect something that we can be sure will happen in the future, but we do not hope for it. The object of hope (5) *lies
beyond the control of the one who hopes.* In ordinary language, no one
speaks of hope in relation to things we are able to bring about ourselves

in a real way, that is, things we are certain we are able to do. The realization of the hoped-for object is subject to a certain degree of uncertainty, which is the result of factors that are independent of the subject who hopes and that lie beyond his own capabilities. For example, a person who knows for sure he can repair a damaged object does not say he hopes it will get fixed. The moment an element of absolute certainty enters in, hope disappears. Every act of hope includes a certain uncontrollability with respect to the hoping subject. The object of the passion of hope (*espoir*), which can be achieved by human means, is also characterized by uncontrollability, although to a lesser degree than the good of the passion of hope (*espoir*) or of fundamental hope acquired due to the power of an other. The final feature (6) of hope consists in the attitude of *expectant waiting*, which can be directed either to a good or an evil. In any event, hope, as we have seen, is always ordered to something that represents a good for the hoping subject (*sub ratione boni*); its contrary is the object of fear.

The enumeration of these six features of hope is not, in my opinion, adequate for an analysis of hope. Not only does Pieper claim to treat them "in passing," he also neglects to study in more depth other characteristics that accompany human hope or belong to it.

2. OTHER CHARACTERISTICS OF HUMAN HOPE

2.1 Hope is an intentional movement toward an object

Hope is characterized by an "intentional" movement toward a preexistent object, a movement that presupposes the hoping subject has perceived the hoped-for object either through the senses, through an estimative faculty, or through the intelligence. It is impossible to hope for something that one has not already perceived in some manner. Every act of hope presupposes the existence of something good, something the subject is aware of before setting off in its pursuit. The individual who knows a good object through his senses or his intelligence already possesses it in a certain sense, but not yet fully in reality. The intentionality of hope, directed toward a particular object, proceeds from a response on the part of the subject to a good that has affected it.[9] The act of hoping is a consequence of a response triggered by an object or a precise situation, a response that nevertheless can also lead to either ordinary or fundamental despair. For this reason, a hope that does not have an object or an intentional movement toward a future, possible, difficult-to-obtain good, would not in fact be hope. This "intentional" movement is not only the foundation for the concrete act of both ordinary or fundamental hope, but also is in the ontological structure of *not-yet-being,* accompanied by the categories of the possible, of the project, and of the realizable utopia.

2.2 Hope and desire

Ordinary language easily confuses the notions of hope and desire, as if they were synonymous. Spinoza defends such an identification. It is true that hope and desire are both characterized by a movement toward a good that lies outside the individual's possession. We can distinguish three sorts of desire that run parallel to the act of hope: (a) a desire that disappears once its object has been achieved or realized: for example, hunger disappears after a good meal; (b) a desire that increases when it is satisfied: for example, desire intensifies in the search for wisdom or for complete happiness; and (c) a desire that continues in the union, and that we find in social hope.[10] Desire and hope are also accompanied by expectant waiting, a feature I will address in a moment.

Though hope presupposes desire as a condition of possibility for its actualization,[11] it is not identical with it, insofar as it includes a certain certitude with respect to the actualization of the hoped-for good. By contrast, desires may be set on illusory objects or on those that will not likely find realization even if certain minimal conditions are met. Indeed, we can distinguish two types of desire. On the one hand, we desire a good even though we know we cannot come into possession of it or bring it about. Such a desire, which is often connected with the faculty of the imagination, may express a flight from the concrete situation into which the human being is projected, a flight from the monotony of day-to-day life or from boredom. On the other hand, we desire an object that is possible, that is, an object characterized by a certain degree of certitude or likelihood that it will be possessed.[12] While we desire something either possible or impossible to bring about, the object of hope is, at least subjectively, able to be realized. Thus, desire is distinguished from hope according to the real possibility of obtaining the object that the subject seeks.

Though Marcel has been falsely accused of failing to distinguish between desire and hope,[13] he places desire in the metaphysical category of having, insofar as desire, in his view, is egocentric and strives after possession. The desired thing or situation is not willed for its own sake, but it is willed in relation to and regarded from the perspective of the desiring subject. Genuine hope, which Marcel distinguishes from desire-hope (*espoir*), is rooted in the metaphysical category of being. It is directed to a "we": "I hope in thee for us."[14] It transcends desire insofar as it refuses to be centered on the person's ego. While desire always aims at a thing or a person, we can distinguish in hope between an "I hope that . . ." and an "I hope . . . ,"[15] between ordinary hope (*espoir*) and fundamental hope.[16] However, Marcel's distinction does not seem adequate to me, since it does not provide a sufficient basis for distinguishing between desire and hope (*espoir*). It seems more appropriate for comparing desire and fundamental hope.

The absent good that constitutes the object of hope is possible and difficult to obtain; this is what in fact distinguishes it from desire. Simple desire cannot aim at the possession of a difficult-to-obtain good insofar as a good of this sort requires the intervention of a faculty capable of surmounting the difficulty involved in acquiring the desired good—namely, it requires the irascible appetite, the source of the passion of hope.[17] Desire is rooted in the concupiscible appetite. While the hoped-for good is a *bonum arduum*, the desired good is a *bonum absolute*.[18]

The adjective *arduum*, as Pieper has stressed, constitutes one of the four ways of describing the act of hope. The *arduum* is not identical to a simple difficulty, but refers, according to Alexander of Hales and Albert the Great, to something elevated, and according to Bonaventure, to something great, eminent, and excellent.[19] This latter in fact designates the *arduum* as the formal object of hope. For Thomas Aquinas, the *arduum* is that which exceeds facile activity or a natural course of operation, and demands from the subject a particular and exceptional effort; and that is why it resides in the irascible power, the faculty that fights for the acquisition of a good.

Thomas Aquinas distinguishes three sorts of good that do not qualify as *arduum*, and thereby as objects of hope. First, there is the insignificant good, whose lack of value is rooted in the subjective attitude of the person who hopes. Second, there is the good we can possess immediately at our own discretion, which is excluded insofar as a hoped-for good requires some degree of effort to acquire it. The third category consists of the goods of which we possess the ineluctable cause.[20]

The difficulty of the hoped-for good entails a certain significance for the hoping subject, a certain difficulty in acquiring it, and also the absence of an ineluctable cause.

2.3 Hope and expectant waiting

Expectant waiting constitutes one of the most important characteristics of the act of hope. Indeed, certain authors maintain hope is a subcategory of expectation.[21] But is it in fact the case that all hope is necessarily an expectant waiting?

Expectant waiting and hope are both oriented toward the future, in which a reality, an event, or a possibility, is to come about. Their directedness toward the future can even be so strong as to render the present "nonexistent," insofar as they desire to reduce the obstacle of time in order that the object they are set on may be realized.[22] In any event, we should notice we can wait expectantly only for something that will take place in the future, while it is possible to hope for something that could already have been realized in the past or in the present. It is possible for me today to hope I passed the exam I took yesterday, even if the professor has already determined the result. Thus, the hoped-for object is in fact already positively or negatively realized, while the hoping subject remains still in uncertainty with respect to the result. We can get a better grasp of this possibility of hoping for something that has happened by considering the distinction Middendorf has drawn between the objective fulfillment of hope, which bears on what may already have taken place, and the subjective experience of the accomplishment of the realization or the nonrealization of the hoped-for object.[23] This differentiation refines the Thomistic definition of hope as a movement toward a *bonum futurum,* a future that is not necessarily the moment in which the hoped-for good will take place, but rather in which the hoping subject will become aware of or rejoice in the fact or the result of the hoped-for good. Expectant waiting and hope are also distinguished with respect to the verb tense they employ. The verb "to hope" is almost never conjugated in the future tense, and when it is used in the past, it is only in the imperfect tense, even though it refers to a precise moment, such as yesterday or this morning. The verb "to wait expectantly" (*attendre*), by contrast, is conjugated in every tense.[24]

Expectant waiting and hope come together in their inclination toward a *good and possible object*. The object of expectation, however, is not always *good*, but can also be bad or indifferent. According to its value, a variety of emotions are attendant upon expectation, such as joy, fear, or dread. In my analysis, I will refer only to the expectation directed to an object that is good, insofar as it is, under this aspect, closest to hope, which is always directed to a good, to something pleasant or enjoyable, thus distinguishing itself from fear, which is the representation of a future destructive or distressing evil. Expectant waiting and hope both moreover take as their object something whose realization is *possible* or whose possession is probable. For example, we don't expect or hope for the arrival of a bus on a corner it never passes or at a time when it is not running.

These two acts are also characterized by their *uncertainty* with respect to the actualization of their object. If I am expectantly awaiting or hoping for the arrival of a friend, I am not absolutely certain he will in fact be there at the appointed time, since external factors, or even ones internal to the person, could arise and change the course of the anticipated events. These two dispositions rest on a certain "promise" that the good awaited or hoped for will be realized. They are at the same time threatened by the possibility of being disappointed by the nonrealization of the good in question.[25] In the case of expectant waiting, we can nevertheless make a distinction between the sort of expectation characterized by a certain degree of uncertainty and the sort that anticipates what will happen in any event. This latter is accompanied by a greater degree of certainty, insofar as it is based on experience or reasoning.[26]

In any event, although expectation and hope are marked by a certain degree of uncertainty, we notice the degree of subjective certainty concerning the actualization of a future object or event is greater for the one who waits expectantly than for the one who hopes. We see this, for example in the following expressions: "I am waiting for the bus," as compared to "I hope that the bus will come." In the first case, I am almost certain the bus will come, and it does not cause me much worry. If it happened not to arrive at the scheduled time, I would begin to grow impatient, my expectation would become increasingly uncertain, and it would eventually give way to hope. The dimension of trust plays an important role here.

In addition to the difference in the degree of certainty with respect to the realization of a particular object, we also notice another difference. Expectant waiting is characterized by strong internal activity, an insistence, and sometimes an impatience, in relation to the actualization of a good that lies outside the control of the individual. Hope, by contrast, is more detached and more flexible. It possesses a certain interior relaxation, accompanied by a patience that accepts the various external and unforeseen difficulties; it exhibits a greater trust in the future on the part of the subject. Expectation and hope are thus distinguished by two different temporal structures: while the former is a closed time, the latter is an open time. Marcel talks about these structures, and I will return to them at a later point. Closed time signifies that the present already contains what will happen in the future, excluding all genuine novelty with respect to what is to come. It is no longer open and disponible toward the future. Open time, by contrast, implies the possibility of receiving something as a gift.[27]

The difference between expectation and hope in degree of uncertainty gives rise in turn to a further distinction. While the actualization of the object expectantly awaited is characterized by a relatively high coefficient of probability, the hoped-for object contains a "superrational" moment (which does not mean irrational). In other words, it does not allow itself to be captured by rational calculation. In order for hope to be able to blossom and for us to be able to rejoice in an object, according to Marcel, we must "be entirely liberated from the chains of possession in all of its forms,"[28] and we must project ourselves trustingly into the uncertainty and unknowability that is an inalienable dimension of the future. The one who bases his activity solely on rational and certain knowledge is one who rejects this "superrational" and unquantifiable dimension, and thereby rejects a metaphysics of openness and trust. Not daring to make the leap into the incalculable void of hope and desiring to escape the anxiety and the fear of existential uncertainty with respect to the future, the most he can do is commit himself to the expectation that appeals to a rational outlook. "So the more we endeavour to live in accordance with the guidance of reason, the more we endeavour to depend less on hope and to free ourselves from fear, to control fortune as much as we can, and to direct our actions by the sure counsel of reason."[29] Hope is reduced in this context to a simple opinion, lacking any scientific value, stripped of certitude, because it arises from the imagination or from simple desires and uncontrollable passions. The goal is therefore "to program hope," to master and possess the future.

The notion that hope is an expectation of the future based on rational calculation is not new. Already for the Greeks of the preclassical period, such as Homer, Hesiod, Theognis, and Pindar, it is accompanied by a logical and provisional determination of how the future will likely unfold. This knowledge of the future is not absolutely certain and remains within the realm of "opinion." Later Greek authors avoid this understanding, and connect hope, which they see as a desire or a wish, with trust, just as they do expectation.[30] We can discern here a shift in perspective with respect to the nature of hope and expectation, which pass from the rational to the appetitive. What implications does this have for the two dispositions—are they acts of knowledge that have a future good as their object, or are they of the order of opinion, or again are they emotions of the appetitive faculty, external and passional attitudes?

After citing three texts from Thomas Aquinas in which he makes expectation an act of the cognitive faculty, Zimara[31] suggests that expectation is in the first place an inclination of the appetite. He bases this suggestion on a passage from Aquinas[32] that states the passion of hope is a movement of the appetitive faculty toward a good, while the cognitive act is a movement in the opposite direction, from the object to the subject. The appetitive act of hope is consequent upon the intellectual grasp of the future, difficult, but possible and attainable good it presents to it. The cognitive faculty takes hold of the good, which becomes the goal for which the appetitive faculty aims, and it determines the chances of possessing it. Hope is, according to Thomas, the extension of the appetite toward this object. Although Thomas does not speak of expectation in this context, but rather of hope, Zimara's interpretation, which affirms that expectation is in the first place an appetitive drive, is correct, for Thomas seems to use interchangeably the passion of hope and the expectation of a possible future good; the latter represents one of the two constitutive elements of hope (the other being trust) and is essentially an active process, an impulse, a *protensio*.

The relationship between hope and expectation will become even clearer in light of the first response to the objections formulated in the passage I referred to above. Thomas Aquinas distinguishes two types of passions of hope. First, the one in which the human being is capable of obtaining the object through his own means and which Aquinas calls pure hope, *sperare tantum,* that is, hope without expectant waiting. This hope is a drive toward a future and difficult-to-obtain good, a drive that originates in the appetitive faculty. Second, there is the type in which the human being cannot attain the object without having recourse to the help of an other. Aquinas calls this second type a relative hope, that is, a hope that includes an element of expectation, an *exspectatio.* While the first type has a single object, namely, the future and difficult-to-obtain good, the second is characterized by two objects: the hoped-for good and the subject from whom one awaits help in view of the actualization of the future good. Thomas names this second movement of the passion of hope an expectant waiting, because of the observation preceding the act of knowing. Expectation is an essential part of any act of human hope requiring the help of an other for the sake of possessing the hoped-for object, but it is absent when the object is actualizable through the subject's own efforts. Thus, it is not the case that all hope necessarily includes the dimension of expectation.

Returning to the question of whether hope is primarily cognitive or appetitive, it seems to me Edmaier gives an improper definition of expectation as an intellectual act regarding the future. His argument refers to the German language, which apparently expresses the notion of expectation as a cognitive act, in contrast to Latin.[33] Although expectation presupposes an instinctual knowledge, expectation is not in itself a cognitive act that, with some degree of certainty, anticipates the unfolding of the future. Rather, it is constituted, like hope, by an appetitive movement. In the context of his understanding of expectation, Edmaier nevertheless sets in relief the fact that it has a neutral value (*Wertneutralität*), which Middendorf had already pointed out before him. A person who waits expectantly has an interest, in the first place, in whether or not the awaited object is realized or not, and remains neutral with respect to its value or its significance. Hope is distinguished from expectation insofar as it is essentially a movement, as I said above, an intentionality that presupposes an object that attracts the subject who perceives it and invites the subject to respond positively to it. The value and the significance of the object perceived are important for the actualization of hope. "Expectation is not an attitude of response on the part of the subject to the meaning or the significance of an object, as it is in the case of hope and desire."[34]

Hope and expectation are preceded by an act of the knowing faculty, which is not something that belongs solely to the human being, but exists in a certain way also in the animal that hopes and expects. If we observe the behavior of animals, we see they possess a certain capacity to be aware of the future. The dog who catches sight of a rabbit does not set off in pursuit unless it "knows" it has some possibility, a certain hope, of being able to catch it. The animal's capacity to be aware of the future is rooted in natural instinct, preceded by an estimative faculty that allows it to recognize whether a perceived thing is beneficial or harmful for its existence. The sheep that spots a wolf runs away, because it grasps through its estimative faculty that the wolf is a natural enemy.[35] The estimative function, though it lies along the path to intelligence, does not know the essence of things, it does not grasp the universal. Limited to a precise place and time, it is bound to matter. The object of the human estimative faculty is the association of the various particular data it connects together. Unable to make the leap that would lead to the universal, it remains with the particular and passes from one singular and concrete fact to another. This natural instinct will be surpassed by the human being's intellectual faculty, which freely determines a goal toward which it strives, expecting and hoping to be able to reach it.

To better delineate expectation, Laín Entralgo correlates it with the various levels of being. While mineral existence does not possess any expectation, living things are determined by the vital cycles of generation (birth, growth, reproduction, decline, and death). We can see something analogous to expectation in the vegetable kingdom because of the passivity of plants. Drawing on the results of Zubiri, Laín Entralgo notes animals are actively oriented toward the future, they exist in a state of *protension,* which is intrinsically related to expectation, and they strive toward their own realization. Animal life is distinguished by its states of awareness of danger or favorable situations. This expectation is determined by specific anatomical structures. The animal waits expectantly, but it cannot hope. Human expectation, for its part, goes beyond animal expectation, even though it remains at the level of the instincts and the senses, for it is "supra-instinctive, supra-situational and open to the infinite,"[36] and thus in a certain sense, indeterminate. Because of the anthropological structure of the body-soul union of the human being and its intellectual principle, human expectation is in a fundamental sense project.[37]

Lain Entralgo grants human expectation the character of a *"habitus* that belongs essentially to [the human being's] first nature,"[38] while hope is a "second attitude of our nature,"[39] which allows the human being to have a veritable trust in the realization of possibilities. Thus, for Lain Entralgo, expectation comes before hope; in other words, hope builds on expectation. In my opinion, expectation can under certain circumstances be constitutive of the passion of hope, without being identical to it; the passion of hope is not a *habitus,* but is, as we will see, a passion of the irascible appetite. The human being, like the animal, is certainly an organism that lives in expectation. Both humans and animals hope with the passion of hope, expectantly awaiting something in the future, something that is good and accessible. The passion of hope nevertheless does not relate to expectation as an act to potency, a "second attitude of our nature" to a *"habitus* that belongs essentially to the first nature," but it is, in my opinion, constitutive of the first nature of the human being.[40]

I thus object to Lain Entralgo's suggestion that "project" and expectation are convertible terms; by contrast, I wish to claim that the human project, which presupposes an intellectual act, is the result that makes expectation possible. It is nevertheless correct to affirm that an antecedent intellectual grasp characterizes both expectation and the passion of hope.

2.4 Hope presupposes at least some degree of certainty and an act of belief, accompanied by an act of trust

As Pieper observed "in passing," the act of hope implies at least some degree of *certainty,* a real possibility, accompanied by a trust that one will obtain one's object. We do not hope for something we know ahead of time we will not be able to possess. Nevertheless, hope also implies a certain leap into the void, insofar as the subject does not know for sure he will really attain the good in question. This uncertainty is due, as we have seen, to a number of factors—both external and internal to the individual—but which are in either case ultimately rooted in existential uncertainty. The moment an act of hope acquires the character of "absolute" certainty, it immediately ceases to be hope and is transformed into knowledge.

The degree of "certainty" that belongs to *ordinary hope (espoir)* arises either from an original trust in one's natural faculties, which seem capable, of themselves, of obtaining the good toward which the subject is striving, or from a certain calculation of the probability the future contingency will come about, a calculation that can also be regulated by the virtue of prudence. On the other hand, the certainty of *fundamental hope* is rooted in the human will's natural inclination toward the *summum bonum*, and also, as Pieper says, in the grounds for fundamental hope, which presupposes a metaphysics of being and of goodness. In other words, the certainty is rooted in an affirmation of reality, in a basic trust in being, in which love, gift, and fidelity all play a primordial role.

The certainty that accompanies the act of hope presupposes the real possibility of obtaining the good toward which the individual is inclined. Many Anglo-Saxon philosophers of hope agree on this point, although their positions differ in certain respects. "One can hope only for what is believed possible,"[41] as Godfrey rightly insists. Harrison maintains that hope implies "x" is neither inevitable, nor impossible.[42] Price takes up the category of "possibility" as the essential element in the act of hope, but he specifies it forms the object of a certain *belief*:[43] "if we hope that *x* will happen, we must at least believe that it is possible that *x* will happen"; in other words, we must believe "x" is logically and causally possible. He continues: "there is another belief factor in hope: the valuational belief that it will be a good thing if *x* happens."[44] Day distinguishes himself from Godfrey and Price by insisting that the category of possibility and the act of *belief* that accompany hope imply, as Locke and Hume have stressed,[45] a *minimum degree of probability* with respect to the actualization of the hoped-for object.

Day's position is nevertheless exaggerated insofar as he affirms the necessity of the probable as an essential element for an understanding of hope. Such a perspective overlooks a category of hope experiences that lack the probability dimension, resulting from prudential and calculating knowledge. It denies the legitimacy of any act of hope that does not possess purely rational reasons. True trust, for example, is given without calculation. It does not demand a single precondition, as we will see. The same can be said for love, for gift, and for "genuine" hope. Pojman, Marcel, and Godfrey are all correct to insist the notion of *possibility* suffices for an act of hope; in other words, it is not necessary to *believe* a proposal is likely in order to act.[46] Indeed, there are concrete cases in which a person throws himself into hope without necessarily weighing its likelihood, or cases in which there is no probability of success whatsoever, or even those in which the likelihood is greater that the hoped-for object will not be obtained: all one can do is hope against all probability. Moreover, it is possible to hope for an object that is unlikely or that has no logical or causal possibility: for example, we can hope for an eternal life that does not belong to the order of temporality or historicity, nor to the order of empirical causality.[47] The object of such a hope depends on a gratuitous gift and remains independent of any causal necessity.

In order for there to be a movement of ordinary hope (*espoir*) or fundamental hope,[48] there must be *some degree of openness* on the part of the subject: the subject must be capable of receiving the hoped-for object he has either acquired through his own efforts or received through the help of the other. Indeed, a person who is not disponible no longer hopes. Being thus closed in on oneself (a state that Middendorf and Bollnow have described,[49] as well as Marcel, when he speaks of a subject who is "unavailable" and "encumbered with one-self")[50] may also be the result of a subjective or objective conviction that the attainment of the hoped-for object is impossible; it may be the result of a lack of trust in oneself or in the subject who makes the object possible, or it may be the consequence of previously disappointed hopes. We find such indisponibility both in the person in despair—who is convinced everything will turn out poorly, that there is nothing one can expect from life or from others—and in one who is presumptuous. Genuine metaphysical hope is not something one can calculate down to the most minute details, it has nothing to do with a subject's belief in what is empirically possible, or even probable; rather, it constitutes a *response* to being, a trusting abandonment founded on an ontology of intersubjectivity. According to Marcel, we can describe such a hope as "essentially the availability of a soul which has entered intimately enough into the experience of communion to accomplish in the teeth of will and knowledge the transcendent act—the act establishing the vital regeneration of which this experience affords both the pledge and the first-fruits."[51] In order for "genuine" hope[52] to flourish, it is necessary, according to Marcel, that the subject be free from "having" in order to be able to turn himself more decisively to the dimension of "being." He thus becomes increasingly disponible, being open to the various possibilities of the future. The act of hope is characterized above all by an attitude of receptivity and openness with respect to the good toward which the subject is striving, a good whose actualization does not depend on the subject's own efforts. Hope is connected with a meta physics of gift, in which the hoped-for object is offered to the individual.

The acts of hope and belief are accompanied by *trust*. The Greek authors of the fourth and fifth centuries before Christ, such as Euripides and Thucydides, were the first to refuse to use the concept *elpis* in its usual sense—as the rational weighing of possibilities in view of attaining a precise goal—in order to add to hope the characteristic of trust.[53] Taking up this long tradition, Godfrey affirms there are two sorts of trust, which are correlated to the two ontologies he distinguishes (the "will-nature" model and the intersubjective model):[54] there is trust as attitude, and trust as relation. The first is a disposition that characterizes the subject, namely, as someone who decides to give his trust. The second expresses an act by which the subject places trust in another not only because he chooses to do so, but also because of the other. This trust is related to love.

Trust is characterized by three factors. First, it implies the difficulty of the hoped-for good, the uncertain possession of which assumes the person depends either on himself or on the other. The possession of a good that is easily available does not necessarily require trust in onself or in the other. Second, trust implies the possibility of the acquisition of a difficult-to-obtain object that is hoped for. If the possession of this object were in principle impossible, there would be no hope for this good. Trust would have no justification, insofar as the good in question is not available. Where objective and/or subjective possibility does not exist, there can be no trust. Third, trust cannot exist insofar as there is an "absolute" certainty regarding the achievement of the difficult good. As I have already pointed out, we do not place our trust in an event that has to occur by nature or one that we can be sure will happen because of information in our possession. The moment a doubt arises, this situation gives rise to a certain degree of uncertainty (which is nevertheless accompanied by a certain degree of certainty) with respect to the acquisition of the difficult and possible good, which allows the manifestation of trust. This certainty, which will however never be absolute and which is accompanied by existential uncertainty, gives hope a certain liveliness with respect to the acquisition of the hoped-for good. Its function is that of a dynamic upsurge that inspires the person to throw himself, in spite of uncertainty, into the pursuit of the hoped-for good. Trust, which implies a certain risk, is expressed by a bold leap into the unknown, by an attitude of self-abandon, either to the course of things or events, or into the hands of someone who may in fact be someone other than the hoping subject.[55]

Trust, which cannot be forced but only awakened, awaits in each of these three instances (the course of things, the other, or oneself) the help that enables it to acquire the difficult and possible good it hopes for. The strongest and most vital trust is that which grows between two persons united in friendship or in love. Strictly speaking, there is no such thing as trust except in relation to a thou.[56]

Hope presupposes a minimum of trust not only in oneself, in an event, or in another person. Being the consequence of an act of freedom following upon disponibility, it implies more fundamentally a *basic trust* in the world, in life, in the whole of reality—in short, in being. Basic trust is not characterized by a precise and contingent object, as in the case of other derivative forms of trust, but by a comprehensive attitude with respect to being in general, an attitude inscribed within the "depths" of the person. Both basic trust and these other forms represent a necessary precondition for the flourishing of the act of hope. It is on the basis of "this basic trust in being,"[57] which enables one to be open to the whole of reality, that the subject strives through his concupiscible appetite toward certain goods. A number of philosophers, as well as psychologists and psychiatrists, have explained this basic trust as one of the elements indispensable to the act of hope and to existence itself. A person is able to hope precisely to the extent that he possesses this basic trust. The question of the origin of this basic trust has provoked various responses.

Certain psychologists and psychiatrists, such as Spitz, Meves, Nitschke, and Revers, maintain trust arises from a good mother-child relationship; in other words, it is an attitude that develops during the first years of an individual's existence. Staehelin, for his part, acknowledges the great influence this relationship has on the flourishing or the impairment of primary trust, the object of which is openness to "reality at the secondary level." He nevertheless observes, in the light of his patients' experiences, that basic trust is essential to human nature, that is, it precedes any relationship, any form of interpersonality. It is an elemental datum. It is not something one acquires on one's own, even though it is possible to reinforce it or diminish it through behaviors one has either undergone or freely chosen. Psychosomatic illness and disturbance, according to Staehelin, are symptomatic of the lack of this basic trust. This lack expresses an uprootedness, the loss of an inner relationship with the absolute; that is to say, it is a lessening of the capacity to live the existential dimension of the infinite.[58]

This observation has been confirmed by the study of the American psychologist Erikson, who has contributed much to the understanding of the development of the person. He notes that the child begins to develop particular trusts on the basis of a basic trust, which is, according to Godfrey's interpretation, essentially a hope. This "basic trust" is a disposition in a certain sense prior to the period in which the child begins progressively to learn in whom and in what he is able to trust.[59] Moreover, trust is indispensable to the child's flourishing. We observe such an attitude of trust and receptivity toward the whole of reality in the attitude of the child who does not start out calling into question the things he perceives, but rather trustingly welcomes them.

The similarity between trust and hope does not imply they are identical, contrary to what Zimara and Bernard claim. Without coming down formally on one side or the other, Edmaier inclines toward a more nuanced distinction between these two attitudes.[60] Hope, which is principally ordered toward the future (though it may also relate to the present or the past), is distinct from trust, which is a present disposition. I also believe that trust always accompanies the act of hope, whether it be understood as ordinary hope (*espoir*) or as fundamental hope, and that it (basic trust) also lies at the origin of hope. Hope presupposes an act that gives credence to reality, that is, a trust in reality. Through this self-surrender, hope is accompanied by an "absolute confidence" that leads to "a security of his being, or in his being, which is contrary to the radical insecurity of *Having*."[61] The loss of trust in onself, in the other, or even in reality in general, leads either to ordinary or fundamental despair, depending on how severe the loss is. Indeed, the person in despair believes "there is nothing in being to which I can give credit, nothing that I can count on."[62] One way to heal this loss would be to help the person rediscover the dimension of trust that leads to hope.

2.5 Hope and fear

Hope—whether fundamental hope or the passion of hope—is always accompanied by uncertainty, as I pointed out above, with respect to the accomplishment of its project. This uncertainty implies a certain degree of fear.[63] While Bloch affirms an opposition between hope and fear,[64] and Marcel describes the human being as wholly "given to fear" only for "moments at a time,"[65] Spinoza by contrast insists on the inseparability of hope and fear.[66] Fahrenbach and Grentrup,[67] however, claim that the act of hope must be accompanied by a fear of the non-realization of the hoped-for object if hope does not wish to become inert. For my part, I believe, with Day,[68] that hope and fear are contradictory, given that a subject cannot simultaneously hope for an object and fear it. The object of hope, which is a good, and the object of fear, which is an evil, cannot coexist at the same time and in the same respect. Nevertheless, the passion of hope (*espoir*), like fundamental hope, may be accompanied by a fear that arises from the uncertainty inherent in the act of hope and that expresses the possibility that the subject may not attain the object it hopes to attain, whether it be for external reasons or reasons intrinsic to the individual. In this case, fear stems from the obstacles that present themselves along the path leading to the possession of the difficult but possible good, obstacles that may in fact keep the subject from enjoying the object in the future. Although fear accompanies the act of hope, hope is nevertheless not a necessary part of fear.

2.6 Hope and love

Hope (both ordinary and fundamental hope) and love are intrinsically connected, both at the level of passion and the level of reason. Hope can nevertheless be in certain cases the source of love, and the reverse is also true. On the one hand, love precedes hope, insofar as the possession of the object of hope depends on human efforts. It is the love of a good that unleashes desire and ends in hope, in a movement of appetite toward the possession of the absent good, the good by which the individual feels himself attracted. On the other hand, hope precedes love, insofar as the possession of the hoped-for good depends on an other. It brings one to love the person who stands at the origin of the future possession of a particular good.

Marcel insightfully grasped the vital connection between hope and love, affirming "it is not possible to sit in judgement on the case of hope without at the same time trying the case of love."[69] He situates hope within the relation between an I and a thou, between two free persons

4

who come together in a "we": "I hope in you for us." Here we see a metaphysics of intersubjectivity that draws on the concepts of availability and fidelity. Hope is indeed always related to a communion, namely, it cannot exist and flourish except insofar as it is related to a "thou" as part of a "we," rooted in love. "There is no hope except in the context of a 'we' . . . of agape, and not at all of a solitary ego preoccupied with his own individual ends."[70] "Hope is emptied of its meaning and virtue if it is not the affirmation of a *both of us,* of *all of us together.*"[71] Marcel is speaking here of fundamental hope, and does not consider the passion of hope.

Hope implies a minimum of love, whether it be a love of desire, which we also find in animals, or a love of friendship.[72] With the notions of gift and fidelity, this latter also provides the foundation for an interpersonal relationship between an I and a thou that is synthesized, as we saw above, in a "we." Hope, as an act of the rational person, cannot be separated from a love that transcends the love of concupiscence, without however destroying it, but rather ordering it rationally. A world in which the love of friendship would be altogether lacking would be a world in which hope is sheer illusion. In such a world, there would be room left only for the passion of hope (*espoir*).

2.7 Hope and optimism

To a person who is in a difficult situation and who, in spite of certain disappointed hopes, nevertheless manages to hold onto hope, we often give the name "idealist" or "natural optimist." We even say a person who is naturally optimistic finds it easier to hope. To what extent are hope and optimism the same, and to what extent are they different?

Pieper draws a distinction between the attitudes of hope and optimism by affirming the degrees of possible dissimulation between hope and despair. It may seem that someone has hope, when in fact there is a profound despair in his heart of hearts—and vice versa. We may wrongly imagine a person in despair is at bottom an optimist because, on the surface, he does not allow the faintest tremor to escape, and thus comes off as an optimist. People today, according to Pieper, seem to be masters of this art of disguise.[73] Pieper transposes this empirical observation from the individual level to the level of human history. He focuses, in particular, on the history of the philosophy of progress, which hides behind a mask of optimism, under the false robes of hope. Pieper goes so far as to claim, too radically in my opinion, that the optimism in the philosophy of the history of progress is in reality rooted in despair.[74]

In order to get a better sense of the distinction between optimism and hope, let us consider for a moment the case of a person who is in a situation in which he has lost hope (*espoir*). Seen from the outside, this seems to be a situation of despair. And yet, in spite of the desperate situation in which the person is imprisoned, he can still be sustained by a hope whose object is his complete and individual fulfillment, which allows him to get beyond the impasse that confronts him. In such a context, optimism would have no persuasive force. What nonsense it would be, for example, to say to a person on his deathbed that things will turn out fine. If, by such a comment, one is referring to the state of affairs external to the one dying, the statement could make some sense. Applied, however, to the dying man's personal future, the comment is too superficial with regard to the immense importance of the act the man is currently living. The terminally ill, the prisoner condemned to death, or the martyr, when they face their difficult moments, do not cling to optimism, as beautiful or useful as it may be; they do not cling to a vague and general object. Rather, they draw strength from a fundamental hope, whose reason provides a certainty with regard to their future, in spite of the inescapable situation in which they find themselves, in spite of death.

The attitude of uncertainty in which people of today have been trapped ever since the detonation of the first atomic bomb is analogous to a limit-situation. Confronted with this concrete historical set of circumstances, it has become difficult for people to believe humanity is traveling slowly but surely down the path to its own fulfillment, toward the fatherland, the "New Jerusalem" on Earth. Moreover, it is not at all evident that at the dawn of the third millennium, given the countless wars of the twentieth century and the increasingly destructive capacities of nuclear arms, the world has achieved a level of civilization any higher than that of the past. To take refuge in optimism in order to keep from falling into nihilism and despair proves to be vain. However much people console themselves with sweet words and dreams of good days to come, they will not manage to overcome the uncertainty that surrounds them on all sides, nor eliminate the ever-threatening possibility of falling into despair.

According to Pieper, fundamental hope alone is able to keep the contemporary human being from falling into despair or from fleeing into a groundless optimism regarding the future of human history.[75] Optimism does not penetrate to the existential and metaphysical depths of the person, but remains on the surface. The optimist is moreover much less personally involved than the one who hopes. He remains, as Marcel has observed, at "a sufficient distance," contemplating things from a distance, so that they lose their harsh character. In contrast to the optimist, the person who hopes is himself "involved in some kind of a process,"[76] and he trustingly hands himself over to it.

In the famous talk he gave on hope, Marcel discusses a counterargument to what we have been saying, one that tends to confuse hope with optimism. Hope, from this perspective, is reduced to a simple psychological, subjective disposition, which stimulates action.[77] Come hell or high water, Marcel defends the metaphysical value of hope, which does not belong in the category of having, but which transcends it. It belongs instead to the metaphysical class of being; as Minkowski says, hope "'opens' the closed world."[78] The optimist is characterized by his faith in the good outcome of events. He is firmly convinced that the things that present themselves to him with all the charm of ease, that is, as self-evident, will turn out well on their own. The various species of optimism, be they sentimental or rational, do not arise from a profound, existential lived experience, but from a detached view of reality.

Natural or theoretical optimism "is not to be confused . . . with hope," because this latter, according to Marcel, is "inspired by love."[79] There is a fundamental difference between the statement "I place my hope in" and the vague affirmation that "in any event, things will turn out for the best"; we can also say "that a certain belief in progress . . . is opposed to true hope."[80] Despite the disappointments that run through human life, and the horrors, wars, and massacres scattered through the history of humanity, Minkowski holds out a hope that "cannot be translated . . . by 'optimism' in the common sense of the term. . . . It is of a different nature. It is the foundation for the future."[81]

The optimist, who posits an act of faith in the future without any rational foundation, is characterized by a vague and uncertain expectation, and for that reason, is constantly subject to the possibility of disappointment. The optimist nevertheless experiences a confidence in the unfolding of the future upon which he has set his eyes, seeing good things ahead. Hope, for its part, at least has a concrete object. While optimism is rooted in having a good attitude or a state of soul by which things are perceived at their best, hope, according to Edmaier,[82] originates in a difficult situation, one that is accompanied by uncertainty and an element of risk and fear. This latter affirmation seems to me debatable, however, insofar as hope is also capable of growing out of an indifferent situation, or even a positive one, as we shall see in chapter three.

3. THE STRUCTURE OF HOPE INHERENT IN PHILOSOPHY AND REASON

Pieper devotes two studies and several articles to the discussion of the nature of the philosophical act, which he compares to the so-called exact sciences. These latter are characterized by the possibility of their research finding completion; in other words, they progress toward a precise endpoint that they are able, at least in theory, to reach in the future. The questions they raise do not normally remain without an answer. From the moment an answer appears, the hope that was driving the research comes to an end, in order to arise again as the impulse for a new question. Philosophy, by contrast, which has as its object an understanding of the totality of the world and of existence, finds itself by nature on a path that is endless in a different sort of way. By its essence, the questions philosophy explores are not the sort that can receive a definitive answer.[83] Pieper rejects the possibility of constructing a philosophical system, because to do so would be to deny the *theoria* aspect of philosophy. Philosophical questions always run up against the mystery that pervades the reality being contemplated, and that gives rise to wonder, which is the essential attitude of philosophy—an attitude found not only at the beginning of the philosophical act, but one that is the abiding principle of its entire unfolding. Once he has understood a phenomenon or resolved a problem that called forth wonder, the scientist ceases to wonder, while the philosopher remains continually in the grip of wonder; the questions a philosopher raises cannot be resolved scientifically.

Wonder expresses a lack of knowledge with regard to a thing, an event, or a cause. It is reflected, moreover, in a distinction I highlighted in the first chapter in relation to the question of the origin of *res artificiales* and *res naturales*. Natural things, which form the primary matter out of which artificial things are "created," have been thought and willed, according to Pieper, by a mind and will other than the human being's. For this reason, the human intellect, which is not their source and is not able to grasp their foundation, sees them in their "blinding radiance" and their unfathomable mystery.[84] A complete comprehension of a *res* will always evade us, the thing will remain for us a mystery we must contemplate in silence.

To be sure, it is given to human beings to understand all things to a certain extent, insofar as their intellect is *capax universi;* but because they are contingent, that is, because their knowledge is limited and they are not the source of either the essence or the existence of *res naturales,* humans are not able to grasp them in all their depth. The very structure of reality prevents people from understanding anything at all in all of its complexity.[85] Human beings thus remain *in via*; their hope remains unconsummated. At the same time, however, this unceasing philosophical exploration and research, accompanied by the certainty of never being able to reach the goal here on earth, does not lead to a situation of despair and hardening: on the contrary, the search for wisdom is driven by the principle of hope. "Consequently, the essence of things and their totality is not given to [them] fully and completely in the purity of the concept: but 'in hope.'"[86] Hope thus resides within the very structure of human thought. Without the principle of hope, the human intellect would not engage itself in pursuit—which is often laborious and thankless—of an answer to the many questions that arise.

Hope is intrinsic to the structure of the philosophical act; the philosopher is someone who hopes. The impossibility inherent in reason and philosophy to comprehend something completely allows Pieper to draw an analogy with the ontological structure of the *status viatoris.* This latter constitutes the foundation that underlies the conception of philosophy as an act of hope, a philosophy characterized, like the itinerant state itself, by *not-yet-being-in-possession.*[87]

Pieper's description of hope as integral to the structure of the philosophical act and of the act of knowing can be found in other thinkers, such as Lain Entralgo and Coreth, writing after Pieper had worked out this idea. However, these other thinkers place a stronger emphasis on hope in the structure of questioning.[88] In his article, "Hope and the Structure of Philosophical Systems," Ricoeur points out that philosophical discourse implies both a beginning and an end toward which it strives, and which represents the fullness of the desire that drives it toward this ultimate horizon. Ricoeur rejects Hegel's position, which promises absolute knowledge and which can be characterized by "a philosophy of reminiscence, for which rationality belongs to the whole as present,"[89] an understanding that entails the rejection of a philosophy of hope; he turns instead to Kant, who treats the hope dimension as one of the principal questions of philosophy. The philosophy of hope implies the rejection of absolute knowledge: "Between hope or absolute knowledge we have to choose. We cannot have both. Either one or the other, but not both together."[90]

Ladrière has recently picked up this theme of hope as a constitutive element of the act of reason in an article entitled "Raison et eschatologie." Following Ricoeur, for whom "the unity of truth is a timeless task only because it is at first an eschatological hope,"[91] he concludes, after a detailed analysis of the act of thought for both theoretical and practical reason, that reason is ordered to knowledge of the true, and in particular to the event of the meaning that forms the heart of its journey:

> The pathway that clings to the demand is a pathway that must believe, that cannot rely on proofs, that trusts beyond and in spite of all appearances—it is a pathway of hope. Now, hope is an expectant waiting, its correlate is a promise, a promise that is not articulated but is recognized. That which is promised and waited for is the coming of an event that is always held in suspense and always proclaimed, it is the event that gives meaning, or perhaps it is better to say, it is the event of meaning itself.[92]

According to Ladrière, reason includes an eschatological structure whose principal driving force is hope. This structure possesses four features: (a) that which is to come is anterior to that which is given, that is, that which has been achieved, and is not solely the actualization of present potentialities, but constitutes a genuine novelty; (b) this novelty is governed by a moment that is to come, a moment that has an assignable place and acts as an event to come rather than as a final cause; (c) the moments of this process are determined with respect to an ulterior event, and in particular with respect to the ultimate event; and finally, (d) "this relationship to the *eschaton* opens up in every moment of the process as a space of trust that gives meaning to action and gives the ability to hope."[93] Reason's movement toward the event of meaning is animated by a desire that gives it the power to hope. The *eschaton* of reason is constituted by the complete mediation of reason and desire, the exact content of which escapes the philosopher, who is confronted with a choice: "an adherence to the necessity that governs the order of things? Or the acknowledgment, in freedom, of a love by which we ourselves have been acknowledged from the beginning of time?"[94] So ends Ladrière's article. It brings out in a remarkable manner the fact that hope is a structure intrinsic to rational, theoretical, and practical knowledge.

NOTES

1. Though Pieper's approach to hope changes over the years, his position remains ultimately the same. In *On Hope* (1935), he posits a priori the definition of fundamental hope as a theological virtue, without, however, specifying explicitly the line of thinking that brought him to this conclusion. He distances himself from this perspective in his article "Hoffnung–auf was?" (160–64), which appeared in 1957, and even more clearly beginning in 1967 with the publication of *Hope and History* (see also "Über die Hoffnung der Kranken," 16–21 and "Hoffnung und Geschichte," 9–10), in which he takes a linguistic approach as a point of departure for his philosophical analysis of hope.

2. Pieper, *Belief and Faith,* 4 [*Werke,* Vol. 4, 200]; see *In Defense of Philosophy,* 97f. [*Werke,* Vol. 3, 138f.]; "Der Philosophierende und die Sprache," [*Werke,* Vol. 3, 199]; "Tod und Unsterblichkeit." In *Catholica,* 87.

3. See Pieper, *Abuse of Language, Abuse of Power,* 15f., 28f., 30f. [*Werke,* Vol. 6, 137, 145, 146]; "Was heisst 'Gott spricht'?"; "Sachlichkeit und Klugheit," 72.

4. Pieper, "Über die Hoffnung der Kranken," 16; see *Hope and History,* 20, 25 [*Werke,* Vol. 6, 381, 384]; *Glauben, Hoffen, Lieben,* 13. "Hoffnung–auf was?," 162; *Belief and Faith,* 4ff. [*Werke,* Vol. 4, 201f.]. We read in his autobiography: "because, for a more penetrating elaboration of a philosophical, and therefore universally significant, theme, there does not exist any other compelling starting point. And, from that point on, I myself tried to stay true to this insight, as much in my later writings as in my academic lecturing," "Josef Pieper," 251. We find this linguistic approach, which characterizes the analytical method of Pieper's post-war thinking, in the way he tries to grasp the nature not only of hope but also of death (*Death and Immortality,* 14ff., 23 [*Werke,* Vol. 5, 295ff., 303]), of faith (*Belief and Faith,* 6ff. [*Werke,* Vol. 4, 202ff.]; *Hinführung zum Glauben,* 6ff.), of sin (*The Concept of Sin,* 1ff. [*Werke,* Vol. 5, 208ff.]; *Sünde–eine Fehlleistung?,* 5ff.); and of love (*About Love,* 3–17 [*Werke,* Vol. 4, 298–313]; "Das Phänomen der Liebe," 1ff.).

5. See Spinoza, *Ethics,* Part Three, Proposition 18, Scholium 2.

6. See Jaspers, "Die Kraft der Hoffnung."

7. See Pieper, "Über die Schlichtheit der Sprache in der Philosophie," 289; *Guide to Thomas Aquinas*, 108ff. [*Werke*, Vol. 2, 251ff.]. Such an approach to hope can be found likewise in several other contemporary philosophers of hope, such as Downie ("Hope," 248ff.), Fahrenbach (*Wesen und Sinn der Hoffnung*, 30ff., 54), Godfrey (*A Philosophy of Human Hope*, 7ff.), Marcel, Middendorf, Minkowski ("L'espérance"), and Quinn ("Hoping," 54f.).

8. See Pieper, "Über die Hoffnung der Kranken," 17ff. *Hope and History*, 20f. [*Werke*, Vol. 6, 381f.]; "Hoffnung und Geschichte," 9f; "Hoffnung–auf was?"161f.; "Über die Kunst, nicht zu verzweifeln," 207f.

9. Hope as an intentional movement toward an object is included under the theme of the desirable in Pieper. The possible but difficult-to-obtain good compels a certain response from the human being, which may take three different forms, according to the importance of the hoped-for object: in relation to the value of the object, to what is important solely for the person, and finally to the objective good of the person. See Middendorf, *Über die Hoffnung*, 43–69.

10. See Godfrey, *A Philosophy of Human Hope*, 15ff.

11. See Day, "Hope," 94. Downie, "Hope," 248, 250. Lynch, *Images of Hope*, 110. Pieper, *Hope and History*, 20 [*Werke*, Vol. 6, 381] and "Über die Hoffnung der Kranken," 18. Wheatley, "Wishing and Hoping."

12. Lynch (*Images of Hope*, 122ff.) introduces an interesting distinction between two types of desire: while the first is an act of reaction (rebellion or conformity) to something another person wants—in other words, the other is always consulted with respect to my desire ("I want what you want")—the second does not depend on the will of the other, even while it essentially requires a context of reciprocity, which culminates in genuine love. See Godfrey, *A Philosophy of Human Hope*, 42ff.

13. See Disse, "Le fondement de l'espérance chez Ernst Bloch," 187.

14. Marcel, *Homo viator*, 60 [81]; *Presence and Immortality*, 231 [183]; *The Mystery of Being*, vol. 2, 155 [Vol. 2, 156].

15. Marcel, *Homo viator*, 32 [43]; see *The Mystery of Being*, vol. 2, 162 [Vol. 2, 163].

16. On the distinction between ordinary hope and fundamental hope, see chapter three.

17. I will discuss the passion of hope in chapter three, section 4.1.

18. *Bonum absolute* indicates something that is good in itself and not necessarily a greater good.

19. See Gauthier, *Magnanimité*, 322f. Zimara, *Das Wesen der Hoffnung in Natur und Übernatur*, 80. On the notion of *arduum* in the twelfth and thirteenth centuries, see Bougerol, *La théologie de l'espérance aux XIIème et XIIIème siècle*.

20. See Thomas Aquinas, *Summa theologiae*, I–II, 40, 1 and 67, 4 ad 3.

21. See Lain Entralgo, *L'attente et l'espérance*, 9, 555f.

22. This attitude obviously applies only for the expectant waiting for an object under the aspect of the good as we will see in a moment.

23. See Middendorf, *Über die Hoffnung*, 17.

24. See Minkowski, "L'espérance," 98f.

25. Through a study of the various reactions a person has when presented with the gift of an empty box, for example, the psychologist Kijm ("L'expérience du vide," 153, 158) notes that uncertainty is intrinsically related to the movement of expectation. If this expectation is disappointed or shown to be in vain, the uncertainty ceases at the same time.

26. On the issue of two types of expectation, see Fahrenbach, *Wesen und Sinn der Hoffnung*, 45ff. Bollnow, *Neue Geborgenheit*, 105. Middendorf, *Über die Hoffnung*, 23. Price, *Belief*, 269. Zimara, *Das Wesen der Hoffnung in Natur und Übernatur*, 79. Uncertainty always remains, however, as I emphasized in the first chapter. The future eludes all absolutely certain human planning. This uncertainty, moreover, originates in the incapacity to take into consideration the totality of data that exert an influence on a future event, and, in a very particular way, in human freedom. We can say, with Jaspers ("Die Kraft der Hoffnung," 219), "we must renounce the security of knowledge in relation to the future." Here, he is in agreement with Pieper's philosophy of history, which I will address in the sixth chapter. The future escapes the human being's grasp; it lies beyond his control.

27. See Bollnow, *Neue Geborgenheit*, 106ff. Fahrenbach, *Wesen und Sinn der Hoffnung*, 46f.

28. "[Because] to hope . . . is to live in hope instead of anxiously concentrating our attention on the poor little counters spread out in front of us which we feverishly reckon up over and over again without respite, tormented by the fear of being foiled or ruined. The more we allow ourselves to be the Servants of Having, the more we shall let ourselves fall a prey to the gnawing anxiety which Having involves, the more we shall tend to lose not only the aptitude for hope, but even I should say the very belief, indistinct as it may be, of its possible reality." Marcel, *Homo viator*, 61 [82].

29. Spinoza, *Ethics*, Part Four, Proposition 47, Scholium.

30. See Menxel, *Elpis. Espoir. Espérance*, 44–94. Woschitz, *Elpis. Hoffnung*, 76ff.

31. See Zimara, *Das Wesen der Hoffnung in Natur und Übernatur*, 73f.

32. Aquinas, *Summa theologiae*, I–II, 40, 2.

33. See Edmaier, *Horizonte der Hoffnung*, 83f. Lopez-Mendez, *Die Hoffnung im theologischen Denken Teilhard de Chardins*, 47.

34. Middendorf, *Über die Hoffnung*, 22; see also 12. "The object of expectation is 'indifferent'; in expectation, our entire interest is ultimately focused

on the realization or the non-realization of something, and we remain neutral with respect to the significance of the object. To be sure, the person can add to his expectation a certain emotional interest in the expected object, but in this case we are no longer dealing with pure expectation, but instead we have the addition of an opinion with regard to the significance of the object. In expectation,—just like, for example, in translation—the subject takes a merely 'theoretical' interest in the object" (22–23). "In pure expectation, for example, the subject indeed aims at the realization of something, but it is . . . not oriented at an object qua significant object, it does not arise in response to the object. In hope, by contrast, the subject's aiming at the realization of an object arises as a response to the significance of the object that has not yet occurred" (13).

35. See Thomas Aquinas, *Summa theologiae*, I, 78, 4. Üxküll, *Streifzüge durch die Umwelten von Tieren und Menschen*, 55.

36. Lain Entralgo, *L'attente et l'espérance*, 459.

37. Ibid., 470–504.

38. Ibid., 505.

39. Ibid., 556.

40. Expectation is distinct from hope in terms of its object (while the object of expectation can be either a good or an evil, the object of hope is always good), even though it is under certain circumstances constitutive of hope without being identical to it.

41. Godfrey, *A Philosophy of Human Hope*, 30; see also 180, 218.

42. See Harrison, "Christian Virtues," 14.

43. The act of hope is distinguished from the act of belief in at least the following three ways: (a) belief, contrary to hope, implies that the proposition in which the subject believes is true, at least subjectively; (b) there are acts of hope that are morally bad, for example, the hope for an atomic war or for the death of a rich parent or of innocent children, while acts of belief cannot be immoral in themselves; (c) hope implies desire, even though it remains distinct from desire, whereas desire is not necessarily included in the act of belief. For further qualifications, see Day, "Hope," 99ff., and *Hope*, 71ff.

44. Price, *Belief*, 268–69. See Sutherland, "Hope," 195ff. Pojman, *Religious Belief and the Will*, 217.

45. See Day, *Hope*, 24, 99, and "The Anatomy of Hope and Fear," where he refers to Russell, Carnap, and Kneale.

46. See Pojman, *Religious Belief and the Will*, 217. Godfrey, *A Philosophy of Human Hope*, 30. Marcel, *Homo viator*, 65 [87].

47. See Sutherland, "Hope," 200. He conceives of hope as "a moral vision of what might be," thus passing from an empirical study to a study of what ought to be.

48. On the difference between these two types of hope, see chapter three.

49. See Middendorf, *Über die Hoffnung*, 76, 80. Bollnow, *Neue Geborgenheit*, 48ff.

50. Marcel, *Concrete Approaches to Investigating the Ontological Mystery*, 193 [86]. See *Being and Having*, 78 [114].

51. Marcel, *Homo viator*, 67 [90–91]. Pieper and Marcel place the notion of prayer (understood as supplication) at the heart of availability. Prayer is related to hope insofar as the actualization of the hoped-for object does not depend on the hoping subject. Prayer is absent from the passion of hope, since its object can be obtained by the subject's own efforts. For Pieper, this available hope lies within the more general context of a world characterized by *theoria*, a world that stands in opposition to the *praxis* that rejects a metaphysics of gift and availability, seeking to achieve the hoped-for object on its own terms. Referring to the ancient distinction between the *artes liberales* and the *artes serviles*, Pieper affirms the existence of activities that are essential to a balanced and integral human existence, activities that one does not undertake in order to achieve something, but which have their goal and their meaning in themselves, such as philosophy, music, art, leisure, and prayer. These activities by nature lie outside the category "for the sake of," which is so characteristic of *homo practicus*. See Pieper, *Arbeit, Freizeit, Musse–Was ist eine Universität?*, 24f; *Leisure the Basis of Culture*, 93–95 [*Werke*, Vol. 3, 20–21]; *In Defense of Philosophy*, 33 [*Werke*, Vol. 3, 93]; *On Hope*, 35ff., 69ff. [*Werke*, Vol. 4, 269f., 286f.]; "Hoffnung und Geschichte," 26; "Hoffnung," 704; *Christenfibel*, 81f. Marcel affirms "the zone of hope is also that of prayer" (*Being and Having*, 74 [108]; see also 94 [136]; "Structure de l'espérance," 80), which is a "receptive disposition" (*The Mystery of Being*, vol. 2, 105 [Vol. 2, 105]) and a "rejection of a temptation" that leads a person "in being shut in on oneself in pride or despair." On the relationship between prayer and hope in Thomas Aquinas, see Bernard, *Théologie de l'espérance selon saint Thomas d'Aquin*, 128–33. For a good treatment of the prayer-hope relationship from a philosophical perspective, see Middendorf, *Über die Hoffnung*, 39ff.

52. Genuine hope is distinct from ordinary hope (*espoir*) insofar as, for the latter, the realization of the object does not depend on the good will of the other, but on the subject's own efforts. On Aquinas's distinction between (a) *sperare tantum* and (b) *exspectatio*, which is developed in our discussion of expectation, see *Summa theologiae*, I–II, 40, 2.

53. See Menxel, *Elpis. Espoir. Espérance*, 86, 93.

54. See Godfrey, *A Philosophy of Human Hope*, 157–68. "According to the will-nature model, what is real is twofold: in the sphere of knowing, there are subjects that know and objects that are known. In the sphere of activity, there are agents that are self-determining and entities that are determined by something other than themselves. 'Will' points to that sort of reality that is capable

of making and using and knowing. Fulfillment lies in mastery, conceptual or operational. 'Nature' points to that which is capable of being modified, used, and known. Fulfillment lies in functioning well for others' purposes, in being a perfect instrument (or in organic self-realization)" (157). This model defends a relation of utility. "The will-nature model takes the subject as free agent and takes the object as the realm in which agency is carried out. The principal relationship that links the model's two poles is *utilization*, the other serves as instrument for the agent's purposes. . . . According to the will-nature model, hope is analyzable without remainder into desiring on the one hand and calculation on the other" (167). The intersubjective model, by contrast, affirms that the relation among persons is characterized by a shared life in which the other is appreciated for his own sake; see also 158. This model "takes realities as related in appreciation, in appreciating and being appreciated, in accepting and being accepted. While the will-nature model's interrelationships admit of further determination as positive, neutral, or negative, the intersubjective model has only positive interrelationship. The type of fulfillment congruent with this model is union rather than successful utilization. . . . The objective of hope that harmonizes with this model is relational benefit or shared life. Hope in this model is hope-in as well as hope-that" (168).

55. In relation to the good that the subject is able to attain on his own, trust lies in the hoping subject himself.

56. See Edmaier, *Horizonte der Hoffnung*, 20. Middendorf, *Über die Hoffnung*, 35. Nitschke, "Angst und Vertrauen," 177. Fahrenbach, *Wesen und Sinn der Hoffnung*, 91f. Marcel, *Homo viator*, 10, 58f. [9, 78f.]. *The Mystery of Being*, vol. 2, 170 [Vol. 2, 171].

57. See Wust, *Dialektik des Geistes*, vol. 3/1, 144.

58. See Staehelin, *Die Welt als Du*, 165ff; *Urvertrauen und zweite Wirklichkeit*, 66f.; *Haben und Sein*, 55, 59; *Der psychosomatische Christus*, 77, 81ff.

59. See Godfrey, *A Philosophy of Human Hope*, 40ff. Edmaier, *Horizonte der Hoffnung*, 104.

60. See Edmaier, *Horizonte der Hoffnung*, 86. Zimara, *Das Wesen der Hoffnung in Natur und Übernatur*, 141. Bernard, *Théologie de l'espérance selon saint Thomas d'Aquin*, 37.

61. Marcel, *Homo viator*, 46 [62].

62. Marcel, *Concrete Approaches to Investigating the Ontological Mystery*, 184 [68]. See Revers, *Über die Hoffnung*, 7. Bollnow, *Neue Geborgenheit*, 20.

63. Pieper does not discuss the relationship between fear and hope (*espoir*), but he focuses his attention solely on the fear of the Lord and its relationship to the theological virtue of hope. See *On Hope*, 77ff. [*Werke*, Vol. 4, 288ff.].

64. Fear and anxiety constitute for Bloch (*The Principle of Hope*, 74f. [83]) the state in which contemporary man finds himself: "Theirs is a state of anxiety; if it becomes more definite, then it is. . . . It is a question of learning hope," he prophesies at the beginning of his work devoted to hope (3 [1]).

65. Marcel, "Structure de l'espérance," 77.

66. Spinoza observes, "hope does not exist without fear, nor fear without hope" (*Ethics*, Part Three, proposition 50, Scholium). He wants to eliminate these two passions that disturb the state of indifference, which is the goal of stoic philosophy and the guarantee of happiness. The human being must overcome these passions through the force of reason. This stoic rejection of all passion is the result of the principle according to which we ought to focus our attention solely on the present moment. Spinoza objects to any striving toward the uncertain future, a striving that, by its essence, includes the acts of hope and fear.

67. See Fahrenbach, *Wesen und Sinn der Hoffnung*, 52. Grentrup, *Hoffen und Vertrauen*, 58, 67. Middendorf (21 fn. 4) is more cautious, refusing to decide whether all hope is tied to fear, and observing simply that they are not mutually exclusive. See Edmaier, *Horizonte der Hoffnung*, 103f.

68. "Although A can—indeed, always does—simultaneously hope that Q but fear that ~Q, and can—indeed, always does—simultaneously fear that Q but hope that ~Q, A cannot simultaneously hope that Q and fear that Q. It is in this sense that Hope and Fear are contraries," Day, *Hope*, 32. Day devotes a chapter to Aquinas's position, but his interpretation is questionable. He maintains that Thomistic thought has remained focused on the passion of hope (*espoir*) and hope. While Thomas does not devote a single question to the passion of hope, he devotes three questions to the passion of fear (*Summa theologiae*, I–II, 40 and 41 to 44), and one to the gift of fear (II–II, 19), not to mention the many references he makes to fear in his writings. Indeed, Day affirms (33), falsely in my opinion as far as Thomas Aquinas is concerned, that "other classic treatments of Hope, notably those of Aquinas, Kant and Mill, dwell almost exclusively on Hope and virtually ignore Fear. But today there is agreement with Hume that Fear is at least as important as Hope." The reason he gives for this shift in perspective is that Aquinas, Kant, and Mill treat human hope within a theological context, while Hume addresses it from a psychological perspective.

69. Marcel, *Homo viator*, 58 [78], 59 [79].

70. Ibid., 10 [9].

71. Marcel, "Structure de l'espérance," 80. "Hope and love are obviously both originally rooted in the personhood of human beings, 'unconfused, but unseparated.' . . . A profound hope also rests in fulfilled personal love, in the self-giving surrender to a 'Thou' and a 'we.' The enduring quality of love and

hope are reciprocally conditioning, the power of each stands and falls with the strength of the other. And both together in turn make possible and determine the personal form and intensity of belief. Thus, it is something we observe even psychologically: If love is compromised, hope grows weak, and finally belief disappears. Hope and love can therefore never be viewed separately from one another or played off against each other," Edmaier, *Horizonte der Hoffnung*, 100.

72. Pieper devotes a study to love (*About Love*), but nevertheless does not address the relationship between hope and love except at the level of *caritas*.

73. See Pieper, *On Hope*, 49 [*Werke*, Vol. 4, 276]. The psychologist Rauchfleisch (*Leiden-verzweifeln-hoffen*, 26f., 38) observes that the human being who is in an extreme existential situation, who plunges into fear and despair, often takes refuge behind a mask of serenity. See Martin, *Self-Deception and Morality*. Day (*Hope*, 86) does not make this distinction (the possibility that an act of optimism could be in fact an act of despair), because in his eyes every act of optimism is "intrinsically good because it is predominantly pleasant, and all pessimism is intrinsically bad because it is predominantly painful."

74. I will return to this point in the fourth and sixth chapters. See Pieper, "Die Verborgenheit von Hoffnung und Verzweiflung," 170f.

75. On this point, see chapter six.

76. Marcel, *Homo viator*, 34–35 [46–47].

77. Ibid., 57f. [76f.].

78. Minkowski, "L'espérance," 107.

79. Marcel, *Homo viator*, 59 [79]; see also *The Existential Background of Human Dignity*, 142 [185].

80. Marcel, *Homo viator*, 57 [76].

81. Minkowski, "L'espérance," 104–5.

82. Edmaier, *Horizonte der Hoffnung*, 48ff.

83. See Pieper, *Leisure the Basis of Culture*, 89, 139–146 [*Werke*, Vol. 3, 17, 51–56]; *In Defense of Philosophy*, 85f., 115 [*Werke*, Vol. 3, 128f., 151]; "Philosophieren heute," 16f; "Philosophieren heute. Die Situation des Philosophierenden heute," 239.

84. See Pieper, *Was heisst Akademisch?*, 27f., 68; *Leisure the Basis of Culture*, 134f. [*Werke*, Vol. 3, 48].

85. See Pieper, *The Silence of St. Thomas*, 62ff., 89f. [*Werke*, Vol. 2, 124ff., 139].

86. Pieper, *Leisure the Basis of Culture*, 120 [*Werke*, Vol. 3, 38–39]; see also 139ff. [51ff.]; *In Defense of Philosophy*, 85f., 94, 115 [*Werke*, Vol. 3, 128ff., 135f., 151]; "Philosophie heute," 239; "The Negative Element in the Philosophy of St. Thomas Aquinas," in *The Silence of St. Thomas*, 68–71 [*Werke*, Vol. 2, 128–129].

87. "The knowing subject is visualized as a traveller, a *viator*, as someone 'on the way.' This means, from one point of view, that the steps he takes have significance, that they are not altogether in vain, and that they bring him nearer to his goal. Yet this thought has to be complemented by another: as long as man as 'existing being' is 'on the way,' just so long is the 'way' of his knowing uncompleted. This condition of hope in every philosophizing search after the nature of things, may it be said once more, is based upon the 'createdness' of the world and of the knowing man himself," Pieper, "The Negative Element in the Philosophy of St. Thomas Aquinas," 69–70 [*Werke*, Vol. 2, 129].

88. See Coreth, *Metaphysik*, 81. Lain-Entralgo, *L'attente de l'espérance*, 474f. Widmer, *Anthropologie der Hoffnung*, 307ff. Smith, *Hope and History*, 58.

89. Ricoeur, "Hope and the Structure of Philosophical Systems," 60.

90. Ibid., 64.

91. Ricoeur, *History and Truth*, 55 [60]. Ladrière ("Raison et eschatologie," 173) affirms that "in all genuine thought, there is aiming at the truth and as it were a partial, provisional, and deficient prefiguration of what it implies, of what it calls for, of what it demands. But the true is not the sort of thing that can be enclosed within a formula, in a system, or in a conceptual framework. It cannot be posited as a graspable ideal object, in the sense of a meaning. It cannot be the object of a vision, its reality cannot be communicated in figures. And yet it is what gives meaning to the endeavors of thought. It is present, but as something withdrawn, it is inspiring, but as lying beyond our grasp. It exists in the mode of what is always to come, making itself felt in the present, but as something distant that will remain out of our reach. The relationship we form with the true is not a relationship of evidence, nor even of belief in the strict sense, but of hope."

92. Ladrière, "Raison et eschatologie," 190.

93. Ibid., 191.

94. Ibid., 192.

3

The Distinction Between Ordinary and Fundamental Hope

1. THE DISTINCTION BETWEEN ORDINARY AND FUNDAMENTAL HOPE IN PIEPER

In the chapter two, I brought out the importance Pieper attaches to ordinary language in discerning the characteristics of hope. Like Middendorf, Minkowski, and Fahrenbach, he draws from ordinary language the distinction between two types of hope, which, although they share certain traits in common, are distinct from each other in terms of their finality, their proper object, and the degree to which they are rooted in the person. Moreover, from the perspective of grammar, they are distinct insofar as one type appears in the plural, while the other is never used except in the singular. In contrast to German, English, Italian, and Spanish, French has two words at its disposal, which allows it to draw a clear distinction between these two types of hope: *espoir* and *espérance.*

We observe that, over the course of a day, the human being hopes for a thousand and one different things: finding a job or an apartment, passing exams, keeping healthy, making it to an appointment on time, keeping peace, having good weather, or getting some rain. Our day is filled with hopes of this sort, with plans for the near or distant future, the fulfillment or nonfulfillment of which affects us to varying degrees depending on how much importance we attach to the thing hoped for. Existence is in large part a tissue of hopes, which arise again and again over the years. Though these hopes are infinitely varied and diverse, they are also more or less the same, not with respect to their object, but with respect to their nature. At the same time, life is also inevitably a tissue of failed hopes, of unrealized plans and daily disappointments. Indeed, even if the human being has lost countless hopes, ordinary

language does not refer to him as being in despair in the strongest
sense of the term, as we see confirmed in the existence of people
trapped in situations that appear inescapable. The human being who
has lost many hopes is yet still able to hope with the hope that remains
unaffected by such disappointments: that is, with fundamental hope.

> Countless hopes can be disappointed, shattered, proven futile and illu-
> sory, without for all that simply driving a person into 'despair'; appar-
> ently there is only one hope, the hope for something the loss of which
> would leave the person absolutely without hope, such that we could say
> of him, and we must say of him that he is now simply bereft of hope.[1]

We encounter the ordinary/fundamental hope distinction throughout
Pieper's writings, even though there are differences in the way he
presents it and the weight he accords it. What he focuses on in his first
work on hope, *Über die Hoffnung* (1935), is the difference between natural and supernatural hope, terms he uses most often in the singular.[2]
He identifies natural hope with the German plural "die Hoffnungen"[3]
and supernatural hope, that is, the theological virtue of hope, with the
singular "die Hoffnung," obliquely introducing the distinction he will
treat more explicitly twenty-five years later. He begins to clarify this
point in *Über das christliche Menschenbild* (1936), in which he distinguishes between natural hope, which he expresses in the plural in
order to specify that its object is various and changing, and supernatural hope, which is singular.[4] We come across this same distinction
("Hoffnung" and "Hoffnungen") in his postwar writings, although
Pieper does not put much weight on it, whether the distinction is
implicit, as in *Über das Ende der Zeit* [*The End of Time*] (1950),[5] or more
explicit, as in "Selbstgespräch über die Hoffnung" (1951),[6] "Über die
Hoffnung" (1957),[7] or "Hoffnung–auf was?" (1957).[8] However, it is not
until the five lectures he gave at the University of Salzburg and published in 1967 as *Hoffnung und Geschichte* [*Hope and History*] that he
makes this distinction truly explicit.[9]

Although Pieper already referred to this distinction implicitly in
1935, he does not introduce any innovations, but rather enters into a
tradition shared by a number of philosophers, doctors, psychologists,
and psychiatrists, who employ this distinction, giving a different name
to each of the two realities. Pieper makes reference to the doctor
Plügge, as well as to the philosophers Marcel and Landsberg, ignoring

thinkers such as Bloch, Bollnow,[10] Camus,[11] Edmaier,[12] Fahrenbach,[13] Godfrey, Lain Entralgo, Le Senne,[14] Minkowski,[15] Möller,[16] Revers, Sonnemans,[17] Teilhard de Chardin,[18] and Zimara. Landsberg, one of Scheler's disciples who had an influence on Mounier, devoted many pages to a discussion of hope within the context of a study on death. Beginning in 1937, he introduced the distinction between the ordinary hope for something that is directed to the world and the fundamental hope that is set on the future of my person.[19] Marcel takes up this distinction, though he does not use the same terminology.[20] Instead, he differentiates between "I hope that" and "I hope" or "I hope in," according to the expression employed.[21]

2. LIMIT-SITUATIONS AS OCCASIONS FOR THE MANIFESTATION OF FUNDAMENTAL HOPE

In his attempt to distinguish between ordinary and fundamental hope, Pieper points to the figure of the martyr, who is in a limit-situation.[22] What is most engaging about the historical and concrete figure of the person who has freely chosen to die[23] is his positive reaction to a desperate situation in which there is no longer any grounds for hope of the ordinary sort. He does not fall into despair, as one would reasonably expect. The hopes that he may have had days or even hours before the decision was made to put him to death are cruelly taken away. Optimism, which affirms that things will work out for the best, would vanish under these conditions. According to Pieper, the future martyr has only one type of hope left with regard to the satisfaction and fulfillment of his person. He must have recourse to fundamental hope.

In order to assure himself of a concrete foundation for his distinction between the two notions of hope, Pieper refers on many occasions[24] to the results of the studies of the German doctor Plügge. The articles present the results the author obtained after a series of experiments in which he observed the reaction of the terminally ill or those who had survived one or several suicide attempts. Analyzing some fifty observations occurring between 1949 and 1950, mostly concerned with young adults, he notes in the first place that these sick people are profoundly skeptical and alone, and do not think very far beyond the present. They are characterized, on the one hand, by an absence of human relations, which implies a lack of self-confidence or trust in others and, on the other hand, by the boredom expressed by a life without a future, as Revers has pointed out.[25] Plügge observes they are torn between the desire to destroy themselves by suicide and the desire, which is accompanied by fundamental hope, to find fulfillment after death. He calls the hope of those who are suicidal a "perverse hope."[26] Those who are suicidal, or at least the majority of them, do not seek their own destruction, but they hope in a fundamental way, despite the desperate situation in which they habitually find themselves, that the depth of their being will be fulfilled after death.[27] Landsberg, who wrote an interesting study on the moral questions related to suicide, comes to the conclusion that "the act of suicide does not, to me, express despair, but rather a wild and misguided hope directed to the vast unknown kingdom on the other side of death. I would even venture on the paradox: men often kill themselves because they cannot and will not despair."[28]

After his careful observation of the terminally ill and his interviews with them, Plügge concludes there are two sorts of hope inherent in the person. They are not contradictory, but they are different with respect to their proper objects. He notices one type of hope that disappears quite quickly in the sick, insofar as the nonrealization of its object disappoints them. However, in spite of these various disappointments that to some degree affect the core of their being, they yet have another type of hope, an invisible force that comes into play and cannot be observed except when they reach a state of classic despair, that is to say, in the moments in which they have lost all the support they might have clung to, the moments in which they feel the presence of nothingness and taste nausea. However paradoxical it may seem, a human being does not become aware of the existence of the basic or fundamental hope inscribed in the depths of his being and essential to his nature except in the moment that his ordinary hopes are annihilated. Plügge is compelled to observe that the moment reason affirms all is lost, that is, the moment there are no longer any grounds whatsoever for hope, another hope springs forth in this existence, which is doomed to an imminent and certain death.

Plügge describes, for example, the case of Madame H. M. Although she knows she is "doomed," and she occasionally falls into despair—which expresses, as Marcel would say, the feeling that one is trapped in a situation that has no way out[29]—she continues to hope with respect to, and in spite of, everything. Her fundamental hope is intentionally directed to a future, which is no longer linked with the possibility of a recovery. Such a reaction seems to us who are looking on to be utterly absurd, since from a strictly rational perspective, H. M. has no chance whatsoever to make it through alive. Why then does she still hold onto hope? Where does she get this hope, which manages to overcome such a despair?

Plügge finds himself not only unable to explain this hope, but even incapable of forming a concept of it. The only thing he is able to observe is that this fundamental hope, which he says is essential to human nature, emerges at the moment in which ordinary hopes, which are distinct from it, are disappointed, that is, when the subject finds himself in a despair phase. He calls the first type of hope common or ordinary hope; it is directed to the world and subject to constant change. The second sort is "true" or fundamental hope, whose object is something indefinite or vague. It expresses the attitude of a subject who places hope in a transcendent reality.[30]

The Swiss psychiatrist Staehelin confirms Plügge's results, although he makes no reference to them. After having spent many years caring for the sick, he too notes the existence of two different sorts of hope, which correspond to two types of reality. On the one hand, there is the fact of "having hope" for something, which he describes as belonging to everyday life or to the world considered under the aspect of continual change, and, on the other hand, there is the state of "being filled with hope," which is due to the fact the human being is constituted as an "indestructible and eternal" entity.[31] This distinction underlies his psychiatric theory, which states that the human being is rooted in a second dimension that transcends and founds the first.[32]

The psychologist Rauchfleisch comes to a similar finding on the basis of empirical experiments. Faced with death, the human being sees various hopes reduced in a moment to nothing, yielding to something new, which ends with the accepting of limits and suffering. In spite of this hopeless situation—which often befalls those who suffer from serious psychological illness, who feel completely isolated, as if they are up against a wall, and no longer see any meaning to their lives—there nevertheless remains a glimmer of hope, however much it may be submerged.[33]

3. THE DIFFERENT OBJECTS OF ORDINARY AND FUNDAMENTAL HOPE

It is useless to try to specify the object of ordinary hope, or even to provide an exhaustive description of it, insofar as it eludes such an attempt by its very nature. It does so not because it is unknowable, but because it constantly takes on new forms according to the time, the place, the circumstances, and the physical, psychological, and spiritual state of the person. While a person may hope for A on one day, the next day he may hope for B or for non-A. Nevertheless, we may describe the object of ordinary hope in terms of the concepts of plurality, diversity, constant change, or nonnecessity or contingency. The contents of ordinary hope are interchangeable;[34] they pass, change, disappear, and reappear in another form. They are all stamped by temporality and are subject to it. The objects of ordinary hope are clearly determined, and this is what allows us to define them, to take stock of them, and to distinguish them. Moreover, ordinary hope belongs to a different future from fundamental hope: while the former is "the future of the world in which we expect various events to take place," the latter is "the future of my very person, in which I must find fulfillment."[35]

In order to grasp the object of the fundamental hope that sustains the person trapped in a limit-situation, such as terminal illness or being condemned to death, I recall Pieper's ontology of *not-yet-being*. This ontology characterizes the human being who exists essentially in the *status viatoris,* and it is based on the concepts of natural desire and of the indeterminate determination that orders the human being toward an ultimate *telos,* in which the person achieves total fulfillment and satisfaction. There are a number of terms and concepts Pieper calls on to designate the object of fundamental hope, which is unique, essentially unchangeable, "totalizing," and final, and the exact form of which remains veiled and unknown:[36] "beatitude,"[37] "full existence,"[38] "the ultimate, decisive, and most profound satisfaction,"[39] "the definitive realization of Dasein,"[40] "the accomplishment of one's being," "the realization of essence," "ultimate realization," "fullness of being,"[41] the "complete, perfect, and ultimate realization and satisfaction"[42] of the person, "future self-fulfillment,"[43] "the sort of complete realization, in which every desire finds satisfaction, such that there remains nothing left to desire either objectively or subjectively,"[44] the "great banquet,"[45] "the new heaven and the new earth,"[46] "Perfect Joy" and "Eternal

Life"[47] or "the ultimate and decisive 'success.'"[48] He also uses another term to designate the same reality, a concept people have always appealed to in order to express what the person hopes for in his heart of hearts: "salvation," a term Pieper identifies with the complete fulfillment of Dasein,[49] with the most profound and decisive satisfaction of the person.[50] He specifies that this notion of salvation is not to be taken in the religious or theological sense, but rather to be understood on an ontological and anthropological level.

> "Salvation" is not understood in a pastoral sense, belonging to a theological realm, something concerned with the 'beyond' and with which we occupy ourselves on Sunday. Instead, it should be understood in the highest sense as something real and serene: "being-whole" or "being-saved" (*Heil-sein*) or "being complete"; the most decisive and profound satisfaction; the possession of that which brings success, not merely in a certain respect, but success in the absolute sense, in being human.[51]

This understanding of fundamental hope as the complete fulfillment of the person is not unique to Pieper, but can be found in the writings of many thinkers who discuss hope on the philosophical, psychological, or medical level.[52] Bloch holds a significant place among them. Basing his ideas on an ontology of *not-yet-being*, on his Left-leaning interpretation of Aristotle and his understanding of matter and the category of possibility, which are themes developed in the preceding chapter, he affirms that history is an open and ongoing process, the endpoint of which is the *summum bonum,* the realization of the identity of things that now stand in opposition to each other: subject and object, individual and collective, and so forth; in short, it is the naturalization of the human being and the humanization of nature that constitute the objects of the hope principle. This ultimate end of the historical dialectical process, this object of the *Principle of Hope,* is at the same time the fullness of the instant, the *nunc stans* of St. Augustine, which is expressed in Faust's exclamation: "Stay awhile. You are so beautiful!"[53]

Bloch makes use of a number of different terms to designate the single object of hope, some of which are figurative: "happiness, freedom, non-alienation, Golden Age, Land of Milk and Honey, the Eternally-Female, the trumpet signal in *Fidelio* and Christ-likeness of the Day of Resurrection which follows it,"[54] the "homeland,"[55] the "Omega," and "Eschaton,"[56] the "*highest good,*" and "the One Thing Necessary,"[57] the "new heaven" and the "new earth,"[58] the "New Jerusalem," "reach home,"[59] "the highest good, bliss let loose such as there has not yet been before,"[60] "absolute satisfaction of needs,"[61] "peace, freedom, bread,"[62] "heaven on earth,"[63] the "restoration of man,"[64] "regnum humanum,"[65] and "the identity of man who has come to himself with his world."[66] He also and especially uses the term "salvation" to designate the object of hope, a term that, along with the notion of liberation, represents "the heart of his thought."[67] Envisioning the world as the "laboratorium possibilis salutis,"[68] Bloch describes salvation specifically as belonging to the world, as the complete fulfillment of nature, and the union of the individual and the species, and thus as the elimination of all antagonism: this is the fatherland.

Pieper's notion of the object of fundamental hope is different from Bloch's both in terms of its content and in terms of the means by which it is realized. On the one hand, while Pieper gives more importance to the actualization of the person, which implies a communitarian dimension, Bloch focuses on the actualization of the community, in which of course the individual will find fulfillment, even if he will disappear paradoxically in a fusion with class consciousness. On the other hand, the actualization of the object of fundamental hope takes place, for Pieper, in the beyond (which he defines as the state of being on the other side of death,[69] and not as a place), and thus is something the human being cannot produce, belonging as it does to the order of gratuity. It is not something one takes, it is something one receives. This conception is based on a metaphysics of being and gift, a metaphysics of openness and receptivity, of assent to the whole of reality, of the interweaving of time and transtemporality. Bloch, for his part, rejects in principle the existence of a "beyond," of an eternity or transtemporality, of a transcendence with transcendence. Reducing the real exhaustively to the temporal dimension, and remaining within the horizon of a metaphysics of having and making, he seeks to erect an immanent city of God, a "messianic kingdom of God—without God,"[70] that is, a "heaven on earth,"[71] built by manual strength, built through *praxis:*

> The goal of all higher religions was a land in which milk and honey flow as really as they do symbolically; the goal of the content-based atheism which remains over after religions is exactly the same—without God, but with the uncovered face of our absconditum and of the salvation-latency in the difficult earth.[72]

Bloch's philosophy is a metareligion, which, like Marxism, is character-ized by a morality of salvation, a salvation that is incorporated into the process of temporal history. It seeks to bring about a synthesis between atheistic Marxism and Christian messianism: it is a sacred history pro-claiming an immanent state of redemption, which will occur with the realization of the socialist revolution, in a classless society. Bloch's notion of hope is above all a political notion, and can be summarized by the famous and lapidary sentence: "ubi Lenin, ibi Jerusalem."[73]

Having thus distinguished between ordinary and fundamental hope, and also between their respective objects, I will now address hope understood as a passion—a definition we find in Pieper, Thomas Aquinas, Hume, and Bloch—and hope understood as a natural and/or theological virtue. I will also address the nature of the relationship between ordinary and fundamental hope.

4. ORDINARY HOPE

Although Pieper on many occasions draws a distinction between natural and supernatural hope, and then, after the Second World War, between ordinary and fundamental hope, describing their acts and specifying their material and formal objects, he nonetheless never attempted to pro-vide a descriptive analysis of ordinary hope understood as a passion, such as it has been defined by the Western philosophical tradition.[74] This is quite strange, given that ordinary hope constitutes the driving impulse of human and animal existence! Nor does he seem very inter-ested in the question of hope understood as a sensation or feeling.[75] Even though, following Aquinas, he specifies that the passion of hope goes hand in hand with the moral virtues of magnanimity and humility, he does not clearly bring out the Thomistic distinction between hope as an irascible passion and hope as a prerequisite for and element of mag-nanimity. It thus seems worthwhile to take a moment to present Aquinas's, Hume's, and Bloch's understanding of the passion of hope.

4.1 The passion of hope in Thomas Aquinas

Following Bonaventure and Albert the Great, Thomas Aquinas situ-ates hope among the passions; specifically, he makes it a central aspect of the irascible power. The word "passion," according to Thomas, indicates an instinctive drive, a movement of the sensible, appetitive power, which originates directly, not in the soul, but in the body, since passion belongs to the soul *per accidens,* that is, insofar as it is united with the body. In virtue of his corporeality, the human being, like the animal, is an organism suffused with passions. They arise from a desire, which itself results from the sensible perception of a reality that affects the impassioned subject. This desire quickly becomes transformed into a movement that can follow two different paths; that is, we can distinguish two different appetites according to the manner in which the subject reacts with respect to the perceived reality. On the one hand, the object of *appetitus concupiscibilis* is something pleasant or good, something painful or simply bad, and the subject thus desires to move toward the object or to move away from it. We can relate this appetite to the internal sense of the animal's evaluative capacity. On the other hand, the *appetitus irascibilis* arises when the possession of the object or the actualization of the event proves to be difficult, or when the evil is hard to overcome. It allows one to surmount the obstacles, before which the concupiscible appetite stands "powerless" to obtain the good or flee the evil. While the first appetite relates itself with ease to something pleasant or unpleasant, the second appetite aims toward the same object or shrinks from it, but under the aspect of its hostility or difficulty to be obtained.

These two appetitive faculties together include eleven *passions,* which can be differentiated, apart from anger, in terms of five pairs. The concupiscible appetite encompasses six passions: *love* (a striving toward the good) and *hatred* (a flight from evil), *desire* (passion for a good that one does not yet possess) and *aversion* (repulsion before a dangerous and threatening evil), *joy* (passion for the possession of a good) and *sadness* (consequent upon evil). Five passions proceed from the irascible appetite: *hope* (before a difficult-to-obtain, future, and possible good), and *despair* (before a difficult good that does not seem possible to obtain), *fear* (the passion stemming from a threatening evil that seems impossible to overcome) and *bravery* (before an imminent danger), and finally *anger* (the reaction to an actual evil, which one can overcome).[76]

Thomas Aquinas includes *hope,*[77] which he distinguishes from desire, among the four most important passions, insofar as it is the last of a series of movements toward a good, which begins with love and proceeds to desire,[78] as well as the first of the irascible passions.

Thomas defines it in reference to its object, which is characterized by the four traits I have already discussed in chapter two. Hope is a movement toward an object under the aspect of *goodness,* and is distinct from fear, which is a movement away from the object. Its object is a *future good,* which allows us to distinguish it from the joy anchored in the present. The moment hope obtains its object, it disappears and gives way to joy. The object of hope is also an *arduous good* (that is, it is a good that is difficult to obtain), as opposed to an easy good, which is the object of desire. Finally, the object in question is a *possible and obtainable good,* as opposed to the object of despair, the possession of which seems impossible. Thus, the object of the passion of hope is a *bonum futurum, arduum, et possibile.*

While the passions of the concupiscible appetite do not necessitate various moral virtues, insofar as their movements are all interrelated, and insofar as they are ordered with respect to one and the same end, namely, the pursuit of a good or the flight from an evil, the passions of the irascible appetite are ordered to different ends.[79] It follows that, if they wish to attain the just mean established by reason, they have to subordinate themselves to various moral virtues.[80] The passion of hope is, on the one hand, moderated by the moral virtue of humility, and on the other hand, reinforced by the moral virtue of magnanimity.

The moral virtue of *magnanimity,* which is rooted in the cardinal virtue of courage, is characterized, like the passion of hope, by a motive force, which urges the subject on toward a natural ideal of greatness, toward a *being-more* through an effort of conquering the arduous good. It expresses the human being's inclination toward the achieving of greatness, the possession of perfection and complete fulfillment. This aspiration to become in actuality what one is in potentiality, to fulfill all of one's potential, is realized by means of the actualization of the virtues. The moral virtue of magnanimity has two objectives: the accomplishment of great deeds, which constitutes its proper end, and the honors that follow upon the achievement of greatness.[81]

The virtue of temperance gives rise to the other moral virtue that moderates the passion of hope: *humility,* which resides in the irascible appetite and which helps the passion of hope to act in conformity with the dictates of reason. It does not stand in opposition to the virtue of magnanimity, but collaborates with it in tempering the subject's inclination toward great things, keeping it from attaining them in a disordered

manner. This virtue, which is an intrinsic attitude that rests on a voluntary decision, is connected with fundamental hope and especially with
the hope that relies on the aid of an other for the actualization of its
object. In this sense, humility presupposes the capacity, or rather the
will, to accept to receive something gratuitously from the other.[82] It
cannot be reduced to humiliation or modesty, but constitutes a primordial metaphysical virtue, a mode of being.

4.2 Hume and Bloch

Hume devotes the second book of his *Treatise on Human Nature*[83] to a
discussion of the human passions, and addresses the passion of hope
in the ninth section of the third part. He enumerates six direct passions
or affections, which form three pairs of contrasting passions: hope and
fear, desire and aversion, joy and suffering. Hope and fear are both the
result of a mixture of joy and suffering, characterized by the degree of
uncertainty regarding the object at which the subject aims. There is
hope when the object is good and probable, and fear when the object
is bad and probable. Joy makes its appearance the moment the subject
strives after an object that is good and certain, while suffering comes
about in relation to an object that is bad and certain. Hume agrees with
Aquinas in situating hope in the category of passion, but he differs
from Aquinas with regard to what represents the contrary of the passion of hope; while, for Aquinas, the opposite is despair, for Hume,
and for Spinoza and Bloch as well, it is fear.

Bloch, in particular, seeks to liberate contemporary man from the
state of fear in which he finds himself, by offering the *Principle of Hope*
as a remedy. The source of the dynamism of this principle, which constitutes the principle of reality, is to be found in Bloch's anthropology,
in which the neo-Marxist philosopher defines Dasein in terms of his
real and yet undetermined *Dass,* which resides, as we saw earlier, in
the "darkness of the lived moment."[84] The human being is not yet fully
himself, but journeys toward the formation and fulfillment of his
essence, the final goal of his existence. His condition of *Dass-sein* urges
him toward a precise *Da-sein,* which lies in an indeterminate future.
For this reason, the human being is essentially characterized by *not-yet-
being.* This situation gives rise to a desire for fulfillment, a striving after
being-complete, which the dialectical materialism of Marxism, with its
praxis and its revolution, is alone capable of bringing about. "The

nature of our immediate being is empty and hence greedy, striving, and hence restless";[85] in other words, "primarily, everybody lives in the future, because they strive."[86] The human being is ontologically characterized by a state of indigence, imperfection, incompleteness, and lack, an unchosen state we may call "hunger."

Hunger, for Bloch, is the symbol and the source of hope, whose object is possession of the human essence, possession of the kingdom of liberty, the *summum bonum*. This is the context in which Bloch discusses Freud's, Jung's, and Adler's psychiatric understandings of the meaning of "instinct."[87] He makes hunger, rather than the Freudian libido, the principal and primary instinct of human nature, from which all other instincts are derived, including the instinct for self-preservation. For Bloch, hope grows out of the fundamental instinct of hunger, which ought not to be understood solely from the physiological perspective, but also from within the context of variable political and economic structures. Whereas Freud develops his theory of the instincts and the libido for the sake of the bourgeoisie that had suffered from sexual repression, Bloch elaborates a theory of the instincts for the working class, the proletariat. The experience of hunger—which expresses not only a physical and psychological, but also a spiritual and metaphysical lack, and which drives the human being toward *Dasein*, toward the possession of what will be filling and satisfying in a comprehensive way—is the basis upon which Bloch develops his philosophy of hope. This state of hunger expresses a "nothingness," a lack of something, but also a flight from this lack. It lies at the origin of the dynamic intentionality of the human being on the way to satisfaction, to the full and eternally present moment, the *nunc stans*. Moreover, it constitutes the key principle of the dialectical process of history. In other words, hunger is the source of the slave's revolt from his master, which occurs in order to abolish the relation of servitude that renders him a victim of oppression.

This hunger, this lack, manifests itself in varying degrees of desire and concupiscence. The first degree of intentionality,[88] which originates with the "that" (*Dass*) and ends with an "impulse" (*Drang*), is constituted by a striving, without yet knowing that which it desires. If this impulse is perceived or experienced by the subject, it becomes a "longing" (*Sehnen*), the object of which is as indefinite as that of "striving" (*Streben*), but which is more directly oriented outward. If the striving is concentrated entirely in itself, it remains a "mania" (*Sucht*). If it strives after an entity, it becomes a "seeking" (*Suchen*) for something it does not yet possess. This seeking is a "drive" (*Treiben*), and Bloch calls the *gefühlte Trieb* a "passion": "If the whole man throws himself into a single emotion, then this becomes a passion."[89] The human being is clearly different from the animal by virtue of his capacity to desire; that is, he is able to pass from "craving" (*Begehren*) to "wishing" (*Wünschen*). The final stage of this dynamic intentionality is the will that leads to activity and work. It is connected with desire, which is anterior to it. Thus, there is a logical progression from one stage to the next: "that" (*Dass*), "impulse" (*Drang*), "striving" (*Streben*), "mania" (*Sucht*), "drive" (*Trieb*), "affect" (*Affekt*), "wish" (*Wünschen*), and "will" (*Willen*).

Bloch places hope within the context of the passions, which are distinct from one another with respect to their degree of intensity in relation to their intentionality. He distinguishes two sorts of passion: the affects of repulsion—such as fear, envy, anger, contempt, and hatred—and the affects of attraction, such as contentment, benevolence, trust, respect, and love.[90] He draws an even more important distinction between a "filled passion," which is characterized by a "brief" instinctive intentionality, a passion whose object is effectively present in the world: jealousy, cupidity, and respect; and an expectant-passion, which is characterized by a much broader instinctive intentionality (a state of anticipation), a passion whose object does not yet exist in reality, but rather lies in the uncertainty of the possibility of its realization: fear, anxiety, hope, and faith. Expectant-passion differs from filled passion in terms of having a greater anticipation with regard to its intention, its content, and its object, and also in terms of an openness to a future reality, that is, to the *not-yet*. The passion of hope enjoys a primacy over the three other expectant-passions. Bloch distinguishes between a positive side (hope and trust) and a negative side (fear, which can turn into despair) in the expectant-passions. The opposite of hope is not despair, which is the contrary of trust, but anxiety, as we have just seen. Nevertheless, the hope that grows into trust is in fact opposed to despair.

Hope is not only a passion ordered to an object that is lacking to the subject, it can also be defined more essentially in terms of its cognitive intentionality, namely, that it is ordered to the making-conscious of that which is not-yet-conscious. It becomes the *docta spes,* the enlightened hope, a cognitive act integrated within the anticipatory consciousness of *Da-sein* and by means of which one can anticipate the various possible futures of being and history. This act aims at the *summum bonum,* the fatherland. Bloch calls it the utopian function of *Dasein.*[91]

Although they agree in viewing hope as a passion, these authors show differences in the way they articulate the structure of the general schema of the passions, their number, their order, their relation, their opposites, and the exact position of hope in this schema. Without discussing the nature, the role, and the content of the passions, Pieper simply refers to and elaborates the position of Thomas Aquinas. Because of his bodiliness, the human being possesses the virtue of hope just as the animal does. This hope can be elevated to a human level, insofar as it is determined according to reason by the two moral virtues (magnanimity and humility) that accompany it and provide its foundation. Hope considered at this level is no longer something animals share. We may at this point raise the question whether it is possible to speak of a natural virtue of ordinary hope. Is the virtue of hope an acquired moral virtue, which the subject brings about through its own efforts, or is it on the contrary an infused, theological virtue, which the subject receives as a gift? When we speak of fundamental hope, what sort of virtue are we talking about?

5. Fundamental hope and the theological virtue of hope

5.1 The loss of an understanding of virtue

Speaking before the Académie Française in 1934, Valéry declared—with a certain exaggeration—that the term "virtue" was dead. We need only observe that the word no longer appears in any of the most read or revered books and that the only place it is used anymore is in operettas, poetry, the catechism, and in the Académie Française.[92] Some twenty years earlier, Scheler had already remarked in his essay, "Zur Rehabilitierung der Tugend," that there was a tendency to deny any reality to the term "virtue," which had lost its most profound meaning. We smile when we hear or read the word. Ordinary language has distorted the term to such an extent that we identify it with an "old, toothless and dreary spinster."[93] Lalande, for his part, claims the concept of virtue has tended "to disappear from contemporary moral discourse. We scarcely use the term except in religious expressions, or else we append a comment about the fact that it has fallen out of use."[94] Even in Catholic theology, the word is surrounded by the "dusty smell of moralizing."[95]

Pieper agrees explicitly with Scheler and Valéry, adding that the concept of virtue (whether intellectual, moral, or theological) has become outdated for those living in the first half of the twentieth century. It no longer resonates with the nobility it had for Greek, Latin, and Christian thought. It has lost a part of its freshness and dynamic force. Pieper observes not only that it seems the name of virtue is dead, banished from common language and emptied of its initial meaning,[96] but also that the use of the particular virtues in ordinary language, as well as in philosophical thinking, has distorted their original meanings to such an extent that we have come to value the opposite of a virtue as being the real virtue. Thus, for example, the first cardinal virtue (prudence) has devolved into the calculation of the best way to obtain a profit or the best means to reach a precise goal, whereas the Ancients saw prudence as an action that conformed itself to reality in order to allow itself to be directed by what reality presented. Something similar has taken place with respect to courage, justice, moderation, and love.[97]

"Is it possible to 'save virtue'?"[98] asks Pieper at several points. He answers in the affirmative. Indeed, one part of his philosophical reflection aims not only at denouncing the betrayal and banishment of the virtues, but also at their rehabilitation. He ends his philosophical work on the four cardinal virtues and the three theological virtues in 1974 with *Über die Liebe* [*On Love*]. There is no question but that Pieper is one of the pioneers who has reawakened interest in the virtues within the context of moral and political philosophy, and the philosophy of law.[99]

5.2 The concepts of habitus and virtue

According to Thomas Aquinas, virtue is a "habit [*habitus*] . . . that is in every case the source of a good human act."[100] In this definition, the genus is *habitus* and the specific difference is the orientation to the good in every case. Virtue is thus the principle of a good action, viewed under the aspect of morality. At another point in the same work, Aquinas affirms that the principle of an act is identical to potency.[101] We ought to ask in what way, then, virtue and potency are related, insofar as they both represent the *principium actus*.

In order to answer this question, let us dwell for a moment on the relationship between *habitus* and *potentia*. *Habitus* relates to *potentia* as the complete to the incomplete (that is, it represents the actualization of that which the potency is not yet). *Habitus* is thus an actualized potency. Since it is actualized in actions, a *habitus* lies between potency and the realization of a capacity for action. In other words, it is an *actus primus,* whereas its operation is of the order of *actus secundus*. It is a disposition that is normally acquired through the long process of repeated activity, by virtue of which the person acts easily, quickly, and surely. Insofar as the soul acquires this firm disposition, a *habitus* is a possession that belongs to the soul as a descriptive quality; in other words, it is a modality of substance, a certain determination, or a disposition that is attributed to the substance and modifies it, or determines it from within.

The *habitus* that leads the person to behave in conformity to an end viewed with respect to its natural finality is called a good *habitus,* or a *virtue,* while the *habitus* that turns it away from its end is called a bad *habitus* or vice. In this respect, the criterion for judgment regarding the moral value of a *habitus* is to what extent the *habitus* is in harmony with the nature of the agent.[102] Virtue is a good *habitus* that acts in obedience to the intellect; it is a perfection of the capacity for action or potency, insofar as potency is ordered to act, to an end that represents the actualization of the potency in a concrete act. Virtue represents the best of what a human being *is able* to be.[103]

5.3 Hope: A natural or theological virtue?

Pieper begins the second chapter of *Über die Hoffnung* [*On Hope*] by presenting a set of alternatives: either we must affirm hope as a theological virtue, or we must deny that hope is a virtue in any sense. These alternatives come from Thomas Aquinas, who affirms that hope, qua virtue, cannot be acquired through human effort alone, insofar as it surpasses human capacity.[104] Pieper elaborates his thesis on the basis of an a priori affirmation, before he demonstrates its validity in a second moment. I will dwell for a moment on his argument, all the while taking account of the perspectives of contemporary thinkers.

The simple fact of affirming a distinction between two types of virtue, natural and supernatural (these latter being a gift), and thereby a distinction between two types of beatitude, does not yet imply that hope can fall only under the latter category. Thus, in order to maintain that one can speak of the virtue of hope only as a theological virtue, Pieper makes reference to an argument based on his definition of virtue. Virtue is a good disposition, which orders the subject in every case to the good. If he assents to the virtue's natural movement, the virtuous human being is not inclined to evil. If, in his freedom, he nevertheless chooses evil, the virtue in question will be diminished, and could even disappear, being replaced by indifference or even vice. A morally good act implies the existence of a corresponding virtue. For example, when the virtue of justice, which is a natural virtue, ceases to aim for the good, the human being immediately ceases to be just. Nevertheless, according to Pieper, we observe that natural hope, even if it is accompanied by the moral virtues of magnanimity and humility, can also be directed to evil, without for all that ceasing to be hope; we need only think of the various and sundry hopes that fill our lives. Thus, natural hope lacks the aptitude for being in every case an act that aims at the good, which is a characteristic belonging to all virtue.[105]

Although Pieper does not say so explicitly, we see here an argument similar to the one he uses with respect to the terminally ill person or the martyr. Both are trapped in a situation in which their hopes have been disappointed. The collapse of their hopes results from a variety of external events, according to the particular case. This shows quite clearly that these hopes cannot be virtues, because every loss of virtue, just like any acquisition of virtue, is due to an interior, personal choice. For example, if I possess the virtue of justice, no external factor can take it away from me in any direct sense. The virtue forms a part of my being, and only a lack of personal attention and repeated acts that lead me away from the dimension of justice can cause me gradually to lose it. The same can be said in the case of the person who is terminally ill. If hope were a natural virtue, it could not simply evaporate as a result of an external cause. But we have seen that the terminally ill person in fact loses hopes, that in the end such a person is left with only one hope, the hope that, being firm and unshakeable, is the root of all other hopes. According to Pieper, hope is a virtue that is offered to the person in this condition, along with its object; and, like all gifts, it can be freely rejected.

Pieper speaks in this context of ordinary hope and not of fundamental hope. Can fundamental hope be the object of a natural virtue? In other words, can it be acquired by one's own efforts? Although

Pieper's argument based on the character of virtue is present throughout the course of his writings, we nevertheless find a somewhat novel approach in those that appear after *Über die Hoffnung* [*On Hope*], in which he places the emphasis on two notions in particular: the gratuitous *gift* of the virtue of hope and *salvation* (that is, in this context, the complete satisfaction and fulfillment of the person), as the object of hope that lies beyond the reach of human effort. Hope cannot be called a virtue except insofar as it helps ordering the human being to his final end, that is, to the complete satisfaction and realization of his being. This explanation rests on Pieper's anthropology and ontology of *not-yet-being*, which affirms both a temporal and transtemporal metaphysical dimension, in which he transposes Bloch's saying, "thinking means venturing beyond," into a surpassing of history through a transcendence with transcendence. In Pieper's eyes, the virtue of hope is not something the subject is capable of acquiring through his own efforts, but it instead possesses a gift-character, it is something that the subject receives from a giver.[106] This gift can be either accepted or rejected: it is precisely here that freedom and the possibility of despair lies. The capacity to receive a gift—which is relevant not only in the context of the virtue of hope, but also in the context of genuine love, the intuitive knowledge of being, and contemplation—is essential to the contingent condition of the human being.

This metaphysics of the gift, which lies at the heart of the notion of fundamental hope, is the subject of an excellent study by Kenneth Schmitz. He distinguishes between *datum* and *donum*. The given (*datum*) belongs to a metaphysics of having and doing, of the simple observation of a fact, or an entity; it forms the material basis of knowledge. However, scientific discourse does not refer to a giver, it does not seek out the ontological cause of the given, but rather contents itself with affirming that it is simply given or posited. Schmitz points out, nevertheless, that it is impossible to give something to oneself, taking "gift" here in the strongest sense of the term. Thus, the *donum*, which must be both given and received, is characterized by gratuity, by its coming from another, by its profound freedom and nonnecessity, by its reception, which presupposes an openness and a disponibility on the part of the subject, by the inherent risk in the possible rejection of the gift by the one to whom it is given, and by the impossibility of giving a *donum* fully in return to the giver.[107]

The object of the virtue of hope does not come about through manual strength, but belongs to the realm of liberality, of gift, which is "a call to which one must respond" and which thus implies freedom: "at the root of hope there is something which is literally offered to us: but we can refuse hope, just as we can refuse love. Moreover, we can no doubt deny hope, just as we can deny or degrade our love,"[108] Marcel notes. An analysis of gift thus implies an analysis of the virtue of gratitude, which is the consequence of an internal attitude toward a gift the subject has undeservedly received—in other words, something that is not the fruit of doing. A genuine gift originates in the freedom of the giver, who offers it without desiring anything in return, without expecting to be thanked.[109]

Bollnow correctly observes that Sartre's atheistic existentialism rejects not only any gratitude, but also any fundamental hope that the human being would receive as a gift. Refusing to depend on any other, the human being, for Sartre, seeks to be absolutely autonomous and free. Now, Bollnow's observation applies not only to the thought of Sartre, but also to any that would teach an unshakable faith in human progress which is realized solely by means of *praxis*. It is in this context we see in a clear manner the opposition between Pieper's understanding of fundamental hope as a gift, the object of which is the complete satisfaction and fulfillment of the person at both an individual and also a community level, and Bloch's understanding of hope, which Marcel, during a public debate with Bloch, claimed to be a "flattening of hope"[110] that attenuates its existential dimension. While Pieper insists it is impossible for the human being to bring about the object of fundamental hope through his own efforts, Bloch affirms this object can be produced by "doing." Although *The Principle of Hope* attempts to catalogue the various understandings of hope, its author leaves out any type of hope that does not depend on human activity, any type that transcends the immanence of *praxis*, any type that leads to a transcendence with transcendence, the object of which would be realized in a transtemporal and transhistorical dimension. Bloch paints hope of this sort as an opium, an illusion, a fantasy, or an "otherworldly" consolation. He reduces hope to that which the human being can bring about with one's own efforts.

In terms of the actualization of the hoped-for object, the reality of the gift is essential as much to fundamental hope as to the passion of hope, which is accompanied by an expectation, an *expectare*, a recourse to the other, by contrast to *sperare*, which reaches its object through its own efforts.[111] The virtue of hope, according to Pieper, is connected with *expectare* insofar as its object is a gift. It will be brought about in its completeness once the subject has crossed the threshold of death, and it cannot be granted by anyone other than an absolute Thou. I will not enter into the arguments behind these affirmations, because I will address these issues in more detail in chapter four, which will discuss the grounds for fundamental hope in the face of the anti-utopia that personal and collective death represents. For Pieper, not only is the object of fundamental hope a gift, but so is its realization. It does not require any effort to obtain this object other than being open and willing to receive freely what the giver offers.

As we have seen, Pieper draws a distinction between two sorts of hope, in fidelity to Thomas Aquinas: fundamental hope, or the theological virtue of hope; and ordinary hope, or the passion of hope. This latter he differentiates further into the simple passion of hope and the passion of hope as accompanied by the moral virtues of magnanimity and humility. The only way, according to Pieper, to speak of the virtue of fundamental hope is to accord it the status of a theological virtue, that is, a virtue that is characterized by a gratuitous gift, or, in other words, a virtue that is not "natural" to the human being. From this perspective, even the possession of the object of this virtue is itself the result of a gift. The fact that the virtue of hope can only be a theological virtue, in Pieper's eyes, is of "capital importance."[112] He is aware that such an affirmation is difficult to grasp in the contemporary mindset, insofar as this notion is foreign to it.[113]

At the beginning of the second chapter of *Über die Hoffnung* [*On Hope*], the precise theme of which is "hope as a virtue," Pieper clearly affirms that the philosopher who defines fundamental hope as a theological virtue can do so only if the philosopher is at the same time a Christian theologian. A few lines later, we read that one can come to knowledge of the existence, origin, and even the object of hope only on the basis of a divine revelation. Pieper also affirms that Christ is the true reason for our hope and its fulfillment. Affirmations such as these are, of course, liable to present some problems, particularly to the extent that they reinforce the reproach that one could make with some justification to Pieper's treatment of hope in *Über die Hoffnung* [*On*

Hope], namely, that it is not sufficiently philosophical. But this judgment could be nuanced: the criticism is justified with respect to the affirmation we have just cited, but it becomes somewhat weakened once we consider that Pieper never uses the same words, nor even the same ideas or thoughts, in his later writings having to do with the theme of hope.[114] His thinking evolves after 1935, and we never again find the affirmation that an appeal to Christian theology is necessary in order to understand hope in its depths. Nevertheless, Pieper continues to insist that if one wishes to accord fundamental hope virtue status, it has to be as a theological virtue. He thus agrees with a certain current of Thomism that seems not to allow any room for a natural virtue of hope.[115]

Pieper's refusal to accept a natural virtue of hope has come under criticism from a number of contemporary authors. Bollnow reproaches him for going beyond the properly philosophical realm in order to enter the realm of theology and for assuming that philosophy is incapable of treating the virtue of hope.[116] He maintains that fundamental hope constitutes the *"fundamental and ultimate supporting structure,"*[117] the *"very center of human Dasein."*[118] Landsberg, who is not thinking directly of Pieper's position, affirms that hope in the singular is constitutive of Dasein, that is, it forms Dasein's fundamental structure.[119] We find a similar idea in the work of Marcel, for whom hope is the stuff of which the soul is made,[120] or again in the work of Le Senne, for whom hope is "consubstantial with our life."[121] For these thinkers, existence is not determined by Heideggerian care, but by the fundamental hope that is not yet supernatural or Christian hope, but rather natural hope.

These two types of hope are characterized by their different degrees of certainty. While the certainty of natural hope is subject to the uncertainty due to the human condition, an uncertainty that can lead to despair, superanatural hope, in Landsberg's eyes, is stamped by a greater degree of certainty, and is incapable of darkening into despair.[122] This same criterion for distinction reappears in Plügge, who holds that fundamental hope, which is distinct from ordinary hope, is not identical with the Christian virtue of hope. He goes further than Landsberg, affirming that fundamental hope is the natural prefiguration of hope understood in the sense of a Christian virtue. It is so to speak the primary matter out of which the Christian virtue can be formed.[123] Wanting to analyze hope from a philosophical perspective, Bollnow, following Plügge, also affirms that fundamental hope is not the theological virtue of hope but its natural prefiguration.[124] All three refer to the French philosopher Maine de Biran's affirmation that "religion has come to confirm the hope that was given by nature,"[125] but they fail to provide a single argument to justify the assertion. The distinction between natural hope and supernatural hope arises from the desire to assure the human being of a fundamental hope that would be constitutive of Dasein, without needing to have recourse to the idea of a Christian supernatural virtue, or to a divine revelation.

Fundamental hope, like ordinary hope, is constitutive of human nature, insofar as it presupposes the original act of trust in being. Bollnow, Landsberg, Le Senne, Marcel, and Plügge are all no doubt correct to affirm the "naturalness" of hope. In reality, Pieper is not in opposition to them on this point; he himself says "fundamental hope is identical with our existence,"[126] insofar as it expresses the state of being "on the way." This does not mean this hope has already acquired the status of a natural virtue that is determined by reason and the possibility of being rejected by the subject.

Pieper's solution, which defines the theological status of the virtue of hope in terms of the aspect of gift, an aspect that applies both to the hoped-for object and to the very act of hoping, does not seem to me convincing for a philosophical approach, one that does not include the transcendent dimension of a Christian God. It is reasonably possible to distinguish various sorts of human hope. The act of natural hope, that is, ordinary hope or hope as passion, is a movement of the irascible appetite, that is, of the will as ordered to a good (*sub ratione boni*), the realization of which or the possession of its object is due either to the subject's own efforts or to a gift from an other. It can be accompanied by the moral virtues (of magnanimity and humility) that correct the possible deviations of the passion of hope, since the passion itself is not directly subject to reason. But this passion of hope, even accompanied by other virtues, cannot be called a natural virtue of hope. Nevertheless, we are able to speak of rational anticipations in connection with this passion. These are rational and calculable expectations that the passion of hope can assimilate in an intrinsic way when the passion is accompanied by the moral virtues of magnanimity and humility, even though it does not incorporate them into its nature. These rational anticipations, which the subject freely posits and of which he attains the object either through his own efforts or through the aid of the other, can be related to the intellectual and moral virtue of prudence. None of these, however, yet constitute a natural virtue of hope. It is nevertheless possible, in my opinion, to speak of a natural virtue of hope, whose object would belong to the order of gift, even though that object would not necessarily be God, as it is for the theological virtue of hope. This virtue would be acquired by the subject through continuous activity in which he places his trust in an other or in the event of a state of affairs. It would represent, as it were, the natural prefiguration of the theological virtue of hope, whose act, and not only whose object, would belong to the order of gift.

The discussion of hope's status as a natural or supernatural virtue seems to rest on the broader issue of the nature-grace relation in general.[127] Pieper starts from a view of the world illuminated by faith and implying a metaphysics of creation, in which the natural is pervaded by the supernatural. He identifies fundamental hope, which is "identical with our existence" and which emerges out of, among other things, limit-situations (as we shall see momentarily), with the theological virtue. This latter is itself, according to Pieper, essential to the person. He takes the notion of *fides implicita* and transposes it into *spes implicita*.[128] For my part, I believe fundamental hope either belongs to the natural constitution of the human being or it forms the basis for a natural virtue that can be transformed, within a theological context, into a theological virtue.

5.4 The relation between ordinary and fundamental hope

Fundamental hope manifests itself most clearly in the context of an existential limit-situation into which the person is "thrown" at a given moment of his existence, without his willing it, and it presents a real possibility of falling into despair. These extreme situations punctuating existence can turn out to be enormously beneficial, for they compel the subject in a radical and sometimes painful way to return to the bare foundation of his existence. They invite him to become aware of himself and of his place in the world, or they reawaken that awareness. They help him to detach himself from the *Umwelt* in order to enter into the *Welt* dimension. Death and *eros* are examples of such profound existential upheavals that are able to turn into beneficial experiences for those who respond positively to them, that is, for those who open themselves up to a new dimension of being that lies beyond the subject and transcends the workaday world.[129] Another possible consequence of these experiences is that one's view of the world, one's understanding of one's place in the world, and the meaning of one's life, can be wholly or partially called into question.

Observing his terminally ill or suicidal patients, Plügge notes that a fundamental hope arises the moment they lose all their hopes in an ordinary sense, because these hopes are frustrated by the non-realization of their object.[130] Rauchfleisch, too, observes that it is in the pit of "ordinary" despair—as opposed to fundamental despair—into which the human being, the victim of solitude and grief, has sunk, that a trusting hope in the future can emerge, if the subject freely wills it.[131] Thus, it is precisely the state of having lost one's ordinary or everyday hopes, a state brought about in an extreme situation, that enables the human being to open up to the fundamental hope that is "natural" to his being, and to become conscious of it to some degree. Although fundamental hope seems to be dormant, giving place instead to the various burning hopes that in fact can only be kept alive because of it, it can itself resurface in the most destabilizing existential moments. Someone suffering from a terminal illness, the martyr, the prisoner condemned to death, in short, any human being confronted with an extreme situation, is able to become aware of his finitude and to enter freely onto the path that leads either to fundamental despair or fundamental hope.

Adopting Plügge's conclusions as his own, Pieper particularly admires his idea that genuine hope arises from the loss of ordinary hopes. What Pieper adds to this experimental observation is the notion of disappointment, which, playing on the words *Enttäuschung* (disappointment) and *Täuschung* (deception), he defines as a deception or illusion. What does this error consist in, this deception that becomes most transparent to the human being in moments of existential shock? According to Pieper, these deceptions lead the human being to believe that the possession of a multiplicity of worldly goods will bring about the object toward which he strives by nature, or at least that possessing these goods is something absolutely necessary. A person is disabused of this illusion when his spirit is opened up so it transcends this world, that is, when he becomes aware that the complete fulfillment of his person does not lie in external things, in a metaphysics of *having*, but in a metaphysics of *being*, of gift, in which the object is not necessarily something that can be measured. Thus, for Pieper, the existential shocks connected with the disappointment of hopes can deliver a person from the traps of deceptions and illusions. They allow him to open himself to fundamental hope and escape from the temptation to despair.[132] But is an experience of existential upheaval such as this sufficient for the human being to open up to fundamental hope? No, because that would deny human freedom; the person is just as capable of opening to the gift of hope as he is of rejecting it and becoming enclosed in the shadows of despair.

Many have pointed to the disappointment of hopes as the privileged means of opening the path to the flourishing of fundamental hope, including Plügge, Evans,[133] Fahrenbach,[134] Marcel,[135] Pestieau,[136] Unamuno,[137] and Vieillard-Baron. This last says, in his work entitled *L'illusion historique et l'espérance céleste,* that disillusion is what characterizes the twentieth century, after a nineteenth century that naively placed its hope in progress. This loss of limited hopes, this disillusionment—which is a consequence of the historical illusion that reduces the whole of reality to the single dimension of historicity and *praxis,* and which expresses an ontological experience of the fragility of Dasein—is necessary for consciousness to be able to perceive the fundamental hope that opens it to the future.[138] We can draw a parallel here with the dramatic and sometimes disturbing position in which contemporary people find themselves, having accumulated war-machines capable of destroying the human race and the entire Earth, the very things they were made to protect. This precarious situation, which could lead to despair and which we could compare to a state of existential upheaval, if it is not something the contemporary person grows accustomed to or forgets altogether, could be a privileged opportunity for him to become aware and open himself up to genuine hope.

Existential shock is not identical to the situation of despair, but it is a possible source of despair, that is, it confronts the subject with a free choice between, on the one hand, an openness of his being to a *being-more,* accompanied by trust, and, on the other hand, a withdrawal into himself and a wallowing in disappointment.

He finds himself at the crossroads between fundamental hope and fundamental despair.[139] It is in this context that we must accept Marcel's affirmation, namely, that "hope can exist only as an active struggle against despair,"[140] that is, that "there can strictly speaking be no hope except when the temptation to despair exists. Hope is the act by which this temptation is actively or victoriously overcome."[141] The temptation to despair is not being affirmed, here, as identical to despair.

As I have already pointed out, Pieper is not so categorical on this subject. He leaves open the possibility that the human being can just as well discover fundamental hope outside of situations of trial and existential shock.[142] He refuses to identify the hopeless situation with despair, insofar as he insists that the former, the existential upheaval, can be—though of course it need not always be—the point of departure for the onset of either despair or hope. Moreover, fundamental hope, as we have seen, is natural to the person; it is an integral aspect of his *status viatoris*. As Pieper puts it, fundamental hope is "the proper virtue of 'not yet,'"[143] of the inclination from *minimal-being* to *being-complete*.

It is possible to ask which comes before the other, fundamental hope or ordinary hope. Pieper observes that the development and maintenance of the virtue of hope necessarily presuppose the two moral virtues of magnanimity and humility, which accompany the passion of hope. The loss of the virtue of hope can occur for two reasons: first, it may result from a lack of magnanimity and humility, and second, it may result from an act of freedom.[144] It would thus seem that, for Pieper, fundamental hope would be posterior to ordinary hope. But if this is the case, how are we to understand his affirmation that fundamental hope is natural to the very being of the human person? Fundamental hope is anterior to ordinary hopes insofar as its object underlies the object of the latter. Indeed, from Pieper's perspective, when I hope with a hope for a difficult and arduous object, I hope at the same time with a fundamental hope that undergirds this hope insofar as I hold that the possession of this good will contribute to my personal completion and fulfillment. It would be possible to draw a parallel here with the happiness sought in all activity.

According to Pieper, it is fundamental hope that sustains every movement of human hope. In other words, without fundamental hope, there would be no hope at all; without fundamental hope, we could not speak of hope at all because there would not even be such a thing as despair, as we will see. "Human hopes cannot be genuine hopes without 'the' hope . . . ordinary hopes are so many reflections of 'the' hope,"[145] as Munos-Alonso says, which is a claim we find as well in Fahrenbach[146] and Le Senne.[147]

Notes

1. Pieper, "Über die Hoffnung der Kranken," 23. *Hope and History,* 26 [*Werke,* Vol. 6, 385]; *Glauben, Hoffen, Lieben,* 13f. In Plato's *Symposium,* Diotima makes the observation that, as the language shows, there is a difference between the multiplicity of people who make many different things and the singularity of the one who alone merits the name "maker," namely, the poet. In light of this observation, she draws an analogy with the distinction between the various types of love and the singularity of the one who loves in the sense of *eros.* Pieper transposes this analogy into the context of hope through his distinction between ordinary and fundamental hope. See Plato, *Symposium,* 205b–d. Pieper, *Hope and History,* 25 [*Werke,* Vol. 6, 384] and "Über die Hoffnung der Kranken," 21f.

2. See Pieper, *On Hope,* 26f. [*Werke,* Vol. 4, 264f.].

3. Ibid., 38–39, 43 [271, 274].

4. Pieper, *Über das christliche Menschenbild,* 65.

5. Pieper, *The End of Time,* 145–48 [*Werke,* Vol. 6, 369–70].

6. Pieper, "Selbstgespräch über die Hoffnung," 90.

7. Pieper, "Über die Hoffnung," in: J. Besch, 81f. and reprinted in *Glauben, Hoffnung, Lieben,* 13.

8. Pieper, "Hoffnung–auf was?," 162.

9. Pieper, *Hope and History,* 26 [*Werke,* Vol. 6, 385].

10. Bollnow (*Neue Geborgenheit,* 99f.) distinguishes between "relative hope" and "absolute hope," and also between "hope" in the singular, or "Zustand des hoffnungsvollen Gestimmtseins" [the state of being full of hope] and "hopes" in the plural, or "einzelnen bestimmten Hoffnungen" [individual, specific hopes].

11. Although he does not formulate it explicitly, Camus adverts to the difference between fundamental and ordinary hope. While fundamental hope is an expectant waiting for a future life, which will arrive once we have crossed the threshold of death and which rests on our trust in God, ordinary hope contents itself with life on earth, rejecting any possibility of a *post mortem,* and being dependent solely on human efforts. (For more references, see chapter five, in particular, the first section, entitled "The human being facing the insurmountable obstacle of death.")

12. Edmaier (*Horizonte der Hoffnung,* 74ff.) distinguishes between "gegenständliche Hoffnung" [objective hope], which is identical to ordinary hope, *espoir,* and "tranzendentale Hoffnung" [transcendental hope].

13. Fahrenbach (*Wesen und Sinn der Hoffnung,* 54, 88ff.) distinguishes between "Hoffnungen" and "Hoffnung" or "Grundhoffnung" [fundamental hope].

14. Le Senne (*Le découverte de Dieu*, 254ff.) distinguishes between an "infinite hope" and "hopes."

15. Minkowski ("L'espérance," 97f.) distinguishes between ordinary and fundamental hope, emphasizing that we find this distinction clearly expressed by the difference in the sound of the voice in the person who speaks about the two notions. Thus, even when it concerns a serious object, ordinary hope is spoken of in tones that do not reach the deep tonality of the voice that speaks of fundamental hope.

16. Möller, *Littérature du XXème siècle et Christianisme*, Vol., 4, 14, fn. 4.

17. Sonnemans (*Hoffnung ohne Gott? In Konfrontation mit Ernst Bloch*, 29) draws a very interesting distinction between "Sachhoffnungen" [various hopes directed to things] and "Hoffnung auf einen, der Du für uns ist" [the hope for someone who is 'thou' for us].

18. Lopez-Mendez, *Die Hoffnung im theologischen Denken Teilhard de Chardins*, 47–66.

19. See Landsberg, *The Experience of Death*, 25ff. [50ff.].

20. Marcel does not affirm an opposition between ordinary and fundamental hope; sometimes he even uses the terms interchangeably for the same reality. See *Being and Having*, 79, 88, 91 (fn. 1) [116, 128, 131 (fn. 1)]. *The Mystery of Being*, vol. 2, 158–59 [Vol. 2, 159]. It seems that Marcel grasps the distinction when he describes the way he understood his famous lecture on hope, which he gave in 1942, but he does not work out its implications: "I had to find the connection the hope (*espoir*) of liberation and hope (*espérance*) in immortality," *Presence and Immortality*, 231 [183].

21. See Marcel, *Homo viator*, 29f., 32, 45, 46 [39f., 43, 60, 62]. We could relate the two ways of hoping with the two ways of believing: "believing that" and "believing in," in *The Mystery of Being*, vol. 2, 77 [Vol. 2, 78].

22. On the notion of 'boundary-situation,' see Jaspers, *Philosophy*, vol. 2, 177ff. (467ff.).

23. The martyr, who lives the virtue of courage in a perfect manner by standing firm in the face of evil, freely accepts the death that is imposed on him from the outside, the death that he might be able to avoid by renouncing the ideal for which he dies. Moreover, he is characterized by his extremely positive attitude toward reality, unceasingly praising the beauty and goodness of creation in spite of the injustice of the evil being inflicted on him. He does not despise the natural reality of this world: see Pieper, "Sur l'Espérance des Martyrs," 82. *In Tune with the World*, 20f. [*Werke*, Vol. 6, 237]; "Die Verborgenheit von Hoffnung und Verzweiflung," 178.

24. See Pieper, *Hoffnung und Geschichte* 26f. [*Werke*, Vol. 6, 385f.]; "Über die Hoffnung der Kranken," 24ff. "Hoffnung und Geschichte," 12f.

25. See Revers, *Über die Hoffnung*, 11. A person who is suicidal, however, is distinguished from the martyr and the terminally ill person (and even from the prisoner condemned death) by the fact that he chooses more or less freely to die, while the others have been forced into it by external factors.

26. Plügge, "Über die Hoffnung," 63. See "Über suizidale Krane," 442.

27. For Pascal the person who hangs himself is in fact looking for happiness by that act. The human being is by nature and structurally a being ordered to happiness, to a meaning. In other words, in one way or another, in everything he does he is trying to acquire complete happiness, and this is true, at least in most cases, even if he decides to kill himself. See Bloch, *Atheism in Christianity*, 249 [329] and *The Principle of Hope*, 195 [224]. Lain Entralgo, *L'attente et l'espérance*, 508, 527. Comte-Sponville, *Le mythe d'Icare: Traité du désespoir et de la béatitude*, vol. 1, 18. Edmaier, *Horizonte der Hoffnung*, 78.

28. Landsberg, *The Experience of Death*, 82 [125].

29. See Marcel, "Structure de l'espérance," 74.

30. See Plügge, "Über suizidale Kranke," 437ff., and "Über die Hoffnung," 61ff.

31. See Staehelin, *Haben und Sein*, 47ff.

32. Ibid., 50; see also *Der finale Mensch*, 17; *Urvertrauen und zweite Wirklichkeit*.

33. See Rauchfleisch, *Leiden-verzweifeln-hoffen*, 36, 38, 78. Reil, a famous doctor and psychiatrist from the eighteenth and nineteenth centuries, observes that the terminally ill may lose their lives, but they never lose their hope: cited by Brednow, "Der Mensch und die Hoffnung," 529, Jaspers, "Die Kraft der Hoffnung," 219, and Lain Entralgo, *L'attente et l'espérance*, 506f.

34. See Landsberg, *The Experience of Death*, 25 [50]. Godfrey, *A Philosophy of Human Hope*, 21. Plügge, "Über suizidale Krank," 437ff.

35. Le Senne, *La découverte de Dieu*, 254.

36. See Pieper, "Über die Hoffnung der Kranken," 32; "Hoffnung und Geschichte," 26.

37. Pieper, *Happiness and Contemplation*.

38. Pieper, "Über die Kunst, nicht zu verzweifeln," 208.

39. Pieper, "Selbstgespräch über die Hoffnung," 90; "Über die Hoffnung," in Besch, 73, 83. *Glauben, Hoffen, Lieben*, 14.

40. Pieper, "Über die Hoffnung der Kranken," 32.

41. Pieper, *Über das christliche Menschenbild*, 65.

42. Pieper, "Hoffnung und Geschichte," 23; "Über die Kunst, nicht zu verzweifeln," 208; *Glauben, Hoffen, Lieben*, 20. "Über die Hoffnung der Kranken," 30.

43. Pieper, "Über die Hoffnung der Kranken," 30.

44. Pieper, "Selbstgespräch über die Hoffnung," 86.

45. Pieper, "Über die Kunst, nicht zu verzweifeln," 211.

46. Pieper, "Die Verborgenheit von Hoffnung und Verzweiflung," 172.

47. Pieper, *Death and Immortality*, 118 [*Werke*, Vol. 5, 396].

48. Pieper, *Glauben, Hoffen, Lieben*, 15.

49. See Pieper, "Über die Hoffnung der Kranken," 32.

50. See Pieper, "Selbstgespräch über die Hoffnung," 90.

51. Pieper, *Glauben, Hoffen, Lieben*, 14; see "Über die Hoffnung," in Besch, 73.

52. Some of these authors describe the object of fundamental hope also in terms of the notion of 'salvation,' which ought to be understood in the sense of the total ontological wholeness of the subject. See, for example, Bollnow, *Neue Geborgenheit*, 147. Edmaier, *Horizonte der Hoffnung*, 33, 67, 72, 100, 124, 133, 140, 200, 206, 210ff. Fahrenbach, *Wesen und Sinn der Hoffnung*, 65, 109, 115. Lain Entralgo, *L'attente et l'espérance*, 325. Landsberg, *The Experience of Death*, 22f., 25ff. [47, 50ff.]. Le Senne, *La découverte de Dieu*, 252. Marcel, *Homo viator*, 30, 185f. [40, 260f.]; *The Mystery of Being*, vol. 2, 172, 180 [Vol. 2, 174, 181]; "Dialogue sur l'espérance. Gabriel Marcel et Ernst Bloch," 44, 58; *Being and Having*, 75, 79f. [109, 116]. Middendorf, *Über die Hoffnung*, 60f. Plügge, "Über die Hoffnung," 62f.; "Über die suizidale Kranke," 438. Revers, *Über die Hoffnung*, 12f. Sonnemans, *Hoffnung ohne Gott? In Konfrontation mit Ernst Bloch*, 34f. Wust, *Ungewißheit und Wagnis*, S. 40f., 97f, 178f, 227f.

53. Bloch, *The Principle of Hope*, 16 [15]; see also 292 [340].

54. Ibid., 1375 [1627].

55. Ibid., 1376 [1628].

56. Bloch, *Atheism in Christianity*, 224, 265 [297, 346].

57. Bloch, *The Principle of Hope*, 16f. [16]; see also 1312ff. [1551ff.].

58. Ibid., 201 [230].

59. Ibid., 7 [6].

60. Ibid., 108 [122].

61. Ibid., 1324ff. [1565ff.].

62. Ibid., 583 [680].

63. Bloch, *Heritage of Our Times*, 138ff. [152ff.].

64. Bloch, *The Principle of Hope*, 582 [679].

65. Ibid., 1367 [1618].

66. Ibid., 316 [368], 313 [364].

67. Pelletier, "Libération et salut d'après Ernst Bloch," 173.

68. Bloch, *Atheism in Christianity*, 221 [293]; see also 254 [334].

69. See Pieper, *Hope and History*, 88 [*Werke*, Vol. 6, 424].

70. Bloch, *The Principle of Hope*, 1200 [1413].

71. Bloch, *Heritage of Our Times*, 142 [157].

72. Bloch, *The Principle of Hope*, 1311 [1550].

73. Ibid., 610 [711]; see also 604 [705].

74. We see a shift of perspective regarding the understanding of human hope, which occurs between his first work on hope, a work of his youth, and his later writings. While in *Über die Hoffnung, [On Hope]* Pieper articulates a tripartite conception of hope (the passion of hope, the passion of hope accompanied by the moral virtues of magnanimity and humility, and finally the theological virtue of hope), his later writings no longer explicitly distinguish anything but two sorts of hope: ordinary hope (under which we may place the two passions of hope) and fundamental hope (which corresponds to the theological virtue of hope). Pieper devotes only a few pages to the exposition of the two moral virtues of magnanimity and humility (*On Hope*, 27–30 [*Werke*, Vol. 4, 264–66]; *Fortitude and Temperance*, 103ff. [*Werke*, Vol. 4, 181f.]; as well as a brief mention in "Selbstgespräch über die Hoffnung," 91).

75. A thesis defended by a small minority of philosophers, such as Day, "Hope," and *Hope*.

76. For Aquinas's treatment of the passions, see *Summa theologiae*, III, 22–25.

77. Ibid., question 40.

78. Thomas names the four passions joy, sadness, fear, and hope (Ibid., q.25, a.4).

79. Ibid., I–II, 60, 4.

80. It is helpful to point out that the eleven passions, which express the reaction of the appetitive faculties with respect to a good or bad object, understood here in an ontological sense, are in themselves indifferent or neutral with respect to their moral value. The human being confers upon them a moral character through his acts. Human passion is morally good, if it is in conformity to reason, and bad if it is opposed to it. This clarification seems to me important for a rehabilitation of the notion of passion, which has too often been defined in opposition to the rational. The moral virtues of magnanimity and humility, for example, come to accompany and sustain the passion of hope, ordering it according to reason. They confer upon it a rational principle. We find this notion already in Aristotle, for whom the appetitive movements have to be subordinated to reason in order to find the just mean, which lies between the two vices that form a contrast with it, one by falling short of it, the other by exceeding it.

81. See Thomas Aquinas, *Summa theologiae*, II–II, 129, 1 and 8; 131, 2, ad 1. Aquinas distinguishes two sorts of moral virtues: those that the human being acquires through his own efforts, and those that he possesses by infusion or by a gift. There are accordingly two sorts of magnanimity, which are distinguished in terms of their origin: acquired magnanimity and infused magnanimity. The first, which is related to hope, differs from the virtue of

fundamental hope insofar as its object of greatness is realized by unaided human effort. The second accompanies the virtue of fundamental hope, which forms the object of a gift. The moral virtue of infused magnanimity nevertheless remains distinct from the theological virtue of hope insofar as it possesses a different direct object, which is the subject of the virtuous act and not God.

82. See Middendorf, *Über die Hoffnung*, 38.

83. On Hume's treatment of the passions, see Cléro, *La philosophie des passions chez David Hume.*

84. Bloch, *The Principle of Hope*, 290 [338].

85. Ibid., 45 [49].

86. Ibid., 4 [2].

87. See Schnoor, *Psychoanalyse der Hoffnung.*

88. See Bloch, *The Principle of Hope*, 45ff. [49ff.].

89. Ibid., 70 [77].

90. Ibid., 73 [81].

91. "Only when reason starts to speak, does hope, in which there is no guile, begin to blossom again. The Not-Yet-Conscious itself must become *conscious* in its act, *known* in its content, as the process of dawning on the one hand, as what is dawning on the other. And so the point is reached where hope itself, this authentic expectant emotion in the forward dream, no longer just appears as a merely self-based mental feeling . . . but in a *conscious-known* (*bewusst-gewusst*) way as *utopian function,*" Bloch, *The Principle of Hope*, 144 [163]. "Thus the utopian function is also the only transcendent one which has remained, and the only one which deserves to remain: one which is transcendent without transcendence. Its support and correlate is process, which has not yet surrendered its most immanent What-content, but which is still under way. Which consequently is itself in a state of hope and of object-based premonition of the Not-Yet-Become, in the shape of a Not-Yet-Become-Good. . . . the *act-content* of hope is, as a consciously illuminated [*Bewusstsein*], knowingly elucidated [*Gewusstsein*] content, the *positive utopian function;* the *historical content* of hope, first represented in ideas, encyclopaedically explored in real judgements, is *human culture referred to its concrete-utopian horizon.* The docta spes combine operates on this knowledge as expectant emotion in the Ratio, as Ratio in the expectant emotion," 146 [166].

92. See Gusdorf, *La vertu de la force*, 1. Pieper refers to this text from Valéry on several occasions: see *Über das christliche Menschenbild*, 17f.; "Die Aktualität der Kardinaltugenden," 33; *Auskfünft über die Tugenden*, 9; "Tugendlehre als Aussage über den Menschen," 151.

93. See Scheler, "Zur Rehabilitierung der Tugend," 15.

94. Lalande, *Vocabulaire technique et critique de la philosophie*, 1203.

95. Pohier, "Psychology and Virtue," 483.

96. See Pieper, "Nachdenkliches über die Klugheit," 93; *Glauben, Hoffen, Lieben*, 18; "Tugendlehre als Aussage über den Menschen," 151. This affirmation has proven to be false in these last decades, which have shown a marked increase of interest in the philosophical investigation of virtue.

97. Simon agrees with Pieper in pointing out that the disappearance of the concept of virtue has been accompanied by the appearance of modern substitutes; he distinguishes three types: *natural goodness, social engineering*, and *psycho-technology* (*The Definition of Moral Virtue*, 2–18).

98. Pieper, "Die Aktualität der Kardinaltugenden," 110; see *Über das christliche Menschenbild*, 18f.; *Auskunft über die Tugenden*, 9ff.; *Death and Immortality*, 101 [*Werke*, Vol. 5, 379].

99. See, for example, Anscombe, "Modern Moral Philosophy." Foot, *Virtues and Vices*. Geach, *The Virtues*. Jankélévitch, *Traité des vertus*. McIntyre, *After Virtue*. Comte-Sponville, *A Short on the Great Virtues*.

100. Thomas Aquinas, *Summa theologiae*, II–II, 4, 5; see also I–II, q.49, q.55, q.56, a.3.

101. Ibid., I, 41, 4.

102. Ibid., 54, 3, and 71, 1.

103. "*Virtue is the highest potential;* it represents the furthest extremity to which *capacity* can be carried, whether this is a capacity for being or for doing. Virtue is the best that one can be," Pieper, "Die Aktualität der Kardinaltugenden," 117.

104. See Thomas Aquinas, *Summa theologiae*, I–II, 62, 3, ad2, cited in Pieper, *On Hope*, 25, fn. 1 [*Werke*, Vol. 4, 263, fn. 15]. For Thomas Aquinas, hope is a theological virtue, on the one hand, because its object (i.e., its material object or final cause) is the *summum bonum*, God, and on the other hand because the attainment of this object lies beyond the capacity of the subject. Since it transcends human effort, this object can only be received as a gift, through dependence on the help of an other (the formal object or efficient cause) [see *Summa theologiae*, II–II, 17, 4. *De Spes*, 1]). Moreover, this very act of hope, qua virtue, is essentially a gift. Pieper adheres to the thought of Aquinas, according to whom there is no virtue of hope in the natural order. In his later writings, Pieper changes the way he presents his position that one can speak of the virtue of hope only in terms of a theological virtue, namely, he makes reference to Ancient philosophy (see Pieper, *Glauben, Hoffen, Lieben*, 18).

105. See Pieper, "Die Verborgenheit von Hoffnung und Verzweiflung," 177. *On Hope*, 26 [*Werke*, vol. 4, 264]. "Hoffnung," in: *Handbuch theologische Grundbegriffe*, 703. "Hoffnung—auf was?," 163. "Sur l'Espérance des Martyrs," 82. *The End of Time*, 151ff. [*Werke*, vol. 6, 373f.].

106. See Pieper, "Selbstgespräch über die Hoffnung," 87ff.; *Glauben, Hoffen, Lieben*, 19; *Fortitude and Temperance*, 43 [*Werke*, Vol. 4, 136].

107. See Schmitz, *The Gift: Creation,* 48ff., 57.

108. Marcel, *Homo viator,* 63 [84]. See ibid., 41f. [56]. *Being and Having,* 74ff. [108ff.]. *Concrete Approaches to Investigating the Ontological Mystery,* 187. [73]. Our discussion of Pieper's notion of gift agrees with Marcel's notion; for Marcel, gift is essential as much to the mystery of being, love, and fidelity, as it is to the act of genuine hope: see *Homo viator,* 50 [67].

109. See Bollnow, *Neue Geborgenheit,* 134ff.

110. Marcel, "Dialogue sur l'espérance. Gabriel Marcel et Ernst Bloch," 67.

111. On this distinction, see chapter two, section 3.3. See also Thomas Aquinas, *Summa theologiae,* I–II, 40–2.

112. Pieper, "Sur l'Espérance des Martyrs," 82.

113. Ibid., 87. "Hoffnung–auf was?," 163. *On Hope,* 31–34 [*Werke,* Vol. 4, 267f.].

114. Pieper speaks of Christ only three times in connection with hope in his writings after *Über die Hoffnung* [*On Hope*], and he does so at the end of the articles in question, specifying that he is going beyond a philosophical context with these affirmations: "Über die Hoffnung der Kranken," 34; "Selbstgespräch über die Hoffnung," 91; "Hoffnung–auf was?," 164.

115. See, for example, Bernard, *Théologie de l'espérance selon saint Thomas d'Aquin,* 37. Glenn, *A Comparison of the Thomistic and the Scotistic Concepts of Hope,* 8. Le Tilly's commentary on Aquinas's *Summa theologiae* (II–II, 17–22), 212ff. Pinckaers, "La nature vertueuse de l'espérance," 196, 208f., 224f., 227, 238f. Urdanoz, "Para una Filosofia y Teologia de la esperanza," 559. Thomas Aquinas specifies that the moral virtue of magnanimity accompanies, provides a context for, and governs the passion of hope (i.e., absolute hope, *sperare tantum* [*Summa theologiae,* I–II, 40, 2, 1], which relies on the individual's own efforts for the accomplishment of its object), but it cannot be identified with theological hope. The second form of the passion of hope is accompanied by *exspectatio* toward an other, i.e., its movement is preceded by an operation of the cognitive faculty. It is not a moral virtue, but remains a passion that can by ordered by reason. Thomas agrees with Bonaventure, affirming in *De Spe* and *Summa theologiae* that the virtue of hope is a virtue insofar as it depends on divine assistance and relies on divine aid through an act of trust. Nevertheless, we could interpret the natural virtue of magnanimity as the natural virtue of hope: see Gauthier, *Magnanimité,* 295ff., 346ff.

116. See Bollnow, *Neue Geborgenheit,* 118.

117. Ibid., 113.

118. Ibid., 110.

119. See Landsberg, *The Experience of Death,* 24, 44f. [49, 74f.].

120. See Marcel, *Being and Having,* 80 [117].

121. Le Senne, *La découverte de Dieu,* 256.

122. See Landsberg, *The Experience of Death,* 27, n. 1 and 49f. [52, fn. 8 and 82f.].

123. See Plügge, "Über die Hoffnung," 66f.; "Über die suizidale Kranke," 438f., fn. 1.

124. See Bollnow, *Neue Geborgenheit,* 101, 116ff., 118.

125. Maine de Biran, *Méditations sur la mort près de sa soeur Victoire,* in: *Oeuvres* (Paris, 1927), cited by Plügge, "Über die Hoffnung," 66. Landsberg, *The Experience of Death,* 80 [122]. Bollnow, *Neue Geborgenheit,* 118.

126. See Pieper, "Über die Kunst, nicht zu verzweifeln," 213; "Selbstgespräch über die Hoffnung," 90.

127. I thus am in agreement with the positions of Edmaier (*Horizonte der Hoffnung,* 33, 75ff.), Lain Entralgo (*L'attente et l'espérance,* 563ff.), and Nink (*Metaphysik des sittlich Guten,* 102ff., 149f., 153f.), who all affirm the existence of a natural virtue of hope. However, they do not provide any arguments for their position. There are also theologians, few though they be, who insist on a natural virtue of hope, such as Wucherer-Huldenfeld ("Beiträge zur Theologie der Hoffnung," 131; he makes explicit allusion to Pieper's position), for example, or Fries ("Hoffnung und Heilsgewissheit bei Thomas von Aquin," 134). Apart from this current of thought that affirms the existence of two virtues of hope (natural and supernatural or theological), there is also another current, which Pieper neglects to mention, that denies that hope is a theological virtue on the basis of the extremely controversial question whether it is possible in a legitimate sense to desire God, a question that is in turn based on the distinction between the love of concupiscence and the love of friendship. Durand de Saint-Pourçain (fourteenth century) affirms in his commentary on the *Sentences* that "hope belongs to the love of concupiscence, by which we desire a good for our own sakes. But God himself cannot be the proximate and immediate object of our love of concupiscence, because God must be loved for his own sake and with a love of friendship. This object (the immediate object of hope) will thus be something else; it cannot be anything but our future beatitude (as distinct from God)," *Sent.,* IV, 1., III, dist. XXVI, q.II, Paris, 1550, fol. 224, cited in Harent, "Espérance," 657. Duns Scotus defends a theologically acquired hope. See Cajetan's response to Durand de Saint-Pourçain (II–II, 17, 5). On this subject, see also Labourdette, *Cours de théologie morale. L'espérance,* 28–35 and Hamonic, "Dieu peut-il être légitimement convoité?" Glenn, *A Comparison of the Thomistic and the Scotistic Concepts of Hope,* 30ff.

128. See Pieper, "Über die Kunst, nicht zu verzweifeln," 212.

129. See Pieper, *Leisure the Basis of Culture,* 95ff., 132f. [*Werke,* Vol. 4, 21f., 46f.]; *Was heisst Akademisch?* [*Werke,* vol. 6, 112f.]; *In Defense of Philosophy,* 21 [*Werke,* Vol. 4, 87ff.]; "Tod und Unsterblichkeit," in *Tradition als*

Herausforderung, 67; "Über den Philosophie-Begriff Platons," 169f.; *Enthusiasm and Divine Madness,* 32f. [62]. Although he does not make reference to Pieper, the psychologist Rauchfleisch (*Leiden-verzweifeln-hoffen,* 90f.) agrees with him in maintaining that it is sometimes necessary to live through extreme and destabilizing situations in order to be able to transcend the workaday world. See also Jaspers, *Philosophy,* vol. 2, 184ff. (475ff.). Augustine's experience confirms this assertion. After the death of his best friend, Augustine experiences, at the age of nineteen, a profound upheaval in the core of his being, which places in question all of the ideas he had formed of himself, of the world, and of God (*Confessions,* IV, 4). We can draw an analogy here between Augustine's situation and that of the terminally ill person. Both undergo, through a precise event, a profound shock that annihilates not only their view of the world and their existence, but also their hopes. It is nevertheless by virtue of the painful experience of a destabilizing event that they are able to transcend their anxiety and solitude, and even their possible falling into despair, in order to attain a new and more profound understanding of reality, an awareness of the existence of fundamental hope, and an openness to it.

130. See Plügge, "Über die Hoffnung," 61, 63; "Über suizidale Kranke," 438. Marcel (*Being and Having,* 93 [135]) speaks of the existential experience of death as the "springboard of an absolute hope."

131. See Rauchfleisch, *Leiden-verzweifeln-hoffen,* 32f., 36, 38, 50, 74.

132. "Every deep disappointment of some hope whose object was to be found in the worldly sphere potentially harbors an opportunity for hope per se to turn, without resignation and for the first time, towards its true object and, in a process of liberation, for existence to expand, for the first time ever, into an atmosphere of wider dimensions. Precisely in disappointment, and perhaps in it alone, we are offered the challenge of entering into the broader existential realm of hope per se," in Pieper, *Hope and History,* 30 [*Werke,* Vol. 6, 387–88]; see "Hoffnung und Geschichte," 13; "Über die Hoffnung der Kranken," 25f., 30f. Fundamental hope cannot be disappointed, but can be rejected by the subject (see *Hope and History,* 31 [also, 388], and "Über die Hoffnung der Kranken," 31).

133. Speaking of despair as momentary in life as opposed to despair as a way of living, Evans (*Existentialism: The Philosophy of Despair and the Quest for Hope,* 43, 66) maintains that despair is an essential moment. He nevertheless admits in other places (26) that there are other possibilities than despair that can lead to the discovery of hope; see also 95ff.

134. "The . . . final hope to make an appearance generally arises only from the disappointment of worldly hopes; thus, it is an experience of self-discovery in the act of placing one's ultimate trust in an essential capacity to hold on. In this experience, a person's self-understanding changes, and so too does his

actual hope: it becomes set on the essential. Hope becomes at this point for the first time in limit situations what it most essentially is," Fahrenbach, *Wesen und Sinn der Hoffnung,* 109.

135. Marcel (*Homo viator,* 47 [63]) agrees with Pieper when he asks whether "this invincible hope is not in fact erected upon the ruins of all human and determinate hopes."

136. Pestieau (*L'espoir incertain,* 206) speaks, at the level of an analysis of society, of "the advent of a way of salvation" (which he does not understand solely in the religious sense) "in a crisis situation, that is, the springs of hope irrupt in the midst of a situation that apparently has no way out." And he affirms that millenarism "is an act of faith through which meaning appears where meaning no longer existed, through which hope is reborn in the midst of a desperate situation."

137. "solo mediante la desesperasíon . . . podemos llegar a la esperanza," [it is only through despair that we can arrive at hope], de Unamuno, *Ensayos,* II (Madrid, 1945), 817, cited in Alfaro, *De la cuestion del hombre a la cuestion de dios,* 250.

138. See Vieillard-Baron, *L'illusion historique et l'espérance céleste,* 142.

139. On this theme, see the psychological discussion of Schnoor, *Psychanalyse der Hoffnung,* 188, 232ff.

140. Marcel, "Structure de l'espérance," 73.

141. Marcel, *Homo viator,* 36 [49]; see also 41 [55]; *Being and Having,* 74 [108].

142. Pieper also takes a position counter to Daniélou's (*The Lord of History,* 342f. [322]), though he does not cite it directly. For Daniélou, fundamental hope can occur only on the basis of a situation with no way out, which he falsely identifies with a situation of despair. As for Marcel, it seems that on occasion he makes hope depend not only on the temptation to despair but on despair itself; in other words, he seems to give despair a priority over hope. Such an understanding implies that hope follows upon despair: "it is only in a situation such as this"—that is, in a world dominated by absolute despair— "that invincible hope can arise." He even goes so far as to say that despair is "the springboard for the highest affirmation" (*Concrete Approaches to Investigating the Ontological Mystery,* 185 [69–70]).

143. Pieper, *On Hope,* 21 [*Werke,* Vol. 4, 262].

144. Ibid., 26–37 [264–70].

145. Munos-Alonso, "Las esperanzas humanas y su fundamento," 153–54.

146. See Fahrenbach, *Wesen und Sinn der Hoffnung,* 57.

147. See Le Senne, *La découverte de Dieu,* 255.

4

The Extreme
Opposites of Hope:
Presumption and Despair

THE ATTITUDES that represent the opposites of the act of hope are presumption and despair. They are both anticipations; while one anticipates the realization of the hoped-for object, either already in the present or in the future, the other anticipates its nonrealization. In this respect, the ontology of *not-yet-being,* with its static-dynamic movement from *minimal-being* to *complete-being* gets reduced, according to Pieper, to a static ontological dimension, whether it be to the *already* or to the *not-yet.* While presumption and despair anticipate either the actualization or the non-realization of a thing, hope strives with openness and trust, accompanied by a measure of uncertainty, toward the actualization of a hoped-for object in the distant or proximate future.

1. PRESUMPTION

Pieper spends more time on the attitude of despair, and devotes little attention to the act of presumption, which he describes as an attitude that rejects the itinerant condition of existence, insofar as it anticipates the fulfillment of human seeking as something already certain.[1] It runs counter to a metaphysics of gift and creation, and remains within the horizon of *praxis.* Presumption takes for granted that the object lies within the reach of the subject's own efforts. I do not believe, however, that the presumptuous person necessarily rejects an ontology of *not-yet-being,* as Pieper maintains. In fact, although he anticipates the realization of the hoped-for object, he too participates in the striving from a *minimal-being* toward his fulfillment and his complete actualization. Presumption, as an attitude that anticipates the possession of the hoped-for object (whether it be the object of ordinary or fundamental hope), expresses a false and hasty sense of security. Rather than coming to certainty in being—which is of course always accompanied by experiences of uncertainty—through a trusting and willing openness to the mystery of reality, the presumptuous person rests on a certainty provided by his own resources. Doing so, he seems to fail to take account of existential uncertainty. The attitude of presumption thus stands in opposition to a certain extent not only to the act of fundamental hope but equally to that of ordinary hope.

2. Despair

2.1 Fundamental despair as the anticipation of nonfulfillment

While fundamental hope affirms that all will end well in relation to the ultimate fulfillment of the person, the community, or reality as a whole, an affirmation that does not arise from a vague optimism but from a trust in being, accompanied by a certainty founded on a reason,[2] despair believes, in advance and before it has gone through the experience, that all will end poorly, in the absurdity of nothingness. Fundamental despair, which is distinct from common or ordinary despair, as we will see, is characterized by a voluntary act that anticipates the nonrealization of the object toward which human nature strives with all its being; it proclaims that there is no fulfillment or complete satisfaction, either for the person or for the community. The existence of a person in despair can be compared to a manufacturing error—an "essential failure"[3]—in human nature, which is caught in the paradox of a desire for fullness that cannot be fulfilled, a paradox that finds its contemporary incarnation in Camus's *Sisyphus*.[4] The person in despair denies the possibility that the object he hopes for, be it fundamental or ordinary hope, can be attained. "The only way to be saved is to renounce salvation," he exclaims[5]—the term "salvation" being understood here as the fulfillment and complete satisfaction of the person. In his eyes, existence is an evil, and "there is no salvation to be expected from it."[6] To borrow Sartre's expression, despair consists in "the belief that my fundamental goals could not be achieved and that, as a consequence, human reality entailed an essential failure."[7]

The attitude of fundamental despair can coexist with a certain optimism with respect to existence. Moreover, it does not necessarily eliminate ordinary hopes, since these keep optimism alive, but it does eliminate fundamental hope, or rather, it rejects the idea that the human being's natural striving may end positively. At the same time, a person in despair may nevertheless lose ordinary hopes as well, thereby rejecting an ontology of becoming, that is, of *not-yet-being,* and replacing it with a static and closed ontology of futureless completeness, in which the category of possibility has been emptied of meaning. His condition can be compared to being dead alive, being "full of death."[8] For Kierkegaard, the person in despair "is mortally ill,"[9] and Marcel sees despair as "anticipating suicide,"[10] comparing it to "death in life, a death anticipated."[11] He is thus in agreement with Jaspers, for whom existence without hope is like a living death.[12] The person in despair brings about a "profound rupture with existence and the movement of becoming,"[13] a "radical negation of the future,"[14] a "total negation of all possibilities of being for the future,"[15] projecting himself into a "closed world,"[16] into a path that has no exit. The situation of despair, far from being an original state into which a person is born, is the result of a rejection, which is not, as some believe, the consequence of a state of soul that lies beyond the activity of the will, that is, a situation for which the subject bears no responsibility and in which he simply happens to find himself one day without having chosen it. Rather, it is the result of a free choice, an act of the will. To despair is "to renounce the idea of remaining oneself, it is to be fascinated by the idea of one's own destruction to the point of anticipating this very destruction itself."[17] This is what Marcel refers to as "a real act of treason" against one's own nature: "it would be to go over to the enemy."[18]

The person in despair has been described as one who is torn apart, who suffers from a self-contradiction, between the desire to actualize one's being (or to actualize something else) and the impossibility of bringing this about.[19] He embodies the act of negation at the core of his being, an act we could, with Marcel, compare to "a certain spiritual autophagy."[20] The situation in which someone in despair finds himself has been related to a neurotic condition. In both cases, the person collapses into himself, the person rejects what Marcel calls "universal communion,"[21] and his will clutches at security. He no longer trusts others. Marked by the metaphysical dimension of having, as opposed to the metaphysics of being, which includes the gift and trust, and also by a closed sense of time in which one is trapped (to a certain extent willingly), the person in despair falls into complete solitude and loses the taste for life. He is marked by depression, "which sees nothing before itself and which expects nothing from anybody,"[22] "a state of being who expects nothing either from himself, or from others, or from life."[23] He disengages from and abandons life.

This relationship between the state of despair and being in a neurotic condition has been brought to light clearly by Revers's psychological studies.[24] He observes that a person's centering himself on his own ego is a constitutive element of boredom, which, as we will see, is both a source and a result of despair. A person who slips into boredom exhibits the traits described above in connection with the person in despair or in a neurotic state. Plügge points out that the suicidal person, just before committing the act, experiences a state of monotony, a profound existential boredom, which leads to a loss of relation to the outside world. The world has become alien, and one no longer feels at home in it. Like the person in boredom or despair, he has lost the capacity to enter into genuine relations with an other, and this indicates a lack of trust and inability to give of oneself.[25] The connection with a thou has become impossible, expressing an impoverishment of the human being's transcendental relations. In other words, the person's development has gone awry. Sartre's play, *No Exit,* depicts in a gripping way the awful situation of the person in despair, for whom the other ultimate represents hell, a situation in which there are no longer any grounds for hope. This situation can be reversed through a connection with reality, from which comes the hope that is capable of healing the mentally ill.[26]

Here we find ourselves standing before two existential and fundamental attitudes—we could even call them two different metaphysics, as I emphasized in chapter three: on the one hand, a withdrawal into onself, which renders the subject incapable of making contact with the world and its mystery, and, on the other hand, a trusting openness to the whole of reality; on the one hand, a metaphysics of despair, and on the other hand a metaphysics of hope—that is, a metaphysics of gift, which is open and available for the dynamic of the actualization of being.

2.2 The root of despair: acedia

According to Pieper, the attitude of despair is rooted in *acedia.* Recalling the way the term was defined by the Ancients, who counted it among the seven capital vices, Pieper describes *acedia* as the expression of a reluctance or refusal to become what the person is in reality, by his very nature. It expresses a negation of the dignity of the individual as a person.[27] Despair is a voluntary attitude that leads both to an inner schizophrenia—manifesting the tension between this refusal and the person's natural orientation to his *telos*—and to a living death. The one who refuses to participate in the realization of his own being, whose finality is given by nature, one who does not accept the fact that the human being is made for a greatness that is offered to him, that he is capable of becoming a person in a full sense, is in Pieper's eyes afflicted with the sickness called *acedia*. This sickness is characterized by a lack of humility and an excess of pride, traits we also find in the presumptuous person: both deny a metaphysics of gift. The "acedic," faced with the vision of his complete actualization, is seized by a sort of angst-ridden vertigo.

Pieper relates *acedia,* which becomes "boredom" in modern parlance, with what he calls the totalitarian worker state. In doing so, he overturns the initial understanding of *acedia,* which identifies it with a lack of industry in work, with the idleness that lies at the root of the vices. Pieper devotes a number of studies to the discussion of such a totalitarianism of work, which banishes any acts or states that have a meaning in themselves, anything that escapes the profit criterion, quantitative productivity, and optimized efficiency. Work is thus established as the supreme measure, the very meaning of human life. Any activity, whether it be artistic, cultural, intellectual, related to leisure or to celebration, is imperiously brought into subjection under it. The human being who is a slave to work denies there is such a thing as activities that are free in themselves, activities whose goal and meaning lie outside the sphere of work. These are, in his eyes, something altogether strange, absurd, and nonsensical, being synonymous with laziness and idleness. Thus, a person who engages in genuine leisure or any other activity that has meaning in itself is comparable to a loafer, who shuns the important work that the building of a more just society of the future requires. We must therefore eliminate all such activities or grant them a utilitarian function, and thus assimilate them into the process of work. The slogan of the man of work is "one does not work to live; one lives to work."[28] This reverses the formulation from one of the greatest thinkers in history: "we engage in work in order to have leisure."[29]

Moreover, the one who exalts work too highly refuses any value to the person except insofar as he is a producer of work, insofar as he is profitable. He thus rejects those who are "good-for-nothing," who prevent business from optimizing its production through technological and human resources. We may think here of the various "parasites" on society: the sick, the elderly, contemplatives of all sorts, such as poets, musicians, monks, and even philosophers, whose activities are at bottom useless, representing a "waste of time." The person is not only reduced to a function, a simple utilitarian value, one object among others, an artificial thing, but is also made a victim of the disease of total conformism, the widespread erosion of differences.

Pieper denounces this erroneous concept of *acedia* as idleness. He cites the Ancients, who emphasized that one of the inalienable characteristics of *acedia* is precisely the impossibility of according an intrinsic value to leisure and accepting it. *Acedia* is, in fact, the origin of and catalyst for the ceaseless frenetic activity or fanaticism for work, the constant inner agitation that knows no rest, which expresses an activity that is no longer rooted in the truth of things. Pieper goes further: he connects *acedia* with a "suicidal" will to work without respite, which characterizes to some extent modern industrial society. Such an unchecked drive toward work for work's sake, toward excessive activity, can be seen as a will to forget oneself, indeed, a refusal to be what the human being is, or even as an attempt to outrun the despair or boredom that fills one's existence.

This observation was not made for the first time in our age; we find it already in Pascal, for whom all of the misery that a human being suffers arises from his unwillingness to "stay quietly in his room."[30] He does nothing but seek out conversations, various amusements, agitation; he escapes into noise and movement, which keeps him from "seeing himself and thinking about what he is,"[31] and from questioning "where they [human beings] come from, and where they are going."[32] In order that the human being may avoid taking the time to contemplate reality (and himself) and the questions related to his essence, his origin, and his end, he must at all costs "keep himself fully occupied."[33] Baudelaire advises modern man to throw himself desperately into work, for work is less boring than amusement. The flight into work and distraction, which is brought on by boredom, the modern term for *acedia,* is presented as a therapy, the goal of which is to make time pass as quickly as possible: when a person is bored time becomes interminable.[34] In order to forget their own existence, "[human beings] need to find new actions and new perceptions. They desire to live in the world and not in themselves. As the great mastodons grazed on forests, so do they graze on the world with their eyes."[35]

We no longer take the time to look, to meditate, to contemplate things in silence, but we often remain at the level of fashion, slaves to the latest taste, which lasts only for a season. In order to outwit the boredom that accompanies this life, we throw ourselves into frenetic activity, into the drug of work and the drug of being constantly on the run. The human being suffering from *acedia* is fundamentally divided in the depths of his being, incapable of remaining in himself. He is driven to leave behind his contemplative inner life in order to flee himself in desperation, thus forfeiting his very being in

> the hurly-burly of work-and-nothing-else, into the fine-spun exhausting game of sophistical phrase-mongering, into incessant 'entertainment' by empty stimulants—in short, into a no man's land which may be quite comfortably furnished, but which has no place for the serenity of intrinsically meaningful activity, for contemplation, and certainly not for festivity.[36]

Anders agrees with Pieper's and Pascal's observations. Contemporary man, who is essentially a consumer, a "hermit in the crowd," is a slave to the technique of entertainment. This technique presupposes a metaphysics of *ubique simul,* which prevents the human being from remaining quietly in himself or in front of something else, whatever it may be. When he comes home from work, he no longer even has the will to rediscover his *proportio humana,* if it still exists. Instead, driven by the *horror vacui,* he throws himself—if he does not go to bed—into a thousand and one things, regardless of what they are, out of a fear of boredom, of being free and autonomous. This escape into distractions is the result of a profound disunity of the person, which Anders defines as an artificially induced schizophrenia.[37]

As a number of thinkers have told us over and over again, boredom has become the modern illness *par excellence.* Relating it to the absurd, nothingness, anxiety, and despair, these thinkers describe it as a "decadent evil"[38] that offers a "foretaste of nothingness,"[39] being the "anticipation of non-being"[40] and revealing to the one who undergoes it the "vanity of the abyss of his actual *not-yet-being.*"[41] This experience has been described as "despair keeping vigil," "the evil of nothingness, 'figlia della nullità, madre del nulla'!" [daughter of nothingness, mother of the nothing].[42] Human existence in the nuclear age has been compared to a "crazy trip down a blood-spattered highway, which starts with substitutes for boredom and ends up in the horror of nothingness," with no traveling companions along the way but "the various figures . . . of Meaninglessness."[43]

Boredom is intrinsically connected to despair. It is the symptom of the desperate attitude that does not know the future; it is an expression of anticipated death, a living death of the subject. The subject, no longer capable of hoping in the fulfillment of his dreams, of his natural strivings that lead him into the future, sinks into the meaninglessness and despair of a return to the nothingness from which he came, the despair of self-annihilation. What happens to someone who is bored to death is a sort of undoing of creation, the act that brings all things into being from the nothing. For someone who is stricken by boredom, "the world seems like death."[44] All finality disappears. The destination of "Professor Nihilism's" journey is the "Valley of Death."[45] Conversely, if the attitude of despair is lacking, genuine boredom cannot exist.[46]

Pieper does not end solely with the notion of *acedia* as the root of despair, but he also addresses the states to which it gives rise: (a) despair, (b) the *evagatio mentis,* the fruits of which are *verbositas, curiositas, importunitas* (spiritual agitation), *inquietudo* (restlessness), *vagacitas mentis* (distractedness of mind), *instabilitas* (instability), the *mutabilitias propositi* (inconstancy regarding plans), (c) *torpor* (inactivity), (d) *pusillanimitas* (pettiness), (e) *rancor* (rancor), and (f) *malicia* (malice).[47] These various Latin terms may seem meaningless to us, things belonging to a distant time and place. Nevertheless, *acedia* affects contemporary culture by means of the states that it causes, as Heidegger has shown. Pieper does not discuss each of these states individually, but focuses on *verbositas* and *curiositas,* making reference to Heidegger's excellent study of the average everydayness of human life. Heidegger himself does not relate his understanding explicitly to that of the Ancients, and abstracts these terms from their religious and transcendental connotations. By means of his analysis, Heidegger has helped resituate these concepts into contemporary philosophical language. He provides a careful description of the notions of "the they," curiosity, distraction, ambiguity, and "never dwelling anywhere."[48] Pieper takes up these terms and develops them within the context of a struggle to preserve the independence, and indeed the primacy, of *theoria* with respect to *praxis,* and also to preserve the intrinsic and fundamental value of activities that promote the dignity of the person and that have their end and their meaning in themselves.

Pieper describes *verbositas* as an abandonment of the silent contemplation of reality for the sake of the idle chatter and noise that lead to a situation in which the word is no longer connected with its source, with the reality that it represents.[49] Heidegger defines *verbositas* as "complete groundlessness" (*Bodenlosigkeit*), the "kind of being which belongs to Dasein's understanding when that understanding has been uprooted."[50] For Comte-Sponville, it represents a cowardice that manifests a "fear of silence, and a fear of truth."[51] The human being caught up in *verbositas* exhibits, according to Pieper, a disjunction with reality, which manifests itself in his language and in the fact that he consumes without taking the time to reflect and to contemplate. He no longer knows how to recollect himself, to keep silent in order better to listen both to reality and to an interlocutor. Only one who keeps silent is able to listen. Every correct word, every word that is well considered and filled with meaning, originates in silence. If one wishes to know the essence of reality (and this is the philosopher's objective, possessed in hope), one must listen in silence, Pieper says, to what reality has to teach us. Reality, for its part, is not silent; rather, it "speaks" and discloses itself to the one who listens. Pieper recommends we rediscover the value of silent solitude in order to achieve a better understanding and internalization of the essence of ourselves and of the world. In order to come to know being, it is necessary, Rassam adds, to create silence in oneself, a silence that is not an escape that grows out of skepticism, relativism, or prideful isolation, but instead a silence that reaches into "the very reality of the things of the world, the presence of beings."[52]

The fact that silence must come first, which Pieper affirms as part of the act of *theoria* and which constitutes the source and the foundation of philosophical reflection, implies a realist theory of knowledge, according to which being, which exists first in itself, is given to the senses and to the intelligence. This attitude of silence entails a metaphysics of gift and disponibility, a "capacity for giving welcome,"[53] for wondering and for lovingly contemplating the world in which *res naturales* do not owe their being to the human mind. The act of silence, which is indispensable to the person's grasp of reality and of self, is not something automatic; rather, it demands an act of the will and a humble docility, a willingness to allow oneself to be penetrated by reality. Indeed, an understanding of the world that considers reality something artificial does not demand such an attitude of silence, for, as I showed in the first chapter, the subject in this case already knows the nature of things, and thus does not marvel at them. A smiling garden, as we saw in our discussion of Sartre, is therefore nonsensical, as is any silent contemplation of reality.

The human being suffering from *acedia* flees the inner life in order to take refuge not only in *verbositas,* but also in *curiositas.* This latter is the attitude in which one gazes upon reality not in order to grasp the truth of things or in order to "come into a Being towards it [reality]," as Heidegger says, "but *just* in order to see."[54] The gaze flits constantly from one object to another, it glances furtively at things, and ends up with an excess of images that threaten to monopolize the subject's existence. In these superficial glances, in this exaggerated curiosity, the human being no longer engages his most profound being; thus, it is left to suffocate.

Pieper concludes his diagnosis of the symptoms of *acedia* with the sickness of despair. Despair is the uprootedness of a person, viewed as a situation that has been profoundly intensified and that threatens to destroy the integrity of the human being as a spiritual entity. The remedy that is able to cure a person in this state and rekindle his hope, Pieper believes, is to learn once again to open one's heart in order to receive the gratuitous being of reality, to rediscover the value of silence and of listening, which implies a metaphysics of consenting to being. The guiding rule for a genuine human existence is expressed externally in this trusting, interior, and hopeful attitude of contemplative and loving silence: "Self-forgetful openness."[55]

2.3 The degrees of despair

We can distinguish two categories of despair: ordinary despair and despair *tout court.* While the former can have a number of objects, which exhibit a great variety and are thus "superficial," the latter has a single object and touches the core of existence. We can draw a parallel between this distinction and that between ordinary and fundamental hope, a distinction that brings out the different degrees that appear in the interrelationship between hope and despair. Fundamental hope is, in effect, able to coexist with a variety of ordinary despairs, which affect being only superficially; fundamental despair, in turn, can coexist with a variety of ordinary hopes that hide themselves, consciously or unconsciously, behind a certain optimism. This makes it difficult to recognize at first glance what disposition a person genuinely has. The dialectic of the "hiddenness (*Verborgenheit*) of hope and despair"[56] excludes the simultaneous coexistence of fundamental hope and fundamental despair or ordinary hope and ordinary despair.

If we consider the dynamic of human behavior for a moment, we observe that despairs arise the moment we experience a disappointment that is due to the failure to achieve the goods we had hoped for. The frustration of a hope yields to disappointment, which is followed by a moment of despair. The length of time this despair may endure will vary, and the degree of intensity of the suffering and pain it causes will depend on the importance the subject has accorded to the hoped-for object. This despair will eventually fade away or will be turned into a new hope. This dialectical play between ordinary hopes and despairs is natural both to humans and to animals, since we are here at the level of passion. Ordinary despairs can also occur when the subject gives up hoping for a difficult-to-obtain good, which is the object of hope. Judging it to be impossible to achieve, he takes flight in retreat.

Fundamental despair, by contrast, does not have its source in the frustration of fundamental hope, or vice versa. Nor does it necessarily come from ordinary despair. Instead, like fundamental hope, it occurs in its paradigmatic sense in the context of a limit-situation. The question that naturally comes up at this point is whether fundamental despair can be comprehensive enough to exclude every hope, including fundamental hope.

The various positions on this question fall into two camps, which are quite distinct from one another. For some, hope exists "underneath" every despair, even the fundamental sort; for others, total despair is capable of destroying all hope (both ordinary and fundamental hope). While these two contrasting positions take for granted that despair is understood as an attitude that runs counter to human nature, certain authors affirm that despair represents the "beatitude" that human beings ought to pursue. In this state of emptiness and nothingness, in which anxiety and sadness are wiped away and replaced by silence and repose, there remains "nothing to hope for. This is despair."[57]

Taking a position that is diametrically opposed to Kierkegaard's, for example, Comte-Sponville denies that despair is a sickness. Instead, he describes it as "the virtue that belongs *to me,* my own health. Hope is the sickness; it is a drug." In order to reach "beatitude," we have to lose hope, and thus anchor ourselves in the eternal present, in despair: "The point of entry is to cease dreaming,"[58] to welcome "despair."[59] It is therefore necessary, he says, to get rid of all hope, to sink into total despair, in order to acquire a taste of perfect wisdom.

A number of philosophers of hope[60] maintain, by contrast, that human existence is essentially pervaded by hope, which is constitutive of life. The human being finds it impossible to despair at the ontological level and insofar as he is alive, because life itself, as Bloch has clearly shown, is made of hope. *The Principle of Hope* is found in the particles and structures that constitute the person. It penetrates human Dasein structurally and ontologically and is the embodiment of the ontology of *not-yet-being,* of the *status viatoris.* Thus, the human being hopes precisely to the extent that he lives. It follows that hope is anterior to all attitudes of hopelessness, such as despair or presumption. From this perspective, it is impossible to have a despair that could completely stifle the principle of hope. Pieper insists, "Dasein itself possesses the structural form of hope."[61] Hope, which is "present at every moment," has merely been "overshadowed"[62] by despair, Minkowski asserts; it "wells up continually,"[63] says Le Senne in turn. According to the poet Leopardi, despair cannot exist without hope, for "man would not despair if he could not hope," "however great it may be, despair is never perfect."[64] We find the same idea in Schiller, and also in Bollnow, Lain Entralgo, Fahrenbach, and Landsberg.[65] It nevertheless seems to me that these authors do not draw an adequate distinction between a fundamental ontological state of being and a state that arises through a free choice.

In order to get a better sense of this distinction, we could return at this point to the distinction discussed in the first chapter in relation to the categories of determination and indeterminacy (freedom), a distinction that allows the possibility, at least in principle, of there being a state of complete despair. On the one hand, we have to agree with those who insist hope is constitutive of human life, with its ontology of *not-yet-being* and its itinerant condition. On the other hand, complete despair belongs to the category of freedom, since the human being is capable, at least in principle, of locking himself up, through a deliberate, voluntary, and free choice of will, in closed time, freely announcing his own "death" prematurely, or in other words, claiming the impossibility of the actualization of the hoped-for object.

Hope is an active and sometimes arduous struggle against the despair that will endure as long as the human being remains in the *status viatoris*. The possibility will always remain for him either to open himself to the dimension of fundamental hope or to close himself up into fundamental despair.[66] As in the case of love, there lies at the root of hope something literally offered to the person, something the person is capable of rejecting to some degree. Although fundamental hope cannot be disappointed, it can nevertheless be lost through a free rejection of this gift, a rejection that opens the door to despair. It is thus possible to live and at the same time to despair in a profound sense. Such an existence, however, would be comparable, as we have already remarked, to a living death.

Even though the concrete situation of complete despair is "scarcely conceivable, as contrary as it is to life,"[67] it remains for all that a real possibility, whose origins lie in the mystery of freedom. However that may be, this despair cannot be called eternal, for the person who experiences it is "en route,"[68] and is able, by retracing his steps, to open himself to receive the gift of fundamental hope. While a human being exists, he cannot extricate himself from a state of existential uncertainty. The attitudes of fundamental hope and absolute despair are never certain and irrevocable. A free decision does not necessarily have to be permanent, i.e., the human being will always retain the possibility, until he draws his final breath, of sinking into despair or being raised up into hope, to establish himself in closed time or in open time. Fundamental hope, inscribed within the being of Dasein through the dimension of freedom, is distinct from "determinate" human hope. The human being is incapable of not hoping, just as he is incapable of not desiring the good, his own happiness. Nevertheless, he remains able to decide, through a rational and free act, that the object of fundamental hope can be neither actualized nor attained.

Notes

1. Pieper, *On Hope*, 65, 70 [*Werke*, Vol. 4, 283, 286]. For a theological analysis of presumption, see Vachon, *La vertu d'espérance et le péché de présomption*, 115ff.

2. On the theme of the grounds for fundamental hope, see chapter five, sections 2, 3, and 4.

3. Sartre and Levy, *Hope Now*, 54 [23].

4. See Camus, *The Myth of Sisyphus*.

5. Comte-Sponville, *Le mythe d'Icare. Traité du désespoir et de la béatitude*, vol. 1, 24; see also 306.

6. Jaccard, *La tentation nihiliste*, 12. See Cioran, *On the Heights of Despair*.

7. Sartre and Levy, *Hope Now*, 54 [23]; see also [81]. Sartre observes that, although he himself has never fallen into despair personally, "ultimately, while writing *Being and Nothingness*, I came to see that despair is nothing but a lucid vision of what the human condition in fact is," 54 [23].

8. Minkowski, "L'espérance," 96. The complete text runs: "C'est pire que la mort, c'est du mort."

9. Kierkegaard, *The Sickness Unto Death*, 21 [179].

10. Marcel, *Being and Having*, 80 [117].

11. Marcel, *Creative Fidelity*, 54 [77].

12. See Jaspers, "Die Kraft der Hoffnung," 219. Evans (*Existentialism: The Philosophy of Despair and the Quest for Hope*, 66) describes constant despair as a "way of life [which] is living death," in contrast to the despair that occurs as a moment in life, which is able to open one up to the dimension of fundamental hope. See also Ellul, *L'espérance oubliée*, 71. Smith, *Hope and History*, 41f.

13. Minkowski, "L'espérance," 106.

14. Lersch, *Aufbau der Person*, 251.

15. Edmaier, *Horizonte der Hoffnung*, 110. Fahrenbach (*Wesen und Sinn der Hoffnung*, 71) describes despair as being torn apart, which he defines as "being torn apart from the ability-to-be in its existentially understood possibilities"; despair is "being (inescapably) closed off from the future of Dasein."

16. Minkowski, "L'espérance," 107.

17. Marcel, *Homo viator*, 37f. [51]; see also 47 [63].

18. Ibid., 48 [65].

19. See Camus, *The Myth of Sisyphus*. Edmaier, *Horizonte der Hoffnung*, 114f. Fahrenbach, *Wesen und Sinn der Hoffnung*, 71. Pieper, *Leisure the Basis of Culture*, 50–52 [*Werke*, Vol. 6, 22–23]; "Selbstgespräch über die Hoffnung," 89; *Glauben, Hoffen, Lieben*, 16; "Die Verborgenheit von Hoffnung und Verzweiflung," 167; *The Concept of Sin*, 34ff., 48 [Werke, Vol. 5, 231ff., 241].

20. Marcel, *Homo viator*, 44 [59]. Schnoor (*Psychoanalyse der Hoffnung*, 212) observes in her psychological and psychiatric studies that "hopelessness indicates a process that becomes active self-destruction on the bodily level, eventually leading to death"; see also 214ff. Fromm, *The Revolution of Hope*, 21 (32).

21. Marcel, "Structure de l'espérance," 80; see also 76. In one of his first philosophical articles ("Sachlichkeit und Klugheit," 74), Pieper describes the person in a neurotic condition as self-centered, in contrast to the healthy human being who is open to community, to being, and to gift (i.e., one who hopes). See also Fromm, Frankl, and Anders, *Die Antiquierheit des Menschen*, vol. 1, 141. Jaccard, *La tentation nihiliste*, 45, 165.

22. Marcel, *The Mystery of Being*, vol. 2, 162 [Vol. 2, 162].

23. Ibid., 158 [159].

24. See for example Revers, *Die Psychologie der Langeweile*, 73.

25. See Plügge, "Über suizidale Kranke," 444ff.

26. "What hope is trying to get at more than anything else, especially amid the hopelessness of mental illness, is the healing power of existence and reality," Lynch observes (*Images of Hope: Imagination as Healer of the Hopeless*, 162). "Reality is healing for those who are without hope, and it is the separation from reality that causes despair" (163). Lersch (*Aufbau der Person*, 256) describes the person with a psychosomatic ailment as similar to a person who is physically and psychologically paralyzed: all the interiority of the foundation of experience has collapsed, making the contemplation of reality impossible. This person's consciousness is afflicted by a internal void, which leads the person to self-destruction. See Bollnow, *Neue Geborgenheit*, 17ff., 139f.

27. See Pieper, "Die Verborgenheit von Hoffnung und Verzweiflung," 167; *Leisure the Basis of Culture*, 48, 51 [*Werke*, Vol. 6, 20, 22]; *On Hope*, 51ff. [*Werke*, Vol. 4, 277ff.]; *Kleines Lesebuch von den Tugenden des menschlichen Herzens*, 48; *Arbeit. Freizeit. Musse—Was ist eine Universität?* 21. Pieper agrees with Kierkegaard, who describes despair as the attitude of one who does not consent to be his own being, but wills "to be rid of oneself" (*The Sickness Unto Death*, 20 [178]). He distinguishes between "despair in weakness," which consists in the feminine form of despair and which finds its complete and perfect form in the masculine sense of despair, in which the ego wants to be itself, but in such a way that the subject aims at making himself whatever he wishes to be on his own terms; in other words, he becomes his own creator. Such an ego proceeds toward self-divinization, taking himself for a *causa sui*. "And this is the self that a person in despair wills to be, severing the self from any relation to a power that has established it, or severing it from the idea that there is such a power. With the help of this infinite form, the self in despair wants to be master of itself or to create itself, to make his self into the self he wants to be, to determine what he will have or not have in his concrete self . . . The

self is its own master, absolutely its own master, so-called; and precisely this is the despair," 68–69.

28. A phrase from Count Zinzendorf, cited by Weber, *Über den Geist des Kapitalismus und die protestantische Ethik,* 171. Cited in J. Pieper, *Leisure the Basis of Culture,* 26 [*Werke,* Vol. 6, 3].

29. Aristotle, *Nichomachean Ethics,* X, 7 (1177b4–5), cited in Pieper, *Leisure the Basis of Culture,* 27 [*Werke,* Vol. 6, 3]; see also 48, 71 [20, 40] and *On Hope,* 52–54 [*Werke,* Vol. 4, 278f.]; *In Tune with the World,* 57f. [*Werke,* Vol. 6, 276f.]; "Die Verborgenheit von Hoffnung und Verzweiflung," 170.

30. Pascal, *Pensées,* no. 136, 67 [no. 139, 109].

31. Ibid., no. 139, 72 [no. 143, 115]; see also no. 414, 148 [no. 171, 119].

32. Ibid., no. 139, 72 [no. 143, 115].

33. Ibid.

34. See Bollnow, *Neue Geborgenheit,* 172. Revers, *Die Psychologie der Langeweile,* 32, 58.

35. Alain, *Propos sur le bonheur,* 101.

36. Pieper, *In Tune with the World,* 21 [*Werke,* Vol. 6, 238]; See "Die Verborgenheit von Hoffnung und Verzweiflung," 169.

37. See Anders, *Die Antiquierheit des Menschen,* vol. 1, 102, 135ff. See Caturelli, *Metafisica del Trabajo,* 154. The psychologist Rauchfleisch (*Leidenverzweifeln-hoffen,* 17f.) describes this "flight forward" into activism as a possible reaction to sickness or death. "For him, it no longer matters *what* he does. All that matters is the fact *that* he is active. . . . Such a person grows ever more deeply dependent on an activity that is 'anesthetizing' in every sense and is at bottom empty. He thus becomes ever more estranged from himself. The noise of the outer world ultimately manages to cover completely over all images and voices that might have been able to rise up from within, and, blinded by the murky light of a world that promises to fulfill all of his wishes, he remains withdrawn in emptiness and slips past any chance of making his own decisions about who he is to become and integrating his suffering into his life."

38. Jankélévitch, *L'aventure, l'ennui, le sérieux,* 110; see also 103.

39. Jaccard, *La tentation nihiliste,* 4.

40. Berdyaev, *The Destiny of Man,* 227 (233).

41. Revers, *Über die Hoffnung,* 7. See the ontology of anxiety developed by Tillich (*The Courage to Be*), who defines it as the "awareness that non-being is part of our own being." He distinguishes three types of anxiety that fill the human heart: ontic anxiety (regarding fate and death), moral anxiety (regarding guilt and damnation), and finally spiritual anxiety (regarding emptiness and meaninglessness). This latter dominates the modern world. This trio of anxieties manifest themselves in the limit-situation that despair represents.

42. Jankélévitch, *L'aventure, l'ennui, le sérieux,* 48.

43. Jaccard, *La tentation nihiliste*, 48.

44. Bollnow, *Vom Wesen der Stimmungen*, 48.

45. Jaccard, *La tentation nihiliste*, 77. Leopardi exclaims, "I am weary of life and I am even more weary of the philosophical indifference that is the sole remedy for evils and for boredom, but which itself ends up in boredom. I have no other plan, no other hope, than simply to die" cited in ibid., 113. "Consciousness suffering from boredom dies the slow death of asphyxiation," Jankélévitsch, *L'aventure, l'ennui, le sérieux*, 115.

46. See Revers, *Die Psychologie der Langeweile*, 57. Plügge, "Über suizidale Kranke," 440. Comte-Sponville, *Le mythe d'Icare. Traité du désespoir et de la béatitude*, vol. 1, 18.

47. See Pieper, *On Hope*, 57ff. [*Werke*, Vol. 4, 281f.]. Thomas Aquinas, *Summa theologiae*, II–II, 35, 4, ad2 and ad3. Here, as he addresses the consequences of *acedia*, Aquinas offers a synthesis of the lists elaborated by Isidore and Gregory the Great.

48. See Heidegger, *Being and Time*, 210-17 [167–73].

49. See Pieper, "Der Philosophierende und die Sprache," [*Werke*, Vol. 3, 198ff.]; *In Defense of Philosphy*, 37ff. [*Werke*, Vol. 3, 96ff.]; *Abuse of Language, Abuse of Power*, 7–23 [*Werke*, Vol. 6, 132–41].

50. Heidegger, *Being and Time*, 212 [169] and 214 [170].

51. Comte-Sponville, *Le mythe d'Icare. Traité du désespoir et de la béatitude*, vol. 1, 19.

52. Rassam, *Le silence comme introduction à la métaphysique*, 13; see also "Le silence." Dauenhauer, *Silence: The Phenomenon and its Ontological Significance*.

53. Forest, *Consentement et création*, 48.

54. Heidegger, *Being and Time*, 216 [172].

55. Pieper, "Die 'gute Meinung' genügt nicht: Im Gespräch mit dem Philosophen Josef Pieper." "And, in an asceticism of silence, which will have to be rediscovered, couldn't there lie the possibility of overcoming, not only the sterility of ordinary idle talk, but also its sibling, hopelessness? . . . [C]ouldn't the 'immediate strict resolution' to keep silence be at the same time a pedagogy in hope?," *Über das Schweigen Goethes* [*Werke*, Vol. 6, 61].

56. The title of an article by Pieper. See *On Hope*, 49 [*Werke*, Vol. 3, 276]; *Glauben, Hoffen, Lieben*, 15; "Hoffnung–auf was?," 162; "Selbstgespräch über die Hoffnung," 90; "Über die Hoffnung der Kranken," 26. Rauchfleisch, *Leiden-verzweifeln-hoffen*, 26ff., 38f. Pieper focuses his reflection on an analysis of fundamental despair, which is the source of every other kind of despair and stands in opposition to fundamental hope, in the context of his ontological approach, and does not linger over a discussion of common or ordinary despairs. Nor does he place any emphasis on the transformation of ordinary despairs into fundamental despair, except to remark that this latter is a free and voluntary act, for which the subject has a certain amount of responsibility.

57. Comte-Sponville, *Le mythe d'Icare. Traité du désespoir et de la béatitude,* vol. 1, 13. "Beatitude is the fulfillment of despair; despair, the place of beatitude," 29; see also vol. 2, 280ff.

58. In other words, to stop hoping, for hope is "folly," "illusory," an "opium."

59. Comte-Sponville, *Le mythe d'Icare. Traité du désespoir et de la béatitude,* Vol. 1, 14.

60. See Bollnow, *Neue Geborgenheit,* 110–13, 116. Fahrenbach, *Wesen und Sinn der Hoffnung,* 115f. Le Senne, *La découverte de Dieu,* 253, 256. Leopardi, *Opere,* vol. 3, 416 and 754, cited in Lain Entralgo, *L'attente et l'espérance,* 223. Marcel, *Being and Having,* 80 [117]. Minkowski, "L'espérance," 96f.

61. Pieper, "Hoffnung und Geschichte," 14; see "Hoffnung–auf was?" 162; *On Hope,* 20f. [*Werke,* Vol. 4, 262]; "Selbstgespräch über die Hoffnung," 89f; *Kleines Lesebuch von den Tugenden des menschlichen Herzens,* 45; "Über die Kunst, nicht zu verzweifeln," 209, 213; "Meditation über das Mirandum," 37.

62. Minkowski, "L'espérance," 106.

63. Le Senne, *La découverte de Dieu,* 266. "We can approach absolute despair, feeling its proximity; but we can never experience anything but a quasi-despair, in which the pure idea of despair is contested by the desire to escape from it," 266; see also 256.

64. Leopardi, *Opere,* vol. 3, 359–60. Cited in Lain Entralgo, *L'attente et l'espérance,* 230.

65. "The Hope first shows him the light of day, / Through infancy hovers before him,/Enchants him in youth with her magic ray, / Survives, when the grave closes o'er him; / For when in the tomb ends his weary race, / E'en there still see we her smiling face!" Schiller, *Schiller's Works,* Vol. 1, 117 (1, 219f.). See Bollnow, *Neue Geborgenheit,* 111, 116. Lain Entralgo, *L'attente et l'espérance,* 236. Fahrenbach, *Wesen und Sinn der Hoffnung,* 117. Discussing the philosophical problem of suicide and concluding that the majority of those who kill themselves do not manifest despair, but rather a hope that is perhaps foolish and perverse, Landsberg (*The Experience of Death,* 82 [125]) affirms that "personally, I go so far as to believe that man never despairs completely, that it is impossible for him and contrary to his essential being, to despair. . . . In my view, despair is not a characteristic of man on earth, but perhaps only of Hell and the Devil."

66. The same can be said for the passion of hope accompanied by the moral virtues of magnanimity and humility.

67. Minkowski, "L'espérance," 96.

68. See Dauenhauer, *The Politics of Hope.*

5

Death as the Enemy of Hope

1. THE HUMAN BEING FACING THE INSURMOUNTABLE OBSTACLE OF DEATH

We can draw a strict correlation between hope and death, which has formed the subject of a number of historical, sociological, theological, and philosophical studies in the past few decades. Death has been described by certain contemporary philosophers as the "final negation,"[1] the obstacle and the "curbstone"[2] of hope, the scorn of hopes. Moreover, death is a sign of contradiction for a metaphysics of having and doing; it renders the contingency of the person and his ontological dependence all the more palpable and significant. Death represents an apparently impassible barrier to the actualization of the object of the hope principle. Bloch sees death—which marks the absolute cessation and annihilation of the dialectical process of both history and the individual, of all possibilities of the *ability-to-be,* all of which are driven by hope—as the "strongest anti-utopia,"[3] the *anti-praxis.* He describes death thus: "not only the corpse is pale but our striving sees itself bled white and devalued for bad and all by its end. The grave, darkness, decay and worms had and still have, whenever they are not pushed out of mind, a kind of retrospectively devaluing force."[4]

Death—which has revealed its horrid face to our age through the experience of two world wars—is, for Camus, the "supreme abuse"[5] or the "ultimate failure";[6] for Bloch, it is the "last fiasco"[7] from which the human being is powerless to escape. The human being is doomed to die from the first moment of his existence: the "cradle has something in common with a sepulcher, and we are covered with the shroud of our mortality at birth";[8] or, as the poet T. S. Eliot succinctly put it, "In my beginning is my end."[9] Death is the assured possibility of the radical impossibility that is written into the fibers of *homo viator.* "*Incerta omnia, sola mors certa.*"[10] Death, this "absent presence,"[11] is an integral part of the human being's ontological condition; it can be compared to the situation "of the person who has been sentenced and who is imprisoned in a cell the walls of which draw imperceptibly closer together at every minute."[12] Indeed, death, inevitability *par excellence,* is one of the most fundamental realities of human existence. To forget it "is always to forget oneself."[13]

If death is the absolute endpoint of existence, if it is understood as the sometimes brutal interruption of the human being's ontological striving toward fulfillment, bringing all possibility of the *ability-to-be* to naught, we can ask ourselves whether the various projects that flow from an ontology of *not-yet-being* have any meaning. Can we entrust ourselves to the natural inclination of the human being that hope represents (whose object is the fulfillment of the individual and/or the human race in general), if death is the definitive end of the journey? If hope were nothing but an aspiration incapable of appropriating anything, it "would earn us nothing but the torture of Tantalus, and would not be distinguishable from despair,"[14] observes Le Senne, who agrees on this point with Alfaro, Emaier, and Landsberg. Pieper, for his part, observes that

> If *the* hope was such that it could not stand fast in the situation of martyrdom (or analogously in the situation of the terminally ill person or the prisoner condemned to death)—then in the end there would be absolutely no hope; there would be no *reason* to hope, that is, there would not be that decisive success of human existence which has forever been known as "salvation"; to put it another way, life would be desperate, it would be hopeless.[15]

Is hope a vice that continually grips and deceives the human being? Is it a chimera that the human being has invented in order the better to survive throughout the duration of his temporal passage, all the while knowing in his heart of hearts that he is heading toward the abyss of Nothingness? "If we live by hope," asks Comte-Sponville, "are we living by an illusion?"[16] Is hope a "promise that cannot be kept"?[17] Is it nothing but a "beautiful idea"[18] lacking any concrete reality, a "lunacy,"[19] a consolation? The greatest enemy of human existence?[20] A "resignation"[21] before life? Is Nietzsche not correct when he says, in his interpretation of Hesiod and Pandora's box, that hope is indeed "the worst of all evils,"[22] insofar as it prolongs human agony? If death were really the final end of existence, an impasse, hope would be doomed from the start. It could do nothing but continually lead the human being astray; it could not be anything but a promise that cannot be kept, a beautiful, but empty, idea. There would be no room in life, as Marcel said, for anything but "puppets and people in despair."[23]

The philosopher who would address the question of hope in its close relation to death stands before a choice between closing oneself off from hope or opening up to it; or, as Bloch says about our age in his last interview, we stand before a choice between "nihilism or a metaphysics of hope."[24] As Marcel says, we find ourselves placed before "the dilemma: plenitude or death . . . death purely and simply is either nothing or is a chance for liberation."[25] On the other side of the frontier of death lies a simple alternative: "Either all or nothing!"[26] as Unamuno exclaims—and he is one who has meditated at great length on death, hope, and absurdity.

Camus brings out this choice by affirming, in the beginning of the *Myth of Sisyphus*, that the only truly serious question the philosopher can pose is the question of suicide, that is, the question concerning the meaning of life. We have to judge "whether life is or is not worth living."[27] Camus penetrates to the heart of the problem of death and existence. Following Sartre, who says that existence is "too much," Camus sees the world as absurd. This absurdity is the result of a confrontation between the irrationality of the whole of reality and the intense and futile desire for clarity, which is rooted in the deepest core of the human being. It is not the conclusion of an argument or a demonstration, but it is an a priori act: "belief in the absurdity of existence."[28]

Camus proposes two possibilities for escaping the absurdity of life: suicide or hope, which compels the human being to a genuine act of transcendence. On the basis of an a priori denial of God, Camus rejects hope, because hope would remove the human being from earthly reality and the obligation to help build it by leading him to take flight in an imaginary "beyond," in the irrational, by leading him to desert the world. Hope keeps him from living his life well, since life belongs solely to the realm of this world. "For if there is a sin against life, it lies perhaps less in despairing of it than in hoping for another life and evading the implacable grandeur of the one we have."[29] Whoever accepts a *post mortem* betrays his responsibility for his own existence and that of others. He flees like a coward from reality, taking refuge in hope, which Camus rejects as a lie and a futile consolation. "I do not want to believe that death is the gateway to another life. For me, it is a closed door. I do not say it is a step we must all take, but that it is a horrible and dirty adventure. Everything I am offered seeks to deliver man from the weight of his own life."[30] Similarly, Camus describes suicide as a "flight."[31]

Rejecting all transcendent hope, and refusing suicide as a solution to the absurdity of Dasein, Camus proposes a "hopeful hope" [*espérance de l'espoir*], which is natural to existence, and which has as its opposite something other than despair. This hope without transcendence expresses the power of the human being's struggle against evil and suffering for the sake of establishing a more human existence and of promoting respect for the other. It makes human existence bearable, in spite of the fact that it is marked by absurdity, which we find expressed paradigmatically in Sisyphus. Nevertheless, nontranscendent hopes do not hold up in the face of death. "There is only one case in which despair is pure: that of the man sentenced to death."[32] If we were to ask whether we are not all in fact condemned to death, Camus would answer "yes." As he says in *The Rebel*, the human condition can be compared to a "mass death sentence."[33] He describes death as the absolute final end of existence, as a "final defeat,"[34] which brings all plans, all meaning, and the human being's profound desire to live forever, to naught. "This idea that 'I am,' my way of acting as if everything has a meaning . . . all that is given the lie in vertiginous fashion by the absurdity of a possible death."[35] Death, with its destructive and ruinous character, remains as the only reality. Camus does not admit that death can itself end in something real, because for him there is no such thing as immortality. Life comes to a brutal end in "a death without hope";[36] there "is no future."[37] But wouldn't this make ordinary human life a situation of pure despair, just like that of the prisoner condemned to death? Wherever there is no fundamental hope to hold fast in the face of death, wouldn't life lose meaning and sink into absurdity and despair?

Sartre, too, sees death as a brutal and contingent fact that arrives from outside of human possibilities, because it destroys all of the possibilities projected by freedom. It abruptly interrupts the human being's striving while journeying toward the free development of his nature. It annihilates the freedom that is no longer able to project itself into the future of its possibilities. Death, which is "the final boundary of human life," is "a door opening upon the nothingness of human-reality."[38] Given that the human being cannot escape death and its character of absolute finality, which wipes out every future and every plan, in other words, from which all fundamental hope has been excluded, life is too much: "it is absurd that we are born; it is absurd that we die. . . . [T]his absurdity is presented as the permanent alienation of my being-possibility which is no longer *my* possibility but that of the Other."[39] Existence is an absurd and short-lived parenthesis in the continuous stream of the nothing.

We find a shift in Sartre's thinking just before his death. He affirms a human immortality, understood not in the sense of the individual but in the sense of historical progress. He also affirms, to the surprise of the readers of *Nausea* and *Being and Nothingness,* that he himself had never experienced despair or anxiety, and that there exists a hope that is not a lyrical illusion but is instead constitutive of the human being. Hope is the principle that accompanies human action, that is, the human being hopes to achieve a goal that he has freely projected, one that will be beneficial both to the community and to himself. Although he states that existence is a failure, he nevertheless insists that hope is constitutive of human activity. In other words, action "cannot in principle be aimed at absolute and certain failure." "The idea of failure is not deeply rooted in me at this moment. On the contrary, what remains most present in my thinking now is hope insofar as it is the relation of man to his goal—a relation that exists even if the goal is not attained."[40]

2. THE GROUNDS FOR FUNDAMENTAL HOPE IN THE FACE OF DEATH

In the course of a public debate with Moltmann in February 1968, Pieper brings up the ambiguities entailed by a stance that is open solely to the future and excludes all past and all *memoria.* He emphasizes that the grounds for the act of hope do not lie in the future, as does its object. Indeed, if the grounds for hope were there, we would have to say that the human being has to have a reason to hope in the future. But reason comes before the act of hope. "The future without origin is empty. And a hope without grounds, without a prior foundation, has equal claim to the name despair";[41] or we could call it a "euphoric illusion."[42] Pieper turns his attention to the past in order to unfold the reason that justifies fundamental hope; in other words, he alludes to a particular understanding of human nature, which is not characterized by total freedom (as it is for Sartre) and the essence of which does not lie in the future (as it does for Bloch). He affirms an ontology of *not-yet-being,* in which the person, as a *viator,* journeys from his *already-being* to his *being-complete.* The reason for hope, in Pieper's view, rests on a specific anthropology, as well as on a metaphysics of being and love, based on creation, as we will see in a moment.

We can thus ask whether there exists a justification for hope that makes the reality of fundamental hope possible and reasonable in spite of the fact that the subject marches resolutely toward death. Pieper never tires of asking, "Is there a reason for hope?"[43] In other words,

> are there grounds for believing that 'things will turn out well, they will have a good ending—for myself and with the world in its totality—a *good* end, "good" pure and simple . . . that the end will be a complete fulfill-ment in which *every* desire will be satisfied in such a way that there will no longer be anything left to desire, either subjectively or objectively?[44]

Pieper not only addresses the relationship between hope and personal death, but also between hope and the possible destruction of the human race due to a human-made catastrophe.[45] The question he rais-es, which reappears in his writings on the philosophy of history, is: In what way is it possible to justify hope in spite of the dramatic and explosive existential situation in which modern man exists, insofar as he remains constantly under the threat of global self-destruction? This uncertainty can give rise not only to fear and anxiety, but it can also possibly lead one to sink into a fundamental despair, a "desperate nihilism." "Can the history of humanity give us anything but despair?"[46] Such a situation makes the question concerning hope, in spite of the pervasive despair, even more indispensable. Pieper observes that "never before have we been in a position to pose the fun-damental question of the possibility and the meaning of human hope with such a sharp urgency."[47] This situation presents the philosopher with the moral necessity to attempt a response. Nevertheless, we ought not to forget that, in terms of existential importance, the possible end of humanity is secondary in relation to personal death.

Pieper denies that hope is an empty promise and that being is ori-ented to nothingness, a nothingness that, as nihilism interprets it, is anterior to being. Confronted with such a hopeless and absurd nihilism, which holds that death will ultimately shatter every hope, especially fundamental hope, Pieper proclaims, in 1951 before a Parisian audience, that "the human being cannot live this way!"[48] His rejection of a metaphysics of the *nihil* stems from a positive and trusting response to reality, that is, from a *metaphysics of being,* according to which being is more fundamental than nothingness, and which implies a consent to the world, that is, an "approach that gives its approval to the world,"[49] which holds that being is essentially good. Reality is welcomed, as Nietzsche puts it, with an "uncanny, unbounded Yes and Amen."[50] Whoever hopes in a genuine sense gives consent to being, to the existence that is perceived as a perfection. He has a primal trust in being, as opposed to the person in despair, for whom there is nothing in reality that warrants his trust. This assent to being, to the whole of reality, is expressed in the formulation: *"everything that is, is good, and it is good to exist."*[51]

This attitude with respect to reality, the world, and oneself, which is not necessarily a conscious attitude, but which shines through in the most humble human actions or responses, is born, according to Pieper, from another consent: love. "[L]oving someone or something means finding him or it *probus,* the Latin word for 'good.' It is a way of turning to him or it and saying, "It's good that you exist; it's good that you are in this world!"[52] This affirmation of love, a primordial act of the will, along with hope, is the primary driving force of human existence. It comes about through a gift[53] that one has the freedom to accept. It is expressed by an expression such as: "I am in agreement with, I consent, I approve, I respond affirmatively, I confirm, I accept, I praise, I glorify, and I celebrate the fact that a particular person or thing exists,"[54] or again by the exclamation that "it is good that you are here, it is wonderful that you exist!"[55] This act lies beyond any instrumentalization, as Brunner's definition of love leads us to see: "I love you for the simple fact that you are there."[56] The act of loving a thing or a person presupposes that the thing's or person's existence is something good or wonderful—in short, it implies a profound "yes" to the existence of the beloved object or subject, which includes an openness to the whole of reality, a consent to the world (*Zustimmung zur Welt*).

Genuine love desires that the beloved should exist and be alive, not only for a certain moment of history, but forever. It is impossible in this context not to think of Marcel's statement, "to love a being . . . is to say you, you in particular will never die."[57] Genuine love wishes to keep its intentional object in existence, as Thomas Aquinas, Nédoncelle, Ortega y Gasset, Soloviev, and Blondel have all said; the idea is summed up particularly well in Blondel's words: "love is, *par excellence,* that which grants existence."[58] This desire for eternal existence, which presupposes a metaphysics of love and an ontology of interpersonality, rejects the idea that personal death is an absolute end, just as it rejects the possibility of annihilation.[59]

The metaphysics of being and of love are part of a more profound metaphysics that forms the heart of Pieper's philosophy: a *metaphysics of creation.*[60] This metaphysics is grasped, first, through an act of *intellectus,* and only afterward does *ratio* attempt to understand it. In contrast to Sartre, for whom the human being has been "projected" into existence by chance, Pieper affirms that the human being has been created *ex nihilo.* Referring to his a priori assumption of a metaphysics of creation, he also affirms that God is by nature love, in contrast to the position Spinoza adopts, namely, that God is incapable of loving anyone.[61] Pieper's God loves his creation in a profound and gratuitous way, without for all that being dependent on being loved in return. He has created the world out of love and in freedom.

In order to get a better grasp of the intrinsic connection that Pieper draws between love and creation, we need to recall what I said in the first chapter on the theme of the relation between the (creative) will and the existence of a thing (*res naturalis* or *res artificialis*), a relation that gives rise to the transcendental affirmation *omne ens est bonum.* In order for a thing to exist, there must be a will that wills it to be. Moreover, I pointed out above that the divine will is characterized by love. Hence, if the divine will accords existence to a thing, it does so through a creative act of love.[62] Every creature is something "creatively willed and affirmed, whose existence depends solely on being so affirmed and loved."[63] The concrete existence of the person means that he is someone loved, someone willed by the wholly Other who loves his creature for its own sake and not for whatever qualities it happens to have, for these qualities did not yet exist *ante creationem ex nihilo.* Pieper's Creator God does not only recognize the intrinsic goodness of things, but he creates this goodness.[64] On the basis of God's free and creative love, that is, on the basis of the interrelationship between the metaphysics of love and of creation, Pieper rejects the possibility that things could be reduced back to nothingness through an act of the divine will. True love, which has its paradigm in divine love, is not capable of annihilating a thing that owes its existence to that love, but on the contrary wills that the thing exist for all eternity.[65]

Pieper thus posits a *Weltanschauung* of creation, of a loving Creator, as an a priori first principle, on the basis of which he develops a metaphysics of love. The certainty of the *reason* felt by the terminally ill person, by the prisoner condemned to death, by the martyr, that they will not sink into nothingness once they have crossed the threshold of death is thus, according to Pieper, ultimately rooted in a trust in being that is more fundamental than nothingness, and in the love of an absolute Thou who has created all things so that they may exist,[66] and who will continue to sustain them in being in spite of death, allowing them to obtain the object of their fundamental hope. The ultimate reason for this is, in Pieper's eyes, a loving Creator God.[67] This reason is not something that can be rationally demonstrated, but it is grasped, according to Pieper, through an intuition that is in fact established a priori. He affirms that philosophical reflection presupposes, at least unconsciously, certain intellectual acts that touch the whole of reality, and which are not solely of the order of knowledge, but also of the order of belief, even when their principle is the negation of a Revelation.[68] In order to give an ultimate response to the question concerning the grounds for hope, Pieper insists that we must assume an a priori position concerning the real. In other words, we have to turn to a *traditum,* a revelation that lies beyond the grasp of pure *ratio.* For Pieper, the human being is incapable of grasping for himself the ultimate grounds for hope. The essential question of whether life has a meaning or not is perhaps a philosophical question, but in the last philosophical analysis one cannot respond to it in a purely rational manner. The response is, as Pieper says, "a *theological* one—or rather, there *is* no response."[69]

In his encounter with the philosophy of despair, Pieper's affirmation that *God is the reason for fundamental hope* is not exceptional within the context of philosophical reflection on hope in this century. Indeed, many authors agree with this position, whether they allude to a leap of faith—for example, Alfaro[70] and Unamuno[71]—or whether, on the basis of a metaphysics of intersubjectivity, they infer the existence of a wholly Other as justifying the reason for hope—for example, Edmaier,[72] Evans,[73] Godfrey, Marcel, and Scherer.[74] I will dwell for a moment on the solution that Marcel proposed, which contains elements similar to Pieper's position, and which he developed a good deal earlier than Pieper. Marcel believes that, if death were the ultimate end of life, all value would be annihilated "in mere scandal" and reality would be "pierced to the heart."[75] In order to get a better grasp of what constitutes the essence of hope, he refers to the experience prisoners of war have of their imprisonment in relation to their being freed. This situation expresses the depths of the state in which each human being finds himself, insofar as he is inexorably approaching death, from which escape is impossible. "To apprehend myself as existing is in some way to apprehend myself as captive."[76] Marcel's notion of hope, like Pieper's, comes to flourish in the context of a tragic and limited state of affairs, a situation that invites despair and that a person strives to overcome by refusing to admit that this situation could be the definitive end of the human journey. Hope, according to Marcel, affirms "prophetically" and with a profound assurance that, "however black things may seem, my present intolerable situation cannot be final; there must be some way out,"[77] a way out that he describes as the complete fulfillment of the person.

Marcel distinguishes two types of time that can be related to death and the two ways that the human being is able to respond to it: on the one hand, closed time, which Marcel connects with despair and which he identifies with hell; and, on the other hand, the open time that he relates to hope.[78] While open time implies the continuation of life, closed time expresses a view of death as the absolute end of existence, and it characterizes the soul as folded back into itself and in despair. This form of time rejects, and fails to see, any positive ending to the limit-situation in which it is trapped. But hope conquers death; it is a "hope for resurrection,"[79] that is, hope is, by nature and not accidentally, hope "in a beyond."[80] Indeed, death is not the absolute end of existence. Rather, it is the "springboard of an absolute hope,"[81] and this is so much the case that, for Marcel, if death did not exist, hope would remain forever in a "larval stage."[82]

In order to give an argument justifying the grounds for hope, Marcel has recourse to an attitude of trusting surrender and openness, which comes about as a result of a positive response to being. Reason consists, initially, in the will to "trust in reality."[83] This attitude can be related to Pieper's notion of attunement to the world (*In Tune with the World*). Fundamental hope is an internal attitude belonging to the person who sets no conditions, establishes no limits, but simply abandons himself in absolute trust, which Marcel compares to a "spirit of childhood."[84] It is essentially an attitude of disponibility with respect to being, to such an extent that, wherever indisponibility comes to dominate over it, hope tends to disappear. Marcel pushes the reason for fundamental hope even further by affirming that it ultimately rests, as it does for Pieper, on a personal relationship with an absolute Thou or the One; in other words, it gives "infinite credit to Him" who is "Absolute Fidelity."[85] The French philosopher affirms that hope appears

> as a response of the creature to infinite Being to whom it is conscious of owing everything that it has and upon whom it cannot impose any condition whatsoever without scandal. From the moment that I abase myself in some sense before the absolute Thou who in his infinite condescension has brought me forth out of nothingness, it seems as though I forbid myself ever again to despair, or, more exactly, that I implicitly accept the possibility of despair as an indication of treason, so that I could not give way to it without pronouncing my own condemnation.[86]

Marcel inserts the reason for hope into his understanding of human life as something characterized fundamentally by intersubjectivity, by the I-thou relationship, that is, a relationship between one who receives and one who gives. This living interaction finds its most fitting and concise formulation in the expression: "I hope in thee for us,"[87] as well as in the dimension of gift, which implies an openness to another "I," a welcoming disponibility, and a reciprocal self-gift between an I and a thou. Hope is essentially rooted in a living relationship, "centered on a *we*,"[88] formed "through a *we* and for a *we*," in short, fundamentally "*choral*."[89] He replaces the "*I think*" with a metaphysics of "*we are*."[90] Intersubjectivity among persons grows into a *coesse*, the core of which is love, fidelity, and disponible openness. Marcel transposes this ontology of the intersubjectivity of contingent thous into a relation between these latter and the absolute Thou. The absolute Thou is the foundation of every I-thou-we relation and it constitutes the guarantee of their unity, their "bond." It is, in Marcel's eyes, the one and only ultimate recourse in a limit-situation with no way out, and it is characterized not as an abstract principle, but as a person whose heart is made of love.

Regarding Marcel's position, Plourde notes that "only the absolute Thou is able to justify absolute hope, and to be its secret spring, because he is *being* and therefore the *salvation* of all finite beings. It is in him alone that reality finds its integrity and its fullness."[91] Marcel summarizes his understanding of hope by pointing out that

> hope is essentially the availability of a soul which has entered intimately enough into the experience of communion to accomplish in the teeth of will and knowledge the transcendent act—the act establishing the vital regeneration of which this experience affords both the pledge and the first-fruits.[92]

For Marcel, as for Pieper, it is the Absolute that ultimately guarantees the actualization of the object of fundamental hope in spite of the destructive character of death. This intense trust in an absolute and eternal Thou, love and fidelity *par excellence,* a person with whom the human being is capable of forming a "we," is what provides the foundation for the reason for fundamental hope. While Pieper takes a certain *Weltanschauung* as his a priori point of departure, namely, the view of creation, at the heart of which lies a metaphysics of intersubjectivity and love, Marcel arrives at God as the reason for fundamental hope on the basis of an analysis of the I-thou-we relation, accompanied by the categories of fidelity, trust, and openness.

Godfrey agrees with the positions of Pieper, Marcel, and Scherer, based on an ontology of intersubjectivity that he contrasts with the "will-nature"[93] ontology that characterizes both Kant's and Bloch's positions. The act of ordinary or fundamental hope implies the notions of belief and trust. Godfrey discusses the issue of knowing whether the act of trust in an other implies a degree of belief in his existence. Could hope be a capacity for apprehension, and would its actuality then represent an indication of reality? On the one hand, in the *will-nature* ontology, in which the subject freely decides to grant his trust, the trust in X implies a certain faith that X is trustworthy and real, but it does not necessarily imply the reality of the object in which the subject places trust and hope. This trust is psychological, that is, it is a mental attitude, in which the subject freely decides to place trust in someone or something. In the ontological model of intersubjectivity, on the other hand, trust in someone no longer implies merely a belief in that person but also in that person's reality: "the actuality of trust necessarily depends on input from the other, and *the fact that there is such a relationship implies the reality of the other.*[94] Indeed, such a trust, according to Godfrey, requires a *cogrounding,* in contrast to the foundation of hope according to the will-nature model, which is the subject's mind. The *ordo essendi* and the *ordo cognoscendi* naturally imply one another in the context of an intersubjective ontology. Trust in someone presupposes the reality of this someone; in other words, it presupposes a "power of apprehending" reality.

While it is possible in the case of the intersubjective model to deduce the reality of a real thou from the act of hope, the same cannot be said with regard to the existence of an absolute Thou, even if that existence is plausible. "Absolute hope does not form the basis of a proof," Godfrey explains, but if the ontology of intersubjectivity is not to be an illusion, "absolute hope is a *sign* of the reality of the absolute Thou—were it not so, then this hope would be the greatest disillusion. . . . If hope is nevertheless to be acknowledged as absolute, it is difficult to see how it could have an adequate foundation other than that of an absolute Thou."[95]

We have seen that, for Pieper, the foundation for the reason for hope lies in a person's attitude of openness, of receptivity, of *theoria* and trusting disponibility in relation to the whole of reality, in an attunement to the world (*In Tune with the World*), the driving principle of which is love, and which rests ultimately on a good Creator God, who is the object of the grasp of *intellectus,* reinforced by the faith in Christian revelation as well as, to a lesser extent, by the arguments of *ratio.* His position runs counter both to fideism and to rationalism. Even though he admits that death is the end of the human journey, Pieper rejects Sartre's position, namely, that the end of the pilgrimage is a waiting for "waitings which themselves wait for waitings."[96] Pieper replies that the end of the *status viatoris* is not a waiting for the journey to come to an end, but a waiting for our arrival at the destination. We reach and we possess the object of the principle of hope.

> Anyone who has taken a road to the end has not merely put something behind him; at the same time something new begins. Behind that idea has always lain the assumption that man's waitings, or more exactly, his hope, is directed towards something. To be sure, he can gain it only in dying, but it lies beyond death and therefore still exists beyond it.[97]

Given that the human being is defined by his *status viatoris,* the end-point of which is death, we could say that the human being is born in order to die, that he is a being-toward-death.[98] This *toward* does not indicate here a unique, final causality that would express the meaning of existence, but its meaning is the attainment of the hoped-for object, the actualization and complete fulfillment of the person as part of a community. The possession of the object of fundamental hope, which happens, according to Pieper, only *post mortem,* assumes that the individual will exist on the other side of the threshold of death, because, in order to possess something and take joy in it, one must exist. Pieper is speaking here of the incorruptibility of the soul, which does not itself imply the actualization and possession of the object of hope (which is a gift). Nevertheless, it does form their condition of possibility.

The choice presented by the anti-utopia of death between a philosophy of hope and a philosophy of the absurd rests on a prior and primordial choice between a metaphysics of being, which implies the primacy of being over nothingness and in which existence is understood as a good, a perfection, and which includes an assent to reality such as it is given, a disponibility and a welcoming receptivity to being, and a metaphysics of nothingness, expressing in various ways a rejection of reality such as it is given and implying the primacy of nothing over being in which existence is an evil, an imperfection, as it is expressed in Schopenhauer's pessimism, which holds that "it would have been better for us never to have existed at all."[99] Such a choice, before which the philosopher of hope stands, can be understood in a certain sense like a wager, for what happens *post mortem* lies beyond the grasp of unaided reason understood as *ratio.* If the philosopher desires to attain an absolute certainty in this regard, he has to take the leap into the realm of prephilosophical data, as Pieper has done in the wake of other philosophers in the Western tradition.

The philosopher of hope, in my opinion, is incapable of demonstrating rationally the absolute falsity of the position that affirms hope and the total absurdity of reality. Instead, the only thing the philosopher can do is to draw attention to the concrete and historical facts that indicate the valid foundation for hope.

3. The Incorruptibility of the Human Being

In Pieper's view, the question of individual immortality is primarily a question of the ontological status and structure of the human soul. The materialists of every age, from Epicurus to certain contemporary philosophers, do not attribute a spiritual quality to the soul that would make it independent of the body. In contrast, the soul's incorruptibility has been affirmed by the Platonic, Idealist, and Thomist traditions. These seem at first glance to defend the same notion, but under closer inspection, an important distinction—indeed, an opposition—between the perspectives becomes evident. For Platonism and German Idealism, incorruptibility is something that belongs to the human soul by nature. In other words, it possesses life by itself and holds itself in existence by its own resources. Pieper distances himself from both materialism and idealism, and prefers instead the solution developed by Thomas Aquinas.[100] Aquinas opposes himself to those who deny the separation of the soul from the body at death (the existence of the *anima separata*); as well as to those who affirm an understanding of immortality that distorts the substantial unity between the body and soul, that is, an understanding according to which death does not affect the human essence, and the soul continues to exist naturally; and finally to those for whom death is total. This death is accompanied at the same time by a resurrection. Pieper focuses his attention on this latter position, which has its champion in the person of the exegete Cullmann.[101]

In his work *Unsterblichkeit der Seele oder Auferstehung der Toten?* (Immortality of the Soul or Resurrection of the Dead?), which provoked a number of reactions when it first appeared, Cullmann affirms that the New Testament does not speak about the immortality of the soul, but rather of the resurrection of the dead, because the human being dies completely when he passes away. He claims to be fighting against a universal error, which attributes "to primitive Christianity the Greek belief in the immortality of the soul,"[102] and insists that "1 Corinthians 15 has been sacrificed to Phaedo."[103] According to Cullmann, there is a radical difference between the two positions, and they cannot be reconciled. We have to choose between two paradigms: Socrates' paradigm of the immortality of the soul or Jesus' paradigm of the resurrection. This affirmation of the destruction of the subject in the moment of death, and this rejection of the immortality of the soul, is

not as new as one might think. We find it already in the Christian
moralists of the seventeenth century, such as Milton, Browne, Hobbes,
and Overton, who were influenced by the English Reformation, as well
as by the Socinians and the Christadelphians.[104] The position that
Cullmann articulates, which reappears in a number of contemporary
philosophers, such as Scherer,[105] has provoked a passionate debate
among certain Catholic theologians, the principal protagonists being
Greshake and Lohfink.[106]

The controversies concerning death and the possibility of the soul's
immortality have their source, according to Pieper, in the anthropological conception one has of the bodily existence of the human being,
and stem from the way one responds to certain questions: to what
extent do the body and soul-spirit form a unity in human nature, and
to what extent are they independent? More precisely, how is it possible to conceive of a subsistent spiritual soul?

Pieper begins by laying out the Platonic anthropology, according to
which the self comprises two distinct poles, which were forced into a
unity: the soul is trapped by force in the body, and waits impatiently
for its deliverance, which will occur in death. In the meantime, the
soul, as the *Alcibiades* emphasizes,[107] uses the body as a tool to serve
its own purposes. Given this particular view of the union between the
body and the soul, death does not affect the being of the human subject, which is the soul; death does not exist for the human being, it is
not a concern. Pieper makes clear that what he is speaking about here
is the Platonic position, and not that of Plato,[108] whose thought is rich-
er and more nuanced. Indeed, although Plato in general also defends
the idea of a distinction and the primacy of the soul over the body, he
seems at the same time to distance himself from this in the *Phaedrus*,[109]
in which he defines the living being as a body-soul unity, which makes
the problem of death a more delicate matter. If the human being is to
be immortal, Pieper observes, it cannot in fact be a part of his nature,
that is, his soul, that is immortal, but the unity of his being, which is
both body and soul. The Platonic position provides an unsatisfactory
description of the human being's situation, according to Pieper,
because death does not affect only a part of the human being, but the
totality, both the soul and the body: *"man dies."*[110] This affirmation
rests on an anthropology that understands the human being as a being
composed of two elements that are intrinsically united. The human

being is a *synolon*, a matter-form composite or, in other words, a body and a soul, which is the life principle.

Rejecting any anthropological dualism, whether of a Platonic or a Cartesian origin, Pieper appropriates the Aristotelian definition of the substantial unity of the human being. This conception of the soul as a form of the body has been sustained and "proven," according to him, by a number of empirical studies done in medicine and depth psychology.[111] The body-soul relation is not, in Pieper's view, a causal interaction or an illusory parallelism, but, as Braine describes in *The Human Person: Animal and Spirit,* it is a fundamental and primary unity, a "psychophysical unity, an incarnate consciousness."[112] In the context of such a "hylomorphic" understanding of the human being, death affects the person as a whole, that is, the substantial unity of body and soul. In the light of this hylomorphic anthropology, we have to conclude that, if one wishes to speak of immortality, only the person, that is, only the body-soul unity, and not a part of it, can be considered immortal.

The two Greek positions, the Platonic and the Aristotelian, each raise a problem. While the former allows us to understand immortality, it reduces the human being in an unacceptable way to the soul, seeing the body as nothing but a prison, a fall, the result of a mishap. While the latter, accounts for the unity of the human being, it nevertheless rests on the slippery slope that leads to a materialistic anthropology. Indeed, insofar as no being can exist except in the mode of hylomorphism, death undermines this substantial union, which means that it entails the disappearance of the whole human being, thus making any immortality impossible.[113] Albert the Great sums up this apparently insoluble conflict: "if we consider the soul as it exists in itself, Plato would be right; if, by contrast, we consider the soul as the form of the body, Aristotle would be right."[114]

Such is the situation facing Thomas Aquinas, who wishes to reconcile substantial unity with personal immortality. To do so, he opens up Aristotle's metaphysical view, according to which every thing that exists, apart from the first mover, is composed of matter and form, and introduces the notion of subsistent form, which is able to exist without matter, but which is nevertheless a composite, like all other things, of essence and existence, neither of which necessarily implies the other. There is only one substantial form in which essence and existence are identical, namely, God. This metaphysical breakthrough allows

Thomas Aquinas to conceive of a subsistent human soul existing in itself, which is not dependent on the body, but which is not, strictly speaking, a complete substance, that is, a complete and self-sufficient being, for it is substantially united to the body it informs. In order to justify this view, Aquinas must prove that the intellectual principle is incorporeal, or, in other words, that there exists a proper activity independent of matter, that is, of the body. To do so, he refers, among other things, to the theory of knowledge, and observes that to know means to possess the other, but to possess it immaterially, in such a way that the knower retains his own form. Given that the intellect can know all things without becoming what he knows in a material sense, the soul does not depend on matter.[115] By thus referring to the distinction between the subsistent form and the form that is integral to a particular matter, Thomas Aquinas maintains both the incorruptibility and the substantial unity of the human being.

The incorruptibility of the soul is not only the object of an act of belief or a postulate of practical reason or an object of intuitive knowledge; it can be "demonstrated," Pieper says, philosophically.[116] It is important to specify that we are not talking about scientific proofs, because its object by nature lies beyond the quantitative dimension. We stand at a level other than that of a measurable experiment, the results of which will never be able to prove or disprove incorruptibility.[117] A rigorous argument would have to show why and how the soul is capable of existing independently of the body to which it is fundamentally united. Although the philosophical tradition has elaborated a variety of rational "proofs" in this regard, such as proofs based on the nature of spirit, on simplicity, immateriality, or the nontemporality of the soul, Pieper prefers the proof that seems to him most compelling, the proof that appeals to the human soul's capacity to grasp truth. We find this proof in Plato, Augustine, and in Thomas Aquinas.[118] The knowledge of truth is by nature an event that occurs independently of the body. Discourse, which is the capacity to "make reality recognizable and to communicate it," presupposes the ability to know the truth, which is itself the recognition of reality. Discourse is not necessarily identical to anything and everything that issues from a mouth. There are, indeed, certain sounds and even words that are the result of a purely physical and psychological mechanism, which are distinct from the genuine speaking that expresses truth.[119]

Interpreting the soul as subsistent form, the hylomorphic anthropology, however, presents a difficulty, one that is not insignificant with respect to the state of the soul *post mortem,* namely, the question of the *anima separata.* The soul separated from the body at the moment of death continues to exist, but its state is no longer that of a person defined by the body-soul union.[120] In exactly what mode does the separated soul exist, and how can it know *res?* Pieper does not answer this question and instead, like the Ancients, takes refuge in silence: "concerning these matters there is no substantiated human knowledge."[121] No one is able to speculate rationally on what will happen behind the veil of death, the veil that silences and confounds the philosopher. Nor does Pieper address the delicate question of personal identity, which has been in recent years the subject of very interesting studies in the context of the analytic tradition.

If we take for granted the truth of the *anima separata* solution, we encounter yet another problem that Pieper did not treat. Since the separated soul cannot be considered in the strict sense a person—only the body-soul union constitutes the person—we can ask ourselves what implications this has for the realization of the object of fundamental hope. This object is not possessed by the *anima separata,* because this latter has not reached its complete fulfillment, which implies the totality of the person, body and soul. Does this mean that fundamental hope is therefore undermined? One solution, if we were to assume that the existence of the separated soul is plausible, could be to accept as a premise that the separated soul (in a nonnatural situation with respect to the body-soul *synolon*) recovers its substantial union with the body—through the resurrection of the body.[122] The object of fundamental hope could not be completely actualized outside of this resurrection. The separated soul continues to hope, in other words, for the recovery of its substantial union with the body, and thus to attain fulfillment.

We ought to recall in this context that Pieper, as a philosopher, does not tire of insisting that what will happen *post mortem* is not something accessible to the unaided human intellect and that one who hopes in the face of death abandons himself in trust to being or to the absolute Thou, in the "certainty" of attaining the hoped-for object. How and in what way this will occur is something that will remain unknown to him. He has arrived at the limit of philosophical understanding and points to the mystery of the afterlife, preserving silence and living in fundamental hope.

4. BLOCH: THE PRINCIPLE OF HOPE IN THE
FACE OF THE ANTI-UTOPIA OF DEATH

Death is practically nonexistent in the thought of Marx, even though it represents in itself the most radical anti-utopia.[123] Having no coherence, it does not represent for Marx a question that can be approached from a philosophical perspective. Nevertheless, one observes in recent decades an upsurge of interest among neo-Marxist philosophers in the problem of death.[124] Bloch's own contribution aligns with this perspective. He addresses death, not as a problem in itself, but in view of founding the *Principle of Hope*.

Death represents, in his eyes, the archenemy of hope, that is to say, it constitutes a constant failure, an ever-present coffin for daily, collective, and historical hope. Understood as an absolute ending that reduces to nothing the dialectical process of history and the individual, the process driven by hope and aiming toward the kingdom of freedom, Bloch sees death as the "anti-utopia" *par excellence,* the *anti-praxis.* "The jaws of death grind everything and the maw of corruption devours every teleology, death is the great forwarding agent of the organic world—but to its catastrophe."[125] If Bloch wishes to maintain his principle of hope, he must therefore find some way or another of staving off death. If this turned out to be impossible, if death were truly the end of all utopia, both personal and collective, his ontology of *not-yet-being* would end its journey in absurdity. *The Principle of Hope* would prove itself to be nothing but an illusion that human beings have clung to since birth:

> What does even the highest moment mean, the "Stay awhile, you are so fair" intended in the most central utopia, when death, without itself being affected, cancels from the capacity for experience with the greatest command of existence its—existence? So no enemy seemed more central, none was so inescapably positioned, no certainty in this thoroughly uncertain life and its formations of purpose is even remotely comparable with that of death. Nothing stands as finalistically as death does at the end, and nothing shatters the work of the subjects of historical purpose-setting so anti-finalistically into fragments.[126]

Wondering where he would be able to find arguments capable of neutralizing the anti-utopic aspect of death, Bloch observes that, until now, we have not yet managed to find any remedy except for the images of the desire for and will to an *Incipit vita nova* that are provided in the different religions. He nevertheless refuses to take into consideration either the "myths" taught by these religions, which, in his view, must be demythologized, or the flight into the afterworld that is taught by Christians, a belief that he denounces as an illusion that functions as a compensation for everything the human being could not possess or achieve while on Earth. Bloch's hope is anchored in the immanent, materialistic, dialectical process that has no earthly limit and that is opposed to any sort of afterworld, in order to arrive at a transcendence without transcendence.

Bloch develops three principal arguments to break through the anti-utopic barrier of death in relation to the principle of hope. In the second edition of *The Spirit of Utopia,* which appeared in 1923, he teaches, first, a metempsychosis, that is, an immortality of the personal human soul, taking a position different from the one he affirms twenty years later in *The Principle of Hope.* In the later book, he rejects the existence of personal immortality in the light of the "Red hero" of Communism, even while he maintains the survival of the individual—this forms the second argument—in class consciousness. The third argument rests on the exterritoriality of death.

Many of the authors who have studied Bloch's thought do not take seriously his affirmations in *The Spirit of Utopia* concerning the personal immortality of the human soul, and for the most part consider only his thought as it was developed in *The Principle of Hope.* It is nevertheless worthwhile to note that, in this first work, Bloch clearly maintains the existence of something that is incorruptible, in the most profound depths of the human being, which constitutes the personality of the individual. This thing he calls the "hidden I." That the human being is doomed to die is, of course, an undeniable fact, according to Bloch; however, it is not possible to deduce the destruction of the soul from the death of the human body. In other words, the affirmation that there is no psychic life except insofar as there exist corresponding acts is nothing but a working hypothesis in physiological psychology. Bloch clearly and unambiguously affirms that the soul is incorruptible in its essence, a position that rests on a dualistic anthropology. He thus differentiates two different ways in which the soul is transposed to a different state: on the one hand, the one that he identifies with the Christian resurrection of the dead, and, on the other hand, metempsychosis, the Ancient view that can be found also in Plato. It is this latter that Bloch defends.

> *That we will be blessed, that there can be a Heavenly Kingdom, that when seen evidently, the dream-content of the human soul also posits itself, that it is correlated to a sphere of reality, however defined:* that is not only conceivable, meaning formally possible, but *simply necessary,* far removed from any formal or real examples, proofs, concessions, premises of its existence, postulated a priori in the nature of the thing, and therefore also having the *utopian,* intensive inclination of a precisely given, *essential* reality.[127]

Bloch distinguishes two types of immortality: *a transphysiological immortality,* which allows the I to continue to exist once the body has ceased to function, and *a transcosmological immortality,* which enables the I to reach its fulfillment in spite of the passing away of the world. The human being travels from the first immortality to the second, which is a goal attained not when a sufficient number of souls have reached it, because it is already reached, but when souls will have become ripe, that is, when they will all have achieved "a final, undefeated, fully matured self-presence."[128] Souls continue to exist through transphysiological immortality and move toward their maturation. The end of this movement is the transcosmological immortality that can be achieved only as a "we"—in other words, only by the whole of collective humanity. The idea of an absolute primacy of the collective consciousness over the individual consciousness reappears in *The Principle of Hope,* though Bloch does not in this later book make allusion to his first argumentation, but replaces it with two others.

Thus, in order to overcome the anti-utopia of death, Bloch refers in the second place to his dualistic anthropology and also to his ontology of *not-yet-being* and coming-to-be. The human being is constituted by a *Dass-Sein,* which is characterized by a *Nicht-Da* and which lies at the basis of all existence. This means that he exists, but that he is not yet really what he is insofar as he has not yet discovered his essence. He exists in a constant striving toward a complete identity of himself with nature, the ultimate goal that Bloch calls *Da-Sein.* The human being, as well as the present obscure and ungraspable moment, is inserted into this dialectic played out by *Dass-Sein* in its striving toward *Da-Sein.*

The unobjectified That, the being-that [*Dass-Sein*] but not yet being-here [*Da-Sein*] of the ground of existence is undoubtedly the driver of *Becoming* in the future series, that is of attempted objectification of being-that [*Dass-Sein*] out into mediated being-here [*Da-Sein*].[129]

The present obscure moment and death are rooted in the same thing: the "still involved being-that [*Dass-Sein*] without being-here [*Da-Sein*]." It is by referring to his ontology of *not-yet-being,* and also to the *Dass-Sein–Da-Sein* distinction that Bloch is able to affirm that the central core of human existence, *Da-Sein,* has not yet been actualized. The human being is not yet in its most profound depths a human being; rather, he is on the way toward being one in actuality. The core of *Dasein,* which exists only in the future, is in this respect not subject to the process of becoming, insofar as it is in a real sense exterritorial with respect to death: "against death it [the core] has the protective circle of the Not-Yet-Living around it."[130] Death does not affect the person.

Bloch finally refers to the figure of the Red hero, who marches consciously and resolutely toward death. He dies for the *Communist cause* without fear, serenely, in peace, but almost entirely without consolation. Lacking any hope in eternal life, because he knows that there is only nothingness awaiting him, he is different from the Christian martyr who dies, according to Bloch, in a complete illusion, believing he will attain heaven. The Red hero is characterized by his faith in a "transcendence without transcendence"[131]: "we are martyrs without an afterlife,"[132] and thus we are completely devoted to life on Earth. Considering the resurrection as a divine myth, he "sacrifices himself without hope of resurrection. His Good Friday is not mitigated or even cancelled out by an Easter Sunday on which he personally will be reawakened to life."[133]

The Red hero's willingness to lay down his life for an ideal that transcends him,[134] even though he knows that his personal existence will be wiped out by death, is rooted in an act of "faith": he believes that he will continue to live in an apersonal manner in the class consciousness that he had identified himself with during his life. The object of the Red hero's hope is not personal immortality, which expresses a "selfish fixation" on the ego, accompanied by the consolation of an afterworld, but an immortality of humanity, of the collective class consciousness in which the individual is grounded, a consciousness brought about through *praxis.* There is no transcendental shore: the only thing that exists is an immanence without fixed end.[135] "Thinking means venturing beyond"[136] is indeed Bloch's motto, but this going beyond always remains within temporal history. It designates a transcendence without transcendence:

> Personal consciousness is so absorbed into class consciousness that to the person it is no longer decisive whether he is remembered or not on the way to victory, on the day of victory. It is not an idea in the sense of abstract faith but concrete communality of class consciousness, the *communist cause itself,* which holds the head up here, without delirium but with strength. And this certainty of class consciousness, cancelling out individual survival, is indeed a Novum against death.[137]

The Red hero is characterized by a fusion between the individual and the collective. This identification expresses a revolutionary, intersubjective solidarity, that is, an individual-collective unity that makes it possible to overcome and conquer death, to die as if one possessed all of eternity.[138] This solidarity is not confined to the present, but is rather transtemporal. In other words, the Red hero is in solidarity as much with the first human beings as with those of the final age. The concrete utopia of the kingdom of freedom constitutes the imperishable core of the consciousness of revolutionary solidarity. The "transcendental" subject is transformed into an "indestructible element of revolutionary-solidaristic consciousness," which means that "the immortal element in the individual is the immortal element in his best intentions and contents." This revolutionary and solidarity class consciousness forms "the soul of future humanity appearing up ahead, which they [the martyrs] have already become by faith unto death."[139]

What is the reason for the Red hero's hope that humanity will in fact reach its hoped-for destination, that the dialectical process of history will reach the fatherland? Bloch makes reference to two human acts: wonder and enthusiasm. The human being, through the course of his life, experiences moments of ecstatic happiness (concrete situations that take hold of him and leave a profound impression), moments that Bloch describes as anticipatory experiences of the fatherland, which is for now hidden within the obscurity of the present.[140] Enthusiasm follows from moments of discovery and inspiration and also from the anticipatory act of the not-yet-conscious, which teaches that reality can be transformed into something completely new. The reason the principle of hope sustains the Red hero is thus rooted in the evidence of the not-yet-conscious, in the act of enthusiasm for the utopic *praxis* that reflects an inner certainty of a supreme good. But this itself is not a sufficient reason for hope, because it ultimately rests on an act of faith that lies beyond all demonstration and on a presupposition based upon a precise experience of the existence of the hoped-for object.

5. A COMPARISON OF PIEPER'S AND BLOCH'S POSITIONS

Bloch analyzes death in connection with hope within the context of a philosophy of progress, in which death appears as part of a supra-individual process, that of the human race en route toward its naturalization, toward that subject-object identity. In opposition to the "religious mythologies" of personal immortality, he affirms an immortality of the collective class consciousness in which the individual is dissolved, no longer existing in a personal mode and no longer benefiting from or personally experiencing the presence of the actualized hoped-for object. The dying person's object of hope, according to Bloch, is the realization of the fatherland of freedom, an object that remains enclosed within a transcendence without transcendence, within the sole dimension of immanence, a dimension that itself has no fixed limit. By virtue of a dogmatic principle, Bloch refuses to traverse the limits of human finitude through genuine transcendence, and remains trapped within these historicotemporal limits. The individual person is instrumentalized, becoming nothing more than an ephemeral manifestation. One no longer speaks of the person except at the level of the new Humanity, of the Human Race. Personal death is regarded as nonexistent and uninteresting in relation to the dialectical process of history, a process of progress; Bloch simply displaces the problem of personal death to the level of the species.

Pieper's critique in Bloch's regard can be illustrated through the hero of the famous novel *Ssanin* (1905), by Artzibaschev, which Bloch claims to be defeatist. The hero of the novel refuses to give up his life so that, perhaps in the thirty-second century, workers may have an abundance of food and sexual pleasures.[141] Pieper insists on the fundamental and irreplaceable value of the free and responsible person as the subject of hope, whose object is his own actualization and complete fulfillment, both at the personal and also at the community level. He integrates this individual hope into the heart of the hope of *humanitas viator*. Only an individual person is able to hope. Pieper refuses to grant the possibility that hope could be something that belongs to a structure that encompasses a certain number of human beings or even all of them together.[142]

Pieper raises the question of how in fact things concretely stand for the person who dies before Bloch's fatherland of freedom and identity comes about. To be sure, the proclamation of the best of all possible worlds in an indeterminate future, this "New Jerusalem" toward which Bloch's process of history is moving, can touch human hearts in a profound sense, and can push them to try to change the reality in which they live. It is of course possible that someone would give his life so that his children or humanity may live in a better future, that he would hope to continue to exist in his descendants, in the work he has accomplished, or in the processes of nature. The human being on his deathbed can, moreover, take joy in the promise that concludes *The Principle of Hope:* since the world is yet only at the beginning, human beings are going to transform it, through their own labor alone, in view of the realization of the fatherland that will arrive at some point in the future. In any event, beyond the obvious worries that the dying person will have concerning the surviving family and friends, concerning the things left unfinished, and even concerning the future of the community in which he lives, or indeed of his country, and humanity as a whole, the dying person can also be preoccupied with the question of his *own* future. Despite the earthly concerns of his final moments, he must face his own final destiny alone: it is in complete solitude that he encounters death, and he will not be accompanied by either relatives or earthly cares. His final preoccupation will be to know whether he will receive the fulfillment and complete satisfaction *of his person.* Renan's exclamation, which could also just as well come from Bloch, cannot ease this torment: "what does it matter if a thousand humanities die? A single humanity will succeed."[143] Thus, "how can one speak of hope," Pieper asks, "when what is hoped for is conceived in such a way that it could not at all be granted to the very being that is solely capable of hoping, namely, the individual, the particular person?"[144]

Aware of this weakness in his argument, Bloch attempts to respond by insisting that the *summum bonum,* which is the complete content of the Whole, the identity of the human being with nature, is the most hoped-for object of hope; in other words, the Whole is what *"people basically want."*[145] He plays with the notions of the individual and the collective, which are nothing but two alternating moments of the process of the development of class consciousness, which come together in an identical union with one another in a third term, namely, the classless collectivity. In one sense, the collective saves the individual from a total disappearance, insofar as the content of the term toward which the dialectical process aims, the term that represents the content of hope, is the "identity of the We with its self and with its world, instead of alienation."[146] His attempt to preserve the individual despite everything in relation to the collective turns out to be fruitless, because the whole of his thinking is sustained by the governing idea of the dialectical dynamism of the historical process toward the Whole, toward the classless collectivity that eliminates the person.

Pieper maintains his distance from Bloch insofar as he conceives the object of hope as something that is as personal as it is communitarian. In fact, although he affirms that the absolute foundation of hope is the person, and that its principal object is the actualization and complete fulfillment of this same person, Pieper also admits that the ego is by its essence ordered to a thou with which it forms a "we," and that the fullness of the person—who in his most profound depths is a being that exists in solidarity, a political and social animal—is actualized within a universal communion with other egos.

Pieper spends almost no time elaborating this communal aspect of the object of hope, placing more emphasis on the personal dimension. Other thinkers have discussed this before him, such as Marcel, who affirms on the basis of his intersubjective ontology that the phrase "I hope in thee for us"[147] constitutes the most precise expression of the act of hope. The positions held by Pieper and Marcel are diametrically opposed to Bloch's notion of hope, which is to be sure also a social notion, but proves to have no regard for the person, whose identity is absorbed without a trace into class consciousness. This conception rests on a "will-nature"[148] ontology, as Godfrey calls it, a subject-object ontology which belongs to the order of system, in contrast to Marcel's and Pieper's ontology, which belongs to the order of intersubjectivity, and in which the other is respected in his integrity within the community relation.

Godfrey distinguishes three types of acts of *ultimate hope,* a disposition directed to a center, a goal, and an objective, in contrast to *fundamental hope,* which has no center, no orientation toward the future: "*hope-for-me, hope-for-another,* and *hope-for-us.*"[149] The first emphasizes the subject, the second the "object"-other, and the third the interpersonal relation. The two first types of acts of hope risk coming into conflict with respect to the goal each pursues, being able to express themselves either in terms of a selfishness or in terms of a loss of a part of the I or a part of the thou: for example, I can hope for *a* to the detriment of *b.* If we relate these two types of hope to the ontological system of *will-nature,* personal hope inevitably finds itself at some moment in conflict with the hope of the other. In this case, the object of hope is understood within the context of a system-ontology, in which the person is instrumentalized. Such is, according to Godfrey, the position of Bloch and of Kant. Drawing on Marcel's notion of intersubjectivity, Godfrey opts for a synthesis between *hope-for-me* and *hope-for-another,* at the heart of which the key realities of love and basic trust become manifest through a shared life in which the person is respected: *hope-for-us.*

> [T]here cannot be any conflict between hope-for-me and ultimate hope-for-us inasmuch as the latter involves love. This sounds a lot like saying that there can be no conflict between individual fulfillment and communal fulfillment if communal fulfillment is given its form by love, and if individual fulfillment is an aspect of communal fulfillment. Indeed, the thesis just enunciated about hopes implies exactly this.[150]

The dividing line is the place or the value the person retains within the community, which we can understand either under the aspect of communion (the mutual respect penetrated by love and trust, by gift, openness, and receptivity), or under the aspect of a system in which the other is instrumentalized. Personal fulfillment and interpersonal fulfillment converge in the ontological model of communion, while they diverge in the ontological model of the system, of will-nature, and of the subject-object relation.

Another contrast between these two German philosophers focuses on the understanding of the present life in relation to the afterworld. Following Marx, Feuerbach, and Camus, Bloch denies the existence of an afterworld, what he calls a "construct . . . of sanctimonious priests,"[151] a religious fantasy,[152] and the "empty promises of the after world,"[153] this transcendent imposture invented by the ruling class in order to keep the people from transforming the world through *praxis* and liberating themselves from alienation. Bourgeois society, which is connected with the priests, exploits and distracts the people, according to Bloch, by promising them goods that they cannot enjoy while on Earth, but which will be given to them in another form on the other side of death, in which all justice will be equitably rendered. It seems that Nietzsche's exhortation has had an impact: "I beseech you, my brothers, *remain faithful to the earth,* and do not believe those who speak to you of otherworldly hopes! Poison-mixers are they, whether they know it or not."[154]

Bloch's rejection of an afterworld, which stems from his awareness of the sabotage and betrayal occasionally indulged in by those in power—"the afterworld has too easily functioned as a compensation"[155]—is without a rational foundation, because a faulty use of this concept does not allow one to conclude that the notion itself does not possess a concrete reality. Indeed, the reduction of the whole of the world to the this-worldly, to immanence, rests on an act of belief in the nonexistence of God, who is replaced by a belief in the social collective and in the dialectical process of history called *praxis.* "God thus appears as the *hypostatized ideal of the human essence which has not yet become in reality.*"[156] God is the "*homo absconditus.*"

The philosophical view of the world that Bloch proposes represents a secularized and immanent religion inserted within a secularized eschatology of history ordered to the Whole and driven by the *Principle of Hope.* His philosophy of hope has its roots in the heart of a *metareligion,* a "*religion as inheritance*" *(Religion im Erbe).*[157] The object hoped for is the eschatological fulfillment, through a movement of transcendence without transcendence, of the "messianic kingdom of God—without God,"[158] of the "heaven on earth,"[159] of temporal millenarianism.

> The goal of all higher religions was a land in which milk and honey flow as readily as they do symbolically; the goal of the content-based atheism which remains after religion is exactly the same—without God, but with the uncovered face of our absconditum and of salvation-latency in the difficult earth.[160]

This desire to build up this sort of kingdom of God is realized through sociopolitical activism, through *praxis,* through the earthly Marxist revolution: "*ubi* Lenin, *ibi* Jerusalem."[161]

Bloch's hope is above all else something political. Fear, the state in which modern people find themselves all too often, constitutes the point of departure for the *Principle of Hope,* on the basis of which the author denounces the bourgeois and capitalistic society, which he accuses of being the source of the nihilism in which we live. "The futility of bourgeois existence is extended to be that of the human situation in general, of existence per se."[162] A statement like this lies within the order of ideology. Bloch analyzes the existential situation of the contemporary human being according to his criterion of class-dialectic; in other words, he classifies the world into two completely distinct worlds: the societies on the rise, such as the countries in the East, and those in decline, such as the capitalistic countries of the West. By affirming that only the societies on the rise are guarantors of genuine hope, while those in decline are responsible for despair, what Bloch is offering here is a simplistic reduction, accompanied by an act of faith without logical argumentation. He lays the blame for our century's pervasive nihilism on certain material, social, and political structures, appealing to the criteria of value, authenticity, and hope.

Moreover, Bloch accuses the Christian view of the world of "taking refuge" in its conviction that the human being will possess his genuine existence in an afterworld, and thus of not giving due appreciation to the goods of this world, and lounging about in the "laziness"[163] of contemplation. This interpretation of Christian hope as a flight into otherworldliness, which we find as well in Camus and Jaspers, does not do justice to the Christian conception of the world, which does not cease recognizing the full value of the this-worldly and its necessary transformation in striving for a better state of things within history. The Christian concept of the "kingdom of God" does not consist solely in the transcendental dimension, but also concerns history. In his philosophy of history, Pieper specifies that, in spite of the possibility of a final future catastrophe in history, Christians who hope in an afterworld nevertheless continue to work concretely within history to change the world. Pieper's philosophy of hope is thus as much opposed to an activism that would reduce all things to a historical immanence and that affirms that hope comes to an end the moment work, action, and *praxis* does, as it is to any escape into a cozy afterworld, accompanied by a refusal to get involved in and struggle for the transformation of the world.

Reversing Bloch's accusation that the afterworld is a fictitious consolation, Pieper affirms that, in reality, it is Bloch's refusal to consider a
genuinely transcendent openness—and thus his withdrawal into the
temporal and material dimension of things alone—that represents a
"'consolation in the hereafter': a completely abstract, deceptive consolation that refers men to something actually situated wholly and utterly 'beyond' their concrete existences."[164] Bloch claims to bring
consolation to those who are dying, even though the *Home* has not yet
come into existence, by promising them that the Whole toward which
the dialectical process of history is moving will be brought about some
day in the future, a promise that is based on an act of faith without reason. Similarly, the Red hero dies for the realization of something in
which it will be impossible for him to participate, something he will not
be able to experience personally.

The death that the Red hero faces is moreover always present in
Bloch's perfectly realized utopia. The problem of personal death and
its character as enemy still represent in the context of a classless society the opposition between the human being and nature. This personal
anti-utopia can no longer be overcome by an act of transcendence in
immanence, as was the case for the Red hero who identified himself
with the class consciousness. Even the one who hopes for a better
humanity—or a better future for his children—must necessarily despair
if his children or the people of a future generation are likewise unable
to overcome the final obstacle of death, which actually confronts them.
Bloch attempts to respond to this problem, though not very convinc-
ingly, by saying that since the this-worldly is without limits,[165] the
human being does not know whether there exists in the process of
human life a possible future transformation that is as yet unknown to
the intellect, which would allow him to conquer death. The human
being of the "New Jerusalem" hopes that he will one day be able to
wipe out death altogether.

This raises another problem: What would become of hope if the
kingdom of freedom, the object of hope in Bloch's sense, never came
to pass—that is, if the human being would use his freedom to destroy
himself, which is quite possible, or some would say even likely, in our
age? What would become of the hope of those who died in the past?
Is it not in the end an otherworldly consolation? The Red hero gives
his life to build the New Jerusalem at some time in the future, a city

in which his descendants will one day rejoice. However, this sort of immortality, made possible by the identification with class conscious-ness, would be in turn reduced to nothingness if the historical process of humanity itself ended in the nothingness of self-destruction.[166] Indeed, a nuclear apocalypse would mean not only the death of the concrete historical person, but also the death of humanity in general. This collective death could no longer be overcome by a collective consciousness greater than that which already constitutes humanity, it would not be able to be transcended without transcendence: here we come to the end of the end. To be sure, Bloch's hope would insist that this will not happen. Let us nevertheless take for granted the pos-sibility of such a destruction, which today is indisputable. Such a pos-sibility would represent for a metaphysics of pure immanence an insurmountable anti-utopia; it would crush Bloch's principle of hope, and transform it into a principle of despair. While Bloch does not seriously consider the possibility that humanity could truly disappear one day,[167] Pieper made it one of the central points of his philosophy of hope and of history.

It is in the context of the contemporary crisis situation that Bloch teaches and promises a "genuine" hope that he brings back to the polit-ical and social level, a hope in the progress of history, colored by a sec-ularized messianism, the goal of which is the construction of a classless society, all the while rejecting an individual hope rooted in an act of love that places its trust in a genuine transcendence. This position reveals a strange paradox: while Bloch wants to end the alienation of the human being by constructing a classless society, he precisely alien-ates the person, who no longer has any existence in himself or any value in himself apart from his function as a tool of the collective. It is not Bloch's hope in the 'new Jerusalem' awaited in a future age—an age *to come,* which seems, like the horizon, to slip away just as one approaches it—that will be able to extend a hand to the human being who has sunk into nihilism and despair, threatened by the atomic bomb, that sword of Damocles. The same can be said for the concrete human being awaiting death in a hospital or in a prison. A genuine fun-damental hope would be one that affirms that death is not the absolute end of existence, both personal and communal, but that it is, instead, a passage, a mysterious emigration.

NOTES

1. Pieper, *Fortitude and Temperance*, 13 [*Werke*, Vol. 4, 114]. For Welte (*Der Ernstfall der Hoffnung*), death, which represents the "serious case of all serious cases" (19) of our existence, is "an absolute no to human life, and, thus, as it seems, to all human hopes. . . . Does it not therefore show a contempt for all human efforts and for all human hopes" (54–55).

2. Marcel, "Dialogue sur l'espérance. Gabriel Marcel et Ernst Bloch," 58.

3. See the second chapter that Bloch devotes to this understanding of death as anti-utopia (Self and grave-lamp or images of hope against the power of the strongest non-utopia: death) in *The Principle of Hope*, 1103–82 [1297–391]; see also 16 [15], 1097–98 [1289–90], 1103 (1297), 1106f. [1301], 1178 [1386], 1181f. [1390]; *Tübinger Einleitung in die Philosophie*, 372; *Atheism in Christianity*, 263 [343]; "Dialogue sur l'espérance. Gabriel Marcel et Ernst Bloch," 58.

4. Bloch, *The Principle of Hope*, 1105 [1299].

5. Camus, *The Myth of Sisyphus*, 90 [168].

6. Camus, *Notebooks. 1942–1951*, 35 [50].

7. Bloch, *The Principle of Hope*, 1106 [1301].

8. In the first sermon on the birth of Bossuet, cited by Jolivet, *Le problème de la mort chez M. Heidegger et J.-P. Sartre*, 19.

9. T. S. Eliot, *Four Quartets*, 23.

10. Augustine, *Exposition of the Psalms*, 38, 19 and *Sermones*, 97, 3.

11. Landsberg, *The Experience of Death*, 6 [23].

12. Marcel, *Creative Fidelity*, 141 [185]. Camus (*The Rebel*, 24 [436]) says that the human condition can be compared to a "mass death sentence."

13. Morin, *L'homme et la mort*, 49.

14. Le Senne, *La découverte de Dieu*, 270. See Edmaier, *Horizonte der Hoffnung*, 141, 204, 207, 215. Alfaro, *De la cuestion del hombre a la cuestion de dios*, 198, 252f. On the basis of his personalism, according to which the human being journeys toward the realization and perfection of himself as a human being through an organic process, Landsberg concludes that "if there were no real possibility to correspond with this tendency, the whole of human existence would perish in the abyss" (*The Experience of Death*, 24 [49]), and that the human being "cannot fulfill his hope," which is the complete actualization of the person, "unless there should be, after all, the possibility of a victory over death" (50 [82]).

15. Pieper, *Glauben, Hoffen, Lieben*, 18. "If historical existence here below is unqualifiedly hope and possesses intrinsically the structure of the *not-yet* . . . if the human being is truly a *viator* 'on the way' until the moment of death, and indeed if even in the final moment of his existence, that which is his own, his completion, still stands before him, then this hope, which is identical with our very Dasein, is *either* absolutely absurd, *or* it finds its fulfillment on the other

side of death! Thus, whoever reduces his field of vision explicitly to this side of the threshold of death, grasps not much more than futility and absurdity," "Über die Hoffnung der Kranken," 13f., 32; "Hoffnung und Geschichte," 23–24; *Hope and History,* 34f., 88, 107 [*Werke,* Vol. 6, 390, 424, 436].

16. See Comte-Sponville, *Le mythe d'Icare. Traité du désespoir et de la béatitude,* vol. I, 14.

17. Desroches, *Sociologie de l'espérance,* 56. Edmaier (*Horizonte der Hoffnung,* 144–45) wonders "whether hope is ultimately nothing but an illusion or whether it is a natural help, which the human being receives in order that he may dominate his Dasein, and a reliable relationship to the objective structure of reality."

18. From a letter from W. von Humboldt to his wife Caroline, dated 1.15.1815 (*Wilhelm und Caroline von Humboldt in ihren Briefen,* Vol. 4, 451).

19. Comte-Sponville, *Le mythe d'Icare. Traité du désespoir et de béatitude,* vol. I, 14.

20. "Two of the greatest enemies of human existence/Fear and hope, bound together." In Goethe, *Faust,* part II, cited in Brednow, "Der Mensch und die Hoffnung," 535.

21. Camus, *Nuptials,* 92 [76].

22. Nietzsche, *Human, All-Too Human,* 82 [Vol. II, 82].

23. Marcel, "Extraits des Entretiens qui eurent lieu à Dijon les 17 et 18 Mars 1973 sur la pensée de Gabriel Marcel," 376.

24. This interview was published in A. Münster, *Ernst Bloch, messianisme et utopie,* 264.

25. Marcel, *Presence and Immortality,* 131f. [105]; see also 243f. [192]; *Man against Mass Society,* 95 [83]. See Scherer, *Sinnerfahrung und Unsterblichkeit,* 16, 26, 175f; *Das Problem des Todes in der Philosophie,* 5; *Der Tod als Frage an die Freiheit,* 140, 170. "Standing before death . . . existence is placed before itself in its unreplaceable individuality, it is exposed to the futility of its meaning and becomes aware through this threat of its hope and its most profound despair.—Thus, the limit-situation of death represents a crisis, in the proper sense of the term; it represents the test of all of Dasein's hope," Fahrenbach, *Wesen und Sinn der Hoffnung,* 98.

26. Unamuno, *Tragic Sense of Life,* 39 [92].

27. Camus, *The Myth of Sisyphus,* 3 [99]. Thibon (*Notre regard qui manque à la lumière,* 68) helps us grasp this fundamental choice in an imaginative way: "There is nothing but appearance and nonsense, and death will be the end of everything. But is death finally reality unmasked or the ultimate appearance? What is at issue is to know—and here lies the borderline shared by the metaphysics of nothingness and the metaphysics of hope—whether the motionless grin of the corpse's skull is our true face . . . or our final mask."

28. Camus, *The Myth of Sisyphus,* 6 [101]; see also 20, 31 [112, 121].

29. Camus, *Nuptials,* 91 [76]. Camus also identifies hope with "resignation" (see also 76), or in other words, a refusal to live.

30. Ibid., 76 [63].

31. Ibid., *The Myth of Sisyphus,* 5 [100: "évasion"]; see *The Rebel,* 6 [416: "fuite"].

32. Camus, *Notebooks. 1935–1942,* 115 [141].

33. Camus, *The Rebel,* 24 [436].

34. Ibid., 15 [425]; see Camus, *Notebooks. 1942–1951,* 230 [293].

35. Camus, *The Myth of Sisyphus,* 57 [140].

36. Camus, *Nuptials,* 76 [63]. In the same work (91 [76]), he says that he has seen two human beings die whose lives were "stripped of all hope." At the moment of death, "they were full of horror, but silent. It is better that way," he concludes. See *Notebooks. 1942–1951,* 35, 230 [50, 293].

37. Camus, *The Myth of Sisyphus,* 58 [141].

38. Sartre, *Being and Nothingness,* 681 [615].

39. Ibid., 699 [631–32].

40. Sartre and Levy, *Hope Now,* 57 [25]; see also 53ff. [21ff.].

41. Pieper, "Herkunftslose Zukunft und Hoffnung ohne Grund?" 195.

42. Pieper, "Über die Hoffnung der Kranken," 34. We find the same idea in Sartre, in his old age, when he writes in his final work of the necessity to have a foundation for hope if one wishes to speak of it and to live it. See Sartre and Levy, *Hope Now,* 109 [81].

43. Pieper, "Selbstgespräch über die Hoffnung," 85; see, *Hope and History,* 90 [*Werke,* Vol. 6, 425].

44. Peiper, "Selbstgespräch über die Hoffnung," 86; see "Die Verborgenheit von Hoffnung und Verzweiflung," 172.

45. I will address this issue in chapter six.

46. Pieper, "Über die Kunst, nicht zu verzweifeln," 196; see also "Sur l'Espérance des Martyrs," 84.

47. Pieper, "Hoffnung und Geschichte," 8; see also *Hope and History,* 17–19 [*Werke,* Vol. 6, 379–80].

48. Pieper, "Sur l'Espérance des Martyrs," 84.

49. Pieper, "Was heisst 'Christliches Abendland'?" 40.

50. Nietzsche, *Thus Spoke Zarathustra,* III, "Before sunrise," 277 [Vol. IV, 208].

51. Pieper, *In Tune with the World,* 20 [*Werke,* Vol. 6, 236].

52. Pieper, *About Love,* 19 [*Werke,* Vol. 4, 314].

53. Pieper describes love as the *Ur-Geschenk* [primal gift] *par excellence.*

54. Pieper, "Das Phänomen Liebe," 3. We find this positive attitude toward reality again in the act of fundamental hope, which, in spite of the subject's

imminent death, exclaims that all will end well, not only for reality as a whole, but also for the person and for humanity. In spite of his approaching death and his awareness of a coming catastrophe, the martyr, for example, does not hate reality, but instead finds it very good.

55. Ibid., 6. See Pieper, *Alles Glück ist Liebesglück*, 8, 11.

56. Brunner, *Eros und Liebe*, 26, cited in Pieper, *About Love*, 55 [*Werke*, Vol. 4, 350].

57. Marcel, *Homo viator*, 147 [205].

58. Blondel, *Exigences philosophiques du Christianisme*, 241. See Thomas Aquinas, *Summa theologiae*, II–II, 25, 7. Nédoncelle, *Vers une philosophie de l'amour et de la personne*, 15.

59. I will return to the possibility of annihilation in chapter six, section 3.2.

60. Though he does not offer a solution or enter into a long discussion for the sake of demonstrating it, Pieper doubts that the understanding of the world as something *created* is already a part of theology, that is, that it forms the object of an act of faith; he leans toward the possibility of giving a rational account of creation, and indeed making it credible (*About Love*, 29f. [*Werke*, Vol. 4, 325f.]. "Kann der Zeitgenosse ein kontemplativer Mensch sein?" 403, and *The Silence of St. Thomas*, 49f. [*Werke*, Vol. 2, 115f.]). He does not use the concept of demonstration, but rather of providing support for a truth. Would he reject a purely rational philosophical demonstration of creation such as Thomas Aquinas advocates—"creationem esse non tantum fides tenet, sed etiam ratio demonstrat"? (*Scriptum super libros sententiarum magistri Petri Lombardi*, II, 1, 1, 2). Pieper confesses that he has mounted indirectly by degrees, in his contemplation of reality, toward the source of all beings, toward the Creator God who represents the reason for the contingency of all creatures. Nevertheless, having grasped the createdness of reality, through a *simplex intuitio*, implied by the Creator-creature relation, a fundamental idea that constantly reappears in his writings, he makes use of *ratio* in order to shed a better light on this intuition and provide discursive reasons in support of the object grasped in *intuition*. In his work on love, he explains that "[i]n any case, the conviction that the universe has been created cannot possibly remain confined to any one special 'sector' of existence—not if it is to be anything more than an abstract tenet carried around in the head. We cannot just file it away in a 'philosophical-religious' pigeonhole. Once it has been thought through to the end, consistently and vitally, it inevitably affects our entire sense of being. For it then follows that all of reality (things, man, we ourselves) presents itself to us as something creatively conceived, something designed, hence something that had a distinct purpose from the start (an idea that, as is well known, Jean-Paul Sartre passionately repudiated). Above all we have then to view all reality, again including ourselves, as something creatively willed and affirmed,

whose existence depends solely on being so affirmed and loved." Pieper, *Faith Hope Love*, 177 [*Werke*, Vol. 4, 325–26]. See also Sokolowski's phenomenological analyses, *The God of Faith and Reason*, 31ff., 41ff., 105ff.

61. See Spinoza, *Ethics*, Part Five, Proposition 17, Corollary.

62. There nevertheless exist emanationist cosmologies that do not posit any love. On this issue, see Scheler's texts on the Christian reversal of the movement of love: *Ressentiment*, 101ff. [71ff.].

63. Pieper, *Faith Hope Love*, 177 [*Werke*, Vol. 4, 326]. "Yes, all human love is an echo of the divine, creative, prime affirmation by virtue of which everything that is—including therefore what we *in concreto* love—has at once received existence and goodness," 171 [320–21]; see also 177ff. [326ff.]; *In Defense of Philosophy*, 53ff. [*Werke*, Vol. 3, 108f.].

64. See Thomas Aquinas, *Summa theologiae*, I–II, 110, 1.

65. "Normally we accept the fact of our own existence unconsciously, as a matter of course, until this vital self-assurance is shaken by outward circumstances. But when that does happen, it becomes clear that our acceptance of our own being, our assent to ourselves, our felling at home in existence (and without self-affirmation, love for another person might not be possible at all)— this very courage for being is ultimately justifiable only by reference to the initial act of the Creator, who brought us into existence as a reality that henceforth can never be removed from the world, that is not susceptible to 'annihilation,' and who with absolute finality has declared it 'good' that we exist," Pieper, *Faith Hope Love*, 194 [*Werke*, Vol. 4, 340].

66. I will return to this assertion in the discussion of the possibility of annihilation in chapter six, section 3.2.

67. "I really do not know how an incorruptible mind, faced with the evil in the world, could keep from utter despair were it not for the logically tenable conviction that there is a guaranteed Goodness of being which no amount of mischief can undermine. But that is the point of view of the man who sees the world as *creatura.*" Pieper, *In Tune with the World*, 62 [*Werke*, Vol. 6, 281]; see *Glauben, Hoffen, Lieben*, 19.

68. I will return to this affirmation in chapter six, section two. See Schumacher, "'Quelle ressemblance y a-t-il entre un disciple de la Grèce et un disciple du ciel?' Le rapport entre philosophie et théologie chez Josef Pieper."

69. Pieper, "Selbstgespräch über die Hoffnung," 88; see also 87. Pieper goes even further into the question of the reason for fundamental hope, which is not simply a creative and loving God. He maintains—knowing full well that he is thus going beyond the strictly philosophical realm, just as Plato himself did countless times when he made reference to myths—that the essential reason for fundamental hope is the resurrection of Christ: hope would be reduced to nothing "if Christ had not been raised up" ([1 Cor 15:15], Pieper

"Über die Hoffnung der Kranken," 34; see also "Hoffnung–auf was?," 164; "Selbstgespräch über die Hoffnung," 90). Pieper's position on the ultimate grounds for hope evolved after his first work on the question. Whereas in *On Hope* [*Über die Hoffnung*] (1935), he affirms that Christ is the foundation or the real reason for and fulfillment of our hope, that is, hope is necessarily rooted in Christ (*On Hope*, 34f. [*Werke*, Vol. 4, 270]), in *Hope and History* [*Hoffnung und Geschichte*] (1967) and *The End of Time* [*Das Ende der Zeit*] (1950), as well as in his articles on hope, Pieper no longer makes reference to Christ except at the end of three of his articles, in which he makes clear that he is no longer operating as a philosopher, but as a theologian. Moreover, after the Second World War, he no longer explicitly takes Christ as the real foundation and fulfillment of hope, but merely underscores—and this is again at the end of the articles in question—the fact of the resurrection of Christ as the ultimate reason for fundamental hope. Pieper thus shows that the philosopher, at a given moment in his reflection, reaches the threshold of mystery and it is at this point legitimate to draw attention to the data of the mystery of faith. In addition, we also observe an evolution regarding the possibility of specifying the contents of hope: whereas in *On Hope*, it was still Christ who formed the content of hope, in the other works Pieper states that the form or the figure of this hope lies beyond our grasp, that it remains veiled and unknown to us, and that no one is able to form a concrete conception of it. The person who truly hopes is characterized by the fact that he "remain[s] open to the possibility of a fulfillment that surpasses every preconceivable human notion," (*Hope and History*, 112 [*Werke*, Vol. 6, 439]); see "Über die Hoffnung der Kranken," 32f.; "Über die Kunst, nicht zu verzweifeln," 213; "Hoffnung und Geschichte," 26. Plügge, "Über die Hoffnung," 58, 61f. Edmaier, *Horizonte der Hoffnung*, 216. Le Senne, *La découverte de Dieu*, 253ff.). Thus, Pieper changes his opinion with respect to the possibility of determining concretely the content of the object of fundamental hope. He even says that he does not trust any limited fixing of the object of human hope, an affirmation that he makes in a certain sense against his own position in 1935, which was in any event a theological position, while his postwar position is philosophical.

70. In his study on philosophical anthropology, Alfaro underscores that personal or collective death, the limit-situation *par excellence* of human existence, places us before two possibilities, or, to use Pieper's words, before two responses to reality: either a withdrawal into oneself, which ends in the despair of nothingness, or an openness to the hope that Alfaro describes as the personal faculty of entrusting onself to "something" that transcends the human being and the world. "This 'something' is experienced as a 'someone' from whom we can hope for the gesture of an absolute gift, that is, as a free person—'Dios a la vista' (Ortega), as hope" (Alfaro, *De la cuestion del hombre a la cuestion de dios,*

198; see also 254). Fundamental hope, if it wishes to transcend death, must necessarily be based on a transcendent reality, which lies outside of human grasp. The human being is not capable of making use of it for himself. He can only abandon himself to it in the attitude of hope and supplication.

71. Unamuno has a clear grasp of this crucial question of the reason for hope and of the tragic character of life, of its absurdity if there could not be a real possibility of transcending death in a "beyond." Despite the destructive character of death, the possibility of a real hope haunted him throughout his life. He was deeply marked by a permanent existential debate between, on the one hand, reason, which denies a personal and conscious continuation of the human being *post mortem* and for which the immortality of the soul cannot be rationally grounded, and, on the other hand, the experience of an intense and invincible desire for eternity, that is, of the hope for a personal and conscious survival of death, the hope to live forever, which is something only God can guarantee. Confronted with the terrible mystery of death, he makes a decision for hope and against reason and his skepticism: "I do not submit to reason, and I rebel against it, and I persist in creating by the energy of faith my immortalizing God" (*Tragic Sense of Life*, 50 [102f.]). Here we find ourselves once again before two ways of responding to reality as a whole, to the question of whether life does or does not have a meaning. For Unamuno, the justification for fundamental hope is God.

72. Edmaier also bases the act of fundamental hope on a consent to being and to oneself, an attitude that is expressed by a basic trust in being. See *Horizonte der Hoffnung*, 206. He observes that "the evacuation and liquidation of its transcendental foundation precipitates human hope into a deadly crisis. Without God, hope appears meaningless and perverse"; see also 13.

73. See Evans, *Existentialism: The Philosophy of Despair and the Quest for Hope*. See also Fahrenbach, *Wesen und Sinn der Hoffnung*, 104ff.

74. According to Scherer, hope calls into question the radicality of the destructive power of death insofar as it rests on a positive interpersonal relationship between an I and a thou, at the heart of which lies love and fidelity. The other is perceived as a person, he is accepted as he is, regardless of the situation—whether it be positive (success, joy) or negative (sickness, death). The *I* grants the *thou*'s absolute right to exist, which is something that Pieper himself has noted, and which is expressed, according to Scherer, by the affirmation of the unconditional obligation to be (*Der Tod als Frage an die Freiheit*, 103). Genuine love, this absolute acceptance of the other, implies an act of hope that affirms that the *thou* will continue to exist forever, in spite of death. Agreeing with Marcel, Scherer states that the *thou* is not able to disappear, neither now, nor in the future, for otherwise it would be impossible to speak of the absolute character of the relationship, of the love between an *I* and a *thou*.

Scherer inserts this horizontal and interpersonal relationship between an *I* and a *thou* into a vertical relationship: the *I* and the *thou* form a *we* in the center of which grows the love and fidelity that are borne, sustained, and founded by an absolute Thou. If an *I* wishes to come to a full understanding of his meaning, that is, to enter into an absolute commitment with a *thou*, the person, Scherer explains, has to be open to the Absolute. If he is not, the contingent human being remains trapped in absurdity, and his love (which is an absolute and free commitment) is reduced by death to nothingness (*Sinnerfahrung und Unsterblichkeit*, 181; see also *Der Tod als Frage an die Freiheit*, 108). The only reason, the ultimate reason, for fundamental hope in the face of death resides in an absolute, free, and faithful Thou, overflowing with a love that wills its beloved to exist for eternity (*Der Tod als Frage an die Freiheit*, 133). "If, in the face of death, there is to be any hope at all for man, it must be founded on an absolute love that refuses to abandon us to death. This implies that the interpersonality lived by human beings enters into the light of absolute interpersonality. . . . If there is any reason at all for hope in the face of death, it cannot lie in human capacity. We will find ourselves on the other side of the threshold of death only if an absolute love, which is able to give being, turns itself to us. If it were not love, it would not desire to conquer our death. If it were not able to give being, indeed, if it were not Being itself, it would be incapable of conquering our death. It therefore follows: If we have any chance of being saved from death, then what comes over us in death is the unhiddenness of being, the truth as absolute love. Thus, being saved from death must at the same time be the definitive confirmation of what we have lived of positive interpersonal relations among human beings," (see, 138–39; see also 122ff., 179). If this Absolute did not exist, Scherer adds, everything would collapse into despair and nonsense; interpersonal relations would be nothing but deception and betrayal, relative and not absolute. See *Das Problem des Todes in der Philosophie*, 204.

75. Marcel, *Homo viator*, 152 [211]; *The Mystery of Being*, vol. II, 146ff., 185 [Vol. II, 147ff., 186].

76. Marcel, *Presence and Immortality*, 175 [139]; see also "Dialogue sur l'espérance. Gabriel Marcel et Ernst Bloch," 43; *Homo viator*, 29ff. [40ff.]; *The Existential Background of Human Dignity*, 142 [185].

77. Marcel, *The Mystery of Being*, vol. II, 160 [Vol. II, 161].

78. See Marcel, "Structure de l'espérance," 76; *The Mystery of Being*, vol. II, 162 [Vol. II, 162].

79. Marcel continues: "These two notions are so closely connected that each can be understood only in terms of the other; there is no hope except for resurrection, and on the other hand, for the fleshly beings that we are, resurrection can be given only in hope," "Structure de l'espérance," 78; see Marcel, "Dialogue sur l'espérance. Gabriel Marcel et Ernst Bloch," 58.

80. Marcel, "Dialogue sur l'espérance. Gabriel Marcel et Ernst Bloch," 58; see also *Being and Having*, 75 [109].

81. Marcel, *Being and Having*, 93 [135]; see, "Dialogue sur l'espérance. Gabriel Marcel et Ernst Bloch," 58.

82. Marcel, *Being and Having*, 93 [135].

83. Ibid., 74 [108].

84. Marcel, "Structure de l'espérance," 77; see also *Homo viator*, 46 [62, 114].

85. Marcel, *Creative Fidelity*, 167, 192 [218, 248].

86. Marcel, *Homo viator*, 47 [63].

87. Ibid., 60 [81].

88. Marcel, "Structure de l'espérance," 76.

89. Marcel, *Tragic Wisdom and Beyond*, 143 [209].

90. Marcel, *The Mystery of Being*, vol. II, 12 [Vol. II, 9]; see also 170 [171].

91. Plourde, *Gabriel Marcel. Philosophe et témoin de l'espérance*, 172. Hope is ordered to an absolute Thou whom the subject is nevertheless free to reject, in an act that implies that he despairs of the Thou.

92. Marcel, *Homo viator*, 67 [90–91]; see also 60, 63 [81, 84].

93. See Godfrey, *A Philosophy of Human Hope*, 157–68. I already addressed these ontologies in the second chapter, section 3.4.

94. Ibid., 183.

95. Ibid., 221.

96. Sartre, *Being and Nothingness*, 688 [622].

97. Pieper, *Death and Immortality*, 94 [*Werke*, Vol. 6, 372]; see also "Tod und Unsterblichkeit," in *Universitas*, 1275.

98. Heidegger's notion of being-towards-death is ontological and thus does not raise the question of meaning.

99. Schopenhauer, *Aphorismen zur Lebensweisheit*, in: *Sämtliche Werke*, vol. IV, 480, cited in Pieper, *In Tune with the World*, 19 [*Werke*, Vol. 6, 235].

100. Basing himself on a metaphysics of the contingency of human being, which implies a particular understanding of the essence/existence relation, Pieper maintains not only that the soul (spirit) does not hold itself in being by itself, that is, that it does not possess existence by nature, but also that it is not capable of returning by itself to the nothing from which it came. The person is incapable of annihilating himself. In fact, only one who creates, in the strongest sense of the term, is able to annihilate. This return to nothing would not be the fruit of an act, but the cessation of an act, namely, the continuous act of creation, of being conserved in being. If God so desired, the human being and humanity in general would return to nothingness. And why does he not so desire? Because "'God created all things in order that they may be,' and not in order that they may be dissolved into nothingness" (Aquinas,

Questiones quodlibetales, 4, 3, 4 [and Wis 1:14], cited in Pieper, *The End of Time,* 63 [*Werke,* Vol. 6, 319]; see also Pieper, *On Hope,* 17ff. [*Werke,* Vol. 4, 261f.]; *Death and Immortality,* 109 [*Werke,* Vol. 5, 387]). I will return to this question of the impossibility of annihilation in more detail in chapter six, section 3.2. Pieper refers to a metaphysics of creation and love, but also to a metaphysics of the immutability of the creative and loving will, which wills being to be. "In creation something happens that absolutely cannot be undone again; the creature which has once entered existence can never again vanish totally from reality," Pieper, *Death and Immortality,* 109 [*Werke,* Vol. 5, 388]. "The individual imperishability of the soul is, of course, likewise something received when the individual was created. That means that it is something given to us as really our own, which is henceforth a permanent part of our beings," (ibid., 110–11 [389]). From the profound relationship between creation and nature (in virtue of which that which the human being possesses through creation he necessarily possesses by nature), it follows that the human soul is by nature incorruptible, because it has its reason in the divine will. With respect to the Protestant position, Pieper stresses that "Thomas himself is of course also convinced of the fact that there is such a thing as a God-given immortality, which belongs to man in paradise, to the man who has been raised from the dead; and this immortality is *not* already given along with the nature of the soul. And I have already said: only this immortality of the whole human being is, for Thomas, immortality in the strict sense. Be that as it may, he would never give up the idea that a natural immortality can be attributed to the soul, which is grounded in its own essence, even though at the same time he is able to claim that this immortality is *eo ipso* 'grounded in the will of God.' To see this and think about it seems to me far more worthwhile in the present context for an understanding of St. Thomas's notion of immortality than a critical evaluation of individual arguments would be, among which moreover even the Platonic arguments find themselves affirmed and reinforced," Pieper, "Tod und Unsterblichkeit," in *Catholica,* 96–97; see also Pieper, *Death and Immortality,* 118 [*Werke,* Vol. 5, 396f.].

101. We find this idea in a whole current of contemporary theology, most notably in Thielicke (*Tod und Leben,* 100, 182), Bultmann (*Theology of the New Testament*), van der Leeuw (*La religion dans son essence et ses manifestations,* 309, 330), Althaus, Brunner (*Das Ewige als Zukunft und Gegenwart,* 111ff.), Jüngel (*Tod,* 57ff.), Moltmann (*Umkehr zur Zukunft,* 92ff.), and Pannenberg (*What is Man?,* 45ff. (34ff.). This position, in Pieper's eyes, is the fruit of a counter-reaction to three tendencies: the Idealist and Platonic notion of immortality, Greek metaphysics, and traditional Catholic theology. In their interpretations of the Platonic understanding of the immortality of the soul, various Enlightenment thinkers, such as Lessing, Robespierre, Reimarus,

Tiedge, and above all Mendelsohn in his work *Phädon oder über die Unsterblichkeit der Seele* (1767), change the initial meaning given to this Platonic reality. In the light of a meticulous comparison of Mendelsohn's interpretation with Plato's original text, Pieper observes that the work undertaken by the former misrepresents the heart of Plato's thought, if it does not undercut it altogether (see Pieper, *Death and Immortality*, 102ff. [*Werke*, Vol. 5, 380ff.]). Pieper rejects both this false interpretation of Plato, which has influenced many thinkers, including Cullman, as well as the view of immortality proposed by German Idealism.

102. Cullmann, *Immortality of the Soul or Resurrection of the Dead?*, 6 (10).

103. Ibid., 8, see also 15ff; and the chapter: "The Last Enemy: Death. Socrates and Jesus," 19–27.

104. See Burns, *Christian Moralism from Tyndale to Milton.*

105. On the basis of the proposition that the soul depends in its essence on the body, that is, that there is no human activity of the spirit that can be understood apart from the body-soul union, Scherer infers that the individual disappears as a whole in death. The only possibility for overcoming death, in his opinion, is the resurrection, which Scherer attempts to justify philosophically by drawing on the notions of interpersonality, freedom, love, and fidelity between two persons, a contingent I and an absolute Thou. The human being hopes for the continuation of his existence not because of the incorruptibility or a part of his being, but because he is sustained by the divine love that will raise him up again in the moment of death. "The immortality of the soul must be understood as a moment of the resurrection," he says; in other words, "in death, the immortality of the soul and the 'resurrection of the body' come together in a single moment" (*Das Problem des Todes in der Philosophie*, 217).

106. See Greshake and Lohfink, *Naherwartung-Auferstehung-Unsterblichkeit*. Boros ("Has Life a Meaning?," 18–19) maintains that: "Hence immortality and resurrection would be one and the same reality . . . [This affirmation] is a personal opinion. But I would also stress that the conception held by many, according to which the soul would exist without a body between death and the universal 'resurrection at the end of time,' and God would specially intervene to keep the soul from inhabiting a body, as is proper to its nature, seems to me bizarre, logically unsatisfactory, and even grotesque." In *Mort, immortalité, résurrection*, J. d'Arc, who is attempting to contribute a "historical illumination by exploring in particular the Old Testament" (12), considers the counter-reactions on the part of certain people who believe that the "moment of our death will be death, judgment, purgatory, and resurrection all at once" (117) to be "arbitrary simplifications" (118). She affirms that immortality can be found in the Old Testament (see 85–94), and maintains that the resurrection of one person "has to coincide with the

resurrection of everyone" (120). In her eyes, "it is impossible to admit a 'resurrection' occurring at the same time as the death of an individual (in spite of
the fact there is a powerful current in this direction, carrying more than a few
of our contemporaries)." See also Benoit, "Resurrection: At the End of Time
or Immediately After Death?" On the debate in general, see Ahlbrecht, *Tod
und Unsterblichkeit in der neueren protestantischen Theologie der Gegenwart.*
Sonnemans, *Seele. Unsterblichkeit–Auferstehung. Zur griechischen und
christlichen Anthropologie und Eschatologie.* Wohlgschaft, *Hoffnung angesichts
des Todes. Das Todesproblem bei Karl Barth und in der zeitgenössischen Theologie
des deutschen Sprachraums.*

107. See Plato, *Alcibiades* 129e, cited in Pieper, "Tod und Unsterblichkeit,"
in *Catholica*, 92, and *Death and Immortality*, 25 [*Werke*, Vol. 6, 305].

108. "Plato himself, however, is no Platonist," Pieper, *Death and
Immortality*, 104 [*Werke*, Vol. 5, 383]. With respect to Plato's thought on death
and immortality, Pieper points out the following differences: "One can—first of
all—no longer say that, for Plato, the continued life of the soul consists in a
mere ongoing existence in the infinite, which occurs by virtue of the soul's natural potency. In the second place, it cannot be legitimately claimed that the
'Greek' teaching on immortality is a 'purely philosophical' teaching in the
sense that it is explicitly founded on experience and rational argumentation;
Plato, at least, clearly did not understand himself this way. And finally, it can
hardly be possible to insist that the 'Greek' and the Christian representations
of what the human soul will experience on the other side of death have
absolutely nothing to do with each other" (382–83). Pieper summarizes his critique in five points: "First: There is in Plato's writings no rational speculation
concerning what will come after death. . . . Second, the mere ongoing existence of the soul is, as Plato explicitly suggests, not in fact what the human
being hopes for when he hopes for life beyond death. . . . Third, as true as it
is that Plato understood the bodily existence of the human being as a soul
trapped inside a body, as he puts it explicitly in various ways, it remains the
case that, oddly, he does not understand death as the mere liberation of the
soul, as a mere transition. . . . Fourth, this world and the world beyond are
not, according to Plato, separated only by the soul leaving the body, but also
through judgment. . . . Fifth, Plato is convinced that, because of what this judgment ordains, there are three forms of life after death," Pieper, "Tod und
Unsterblichkeit," in *Catholica*, 88–92.

109. See Plato, *Phaedrus*, 246cff., cited in Pieper, "Tod und
Unsterblichkeit," in *Catholica*, 87–88; see Pieper, *Death and Immortality*, 104f.
[*Werke*, Vol. V, 383–84].

110. Pieper, *Death and Immortality*, 28 [*Werke*, Vol. 5, 308]; see also 27
[307]; "Tod und Unsterblichkeit," in *Catholica*, 93–94.

111. See Pieper, *Death and Immortality*, 31ff. [*Werke*, Vol. 5, 312ff.]. Pieper does not document his references. "Indeed the different forms of dualism and monism proposed in the history of philosophy all suffer, for one reason or another, from the pitfalls of some reductionism or other. Spiritual monism, which claims that man is reducible to soul, knocks against our deep feeling that our body is not all alien to us. . . . Materialistic monism knocks against our equally deep feeling that there are features in us which cannot be reduced to those functions that are to be found in the realm of material things, or even in the realm of animals. Cartesian dualism, on the other hand, does not solve this difficulty, because it is not an overcoming of the two said monisms, but rather a juxtaposition of both; and in this sense it is simply a duplication of opposite reductionisms. . . . Even when dualism is coupled with 'interaction-ism' it remains unsatisfactory, for it is indeed the specific interaction between soul and body which remains obscure," Agazzi, "Mind and Body: a Philosophical Delineation of the Problem," 18–19.

112. Braine, *The Human Person: Animal and Spirit*, xx.

113. Aristotle was aware of this problem. He attempted to resolve it by affirming the existence of a human faculty, the intellect, which possesses certain faculties that can be engaged independently of the body, and thus which seems to be another sort of soul, able to exist *post mortem*. There would, in this sense, be a part of the soul that would be bound substantially to the body, and another part which would be incorruptible, that is, it would not be affected by the death of the body. Here we stand at the origin of the Averroist controversy, in which the question of the immortality of the human person was at stake.

114. "Animam considerando secundum se, consentiemus Platoni; considerando autem eam secundum formam animationis quam dat corpori, consentiemus Aristoteli," Albert the Great, *Summa theologica*, II, tr.12, q.69, m.2, a.2.

115. See Thomas Aquinas, *Summa theologiae*, I, qs. 75 and 76; *Quaestiones disputatae de anima*, I. On Aquinas's position regarding the soul and body, as well as regarding immortality, see Bernath, *Anima forma corporis*. Kluxen, "Anima separata und Personsein bei Thomas von Aquin." Mundhenk, *Die Seele im System des Thomas von Aquin*.

116. Various authors maintain the mortality of the soul in different ways from a rational perspective: de Harclay, Ockham, Luther, Cajetan, Burian, and Pomponazzi, as well as Hobbes and Unamuno. See Pluta, *Kritiker Unsterblichkeitsdoktrin in Mittelalter und Reneaissance*, 1–65.

117. Pieper observes that the notion of experiment needs to be "de-dogmatized," namely, it does not necessarily need to be understood from the perspective of what is measurable; see Pieper, "Philosophie heute. Die Situation des Philosophierenden heute," 242ff. *In Defense of Philosophy*, 95ff. [*Werke*, Vol. 3, 136ff.].

118. Plato, *Phaedo*, 79. Augustine, *De Trinitate*, 13, 8. Thomas Aquinas, *Summa theologiae*, I, 61, 2 ad3.

119. See Pieper, *Death and Immortality*, 116–17 [*Werke*, Vol. 5, 394–95]; "Tod und Unsterblichkeit," in *Universitas*, 1277ff. Following a number of authors who have addressed the issue of the incorruptibility of the soul by showing in one way or another that the soul is capable of certain operations that it can perform independently from the body, Braine (*The Human Person: Animal and Spirit*) comes to the identical conclusion. He engages a discussion with dualists, contemporary analytical philosophers, and also philosophers of artificial intelligence. He demonstrates that the human being is able to engage in operations at the level of the understanding of language and of thinking in terms of words, which are not operations of the body, but transcend it; See Braine, *The Human Person*, chapters XII (447–79) and XIV (512–531).

120. See Thomas Aquinas, *Quaestiones disputatae de potentia Dei*, 9, 2 ad14; see also *Summa theologiae*, I, 29, 1, ad5 and 75, 4, ad2.

121. Pieper, *Death and Immortality*, 116 [*Werke*, Vol. 5, 394].

122. See Thomas Aquinas, *Summa Contra Gentiles*, IV, 79. For Aquinas, the goal of the natural striving of the human being is not the incorruptibility of the soul, but its reunification with the body, which brings fulfillment to the person. Studying this question in the light of texts from Aquinas and his commentators, Scheffczyk (*Unsterblichkeit bei Thomas von Aquin auf dem Hintergrund der Neueren Diskussion*) concludes that "if human striving, which aims beyond death, is not, however, to be disappointed, there must in addition be a principle that endures through death, which remains a bearer of the longing for perfection in its even more intensified state of neediness, a longing that can find its fulfillment only in the event of grace known as the resurrection" (51). "The Thomastic teaching, which admittedly ought to be affirmed in a complete sense only in the light of the theological endpoint to which the whole is pointing, is not established on the proof of a perfect and happy 'immortality' of the soul in its liberation from the body (which for Thomas does not exist), but on the resurrection of the body. This can be (theologically) achieved only if the spiritual soul does not perish in death" (45).

123. See Fetscher, "Der Tod im Lichte des Marxismus," 283–317. Ormea, "Marxisten angesichts des Todes," 98. Martelet, *Victoire sur la mort*, 43–84. Reisinger, *Der Tod im marxistischen Denken heute*. Rolfes, *Der Sinn des Lebens im marxistischen Denken*, 125. Ruiz de la Pena, *Muerte y marxismo humanista*.

124. See, for example, Kolakowski, Schaff, Garaudy, Garrdavsky, Machovec, and Murry.

125. Bloch, *The Principle of Hope*, 1107 [1301]; see also 312 [363].

126. Ibid., 1107 [1301]; see also *Atheism in Christianity*, 249 [329].

127. Bloch, *The Spirit of Utopia*, 276 [343–44]; see also 253 [315ff.].

128. Ibid., 264 [329].

129. Bloch, *The Principle of Hope*, 1178f. [1387]; see also 287 [334].

130. Ibid., 1181 [1390]. "But because the *central moment* of our *existence* has not yet started out in the process of its objectification and, ultimately, of its realization, it cannot *itself be subject to transitoriness* . . . the core of our existence, which has not entered into process does not encounter the process with its transitoriness, and consequently it is not encountered by them either. Something immediately sealed within itself, a Being which is not in being-here [*Da-Sein*], may have death as another kind of this involutio, as its neighbour, but it cannot have death, as the annihilation of a being-here" (1179 [1387]). See Bloch, *Atheism in Christianity*, 261 [341]. This argument is part of the line of thought stemming from Lessing and Kant, and even from Fichte, who maintains that death belongs to the category of phenomena and thus is radically incapable of attaining the Ego.

131. Bloch, "Dialogue sur l'espérance. Gabriel Marcel et Ernst Bloch," 69; see also 70; *The Principle of Hope*, 1288 [1522]; *Atheism in Christianity*, 258 [338].

132. Bloch, "Dialogue sur l'espérance. Gabriel Marcel et Ernst Bloch," 59.

133. Bloch, *The Principle of Hope*, 1172 [1378]; see also 1106 [1300]. Bloch devotes many pages to the Christian desire for resurrection, see also 1125–33 [1323–33]; *Atheism in Christianity*, 257f. [337f.].

134. On the hope held by the Red heroes during the last world war, see Ormea, "Marxisten angesichts des Todes," 107f. Malvezzi and Pirelli, *Lettere di condannati a morte della Resistenza italiana*.

135. See Bloch, *The Principle of Hope*, 1180f. [1389], 1108f. [1303], 1175 [1382].

136. Ibid., 4 [2].

137. Ibid., 1173 [1379–80]; see also 1176 [1383]. It is interesting to observe that Bloch's conception of the Red hero is similar to the Jewish understanding of the hero *ante christum*. The Jewish martyr offers up his life for the sake of obtaining, not his own salvation, but that of others. He does not find his identity in his relation to God but with his people. He does not believe in a personal existence *post mortem*, since death means for him, as for Bloch, the definitive end of his existence. He thus places all of his hope in the community in which he will in a sense continue to live. See Horkheimer, *Die Sehnsucht nach dem ganz Anderen*, 62, 82. Brantschen, *Hoffnung für Zeit und Ewigkeit*, 60ff.

138. See Bloch, *The Principle of Hope*, 1174 [1381], 969 [1139]. "This living synthesis is itself nothing but the classless collective, as noted. But it is new, classless, and open-utopian, so that partial individuals, partial collective can no longer appear in dualistically reified form, as rigid equivalents. This synthesis between individuals and collective, the resolution of these falsely reified and

dualized social elements, *can however itself only be the collective again, the class-less collective,* because it represents the triumph of community, therefore the absolute side of society; but this triumph is equally the salvation of the individual. In the classless synthesis the sought-for Totum is at work, that which according to Marx liberates both the totally developed individual and real generality. And ultimately it is a Totum because it is a Totum of the goal-content, of the human content, which is still circulating but has not yet been fixed. Within it resounds or dawns the general, that which concerns every human being and constitutes the hope of final content: identity of the We with its self and with its world, instead of alienation" (972f. [1142–43]).

139. Ibid., 1174 [1381].

140. Ibid., 288f. [336f.].

141. See ibid., 1173 [1379]. Studies by doctors and psychiatrists support Pieper's thesis, according to which what interests the human being in the most profound depths of his being is not that humanity as a species may one day arrive at the fatherland of freedom, but that he himself will achieve complete personal fulfillment. See, for example, Plügge ("Über die Hoffnung," 56–62) and Staehelin (*Die Welt als Du,* 163f.).

142. See Pieper, *Hope and History,* 83f., 87, 89f., 99f. [*Werke,* Vol. 6, 421, 423, 425, 431f.]; "Hoffnung und Geschichte," 18f.; "Über die Hoffnung der Kranken," 15; *Death and Immortality,* 94f. [*Werke,* Vol. 5, 373]. We find a similar defense of the primacy of the person over the collective in various thinkers of hope, such as Landsberg (*The Experience of Death,* 21ff. [45ff.]), Plügge ("Über suizidale Kranke," 438), Fahrenbach, Marcel, Scherer (*Sinnerfahrung und Unsterblichkeit,* 194ff. *Der Tod als Frage an die Freiheit,* 124ff.) or Edmaier (*Horizonte der Hoffnung,* 71, 122, 221), for whom the person is the original principle of hope. The object of hope, according to Pieper, is not personal fulfillment alone, but also implies a communion with other 'I's, a notion one finds already in Plato, who speaks of a great banquet in which there will occur the *synousia* between the gods and human beings, as well as the contemplation of true being. See Plato, *Phaedrus,* 247a–e. Pieper, *Hope and History,* 109ff. [*Werke,* Vol. 6, 437ff.]; "Hoffnung und Geschichte," 24ff.; "Über die Kunst, nicht zu verzweifeln," 211ff.

143. Finkielkraut, *Le mécontemporain,* 170.

144. Pieper, *Hope and History,* 87 [*Werke,* Vol. 6, 423].

145. Bloch, *The Principle of Hope,* 316 [368].

146. Ibid., 973 [1143].

147. Marcel, *Homo viator,* 60 [81].

148. On the distinction between a *will-nature* ontology and an ontology of intersubjectivity (which I addressed in chapter two, section 2.4), see Godfrey, *A Philosophy of Human Hope,* 157–68.

149. Godfrey, *A Philosophy of Hope,* 134. Regarding the distinction between *ultimate hope* and *fundamental hope,* see also 55–65.

150. Ibid., 136–37. We already encounter the communal dimension of hope in the writings of Augustine (*De fide, spe et charitate,* col. 234f.), and it is taken up as well by Thomas Aquinas, who makes hope for the other possible precisely because of charity (see *Summa theologiae,* II–II, 17–3). This latter draws a distinction between *absolute* hope and a hope *praesupposita unione amoris.* This question raises the problem of the distinction between interested and disinterested love. Lynch (*Images of Hope*) emphasizes for his part that "Hope cannot be achieved alone. It must in some way or other be an act of a community. . . . People develop hope in each other, hope that they will receive help from each other. . . . We tend always to think of hope as that final act which is my own, in isolation and in self-assertion. But it is not this at all. . . . Hope is an act of the city of man, an act of what I call the public order, not in the external sense of that word but in the sense that it must occur between persons, whether they be man or God. . . . That human societies and hope would rise and fall together" (19–20). "This is our great hope: to venture without cutting ourselves off from human society, to join human society without destroying our own identity, without annihilating ourselves" (206).

151. Bloch, *The Principle of Hope,* 1198 [1411].

152. Ibid., 1108 [1303].

153. Ibid., 510 [592], 514 [596].

154. Nietzsche, *Thus Spoke Zarathustra,* 292 [Vol. IV, 15].

155. Bloch, "Dialogue sur l'espérance. Gabriel Marcel et Ernst Bloch," 60.

156. Bloch, *The Principle of Hope,* 1289 [1523].

157. Ibid., 1288ff. [1521ff.]; see also 1193 [1404].

158. Ibid., 1200 [1413]. "The utopia of the kingdom destroys the fiction of a creator-god and the hypostasis of a heavenly god, but not the end-space in which ens perfectissimum contains the unfathomed depth of his still unthwarted latency. The existence of God, indeed God at all as a special being is superstition; belief is only that in a messianic kingdom of God–without God. Atheism is therefore so far from being the enemy of religious utopia that its constitutes its precondition: *without atheism messianism has no place.*"

159. Bloch, *Heritage of Our Times,* 138 [152].

160. Bloch, *The Principle of Hope,* 1311 [1550]. See Viviano, *The Kingdom of God in History.*

161. Bloch, *The Principle of Hope,* 610 [711].

162. Ibid., 4 [2].

163. Ibid., 955f. [1122]; see also 1280 [1511].

164. Pieper, *Hope and History,* 90 [*Werke,* Vol. 6, 425].

165. Bloch, *The Principle of Hope,* 1108f. [1303], 1175 [1382].

166. Although in the second edition of *The Spirit of Utopia* (1923), Bloch maintains, as we have seen, a personal immortality of the human soul and its fulfillment in a transcosmological immortality, he never comes back to this position in his most significant work, *The Principle of Hope* (1959).

167. It is appropriate however not to forget that Bloch considers the real possibility that the dialectical process may not in fact reach its goal in the second version of *The Spirit of Utopia.* "One knows, one can definitionally know, that the world as a process begins as well as ends in time; the unknowing that maintains it is, in its seething relationality, not a permanent state, and must find its metacosmic limit point in either an absolute In Vain or an absolute Absolute" (272 [338]).

6

Hope and History

1. A PHILOSOPHY OF HOPE AND OF THE
END OF HISTORY AFTER HIROSHIMA

A philosophy of hope is not confined solely to the context of the personal destiny of the temporal and historical individual. Indeed, following the Second World War, Pieper sought a foundation for hope in relation to the future of humanity in general, which is itself projected into a situation of profound uncertainty with respect to the possibility of history's coming to an end—a possibility that some claim is imminent.

While a number of thinkers before Hiroshima affirmed such a possibility, most of them nevertheless envisioned it as the consequence of a cataclysm independent of the human will: a flood, a planetary collision, an atmospheric change, an epidemic, and so forth.[1] The nineteenth-century novels about the end of the world, the most striking of which is Flammarion's *La fin du monde* (1893), betray a process of secularization in the way the end is conceived, insofar as they depict it not so much as a result of the divine will but rather as the natural consequence of the evolution of the world.[2] We find here the underlying theme of a cosmology that holds that, by virtue of the second law of thermodynamics, of entropy, energy that is spent can no longer be recovered and that the universe is therefore heading toward a thermal death, toward a state in which all movement will be impossible. The drama of this view of the end of the universe has been tempered somewhat by the fact that it is predicted to begin in the very distant future, the actual date varying according to the theory.

The contemporary situation changes the problem to a certain extent. Despite the reassuring affirmation that the universe, according to the most recent cosmology, is constantly expanding, moving therefore ever further from the possibility of a thermal death, and thus making a certain "eternity" of the human species probable,[3] ever since August 6, 1945, people have begun to realize that humanity has become for the first time in history the "master of the apocalypse,"[4] able to bring about the self-destruction of the human race. Oppenheimer observes that "no world has ever faced the possibility of destruction—in a relevant sense annihilation—comparable to that which we face, nor a process of decision-making even remotely like that which is involved in this."[5] The astrophysicist Reeves asks in turn whether the principle of complexity, which has been operative in our universe for 15 million years, will ultimately end with the complete self-destruction of the world: "The purpose of *all this* is to culminate in nuclear annihilation? . . . could intelligence emerge only to commit suicide in a few minutes? . . . If this turns out to be necessarily and fatally the case, then it would be fair to say that 'meaning' is a disastrous illusion and God a pitiful cheat."[6] This post-Hiroshima situation prompted Jaspers to note, at the beginning of the sixties, that the world as a whole seems to be in a worse state now than it was before. He concludes that "the situation is irrevocable: the human being is capable of wiping out, of destroying, humanity and all life on earth by his own actions. Reason, by itself, tells him that it is likely that this end will occur sometime in the next few decades."[7] Other thinkers, such as Toynbee or Born, maintain that the human being in the nuclear age is forced by historical facts to choose between "political unification or suicide."[8] The device that has brought about human mastery of nature has become itself the master of the human mastery of nature.

For Anders, who has devoted many works to a "philosophy of Hiroshima," the atomic bomb represents a metaphysical sea change, which he interprets as being fundamentally atheistic and nihilistic: it is no longer God who decides the end of time, history, and human destiny, because the human being in the nuclear age has managed, thanks to science, to take this decision into his own hands. He has granted himself the divine power of annihilation. The human being has become "*modo negativo omnipotens.*"[9] In other words, his supreme power—and herein is the paradox—reverses itself into a total impotence, a non-freedom, the incapacity to master the use of that which he himself has invented, and to control the powers that possess this destructive potential. Ever since Hiroshima, the period Anders calls the "end of history," time belongs to the human being to the extent that he, instead of God, decides in freedom whether he wishes to continue to exist as a species. The human being has become, in a negative sense, the master of his own temporality, of History, and of his ultimate destiny.

Setting aside for the moment the metaphysical conclusion Anders himself draws, I would like to emphasize the fact that in the face of the real possibility of self-destruction, to which the human being of the nuclear age seems chained and which is confirmed by a vast amount of literature in these past few decades, both the question of the end of history and the question of hope have become the most urgent ones of our time and our existence. As Pieper puts it, "here, too, we can speak of unprecedentedness—*for the first time;* never before, it seems, has it been possible to ask the question about the meaning and justification with such acute urgency."[10]

Confronted with the antihope and the anti-utopia that Hiroshima represents, this death on a global scale, which seems inevitable to some and which cannot be transcended within the horizons of time and history by a collective consciousness, we could ask if there is any room left for a glimmer of hope, or if, on the contrary, all that is left is a vision of despair, nothingness, and annihilation. "Is human history, then, a 'cause for despair' after all?"[11] In other words, "is the history of man perhaps of such nature as to offer no grounds for hope?"[12] Pieper asks an age that seems more than any preceding it to be exposed to the temptation of despair. Would the *Principle of Hope* be reduced to nothing, yielding its place to nihilistic despair, or is it possible to transcend this view of things in spite of everything? Are we not compelled to say that, in the end, the metaphysics of nothingness, nihilism, and despair is right? Is the human being doomed to lower his arms and wait bravely for the end that he will have unleashed upon himself? Or, on the contrary, in spite of the tragedy of the situation, should we not say that the proclamation of "faith" by various currents of thought are right—those who preach an optimism, an "infinite" progress, a secularized eschatology in which humanity is on a journey toward the "New Jerusalem" by means of reason, science, technology, and development? Faced with these possibilities, we must analyze the reason for hope that lies at the foundation of the understanding of the end of history.

Pieper addresses the question of a philosophy of history immediately after the Second World War, focusing his attention on a Germany, a Europe, indeed, a world in ruins, and in fear of the possibility of an atomic world war. A metaphysics of *theoria,* of a veritable leisure—the foundation of all real culture, and essential to the development of the person—as well as a philosophy of history that contemplates the future in the light of an uncertain historical situation, constitute the great themes of the works by Pieper to appear after the war. They inaugurate a shift of perspective in his philosophy. *Leisure the Basis of Culture* (1948) and *The End of Time* (1950), which was completed by *Hope and History* (1968), constitute a response to the two historical events of Hiroshima and Auschwitz. Pieper distances himself from the two possible approaches to the end of history that stand opposed to each other, namely, the optimism of progress and the pessimism of decline, of annihilation. He proposes a *via media* founded on a philosophy of hope stripped of every illusion, but allowing the human being of the nuclear age to live with confidence despite the omnipresence of the redoubtable threat of the atomic bomb, that sword of Damocles that never ceases to weigh on his conscience and which could unleash the nuclear apocalypse at any moment:

> And if it is correct to say that throughout the parts of the world dominated by European thought the notion of history founded on the Enlightenment's faith in progress is still the one actually valid, then the prime necessity is to add to it the other dimension, readiness for a catastrophic end of time within history. This does not mean that a true philosophy of history must be erected "on the firm foundation of unrelenting despair"; this is precisely what it does *not* mean. Neither does it imply a renunciation of activity within history. It certainly does not signify that this present era, whose catastrophic features nobody will of course contest, must be construed as the "end-period" in the exact sense. What is meant is that the sempiternal proximity and permanent possibility of a catastrophic end of time must be borne in mind.[13]

2. THE PHILOSOPHY OF HISTORY

In reaction to the theological conception of history, which stems from de Bossuet's *Discours sur l'histoire universelle* (1681) and whose masterpiece and model is most certainly Augustine's *City of God,* Voltaire invents the concept of the philosophy of history.[14] He gathers into this category the sciences of history and philosophy, in accord with the rational conception of the world affirmed in the age of the Enlightenment. Kant devotes many works to the philosophy of history, and we find a similar inspiration in the work of Proudhon, Condorcet,

Turgot, Lessing, Fichte, Schelling, Schiller, Herder, and Vico. It receives its credentials through the thought of Hegel, who tells of progress through negation, in which life is reborn out of death and in which decline leads to the ascension of the Spirit to full self-consciousness, to complete autonomy. This is, according to Hegel, the final end of History, which comes about through action in the unfolding of individual history: "History is the process whereby the spirit discovers itself and its own concept."[15] The second half of the nineteenth century and the first half of the twentieth witness the appearance of various philosophers of history and historians such as Humboldt, Nietzsche, Burckhardt, Dilthey, Spengler, and Toynbee.

Pieper offers a conception of history, and of its philosophical significance, that stands apart from the conception proposed by the majority of his predecessors, and he is one of the first, with Jaspers, to reflect on the end of history after Hiroshima and Auschwitz. Pieper, however, does not address the problematic of a philosophy of history within the context of past history, but he focuses his attention on the future, which he considers as the discipline's proper object. According to Pieper, the philosopher of history is distinct from the historian both in his method and in the object of his research. The historian makes empirical observations and analyses of concrete, historical events in the past in an attempt to reconstruct them in a faithful manner, all the while remaining convinced, as Nietzsche says, that the reconstruction of the past is not an end in itself, but that it serves an end that is relevant for the situation of the present time. The philosopher of history, by contrast, is primarily interested, not in the historical events as such, though they are of course indispensable for his project, but in their meaning. His principal interest, in fact, lies in the questions concerning the meaning and the end of history.

Pieper immediately dismisses a cyclical view of history as the eternal return. He opts instead for a linear sense of history, which is bounded by both a beginning and an end. History is considered as a process that has a point of departure, and moves toward a final state.[16] The notion that history is moving toward an end (whether it is understood as a perfection or as a nothingness) is inherent to the thought both of the Fathers of the Church and of the Middle Ages, and also to the modern and contemporary understanding of history in the West. This finality is the expression of a consciousness that, in contrast to the

Greeks who were more interested in the world's *proton*,[17] is concerned with the fundamental question of the *eschaton* that we find either in the philosophers of progress or in the nihilists.

The question of the future, which acquires a new tone after Hiroshima, has become increasingly urgent over the course of the twentieth century, eventually becoming one of the most widely discussed topics, having recourse to science-fiction, prediction, future planning, utopias, or futurology, which professes to be the science of the future. The more hope in progress gets transformed into a fear of progress, the more pressing becomes the question of the future and the possibility of hope. The majority of modern philosophers of history refer to a teleological and eschatological dimension as part of the process of history and the unfolding of time, that is, a process without a real 'beyond,' the final goal of which is either the complete fulfillment of the human being (which is commonly seen in terms of a sort of secularized kingdom of God), or the total destruction of the human being, a return to nothingness.[18]

Pieper's philosophical reflection on the final state of the unfolding of history, which he considers from the perspective of hope, is a reaction not only to the disturbing historical events of Hiroshima and Auschwitz, but to the "social religions" that await for and promise a "salvation," a fulfillment within historical temporality. He also calls into question any latent optimism or especially any profound pessimism, which, on the heels of the Second World War, is accompanied by a temptation to despair. Moreover, he rejects the solutions to the problem of history that he describes as "unhesitating constructivism"[19] Reflecting on the final state of history, he offers a realistic view, which includes hope but without any illusion that would lead to a cheerful optimism. He is not interested in analyzing history according to the sociological rules governing the study of civilizations, or according to psychological, political, or economic categories, in virtue of a claim that what is really going on at the heart of the unfolding of history is the decline of a civilization, the ascent of a universal empire, a class struggle, or an economic evolution. Pieper is in agreement with Weber's observation, that the philosopher of history has disappeared, yielding its place to a sociology of civilizations. Pieper in fact goes so far as to speak of a decadence of the philosophy of history, a theme that is taken up by Aron, who notes "the absence of and the need for a philosophy of history"[20] in an age in which there is no longer any historical unity and in which the human being is sent out "alone and naked, facing a mysterious destiny, . . . into an adventure in which it [humanity] stakes its soul and its existence."[21]

A philosopher of Western history, which is thoroughly penetrated by the Judeo-Christian tradition, is not able to leave the question of the final state of history hanging in suspense, according to Pieper; the philosopher "*must* ask this question"[22] of the end of time, which represents the proper object of a philosophy of history. Nevertheless, one may rightly raise the question whether it is possible to respond philosophically to this questioning. In contrast to Gouhier, who denies the possibility of a philosophy of history, which could never amount to anything more than "a more or less disguised theology of history,"[23] and in opposition to Marquard,[24] according to whom the world ought to be spared a philosophy of history, Pieper believes that such a philosophical reflection on the end of time is possible. In order to carry it out, he refers to the philosophical act's essential openness to pre-philosophical data, which become particularly intense in the realm of the philosophy of history, and become especially precise in relation to its proper object, which is the final state of the process of history. Developing a "polyphonic counterpoint"[25] between the sciences of philosophy and theology, Pieper defends the legitimacy of integrating teachings regarding the world that cannot be proven either empirically or by unaided reason, but which come from a tradition, a belief, or a theology, and enter into the heart of philosophical reflection.

Pieper describes the philosophical act as a reflection on the whole of reality; the object of this act is the whole of being, the ultimate foundation of the totality of the world and of the human being. If the philosopher reflects on a particular subject, he must take into consideration all the possible data that the human being possesses in relation to this topic, data that come, for example, from psychology and history, from psychiatry and medicine, from ethnology and cultural anthropology, from sociology and biology, as well as from theology. If he had to bracket out the data provided by this latter, or other known data, whether they be experimentally demonstrated or matters of belief, he could not claim to be a philosopher in a genuine sense, given that he would no longer be considering the object of his investigation in a philosophical sense from the various possible perspectives in order to achieve a profound grasp of it.

In this context, it is not a matter of elaborating a systematic philo-sophical investigation into the question whether there exist theological data within philosophy, but rather whether, in his reflection, the philos-ophizing subject considers the data given by faith that he carries with-in himself. Pieper does not speak in this respect about philosophy as such, but rather—and this is a crucial distinction—of the person who philosophizes; he thus agrees here implicitly with Maritain's distinction between the nature and the state of philosophy, between its specific order and its exercise.[26] In effect, if the philosopher who believes in one way or another—excluding, of course, casual or uncritical belief—in the truth of data concerning the world that form the object, not of a purely rational knowledge, but suprarational or a priori, if such a philosopher had to exclude these data from his reflection, according to Pieper, he would ipso facto cease to philosophize. Bracketing out knowledge that he considers true, he would in effect no longer be con-sidering his object (reality in its totality) under every possible respect.

The philosopher's openness to theology, this recourse to prephilo-sophical data, however, does not mean that he ceases to be a philoso-pher and changes at that moment into a theologian. Pieper is not doing theology when he appeals to these sorts of data, anymore than Plato is doing theology when he makes reference, as a philosopher, to myths whose content he takes to be revealed and true,[27] or Sartre when he appeals a priori to the nonexistence of God. Indeed, one could just as well ask whether the philosopher who takes seriously the facts of med-icine or psychology is in fact doing medicine or psychology.

The demand that the philosopher not formally exclude from reflec-tion any accessible knowledge in relation to a given subject is intrinsic to the structure of the philosophical act. Philosophical reflection pre-supposes, at least implicitly, a certain measure of a priori knowledge that applies to the whole of being and that does not lie solely within the order of demonstrable knowledge, but is also part of belief, even if that knowledge takes as its principle the negation of a revelation. Indeed, to engage in philosophy, which is an activity that represents a type of fundamental relation with reality, is not possible—and this point warrants emphasis—except on the basis of the totality of human exis-tence, which of course implies taking positions with respect to what is ultimate, acts that belong to the order of belief, whether in a positive or in a negative sense. Pieper is opposed to the ideal of the absolute neutrality of philosophical knowledge, which refuses, in principle and a priori, to take account of positions with respect to what is ultimate, which are taken on the basis of acts of belief. It is by virtue of this openness to prephilosophical data, to a vision of the world that is initially accepted without critique, that the philosopher becomes increasingly alive, according to Pieper, and he receives from this his *impetus*.

The ordering of the philosophical act to prephilosophical data is particularly significant, according to Pieper, when the philosophy of history is at issue, or more specifically, when one is addressing its proper object, which, for Pieper, is the ultimate state of the process of history. In order to justify this opinion, Pieper observes that there are no experiences bearing upon the beginning and the end of history; these lie outside of any rational and experimental investigation. How is it possible to know the final state of history, which is to some extent determined by freedom? Predictions and statistics, for example, are not capable of grasping a future event, which is determined, in its totality and in all of its relations, by an act of freedom. The sole possibility for coming to any knowledge about the end, according to Pieper, is by appealing to a prephilosophical understanding of reality, that is, to a prophecy, which represents the only form of prediction possible within the framework of history. The philosopher of history thus finds himself confronted with the following dilemma: "they [the beginning and the end of history] are either 'revealed,' or they are inconceivable."[28] There is no intermediate possibility.[29]

The consideration of prophecy in a philosophy of history raises a fundamental question about the validity or credibility of that philosophy: if there were no underlying reason supporting prophecy, it would be without foundation, and the philosophy of history would become a mere opinion. To respond to this question, Pieper refers to the ultimate foundation of his philosophy, that is, creation, and claims that prophecy is "either . . . divinely certified information or does not exist at all. On what other basis, incidentally, would it be likely to be supposed credible?"[30] Only a God who speaks to the human being, in Pieper's eyes, can justify prophecy and grant legitimacy to such prophecy.

Prophecy concerning the end of history, such as we find in the Christian tradition to which Pieper refers, is not a message with an easily discernible meaning, able to be encapsulated in precise formulations. The meaning of prophecy cannot be exhausted by the human

being *in via;* it cannot be imprisoned in language. An interpretation of
the Apocalypse that would describe in the tiniest of detail the concrete
events of the final phase of history, and which would establish when
and where such an Apocalypse will take place, ought to be rejected as
false. No one can know, Pieper explains, when or where the end of
time will come about. The content of prophecy will disclose itself only
gradually as things unfold in historical time. For Newman, it is only
"the event [that] is the true key to prophecy,"[31] that is to say, the meaning of a prophecy will appear in all of its clarity only retrospectively. It
can be deciphered with the flow of historical time.[32] Like all things
revealed, it is and will always be something mysterious. History will
remain an enigma, and it will always contain a "hidden meaning."[33]

3. THE PHILOSOPHY OF PROGRESS

3.1 The philosophy of progress in modern thought

The Church Fathers and the philosophers of the Middle Ages maintain
that the end of history is imminent and that it will come about through
a catastrophe that occurs within the horizon of time, though this does
not constitute the whole of history, that is, the ultimate end of the
process of history. Temporality is, in their eyes, pervaded by what lies
beyond time, by the transhistorical. The Renaissance brings about a
shift in perspective regarding the understanding of the final object of
history. It no longer considers the present as the final period before the
end of history and the catastrophe that brings it about, but rather as a
stage in the evolution of history, which will not end in total absurdity,
but in a perfect fullness; the new heaven and the new earth that humanity is waiting for will come about at a particular time in history. The
past is considered an inferior phase in the development of progress
with respect to the present, just as the present is considered inferior
with respect to the future. A group of modern thinkers take issue with
the medieval understanding by limiting history solely to the temporal
dimension and making human beings the masters and possessors of
history and time. Here we encounter the problem of the relationship
between this world and the afterworld, which I addressed in my discussion of Bloch's position. We witness an inversion of the notion of temporality, which Berger summarizes thus:

... modernization everywhere ... means a powerful shift in attention from past and present to the future. What is more, the temporality within which this future is conceived is of a very peculiar kind—it is precise, measurable, and, at least in principle, subject to human control. In short, it is time to be mastered.[34]

We could refer in this context to the famous "quarrel" between the Ancients and the Moderns,[35] a quarrel that the latter won. The Moderns have an advantage over the Ancients because they have more knowledge than their opponent. The son knows more than the father. The progress of knowledge moves from the level of the person to the level of humanity. One believes that the future will be better than the past. The Golden Age is no longer something to be found in the distant past, but in the future, as Iselin affirms, for example, in *Über die Geschichte der Menschheit* (1764). This idea of progress is equally well expressed in *The Nineteenth Century–A History* (1885).

Human history is a record of progress—a record of accumulating knowledge and increasing wisdom, of continual advancement from a lower to a higher platform of intelligence and well-being. Each generation passes on to the next the treasures which it inherited, beneficially modified by its own experience, enlarged by the fruits of all the victories which itself has gained.[36]

The notion that history is progressing toward a better state of humanity represents the fundamental creed of most European thinkers, and has been nearly universally accepted ever since the appearance of the celebrated work of Turgot, *Plan de deux discours sur l'histoire universelle* (1750). This work, which Turgot wrote when he was only twenty-three, purports to "correct" Bossuet's *Discours sur l'histoire universelle.* Turgot's notion of progress is clearer and more complete than that of his predecessors, such as Bodin, Bacon, Pascal, Fontenelle, the abbé de Saint-Pierre, and Leibniz. He does not restrict progress to a determinate place or a particular culture of historical time, but locates it within history itself, within the march of humanity. Following in Turgot's footsteps, Condorcet, the last of the philosophers who took an active role in the French Revolution, synthesizes the doctrine of Turgot, as well as that of Voltaire, Helvetius, Condillac, Bailly, Price, and Priestly, on the eve of his death, in *Outlines of an Historical View of the Progress of the Human Mind* (1795).

By appealing to facts and to reason, Condorcet seeks to demonstrate that human faculties are open to being infinitely perfected; in other words, the perfectibility of the human being is unlimited in a real sense, and the march of progress can never be reversed. For him, humanity—with a certitude founded on the analysis of the laws of nature and of the progress achieved by the Enlightenment thinkers, and not on some a priori law that would imply a metaphysical or theological system—is marching toward a state of human perfection and happiness. Advancing a conception of progress modeled on mathematics, and thus persuaded that real progress comes only through the replacement of philosophy by experimental science, Condorcet establishes a dogma of the so-called infinite perfectibility of human nature. We find this same idea of progress in the writings of Constant, Saint-Simon or Comte, according to whom humanity is progressing from the theological era to the positivistic era, ending with the establishment of an earthly paradise in which Order and Science will rule.

Five years before Condorcet's work appeared, in 1790, just after the beginning of the French Revolution, the young Hölderlin wrote to his brother:

> I love the generation of centuries to come. For this is my most blessed hope, the faith, which keeps me strong and active, that our grandchildren will be better than we. . . . We live in a period of time in which everything is working toward better days. These seeds of Enlightenment, these mute desires and aspirations of individuals for the improvement of the human race, will spread and grow strong and bear glorious fruit.[37]

We find this faith in progress also in the German philosophers. Herder, for example, affirms that history is subject to an inner law, the law of constant progress toward betterment, which will end thanks to reason in the inauguration of the reign of fraternal friendship and solidarity. Fichte agrees with him in affirming that the final state of history will be the age of reason. Marx and Engels prophecy the dawning of a new day for humanity once the proletariat has been delivered from slavery.

A philosophy of history that exalts progress had not only penetrated the eighteenth century and known a widespread influence in the nineteenth century; but can be found also in the twentieth century, in spite of the harsh tests (two world wars and other contemporary monstrosities) to which it has been put. It is nevertheless necessary to point out that progress is understood differently in the various philosophical schools and that not all of the theories necessarily deny a transcendence with transcendence: for the French Enlightenment thinkers and some of the English Enlightenment thinkers, who are hostile to a divine and providential plan of progress, progress is above all something technological, something one can grasp as an experiential datum; for the Leibnizians and Kantians, and also for certain English philosophers such as Hume and Shaftesbury, progress is something immanent to the human species; for Iselin, Herder or Lessing, progress is the realization of nature, while for Kant, Schiller, Hölderlin, or Fichte, progress is the result of a free initiative of the will, reason's rejection of inclinations that are alien to it.[38]

This faith in the unlimited perfectibility of the human species or in inevitable progress results more generally from a convergence between the "omnipotent" science that enables mastery of nature, the process of the "revolution" of the eighteenth century, atheism, and the Judeo-Christian theological conception of history in its eschatological dimension. The theory of the continuous progress of humanity toward its complete fulfillment within the temporal and historical dimension alone represents, according to various commentators, a secularization of Christian theology, specifically of its eschatological paradigm, which promises the realization of the new heavens and the new earth. As Ricoeur succinctly puts it, it is a "secularization and . . . a rationalist corruption of Christian eschatology."[39] Pieper agrees with his interpretation, affirming that

> the historical process itself, with greater or lesser necessity, but in any case on the basis of forces operating within history, is leading to an end-situation "in which all demands of a religious, moral, artistic, economic, and political nature are fulfilled." All these opinions rest upon the dissolution of the Christian view of history, from which the element of the catastrophic end within history has been expunged, while the notion of a "City of God" outside Time has been completely inverted to reemerge as the concept of an ideal social condition which can be realized within Time through cultural, political, and economic progress.[40]

I have contented myself in this context with giving a quick overview of the basic lines of the philosophy of progress in modern thought, not wanting to spend time on a critical analysis of the notion of progress and its various interpretations in the different schools, which would lie outside the framework of my study.[41] I will turn my attention to three authors with whom Pieper has entered into dialogue and who have affirmed that progress is inherent to the passage of history: Kant, Teilhard de Chardin, and Bloch.

3.2 Kant and the end of history

Although Kant, in contrast to both Hegel and Marx, does not attach the same importance to the philosophy of history as he does to moral philosophy and the philosophy of knowledge, he nevertheless devotes various scattered—and some would say marginal—texts to the subject in the last period of his life.[42] Aware of the arguments against the thesis of continual progress toward betterment, Kant continues to insist on it repeatedly, and especially in his works devoted to the philosophy of history, in which he investigates the future, which receives its meaning and justification from the past. I will analyze in greater detail the second section of the *Conflict of the Faculties* in which Kant raises the question whether the human species is progressing constantly toward a better state. Nevertheless, before addressing this work, I will lay out a few preliminary ideas regarding Kant's understanding of history.

Kant, first of all, paints a picture of historical reality that inclines toward despair, for history seems to be in his eyes "woven together from folly and childish vanity and often even childish malice and destructiveness."[43] In spite of this realistic impression, which the outbreak of wars never ceases to confirm, Kant attempts to find an ultimate meaning of the history of humanity in general, not of the human being taken individually. Given that there is no direct source concerning the beginning of human history, he refers to the Bible, which he takes to be the most ancient and respected document available, and draws especially on the book of Genesis.

The human being lives in paradise without being aware of his freedom or his reason, and follows only his animal instinct. He is happy without being free. The fall, according to Kant, expresses the transition from the state of nature to the state of freedom, from the human being as animal to the human being as rational. The problem that occupies the *Speculative Beginning of Human History* is that of the "transition from the raw state of a merely animal creature to humanity, from the harness of the instincts to the guidance of reason—in a word, from the guardianship of nature to the state of freedom."[44] Kant sees the meaning of the history of humanity in his march toward the complete state of freedom, which, after the fall, exists only as a sketch, and which the *Aufklärung* represents, by appealing to the use of reason for the sake of becoming free, as a progression toward total freedom. In effect, he defines the *Aufklärung* as

> *man's emergence from his self-imposed immaturity. Immaturity* is the inability to use one's understanding without guidance from another. . . . *Sapere Aude!* "Have courage to use your own understanding!" that is the motto of enlightenment.[45]

This maturity (*Mündigkeit*) does not consist in a slow maturation promised by the education of humanity; rather, it already exists. What one must do is simply become aware of it. The human being must take hold of his autonomy through freedom, he must make himself independent with respect to the tutors who keep him in hand[46] and must become capable of thinking for himself.[47] History acquires all of its meaning in the Enlightenment project: it marches toward the accomplished state of freedom, of human autonomy.

The *Aufklärung* marks the event of the enlightened spirit, free from all superstition, the state in which reason has been delivered from its dependence on natural dialectic in order to become conscious of its own structures or precepts, which it consciously projects into the future. The program of the *Critique of Pure Reason* is the elucidation of the knowledge of all things through critical reason, which enjoys complete trust, and by which the human being must acquire his autonomy in all domains, including the domain of legislation and above all of religion (by freeing oneself from superstitions). After critical reason has taken over, rational consciousness no longer has any need to rely solely on the "cunning of nature,"[48] but it is capable of projecting a conscious historical design and to work deliberately for its realization; it constitutes the motor of historical action.

Kant brings about a Copernican revolution in rationality: while, traditionally, one has affirmed the existence of an objectivity inherent in things themselves, and believes that moral norms come from outside, that is, that they are independent of the will, Kant affirms that it is human subjectivity that constitutes objects as objects of knowledge and that the root of moral value is to be found in the rational will, which is a legislator. The human being's task is not to discover a preestablished harmony in the world, but to create it. In other words, he is called on to impose upon the causal system of nature a rational finality. Reason, which is fundamentally autonomous and free, chooses its own objectives; they are not imposed from the outside. Reason is the sole captain aboard the ship of history. The human being must gain dominion over nature in order to reform it in conformity to reason. In the final analysis, it is the human will that decides how the future world will be, and it has indeed the power to transform it as humanity will. Yovel thus summarizes Kant's position:

> Kant makes this idea of subduing nature and reshaping it in accordance with human reason the principle of critical history. The natural, cosmological world follows pure and mechanistic laws and has, as such, no teleological significance. Only human reason and praxis can endow it with ends. Man discovers in himself not only an understanding that can know nature, but also a moral reason that demands that its aims be realized in nature and the world be reshaped according to its laws. Moral or teleological reason thus is now understood as the principle of *will*. The end of the world lies in something beyond itself, in something it has yet to become, and the power which has to transform it is the human will, functioning as practical reason.[49]

Having set up a few preliminary markers to provide a better understanding of Kant's philosophy of history—its origin, its striving toward the state of freedom, and human reason, as proclaimed by the *Aufklärung*—I will focus my attention on the notion of progress developed in the *Conflict of the Faculties*.[50] Kant does not ignore the fact that the "religion" of progress maintained by his predecessors raises problems that he takes into account in his own writings. He expresses his doubts through brief, off-handed remarks, asking, for example, whether eternal peace might not be just a beautiful dream of philosophy,[51] or remarking that one cannot die through pure amelioration,[52] or yet again doubting that it is possible to transform the gnarled wood that makes up the human being into a straight board.[53] Nevertheless, he seriously considers the question introduced by the subtitle of the second section of the *Conflict of the Faculties,* a question that forms the guiding thread of his discussion of progress: "Do mankind's natural tendencies allow us to infer that the race will always progress toward the better . . . ?"[54] What interests him is the historical space that the human being has not yet covered, that is, future time, and he brackets out the natural history of the human being. The question addressed does not concern the human being understood as a biological organism, but rather concerns the event that the human being masters, or, more precisely, it concerns history in its moral dimension, which is not related to the individual person, but to humanity as a whole. What is at issue here is the concrete striving of the human race as a supraindividual unity, of the history of the world and not concrete, individual history.[55]

Thus, to the fundamental question whether humanity is constantly making progress, Kant sees three possible answers: the first, moral terrorism, maintains the possibility of a perpetual regression towards a worse state; the second, eudaimonism, affirms a constant progress toward a better state; and, finally, abderitism states that everything will always remain in an identical state.[56] He rejects the first possibility, because humanity would thus be heading toward extinction, and this, in Kant's eyes, is inconceivable. The instinct for preservation gets the upper hand on the instinct for destruction, which represents for the human being in the nuclear age an unrealistic act of blind faith. Kant also rejects the third possibility, insisting that there is in the human being a certain measure of evil that cannot be overcome. Because a mixture of good and evil, in unknown proportions, lies in the human heart, humanity remains uncertain regarding the future usage humans will make of their freedom.

Is it thus impossible for the philosopher to know whether humanity is progressing toward the better? Kant rejects the possibility of determining through experience the truth of one of the three propositions, for it is always possible that a "turning" point, caused by human freedom, will arise in the future and change the course of history. Given that human beings are free, it is impossible to know what they will do, though it is clear from a moral perspective that one can know what they *ought* to do. It follows that historical events cannot illuminate the future direction of human history.[57] It nevertheless remains the case that knowledge of human dispositions allows us to predict the general direction of history.

To show this, Kant looks for a historical sign[58] that would capture such a human disposition, taking as a point of departure the proposition that "an event can be predicted as the effect of a given cause only when the circumstances that help to shape it actually arise."[59] He thus seeks in addition a concrete event "which would indicate . . . irrespective of the time at which it might actually operate" the existence of a

cause of the advancement of the human species toward a better state
as well as that "it is causally active within the human race."[60] This
would allow him to maintain that the thesis of constant progress toward
a better state is not in vain, but that it is something one can reasonably
hope for. Such a precise event would not, of course, represent a *cause*
of progress, but rather an "indication" of it, a *"historical sign"* that
would prove "the existence of a *tendency* within the human race as a
whole" toward a better state. Such a historical sign accessible to experience, however, does not consist, Kant explains, in an important historical event that human beings would have caused to happen, but
simply in the "attitude of the onlookers as it reveals itself *in public*" during this event. The bias of the witnesses in relation to this event, which
"could be of great disadvantage to themselves," according to Kant,
manifests "universal yet disinterested sympathy for one set of protagonists against their adversaries."[61]

This attitude of "enthusiasm" in the witnesses, which has its origin
and cause in a disposition of the human race, forms the pivot of Kant's
argument, since it brings to light the moral character of humanity.

> Their reaction (because of its universality) proves that mankind as a
> whole shares a certain character in common, and it also proves (because
> of its disinterestedness) that man has a moral character, or at least the
> makings of one. And this does not merely allow us to hope for human
> improvement; it is already a form of improvement in itself.[62]

Kant affirms here that the element of disinterestedness constitutive of
the generality of the witnesses' enthusiasm suffices to apply a moral
character to humanity as a whole.

But what is it that the witness is watching? What is he directing his
desires toward, his desires, which border on enthusiasm, without
becoming himself a participant in the event? The event is the French
Revolution.[63] A question inevitably arises: is it legitimate to affirm as a
key proposition of the argument the statement that "all spectators"[64]
participate in an enthusiastic way in the French Revolution?

The "moral" reaction of the sympathizing witnesses to the
Revolution, their enthusiasm, is brought about by two principal factors:
the autonomy of the French state, which becomes actual in the rights
of the people, and the adoption of a republican constitution, which
aims to inaugurate the reign of peace. The enthusiastic witness to the

French Revolution, which symbolizes the revolutionary process in general and is interpreted as a sign of progress, serves as a guarantee that the attitude of the French populace conforms to that of the human race. Supposing a concrete possibility for its actualization, each country will adopt a republican constitution on the French model. The concept of right in which it is rooted is the result of the evolution of a natural disponibility of the people, who have become sovereign and who approach the ideal at which historical development aims.

Kant does not refer solely to the evolution of the dispositions of humanity in order to "prove" that humanity is moving toward a better state, but he alludes as well, significantly, to the memory of an event of a sort that can never be forgotten.

> Even without the mind of a seer, I now maintain that I can predict from the aspects and signs of our times that the human race will achieve this end, and that it will henceforth progressively improve without any more total reversals. For a phenomenon of this kind which has taken place in human history *can never be forgotten*.[65]

Kant even goes so far as to conclude that the proposition "that the human race has always been progressively improving and will continue to develop in the same way is not just a well-meant saying to be recommended for practical purposes. Whatever unbelievers may say, it is tenable within the most strictly theoretical context."[66] The fact that Kant insists that progress toward a better state represents the most rigorous theory [*die strengste Theorie*], as well as his usage of the verb "to prove"[67] seems to me, however, to suggest a dogmatism that has not been sufficiently argued for.

Once he has "proven" that humanity is moving toward a better state, Kant infers two implications: (a) the French Revolution represents a stage along the way toward the establishment of an ideal constitution, which will be republican and peaceful and will rest on the will of the people; and (b) the moralization of humanity represents the most noble purpose of history and the ultimate objective of the world, given that Kant understands progress toward a better state as a moral striving of the human species rooted in freedom.[68] The ultimate goal of history, as Kant understands it, is not restricted to the political domain, to the establishment of States of right,[69] as certain texts might lead one to believe. In reality, Kant's philosophy of history comprises two interdependent systems, which are not opposed but rather complement each other: an internal one, having to do with the moral aspect of the question, and an external one, which concerns its legal aspect. History is moving, on the one hand, toward the actualization of an intersubjective system in which each free individual acknowledges the equality of the other, and, on the other hand, toward the establishment of an external system that embodies the moral form, that is, toward the formation of a civil constitution that rests on freedom, on a rational justice, as well as a universal confederation that would preserve a universal peace. The external system is nevertheless secondary with respect to the internal system.

Here, Kant alludes to what Yovel calls "the historical imperative," that is, a general act whose goal is the moral progress of humanity; it is something that escapes the "cunning of nature,"[70] even while this latter brings it to completion. Reason, which is autonomous and free with respect to nature, strives for mastery over history. It is reason that directs the progressive actualization and fashioning of the world in conformity with the sovereign good, which is the complete harmonization of the systems of nature and morality, and which constitutes the governing idea of history. "History is the process in which the highest good should be realized, and in which the free, formative activity of practical reason remolds the given world into a new, moral world."[71]

The sovereign good, the goal of the human race, is also called by Kant an ethical community, an invisible and universal church, the kingdom of ends, or yet again the kingdom of God on earth,[72] the result of the autonomous exercise of reason freed from a heteronomous morality. This secularized transposition of the religious ideal of the kingdom of God on Earth, which must be built by *praxis* alone (without the aid of grace and the gift of God),[73] represents the heart of Kant's religious thought, which we find over the course of the whole nineteenth century. The ethical community, which is brought about politically by the establishment of a global, federal, political community, gradually comes together as one passes from the faiths of the churches—which are essentially faith in a dogma founded on a revelation and rest in general on the "servitude" of reason—to the exclusive reign of pure religion, which is the "reasonable" religion, that is, the morality that allows us to overcome social evil. Having before his eyes the historical event of the French Revolution, the brilliant victory of the Enlightenment and Rationalism, Kant states that "we have good reasons to say, however, that 'the kingdom of God is come unto us' once the principle of the gradual transition of ecclesiastical faith to the universal religion of reason, and so to a (divine) ethical state on earth, has become general and has also gained somewhere a *public* foothold, even though the actual establishment of this state is still infinitely removed from us."[74] The final state of history, the result of human efforts, is to develop solely within the dimension of immanent history.

Kant's optimism in the continuous progression of humanity toward the sovereign good of the "kingdom of God" is summed up well in this famous anecdote:

> [a] doctor who used to console his patients from day to day with hopes of imminent recovery . . . [and who] received a visit from one of his friends. "How are you, my friend, and how is your illness?" was the first question. "How do you think," was the reply. *"I am dying of sheer recovery!"* I do not blame anyone if political evils make him begin to despair of the welfare and progress of mankind. But I have confidence in the heroic medicine to which Hume refers, for it ought to produce a speedy cure. "When I now see the nations engaged in war," he says, "it is as if I witnessed two drunken wretches bludgeoning each other in a china-shop. For it is not just that the injuries they inflict on each other will be long in healing, they will also have to pay for all the damage they have caused." *Sero sapiunt Phyrges.* But the after-pains of the present war will force the political prophet to admit that the human race must soon take a turn for the better, and this turn is now already in sight.[75]

On this score, Pieper asks whether there exists today anyone who is still capable of believing that, if another world war were to erupt soon, it is not only a porcelain shop that would be destroyed, but the entire Earth.[76] Indeed, the human being has become the master and possessor of the instrument of the possible destruction of the human species. A century that has experienced this great progress of human reason brought about by the invention of the first atomic bomb has also witnessed a decline in human morality; this is a century among whose "mistakes" we can mention Hiroshima, Nagasaki, Verdun, Auschwitz, and Rwanda, to name only a few. It would be utopian to say that at a given moment the moral development of humanity will inevitably overtake technological progress; or in other words, the last day "will make its appearance and bring about the end of all things with an ascension of Elijah, rather than with a journey to hell like that of the company of Korah."[77] Before such a certitude of faith in progress, it seems opportune to recall the question that Freud raised in 1929 in relation to the lot of the human species: "will the progress of civilization be able, and to what extent will it be able, to dominate the disturbances brought to common life by the human drives of aggression and self-destruction?"[78] And nine years later, he affirms that "we live in a particularly curious time. We discover with surprise that progress has made a pact with barbarism."[79]

3.3 The evolutionism of Teilhard de Chardin and Lorenz

The notion that humanity is progressing toward a better state saw a resurgence in the twentieth century in the work of a scientist, philosopher, and theologian, a man who had a moment of glory before disappearing in a certain respect from the public eye: Teilhard de Chardin. Pieper does not discuss the validity of Teilhard's basic positions on the evolution of the cosmos and of humanity, which have been the theme of countless scientific and polemical studies; rather, he is interested solely in Teilhard's understanding of the final state of history and its relation to hope. The two thinkers never met personally, not even at an international colloquium held in Paris in 1951 on the theme: *Human Hope and Christian Hope.* At this colloquium, Pieper argued the thesis that it is vain to call something hope if it fails a person who finds himself in a limit situation.[80] Teilhard, who was present at the colloquium, criticizes Pieper's position in a letter dated June 2, 1951, in which he explains that in the twentieth century, we can distinguish two different Christianities that stand in confrontation: one that he describes as "disdain for the World (or a Christianity of evasion)," making allusion to the position Pieper defended, which Teilhard rejects, and one of "transcendence (or a Christianity of evolution)." In his opinion, the fundamental question, which was not raised during the colloquium, is to know

> what Man (objectively, apart from all sentimentality, philosophy, and mysticism) has a bio-cosmological right to hope for. From an experimental perspective, what are we dealing with in the Man of the "*hic et nunc*"—a baby, a young man, an adult, . . . or an old man? In other words, what, from the evolutionary perspective of 1951, is the likely human potential?—I will scream it out, unto my dying breath, to all those who have grown deaf through a pseudo-existentialism and a pseudo-Christianity: the whole question lies therein.[81]

Pieper interprets this text—which affirms that humanity, from the perspective of evolutionary potential, is still young, and that this youth constitutes the reason for hope—as the confusion of the notions of history and evolution. The concept of history, according to Pieper, does not mean a simple natural development within the context of temporality, such as, for example, a lightning bolt or a stream of water, but the combination of what happens to the human being, and the response he makes to these events. In other words, it is the "unique commingling of free decision and fate."[82] The categories of freedom, uniqueness, individuality, responsibility, the possibility of rejection or acceptance, good and evil, all make up the intrinsic course of history. History is not something that flows from an acquired principle, nor is it something that follows a line inscribed in nature; the pivot point of its action is the freedom that cannot be fully integrated and predicted within a design for the unfolding of the future. A historical event, for Pieper, is an act born from the free decision of a human being facing realities that he encounters over the course of his existence and before which he is responsible for his action.

According to Pieper, history and evolution belong to different dimensions. Here we see once again the freedom-determinism dialectic I elaborated on in chapter one. Once we introduce the notion of freedom into a philosophy of history, it is no longer possible to predict, from an evolutionary perspective, how the future will unfold, nor is it possible to know whether it will lead to progress. The existential uncertainty in which the human being of the nuclear age lives is not a result of calling into question the evolutionary potential of the human intelligence, which is capable of constructing increasingly sophisticated bombs able to destroy humanity increasingly quickly and totally, but it originates in human freedom. Even if, from an evolutionary perspective, we could predict that the behavior of nature would follow a certain trajectory, such a prediction would become impossible the moment we introduce freedom. On the basis of this confusion between evolution and history, Pieper, who nevertheless does not deny that evolution is a cosmic phenomenon, detects a sophism in Teilhard's position. He describes this sophism thus: "Take a look at evolution up to the stage of man, at how unerringly it has pursued its course—and you will then be assured that, regarding human history as well, there can be no catastrophic end."[83]

If we had to take this only natural evolutionary tendency into consideration, we could set a confident eye on the future, despite the atomic threat. The fact that all things must turn out for the best, that evolution is moving toward the *summum bonum* that Teilhard calls the "Omega point," a fullness and completion of humanity and the universe as a whole, is inscribed within the evolution of nature. Teilhard, following Condorcet and his disciples, affirms an irreversible, predictable, and organic progress of nature in general and humanity in particular. He affirms that the future convergence of the cosmos is inevitable, and considers the past stages of evolution as necessary and inexorable. For him, evolution does not represent a simple hypothesis or theory, but a certitude, which has its foundation in science, in a "strong scientific proof,"[84] which is ultimately based on the conviction of his personal faith in an omnipresent God.

Addressing the question of the end of history, Teilhard proposes two opposed models. According to the first, which, the author says, is more harmonious with his own vision of the world, evil will be reduced to a minimum level. Sickness, hunger, hatred, and internal wars among human beings will be done away with by scientific progress. The reign of peace will be achieved under the ever-warmer rays of the Omega. According to the second model, evil will grow over the course of history in tandem with the good,[85] reaching a culminating point at the end, when the "Noosphere" will divide into two zones. These zones will be attracted "toward two antagonistic poles of adoration," and will be expressed by the crucial choice between the "refusal or acceptance of Omega."[86] This second possibility, he explains, is more in conformity with "the apocalyptic traditions."[87] Teilhard rejects this latter option, because for him the course of the unfolding of time cannot end with "an attitude of rejection and revolt," but on the contrary must be directed toward the convergence of the human being toward his cosmic fulfillment. This fulfillment represents, in Teilhard's eyes, a "major and indisputable fact,"[88] which rests, as I have already remarked, on a "strong scientific proof."[89] *"Humankind has to succeed,* probably not necessarily, but infallibly."[90]

It is to Teilhard's credit that he had the intellectual honesty to propose this second possibility of the final state of history, rather than simply passing over it in silence. He nevertheless considers the possible global self-destruction symbolized by Hiroshima a simple "strike" or an "organic crisis in evolution."[91] But is it possible today to refer to the apocalyptic destruction of the world through an act of human freedom as a simple "strike," an accident along the way, a "premature accident or decline,"[92] or indeed as something that "may be ignored"?[93] To maintain his hope, Teilhard refers moreover to evolution, to the fact that there remains "an instinct of planetary preservation,"[94] that is, that the human Energy, this "expression of a movement as irresistible and infallible as the universe itself . . . cannot possibly be prevented by any obstacle from freely reaching the natural goal of its evolution."[95] Teilhard bases his incurable optimism toward the future on his "faith" in his evolutionary theory, according to which both the universe and humanity find themselves on an ascending path of love, as well as on his faith in a transcendent God. He thus distances himself from Pieper, who, though he has the same faith in God, accepts the concrete possibility that the course of history will end catastrophically.

Pieper is also opposed to the evolutionary ideas of Konrad Lorenz, who attempts, like Teilhard, to establish a reason for hope that the final movement of history will end well. He seems at first glance to be more realistic than Teilhard, describing the contemporary human being as an animal that holds in its hands a thermonuclear bomb, and whose heart is marked with an instinct for aggression, which eludes reason and can never be completely overcome. Nevertheless, Lorenz maintains, in his same work on the notion of aggression, the possibility of an attitude that would prevent the development of this instinct for aggression toward a particular person or toward all human beings: the instinct of love. To be sure, he recognizes that no one is able to love every individual—love is always limited, at least for now, to a finite number of concrete individuals. Experience teaches us that love does not extend to humanity in general. The scope of love, according to Lorenz, can however change in the process of evolution. In other words, it can lead the human being to love humanity. Here is his profession of hope, and the reason that leads him to believe that the final state of history will end well: "That's what evolution can do!"[96]

> I believe in the power of human reason, as I believe in the power of natural selection. I believe that reason can and will exert a selection pressure in the right direction. I believe that this, in the not too distant future, will endow our descendants with the faculty of fulfilling the greatest and most beautiful of all commandments.[97]

The reason for Lorenz's hope does not seem to me to have a sufficiently solid foundation. It is not based on science, on demonstrable empirical data, as its author wishes; instead, it is based, like Teilhard's, on an act of belief, a term he himself uses repeatedly.

3.4 Bloch and the end of history

Since I have treated Bloch's position at length in earlier chapters, I will say only a few words here on his understanding of the end of history. Let us simply recall that he develops an essentially immanent philosophy of history, rejecting a priori any real transtemporality. The final destination of the movement of history, of the dialectic founded on an ontology of *not-yet-being,* in which matter is primary and indeed identified with God, is the construction through *praxis* of the kingdom of freedom, of the kingdom of God without God, of heaven on earth. Bloch reduces reality to the sole dimension of the "this-worldly," excluding any "afterworld," which, according to him, is nothing but an illusion, an invention of the priests and the ruling class. Let us recall his famous exclamation: "Ubi Lenin, ibi Jerusalem."

Moreover, Bloch never takes the historical event of Hiroshima seriously, nor does he consider the possibility of the self-destruction of humanity,[98] in spite of the fact that he works out a philosophy of hope at the level of humanity marching toward the "New Jerusalem."

4. Nihilism: Despair and history

While the philosophy of progress triumphed in the last two centuries, it has been deeply shaken, primarily by the explosion of the first atomic bomb, an event that announced an age in which the self-destruction of humanity is a real possibility, and also by Auschwitz, in which the person was reduced to a thing that one can dispose of at will. The human being in the nuclear age seems to be projected into a situation similar to that of the person condemned to death, awaiting an imminent execution. In a certain sense, Hiroshima thus expresses one of the culminating points of the philosophy of nihilism, a philosophy whose paternity in the modern age can be traced back to Nietzsche, who called himself a "annihilator *par excellence.*"[99] Nietzsche dreamed of an army of exterminators dominated by a "will to nothingness"[100] and by "even a joy for annihilating."[101] Such a will to total destruction, the annihilation of life, has been celebrated, according to Pieper, by some as the "anticelebration" *par excellence*.[102]

Pieper draws our attention to the aptness of Nietzsche's description of the end in the absolute sense through the image of "destruction by hand," and points out that this has even become for certain contemporary thinkers something desirable.[103] While Klima dreams of an annihilation of the whole of humanity,[104] and Wolfson wishes for an "emptiness-therapy," which would be externalized through a global euthanasia in order to bring this torture-filled existence once and for all to an end,[105] Cioran would love, for his part, to see the time of the "triumph of nothingness and the final apotheosis of nonbeing"[106] finally arrive. The nihilist desires such a nothingness, which represents the *summum bonum*, "beatitude." The life of human Dasein is perceived as a temporary illusion, an ephemeral appearance, heading toward its own annihilation and not toward being. The nothing has more value than the will-to-live; human existence is not only an evil, "at bottom useless and unintelligible,"[107] something we could liken to a "reeking urinal" (*croupissoir*),[108] but it is also accompanied by boredom[109] and disgust.

This radicalization of nihilism, the fruits of which are despair, anxiety, and fear, could not really have come about, says Pieper,[110] except on the basis of an inversion of an understanding of creation, namely, into annihilation. The nihilism that posits the possibility of annihilation translates, in Pieper's eyes, an attempt to be like God—a notion that is likewise tied to the idealistic absolutization of human nature against which nihilism is a reaction[111]—by eliminating God for the benefit of the human being, who thus becomes his own God. In effect, the nihilist believes in a metaphysics of nothingness, on which rests his hypothesis that the human being, who all the while remains aware that he is not the source of his own existence, possesses the faculty of nonbeing, this *potentia ad non-esse*. We find this notion in the writings of Anders,[112] for whom the explosion of the first atomic bomb gave the human being, *modo negativo*, the divine power of annihilation. Pieper is opposed to this exaltation of the power of annihilation. Only the one who possesses existence, who is at the origin of existence, is capable, Pieper insists, of definitively wiping it out through an act of annihilation. Contingent being can neither grant itself existence out of nothing, nor can it take it away in order to return to nothing.

The understanding of contemporary nihilism nevertheless contains, for Pieper, a grain of truth, which we see in the philosophical and theological conception of the *annihilatio* of the Ancients, and more specifically in Thomas Aquinas. In the first place, the creature does not possess its existence by nature (its existence and its essence are not identical). It does not have the capacity to remain in being on its own, but can return to the nothing. This return is of the order of possibility, and not, as nihilism maintains, of necessity. Secondly, the creature's return to nothingness is not, considered in itself, an evil, because, for Thomas,[113] it can be understood as an act of justice in relation to sin.

Pieper does not directly address the manifestations of nihilism that pervade human consciousness and the structures of the world. Nor does he discuss the different versions of nihilism in the modern and contemporary periods.[114] Instead, he examines the general issue of nihilism in his defense of the truth of things and actions, which have their meaning in themselves, and especially in his discussion of the philosophy of history. The fundamental and crucially important question regarding the attitude of despair or hope in relation to the end of history that the human being is able to bring about, is to know whether it is legitimate to speak of an annihilation, that is, an absolute end of human existence and of all living things.

We must first of all emphasize that the concept of *annihilatio* does not have to be understood in the sense of the death of an individual, who "changes" form without losing existence, but in a more radical sense: that of a total disintegration of the living thing, a disintegration that would terminate in the complete elimination of both form and matter. We find this distinction in the notion of creation, which can be understood in an improper sense—that is, a creation, or production, out of preexisting elements—or in the proper and absolute sense, in which creation is conceived as an act that brings something into being out of nothing. Pieper focuses his answer to the problem of the possibility of annihilation on the metaphysics of creation in the proper sense, drawing on Aquinas's argument for the preservation of the creature's existence by the Creator. Pieper's point of departure is the affirmation, as we have seen, that only one who can create—in the strongest sense of the verb—is capable of annihilating; this return to the nothing is not the result of an act, but rather the cessation of an act, namely, the act of continuous creation, of preservation in being. The subject capable of annihilating a creature, not to mention the whole of reality, is not the human being but God alone. Pieper thus posits the theoretical possibility that history would terminate in the nothing if the divine will decided no longer to preserve creation in being.

The argument Pieper offers to counter the nihilistic position and to save the principle of hope in relation to the future of humanity is based on two complementary metaphysics, which I mentioned at greater length in chapter five: whereas, in *On Hope* (1935) and *The End of Time* (1949), and even in the third edition of this latter book (1980), he refers to his metaphysics of creation and his ontology of *not-yet-being,* he changes his argument in *About Love* (1972). Here, Pieper starts from a metaphysics of love and interpersonality. These two metaphysics (of creation and of love) allow him to affirm that beings will continue to exist (because the Creator created them in order that they be and not in order that they return to nothing) and thus to undermine the metaphysics of despair.

Pieper appeals to a quotation from Thomas Aquinas, which takes up in part a sentence from the book of *Wisdom:* "'God has created all things that they might be,' . . . not that they might crumble into nothingness."[115] It seems as though Pieper rushes his argument somewhat in order to justify a rejection of the possibility of annihilation. A few pages further on, he specifies clearly that "it must be seen, no, believed, that God has created things 'that they might be,'" and that "[n]o one can say there is no end of history in the absolute sense unless he believes in the Creator."[116] To refute nihilism and its project of annihilation, it seems that one must rely on an act of faith in God.

The Thomistic notion that God in his wisdom and providence preserves the creature in being (though, because of his omnipotence, he could just as well annihilate it), rests on two arguments. The first stems from the immutability of the divine will, on which the existence of all things depends. Being sovereignly free, the divine will possesses an unchangeability, an eternal character, even though it is not necessary that it will forever what it wills in a precise instance. It is by this eternal and invariable will that God wills creation for its own sake. The second argument originates, according to Aquinas, in the nature and the order of the things willed by God in his wisdom. God willed a precise order of the world, which is reflected in the nature of creatures, an order that he is not able to contradict without contradicting his own wisdom.[117]

Apart from these allusions to the metaphysics of creation and of love, Pieper also appeals to his ontology of *not-yet-being*. This ontology reveals that the living thing is by nature ordered to the flourishing of its being, to its fulfillment, and not to nothingness. Pieper thus takes a stand against the positions that one finds in certain works of nihilistic existential philosophy, which hold that existing things are heading toward nothingness. Pieper points out that Thomas Aquinas had already considered this opinion in one of his objections: "the proper movement of nature since it proceeds from nothing is to return to nothing."[118] This opinion, which Aquinas answers by referring to the observation that all movement tends by nature toward the good, which is always a being (*omne ens est bonum*), and that therefore movement toward the nothing can come about only through a free decision, goes against the most profound nature of being. This argument is rooted in the transcendental *bonum,* toward which all things tend by nature. Each existing thing wishes to attain perfection, its *being-more*. Although the human being is able, through a free act, to move toward nonbeing, he is ordered by nature— by the very source of his freedom—toward *being-complete*.

5. PIEPER'S HOPE AND THE END OF HISTORY

The situation of uncertainty in which the human being has been immersed ever since Hiroshima is accompanied by a conflict between two basic, and opposed, tendencies, two visions of history and its ultimate destination: the rationalistic philosophy of progress, which has lost its seductive power, and nihilism, which affirms the absurdity and nausea of personal and social existence. Such is the concrete situation on the basis of which Pieper elaborates his philosophical essay on the end of history and its relation to hope, which perdures through crisis and which, in spite of uncertainty, inspires an increasing interest. He wishes to respond to the historical, existential situation by maintaining a distance from both optimistic and pessimistic currents of thought, both of which, he believes, rest on a hope or despair that lacks an ultimate ground. At the same time, he seeks to justify a hope that gives meaning to concrete historical activities, even while considering the real possibility of a catastrophic end of history. Pieper does not altogether reject these two philosophies of history (optimism and pessimism), but he integrates them within a vision of history that is ultimately marked by enigma.

Pieper accepts the possibility of a temporal end of history, which will not end in the victory of good over evil, in the triumph of reason and justice, of morality and truth (as the philosophy of progress would have it), but in a catastrophe—be it natural or the result of human freedom. This idea has not only been the object of prophecy and the Christian tradition, from John of Patmos to Soloviev, but it is also conceivable on the basis of the situation in which the contemporary human being finds himself, who sees the historical signs pointing to such a possibility in the future: whether we think of Auschwitz or of totalitarian States. The dominant mentality of the twentieth century is no longer the optimism of the philosophies of progress, but rather a mentality that sees a catastrophe immanent in history as increasingly probable—some would say even inevitable. We might think of the nihilistic writers referred to above, whose views, in some cases, end in an ultimate despair with respect to the historical process of humanity, or of the thinkers who have contemplated the implications of the atomic bomb. This final catastrophic state of history must nevertheless not be understood solely as the possibility of thermonuclear self-destruction, but also as the decline of civilization or culture, or even as the installation of a global and totalitarian tyranny that would lead to a progressive dehumanization destructive of the reality of the person.

While Cortès sees humanity "hastening with great strides toward the certain fate of despotism," which will "evolve a power of destruction greater and mightier than anything we have heretofore experienced,"[119] Nietzsche speaks of a threatening order established by a political power by violent means,[120] as well as of the paradoxical establishment, by the democratization of Europe, of a highly developed slavery, which produces tyrants.[121] Kafka predicts that "the lie will take on global proportions," and Haecker foresees the age of "the horrors of desolation."[122] Rauschning suggests the likelihood of a "world-wide material gratification, based upon progressive dehumanization and absolutely subject to the total power of a World Grand Inquisitor,"[123] an idea that we find in Dostoevski's work in the legend of the Grand Inquisitor, and also in Soloviev, in his work *Three Conversations on War, Morality, and Religion,* written one year before his death, in which he speaks of the reign of the Antichrist.[124]

The establishment of a universal totalitarianism is thinkable at the dawning of the third millennium.[125] Such a world would reduce the person to a thing, and human beings to a mass, as Ortega y Gasset put it. Huxley, twenty years after writing *Brave New World,* observes that his earlier predictions, describing a "completely organized society, the scientific caste-system, the abolition of free will by methodical conditioning, the servitude made acceptable by regular doses of chemically induced happiness, the orthodoxies drummed in by nightly courses of sleep-teaching,"[126] are not things that may come about tomorrow or the day after, but already stand at our door. "The nightmare of total organization . . . is now awaiting us, just around the next corner."[127] These citations, of course, do not prove that such a vision of the final state of history is exactly the way things will be, but they are, in Pieper's eyes, concrete signs that express one of the contemporary human being's attitudes toward the future.

The question that arises of the concrete perspective of a catastrophe within history brought about through human freedom, whether it be in the form of global totalitarianism or thermonuclear self-destruction, is the question: What will come of hope? Should we not instead agree that the attitude of despair in the face of such a future state of history is the right one? Wouldn't it make more sense simply to give in to despair? Isn't the history of the human race something ultimately to despair over? What reason could there be for the human being to hope that all will end well for humanity, in spite of a historical catastrophe, comparable by analogy to personal death?

Pieper affirms a hope at the heart of history, even though he remains aware that, according to the Christian prophecy in which he places his trust, it will end in a catastrophe that does not represent the final goal of the process of history. In order to keep hope, he refers to the distinction between two types of end: the terminating point and the goal. A process could come to an end without necessarily attaining its goal. Pieper integrates these two ends into a metaphysical understanding that conceives of a historical end (that is, terminating point) as well as a suprahistorical end (the goal). The first is pervaded by the second, which is founded on the wholly Other. The existence of these two levels of reality, namely, the "this-worldly" and the "other-worldly," allows Pieper to maintain a transfiguration of the historicotemporal dimension into the supratemporal dimension. Such a transfiguration, the mode of which is the theologian's concern, will not come about by means of a historical power, even though it is not without relation to the unfolding of history. Instead, it is made possible only by a direct intervention by the wholly Other. This Other undertakes the salvation of temporal history in order to transpose it into nontemporality.[128] If the possibility of such a salvation did not exist, there would be no foundation, no ultimate reason, for historical hope.

In spite of his view of a final catastrophic state of history, Pieper observes that historical activity does not become paralyzed, but that the individual continues to transform the world, just as he continues to celebrate reality through an act of consent to being. He is thus opposed to the notion that whoever affirms the existence of an afterworld, a supratemporal destination of the process of history, wallows in a bed of idleness, waiting with arms crossed for the New Jerusalem, which will be handed to humanity without any effort. Yet the historical human being does not despair, Pieper says, of attaining the object of his hope, toward which he strives with all his being. The hoped-for object consists as much in the fulfillment of the individual as it does in that of humanity; thus, hope has a social dimension. But, Pieper insists, the content of such a fulfillment, as well as the moment it will come about, eludes human grasp.

The possibility of a catastrophic finale to history presents us with a problem that is similar to the one we addressed in the question of personal death, the difference being that the death of humanity, were it really to happen, would no longer allow Bloch's recourse to overcoming it through a transcendence without transcendence. This total death reduces to nothing any philosophy of hope rooted in immanence. Atomic death cannot be overcome except by refusing to enclose history within the sole dimension of temporality; in other words, except by opening it up to the gift of a transcendence with transcendence. Only the acceptance of a creator God who is love is able, in Pieper's eyes, to constitute the ultimate foundation of a philosophy of history and of hope.[129]

The death of humanity, whether brought on by external causes or by individual freedom, would represent an antihope, a destruction of its projection toward a future that could no longer be transcended without transcendence, a destruction that would end either with the attainment and possession of the hoped-for object toward which the person and humanity were striving, or with despair. Such an ultimate catastrophe would compel a fundamental option between two metaphysics: either a metaphysics of openness and gift, which implies the disponibility and trust of an I in relation to an absolute "Thou," a metaphysics that presupposes that there is more than just the "this-worldly," a metaphysics founded by a wholly Other—or a metaphysics in which history is understood as something purely immanent, the death of the human race thus appearing as the ultimate destination of its advance, a brutal interruption of its projection toward the new earthly Jerusalem, in which both the person and the community would find perfect fulfillment. Such a choice implies yet another: is hope, in the face of the end of history, founded on a faith in the human being and human morality, on the trust that humanity will not send its species to destruction? Or is it founded on trust in the Other, who, despite the bad choices the human being makes in his freedom, and despite the hypothetical event of self-destruction, will watch over humanity and ensure that it reaches its final state? For Pieper, the choice is clear: only the "one who has been initiated into the mysteries," that is, the one who "returns to a traditional fund of truth believed to have been revealed,"[130] a truth revealed by the wholly Other, is capable of "really" existing—existing as a person within the realm of real history.

NOTES

1. See Boia, *La fin du monde: Une histoire sans fin.* Guise, "Les romans de 'fin du monde': le problème de la mort collective dans la littérature et l'imaginaire au XIXième siècle," "Les écrivains de la fin du monde de l'Apocalypse à la bombe atomique." Versins, "Fins du monde."

2. At the end of the nineteenth century, several novels appeared already with the premonition that an improper use of science could be one of the causes of the end of the world; these prophecies became more common after 1900, and proclaimed not only the end of a civilization, but also the end of history.

3. See Reeves, *The Hour of Our Delight. Cosmic Evolution, Order, and Complexity,* 66ff., 171f. [84ff., 206].

4. Anders, *Die Antiquiertheit des Menschen,* vol. I, 239.

5. Oppenheimer, *The Flying Trapeze: Three Crises for Physicists,* 63. See Born, "Die Hoffnung auf Einsicht aller Menschen in die Grösse der atomaren Gefährdung," 130. Sakharov, "L'humanité a la possibilité d'éviter son anéantissement," 130.

6. Reeves, *The Hour of Our Delight. Cosmic Evolution, Order, and Complexity*, 159 [194].

7. Jaspers, "Die Kraft der Hoffnung," 41. See *Die Atombombe und die Zukunft des Menschen–Politisches Bewusstsein in unserer Zeit*, 17ff. Lorenz ("Die Hoffnung auf Einsicht in das Wirken der Natur," 147–48) describes modern man as one who has "in his hand the hydrogen bomb, which his reason has bestowed upon him, and in his heart the instinct for aggression, which he inherited from his humanoidal ancestors, and which the aforementioned reason is unable to control–truly, there is no reason to think he will live for long." See Marcel, *Man against Mass Society*, 64ff., 76, 170, 172 [60f., 71, 138, 141]. *The Mystery of Being*, I, 22f. [Vol. I, 30]. *Problematic Man*, vii [II]. The 1972 M.I.T. report for the Club of Rome is even more categorical: "the imminent future of humanity, to the extent that it is possible to formulate predictions in the light of the present situation, because of the direction in which it is heading, its development, and the constantly accelerating momentum of that development, seems to have no other possible conclusion than a general catastrophe, a veritable apocalypse capable of extinguishing the faintest glimmer of life from the face of the earth and thus to make it a planet as dead as its moon," *Comprendre*, 1974 (24), no. 39/40, 157. Campagnolo ("La crise de notre temps et son utopie," 15) affirms that "there are many who predict a total catastrophe, the apocalyptic end of the human race, sometime in the next fifty or a hundred years."

8. Toynbee, "Un 'Etat mondial' est-il réalisable?" 5. See "Sinn oder Sinnlosigkeit," 84ff. We find the same idea in Born ("Die Hoffnung auf Einsicht aller Menschen in die Grösse der atomaren Gefährdung," 137), for whom "the one thing that can save us is the ancient human dream of *world peace* and *world organization*. . . . World peace, in a world that has grown smaller, is no longer a utopian dream, because it is a necessity, it is a precondition for the survival of the human race." The British Council of Churches, composed of both theologians and scientists, observes in 1948 in its report that "we have to reckon with the possibility that men, in their folly or wickedness, will destroy civilization and culture, or even put an end to the existence of the human race." *Das Zeitalter der Atomkraft*, 29, cited in Pieper, *The End of Time*, 77 [*Werke*, Vol. 6, 328].

9. Anders, *Die atomare Drohung*, 93; see also 66, 205. "The *creatio ex nihilo* that expresses omnipotence has been replaced by its counterforce: the *potestas annihiliationis*, the *reductio ad nihil*–and this latter has indeed come to be a power that lies in our own hands. The omnipotence that humanity has longed for since the time of Prometheus has truly been given to us, albeit differently than we had hoped. Because we possess the power to prepare an end for one another, we have become the *Lords of the Apocalypse. We are the*

Infinite"; see also *Die Antiquierheit des Menschen,* vol. I, 239. "The goal that we have to reach cannot consist in the *non*-possession of the 'thing'; rather, it can only consist in never making use of the 'thing' even though there is nothing we can do about the fact that we have it; never making use of it, even though there will never again be a day in which we *couldn't* use it," *Hiroshima ist überall,* 226.

10. Pieper, *Hope and History,* 17 [*Werke,* Vol. 6, 379f.]; see "Hoffnung und Geschichte," 8.

11. Pieper, *Hope and History,* 107 [*Werke,* Vol. 6, 436]; see also "Über die Kunst, nicht zu verzweifeln," 196 and 207.

12. Pieper, *Hope and History,* 71 [*Werke,* Vol. 6, 413].

13. Pieper *The End of Time,* 116–17 [*Werke,* Vol. 6, 351–52].

14. See Voltaire, *The Philosophy of History (1765)* and *Essai sur les moeurs et l'esprit des nations (1756).*

15. Hegel, *Lectures on the Philosophy of World History. Introduction: Reason in History,* 62 [72].

16. See Pieper, *The End of Time,* 13 [*Werke,* Vol. 6, 288]. Bernstein, *Progress and the Quest for Meaning,* 225ff. Bury, *The Idea of Progress,* 20ff. Eliade, *The Myth of the Eternal Return or, Cosmos and History.* Löwith, *Meaning in History. The Theological Implications of the Philosophy of History,* 3ff. [13ff.] and "The Theological Background of the Philosophy of History," 54. Madaule, "Est-il encore possible de donner un sens à l'histoire?," 82–85. Maritain, *On the Philosophy of History,* 35–37 [X, 643–44].

17. We could think here of Plato and his dialogues, such as the *Timaeus,* the *Critias,* the *Statesman,* and the *Laws,* or to the Epicurean description of the origins of the various civilizations.

18. We will return to this assertion in sections three and four. Concerning the theme of the meaning of history, one can ask whether it exists independently of the human being, or, on the contrary, whether it is the fruit of his freedom (as Sartre maintains, insofar as the human being, in his eyes, establishes his own ends and eliminates any pregiven ends), or even whether it is a synthesis of these two alternatives. Popper, for instance, denies in his critique of historicism that there could be a meaning of history that would exist in itself. He maintains that the human being must give a meaning to history, just as he must determine its ends. See Popper, *The Open Society and its Enemies,* vol. II, 278. For a critique of Popper's position, see Lash, *A Matter of Hope,* 65–71. Kant also maintains that the human being determines the ultimate goal of history. On this, see Yovel, *Kant and the Philosophy of History,* 135ff.

19. Pieper, *The End of Time,* 110 [*Werke,* Vol. 6, 347]; see also 11, 20ff., 26ff. [287, 292ff., 296ff.].

20. Aron, *Dimensions de la conscience historique,* 29.

21. Aron, *Dimensions de la conscience historique*, 29.

22. Pieper, *The End of Time*, 48 [*Werke*, Vol. 6, 309]. See Landgrebe, "Das philosophische Problem des Endes der Geschichte." Djuric, "Die Frage nach dem Ende der Geschichte," 172.

23. Gouhier, *L'histoire et sa philosophie*, 128.

24. *Schwierigkeiten mit der Geschichtsphilosophie.*

25. Pieper, *In Defense of Philosophy*, 118 [*Werke*, Vol. 3, 154]. See Schumacher, "'Quelle ressemblance y a-t-il entre en disciple de la Grèce et un disciple du ciel?' Le rapport entre philosophie et théologie chez Josef Pieper."

26. See Maritain, *An Essay on Christian Philosophy*, 11ff. [V, 240ff.].

27. See Pieper, *Über die platonischen Mythen;* "Über die Wahrheit der platonischen Mythen," 289–96; *Überlieferung* [*Werke*, Vol. 3, 236–99]; *Leisure the Basis of Culture*, 151ff. [*Werke*, Vol. 3, 60f.]; "Über den Philosophie-Begriff Platons," [*Werke*, Vol. 3, 156–72].

28. Pieper, *The End of Time*, 20 [*Werke*, Vol. 6, 292]; see also 58, and "Sur l'Expérience des Martyrs," 77; *Hope and History*, 93, 99f. [*Werke*, Vol. 6, 427, 431]. Pieper also refers to two other arguments, which seem to me to be more problematic. The first begins by pointing to the scarcity of responses to the question concerning what ultimately occurs in the process of history, and states that this process can in the end be reduced to a small number of major events such as the decline of a civilization, class struggle, or the establishment of a universal empire. In order to grasp this reality, one has to go beyond the economic, political, social, or psychological level in order to turn one's attention toward prephilosophical data that teach that "what really and in the deepest analysis happens in history is salvation and disaster" (*The End of Time*, 20 [*Werke*, Vol. 6, 292]), notions, according to Pieper, that the human being cannot avoid thinking about and even come back in the form of dreams. The philosophy of history that refuses, in principle and a priori, to consider the salvation and destruction of the human being, knowledge of which is not restricted to believers alone, can no longer say, in Pieper's eyes, that it seeks to get to the ultimate foundation of things; in other words, it thereby ceases in fact to be a philosophy in the genuine sense. The second argument rests on the fact that Revelation does not teach us what things ultimately are, but what has happened and what will happen in the historical future. The philosopher of history who wishes to be a genuine philosopher, that is, one who seeks a knowledge of history with respect to its ultimate basis, who desires to take in the whole of history in his vision and whose object is the knowledge of its ultimate state, must make reference to a pre-philosophical body of knowledge to do so.

29. Many philosophers of history defend a position similar to Pieper's. See, for example, Calderon Bouchet, *Esperanza, historia y utopia*, 9ff. and 339ff. Callot, *Les trois moments de la philosophie théologique de l'histoire*, 25, 303.

Cottier, *Histoire et connaissance de Dieu*, 104. "A philosophy of history is not for all that a bashful theology that is afraid of uttering its own name. It is a genuine philosophy, but one that recognizes above itself sources of knowledge that transcend it without calling it into question. It is significant that Hegel had reversed this relationship: according to him, the supreme and sovereign discourse is that of philosophy, while religion is subordinate to it," 254. See Kuhn, "'Veritas filia temporis.' Über die Glaubwürdigkeit der Geschichtsphilosophie," 15ff. Maritain, *On the Philosophy of History*, 41, 170f. [X, 647, 756]. For Schlegel, the philosophy of history "must be deduced from real historical events," but, without faith in Christian dogmas, "the whole history of the world would be nought else than an insoluble enigma—an inextricable labyrinth—a huge pile of the blocks and fragments of an unfinished edifice—and the great tragedy of humanity would remain devoid of all proper result." It is therefore necessary to "tacitly pre-suppose the truth of that mystery [the mystery of grace in the divine redemption of mankind]." "If we once remove this divine key-stone in the arch of universal history, the whole fabric of the world's history falls to ruin," in Schlegel, *The Philosophy of History*, 65, 277–279 (7, 227f.).

30. Pieper, *Hope and History*, 96 [*Werke*, Vol. 6, 429].

31. Newman, *An Essay in Aid of a Grammar of Assent*, 446, cited in Pieper, *The End of Time*, 40 [*Werke*, Vol. 6, 304].

32. "One finds himself challenged to conceive as concordant what initially seemed contradictory: one is supposed to regard the ultimately indecipherable, namely history, as nevertheless not inherently unintelligible or even confused; one is supposed to refrain not only from easily manageable explanatory formulas but also from agnostic resignation; one is supposed, regarding the end of history, to respect, in faith, certain trans-empirical reports that claim to reveal the future while nevertheless not actually showing it and that, while not depriving what is to come of its futurity (indeed, while even reinforcing that), nevertheless lay claim to illuminating the darkness of what lies ahead." Pieper, *Hope and History*, 98f. [*Werke*, Vol. 6, 430]. The philosopher of history who appeals to the data of prophecy, in spite of the enigmatic character inherent to it, is able, Pieper remarks, to see and to know the process of history better than one who contests the validity of prophecy. Historical events unveil relationships with the end of time to the philosopher of history's understanding. See Pieper, *The End of Time*, 38ff. [*Werke*, Vol. 6, 303ff.].

33. Ricoeur, "Hope and the Structure of Philosophical Systems," 69. See Pieper, *Hope and History*, 45 [*Werke*, Vol. 6, 397].

34. Berger, *Facing up to Modernity*, 73. See Dupré, *Passage to Modernity*, 156ff., 163.

35. See Jauss, "Ursprung und Bedeutung der Fortschrittsidee in der 'Querelle des Anciens et des Modernes.'"

36. Mackenzie, *The Nineteenth Century,* 459.

37. *Gesammelte Briefe* (Insel edition), 88, cited in Pieper, *The End of Time,* 73 [*Werke,* Vol. 6, 325].

38. See Gueroult, *L'histoire de l'histoire de la philosophie,* vol. II, 369f.

39. Ricoeur, *History and Truth,* 81 [81]. Pieper emphasizes that the rationalistic doctrine of progress, by which he means in particular the position of Kant and his conception of the kingdom of God, "rested upon a secularization of Christian theology, more precisely, of the theology of the Last Things," Pieper, *The End of Time,* 95 [*Werke,* Vol. 6, 340]. Providing references in support, he shows that Kant brought about a reversal and a secularization of the meaning of certain concepts belonging to Christianity (see also 95ff. [340ff.] and *Hope and History,* 54ff., 60f. [*Werke,* Vol. 6, 402ff., 406]). On Kant's position, see the analysis by Hirsch, *Höchstes Gut und Reich Gottes in Kants kritischen Hauptwerken als Beispiel für die Säkularisierung seiner Metaphysik,* and Weyand, *Kants Geschichtsphilosophie,* 16. This position, which Pieper adopts and which is maintained by various later studies on Kant's philosophy of history, runs counter to the interpretative opinion that Riedel offers ("Geschichtstheologie, Geschichtsideologie, Geschichtsphilosophie," 211). Riedel states that "Kant's history of philosophy does not arise out of the secularization of an older, theological-metaphysical discipline; independently of this prior form, it is properly founded only on the ground of a specifically modern understanding of history and science." Gueroult concludes, by contrast (*L'histoire de l'histoire de la philosophie,* vol. II, 353), that the philosophy of the German Enlightenment stripped the ideas of the omnipotence of reason, of development, and of progress "of their theological and metaphysical substructure; naturalism and atheism caused the disappearance of their providential character, and, if not their necessity, at least their internal necessity." See also Gueroult, "Les postulats de la philosophie dans l'histoire," 441f. Löwith, *Meaning in History* and "Vom Sinn der Geschichte," 37ff. Lübbe, *Säkularisierung. Geschichte eines ideenpolitischen Begriffs,* 34ff. Nisbert, *History of the Idea of Progress,* 172f. Cohen summarizes the transition from the Greek view of history, which was directed toward the *proton,* to the Jewish and modern view "that the modern philosophy of history springs from a fulfillment of biblical faith and that it ends with the secularization of its eschatological paradigm," (*Die Religion der Vernunft aus den Quellen des Judentums,* 11–12); in other words, belief in providence was replaced by belief in progress, and "the rationalistic thesis of history as a genuine theodicy represents a blasphemy against providence" (Cottier, *Histoire et connaissance de Dieu,* VII). "*History* is in the Greek consciousness identical with knowledge simply. Thus, history for the Greek is and remains directed only toward the past. In opposition, the prophet is the seer. . . . Their vision begot the concept of history, as the being

of the *future* . . . Time becomes future . . . and future is the eminent content
of this notion of history. . . . By means of the eschatological future, the true
historical existence on earth takes the place of a golden age lying in the mythological past," Cohen, *Religion of Reason Out of the Sources of Judaism*, 261f.
[308 and 293ff.]. See also Blumenberg, *Säkularisierung und Selbstebehauptung*
and *The Legitimacy of the Modern Age,* and the critique by Löwith,
"Besprechung des Buches *Die Legitimität der Neuzeit* von Hans Blumenberg."
Rapp, *Fortschritt*, 116–28. Baumgarteern, *Was darf ich hoffen?*, 171ff.
Baumgartner, "Die Idee des Fortschritts," 157ff. Bury, *The Idea of Progress*, 73.
Demandt, *Endzeit? Die Zukunft der Geschichte*, 34ff. Inge, *The Idea of Progress*.
Rotermundt, *Jedes Ende ist ein Anfang. Auffassungen vom Ende der Geschichte,*
5. Salomon, "The Religion of Progress." Dupré, *Passage to Modernity*. Callot
concludes his analysis of the philosophies of history of Augustine, Vico, and
Herder with the affirmation that the modern philosophy of history ends with
a "sort of rational theodicy" which "certainly represents the lowest point a
reflection on history can reach; it thereby seems quite clearly to mark the end
of this sort of speculation and, through the evacuation of any transcendence,
ultimately to coincide with the positivistic philosophy of history" (*Les trois
moments de la philosophie théologique de l'histoire. Augustin-Vico-Herder.
Situation actuelle*, 279–80). "Man removes himself from subjection to a creator
and thus makes himself, relative to his proper mode, which is historical, into
the God of this history" (356). "History which organizes itself around man as
author and no longer around God and his Providence" (364).

40. Pieper, *The End of Time*, 90–91 [*Werke*, Vol. 6, 337]. This observation
is in agreement with the one Weyand (*Kants Geschichtsphilosophie*, 16) offers
in his historical study on Kant's philosophy of history, in which he affirms that
"the new determination of the *telos* of history acquired a great significance.
The old Christian-eschatological meaning of history was replaced by a purely
immanently ordered meaning, since the new, better life was not something
one achieved only after death, but is rather already to a large extent possible
on earth. Thus, the Enlightenment carried out a secularization of the goal of
history, the significance of which cannot be overestimated; all of the subse-
quent interpretations of the philosophy of history, even into our own age, have
basically followed the example of the eighteenth century. *Progress* was the
great magic word; in the eighteenth century, history was viewed in its light."
See Baumgartner, "Die Idee des Fortschritts," 157ff. Pieper sees in the philosophy of the history of progress a "straightforwardly 'optimistic' simplification"
(*The End of Time*, 88 [*Werke*, Vol. 6, 335]) of the conception of history and
remarks that the decline of this rationalistic idea of progress produces an
"extreme pessimism" (79 [330]), which is pervasive in today's world; according to Pieper, at the root of this notion of progress, this boundless optimism

and this blind trust in Reason and Science, accompanied by the idea of Revolution, lies an attitude of despair.

41. On this subject, see Adorno, "Fortschritt." Bäumer, *Fortschritt und Theologie. Philosophische und theologische Überlegungen zum Fortschrittsgedanken.* Baumgartner, "Die Idee des Fortschritts." Bernstein, *Progress and the Quest of Meaning.* Blumenberg, *Säkularisierung und Selbstbehauptung* and *The Legitimacy of the Modern Age.* Bury, *The Idea of Progress.* Canguilhem, "La décadence de l'idée de Progrès." Cesana, *Geschichte als Entwicklung? Zur Kritik des geschichtsphilosophischen Entwicklungsdenkens.* Cottier, "Le vrai sens du progrès" and "L'inversion du progrès." Delfgaauw, *Geschichte als Fortschritt.* Delvaille, *Essai sur l'histoire de l'idée de progrès jusqu'à la fin du XVIIIième siècle.* Kuhn and Wiedemann, eds., *Die Philosophie und die Frage nach dem Fortschritt.* Lasch, *The True and Only Heaven: Progress and Its Critics.* Lübbe, *Fortschritt als Orientierungsproblem. Aufklärung in der Gegenwart.* Nisbert, *History of the Idea of Progress.* Pollard, *The Idea of Progress.* Rapp, *Fortschritt. Entwicklung und Sinngehalt einer philosophischer Idee.* Sampson, *Progress in the Age of Reason: The Seventeenth Century to the Present Day.*

42. Kant expounds his philosophy of history in several works: *Idea for a Universal History with a Cosmopolitan Intent* (1784); *An Answer to the Question: What is Enlightenment?* (1784); *Speculative Beginning of Human History* (1786); *The End of All Things* (1794); *To Perpetual Peace: A Philosophical Sketch* (1795); and *The Contest of the Faculties* (1798).

43. Kant, *Idea for a Universal History with a Cosmopolitan Intent,* 29–30 [A.B., VIII, 18].

44. Kant, *Speculative Beginning of Human History,* 53 [A.B., VIII, 115].

45. Kant, *An Answer to the Question: What is Enlightenment?,* 41 [A.B., VIII, 35].

46. "It is so easy to be immature. . . . I need not think, if only I can pay: others will readily undertake the irksome work for me. The guardians who have so benevolently taken over the supervision of men. . . . Having first made their domestic livestock dumb, and having carefully made sure that these docile creatures will not take a single step without the go-cart to which they are harnessed, these guardians then show them the danger that threatens them, should they attempt to walk alone," ibid., 41 [A.B., VIII, 35].

47. "*Thinking for one's self* is to seek the chief touchstone of truth in one's self (*id est,* in one's own reason); and the maxim, to think for one's self at all times, is ENLIGHTENMENT," Kant, *What Means, to Orient Oneself in Thinking?,* 407 (fn.) [A.B., VIII, 146].

48. See Yovel, *Kant and the Philosophy of History,* 137ff., 175ff.

49. Ibid., 135. On Kant's Copernican revolution, see Vlachos, *La pensée politique de Kant,* 98–131.

50. Kant denies that the notion of progress can be applied to language, biology, or technology, since he accepts progress only in morality, a conception that follows from the *Critique of Pure Reason*. See Philonenko, "L'idée de progrès chez Kant." Pieper (*The End of Time*, 92 [*Werke*, Vol. 6, 338]) dwells at length on Kant's position because he is the most important representative of this current of thought, one who is capable of expressing the concept of progress in an intelligent and nuanced manner, and above all because he has had a considerable influence, both directly and indirectly, on contemporary thinking.

51. See Kant, *To Perpetual Peace: A Philosophical Sketch*, 107 [A.B., VIII, 343].

52. See Kant, *The Contest of the Faculties*, 189 [A.B., VII, 93].

53. See Kant, *Idea for a Universal History with a Cosmopolitan Intent*, 33–34 [A.B., VIII, 23].

54. This theme is not new in his writings; he already addressed it in 1793 in the third paragraph of *On the Proverb: That may be True in Theory, but is of no Practical Use*, 85 [A.B., VIII, 307], in which he asks whether there exist "in human nature dispositions that authorize one to conclude that the species is progressing constantly toward a better state."

55. Kant here reaffirms one of the theses of his pragmatic anthropology, which he elaborated in the *Idea for a Universal History with a Cosmopolitan Intent* (1784). After having posited as certain the principle of a teleological nature, according to which the natural dispositions of every being are ordered to their fulfillment, Kant affirms that, in what concerns the human being, the natural dispositions, which have the use of reason as their goal, and thus serve to distinguish the human being from the animals, are only fully developed in the species and not in the individual (see *Idea for a Universal History with a Cosmopolitan Intent*, 28–29 [A.B., VIII, 18–19]). The historical individual is always imperfect with respect to the species, for he is fundamentally limited by obstacles such as sickness or death. He forms a cog in the ascent of humanity toward the supreme good; in other words, it is not the individual, but rather the species, that attains its destination. This separation of the individual person from the process of the history of humanity occurred under the influence of Ferguson. Kant continues by affirming in a second proposition that nature created the human being in such a precise way that everything the human being does not share in common with the animals is something he must develop by himself. A third anthropological premise is the insociable sociability of the human being, or the antagonism of the human being in society—that is, his "tendency to enter into society, combined, however, with a thoroughgoing resistance that constantly threatens to sunder this society" (32 [A.B., VIII, 20]).

56. "The human race is either in continually *regressing* and deteriorating, continually *progressing* and improving, or at a permanent *standstill,* in relation to other created beings, at its present level of moral attainment (which is the same as continually revolving in a circle around a fixed point)," Kant, *The Contest of the Faculties,* 178 [A.B., VII, 81]. Pieper raises this question at the beginning of *Hope and History,* 13 [*Werke,* Vol. 6, 376] and *The End of Time,* 97 [*Werke,* Vol. 6, 341].

57. Kant, *The Contest of the Faculties,* 180 [A.B., VII, 83].

58. Kant takes a distance here from his work *Idea of a Universal History From the Cosmopolitan Perspective* (written thirteen years earlier) in which he does not give much credit to the signs that disclose a certain progress in history. He refers to an "idea of reason" that rests on the assumption that the natural human capacity is going to develop completely (which is something one might call into question), that is, human reason is destined to make progress. Promoting such a development requires a social and political structure, which is the goal of a plan hidden in nature. He thus concludes that one may reasonably accept the notion that history is progressing. "One can regard the history of the human species, in the large, as the realization of a hidden plan of nature to bring about an internally, and for this purpose, also an externally perfect national constitution, as the sole state in which all of humanity's natural capacities can be developed" (*Idea for a Universal History with a Cosmopolitan Intent,* 36 [A.B., VIII, 27]), adding that "philosophy also has its chiliastic vision." Apart from this reference to a natural teleology, Kant appeals to a practical reasoning: to the extent that the human being lives according to this "idea of reason," he contributes to the realization of progress. The human being thus has the moral obligation to act in such a way that the future will be better than the present, to act so that the natural capacity of human reason reach a better development.

59. Kant, *The Contest of the Faculties,* 181 [A.B., VII, 84].

60. "In human affairs, there must be some experience or other which, as an event which has actually occurred, might suggest that man has the quality or power of being the *cause* and (since his actions are supposed to be those of a being endowed with freedom) the *author* of his own improvement. But an event can be predicted as the effect of a given cause only when the circumstances which help to shape it actually arise. And while it can well be predicted in general that these circumstances must arise at some time or another (as in calculating probabilities in games of chance), it is impossible to determine whether this will happen during my lifetime, and whether I shall myself experience it and thus be able to confirm the original prediction," ibid., 181 [A.B., VII, 84].

61. Ibid., 181–182 [A.B., VII, 84–85].

62. Ibid., 182 [A.B., VII, 85].

63. On Kant's relation to the French Revolution, see Weyand, *Kants Geschichtsphilosophie,* 186–91. Burg, "Kants Deutung der Französischen Revolution im 'Streit der Fakultäten.'" Fetscher, "Immanuel Kant und die Französische Revolution."

64. Kant, *The Contest of the Faculties,* 182 [A.B., VII, 85].

65. Ibid., 184 [A.B., VII, 88].

66. Ibid., 185 [A.B., VII, 88]. Pieper discusses *The Contest of the Faculties* in *The End of Time,* 97–101 [*Werke,* Vol. 6, 342–43]; *Hope and History,* 56–59 [*Werke,* Vol. 6, 403–5]; "Dialog the End of Time," 15–20.

67. Kant employs the verb "to prove" twice: *The Contest of the Faculties,* 181 [A.B., VII, 84], and 182 [A.B., VII, 85].

68. There exists a parallel between the historical fact of the French Revolution and the revolution in thinking provoked by the *Critique of Pure Reason,* and also the Kantian program of *Aufklärung.* Both express, indeed, a revolutionary turning both on the historical level and also on the level of the history of thought (the Copernican revolution), which brings the human being from the *status naturalis* to the *status civilis.* Heine wrote in 1835 (*Zur Geschichte der Religion und Philosophie in Deutschland,* in Kaufmann, ed., *Sämtliche Werke,* Munich, 1964, vol. IX, 236) that "in the same year (namely, 1781), there appeared in Königsberg the '*Critique of Pure Reason*' by Immanuel Kant. With this book, . . . an intellectual revolution began in Germany, which offers the most peculiar analogies with the material revolution in France." Cited in Brandt, "Zum 'Streit der Fakultäten,'" 39. Proust (*Kant et le ton de l'histoire,* 10) observes that, "once it appeared in Germany, the *Critique of Pure Reason* was understood as the opportunity for a beginning of history and thought. Fichte hails it as "an incomparably more important" revolution than the French Revolution. Hölderlin sees Kant as the "Moses of our nation." Each hears in the *Critique* the starting pistol not so much of a new thought as of a *first* thought. Kant is not only considered to be the first German philosopher, he is read as the philosopher of a nation to come, a nation in the process of being born."

69. In the light of the third anthropological presupposition presented in *Idea of a Universal History From the Cosmopolitan Perspective,* that of insociable sociability, Kant addresses the origin of wars: the affirmation of each State toward the other States. To the extent that the danger of war among diverse nations is not eliminated by the establishment of a world confederation, no State will be able to enjoy total freedom. Just as the evil of associability has led human beings to make an association of States, a grouping together of sovereign States, it will also lead to the elimination of wars. The direction of history, in Kant's eyes, which takes a decisive turn in the French Revolution, suggests the establishment of a Society of Nations, a world federation of States of right

and justice which will guarantee complete freedom, coupled with an eternal peace, allowing, as I have already noted, the fulfillment of human dispositions.

70. Yovel explains that "the cunning of nature is only a vehicle of *political* progress and of the rise of external 'civilization,' not of history in the moral sense; . . . ever since the Enlightenment–with philosophers (that is Kant) deciphering a 'hidden plan of nature' corresponding to the ideal of practical reason, the cunning of nature is no longer an *exclusive* vehicle of progress even in politics, but makes way to the complementary principle of conscious praxis" (*Kant and the Philosophy of History*, 141). Yovel summarizes his interpretation of Kant's philosophy of history by stating that "the origin of historical progress is seen to reside in the action of man, both as a rational being and as a free agent transcending nature; as a free being he advances, at least ever since the Enlightenment, to realize his internal and external freedom through conscious intention. The goal of historical progress is the highest good, built as a synthesis of two systems, internal and external. The former, the ethical community, totalizes the relations of morality proper, as subjective interpersonal dispositions; as such it is also called an invisible church and the kingdom of ends. The latter, the political community, is an analogue of the moral totality in the world of external institution; it includes a world confederation of states, each having a constitution of civil society; and it is based upon labor, technology (the manipulation of nature), property, and rational jurisprudence" 194–96.

71. Ibid., 31. "(a) The highest good is no longer a separate, transcendent world, but becomes the consummate state of *this* world, to be realized through a concrete development in time. (b) The progressive power of history is ascribed not only to a hidden 'cunning of *nature,*' but also to the conscious work of practical *reason.* And (c) the concept of happiness loses its central position and is replaced by nature in general as the empirical component of the highest good. . . . History is the process in which the highest good should be realized, and in which the free, formative activity of practical reason remolds the given world into a new, moral world. . . . History is thus the process where the required 'synthesis' of freedom and nature should occur. . . . Thus the ideas of the highest good and history, far from being marginal, become the systematic apex of Kant's whole critical endeavor. True, the historical meaning of the highest good is not the only one, but it is the most comprehensive and includes if not 'sublates' all the others," ibid., 30–32. See also his analysis of the sovereign good as an idea of history, 29–80.

72. See Kant, *Religion Within the Limits of Reason Alone,* 122 [A.B., VI, 131].

73. According to Yovel, "the task is to establish the 'kingdom of God on earth'–a metaphor that expresses the secular moral idea implied in the sovereign good," in *Kant and the Philosophy of History,* 7. Regarding Kant's position,

he concludes (172) that "the ethical community transposes the religious ideal of the kingdom of God on earth into its secularized equivalent, founded by man's autonomous reason." See also Habichler, *Reich Gottes als Thema des Denkens bei Kant,* which affirms that the idea of the "kingdom of God" in Kant "is almost a 'cryptical' thought, which always emerges very discretely only on the 'surfaces' of this thinking, but which, secretly, has become a very decisive vector in Kant's philosophy" (13). Hirsch, *Höchstes Gut und Reich Gottes in Kants Kritischen Hauptwerken als Beispiel für die Säkularisierung seiner Metaphysik.* Viviano, *The Kingdom of God in History,* 102, 122, 150. Maritain, *On the Philosophy of History,* 150ff. [X, 739ff.].

74. Kant, *Religion Within the Limits of Reason Alone,* 113 [A.B., VI, 122]. After having been rejected by the Berlinischen Monatsschrift, the work from which the citation is drawn (*The Triumph of the Good Principle Over the Evil One and the Foundation of a Kingdom of God on Earth,* a work composed in 1792), appears in the third part of the *Religion Within the Limits of Reason Alone.* In this text, Kant reverses the original meaning of one of the most fundamental notions of the New Testament for the sake of an argument that Pieper calls "crudely rationalistic." This latter continues, affirming that, in Kant's argumentation, one looks reasonably "in surprise at this shallow and over-hasty misinterpretation of the enigma of history," Pieper, *The End of Time,* 97 [*Werke,* Vol. 6, 341].

75. Kant, *The Contest of the Faculties,* 189–190 [A.B., VII, 93–94].

76. Pieper, *The End of Time,* 100f., 104ff. [*Werke,* Vol. 6, 342, and 345f.].

77. One of Kant's expressions, cited in Pieper, *The End of Time,* 105 [Kösel edition, 121].

78. Freud, *Unbehagen in der Kultur,* 270. See Lorenz's reaction in this regard, "Die Hoffnung auf Einsicht in das Wirken der Natur," 147–48.

79. Freud, *Der Mann Moses und die monotheistische Religion,* 503.

80. I presented this thesis in chapter five.

81. Cited in Cuénot, *Pierre Teilhard de Chardin,* 316.

82. Pieper, *The End of Time,* 33 [*Werke,* Vol. 6, 300]; see Pieper, *Hope and History,* 33 [*Werke,* Vol. 6, 389], and "Hoffnung und Geschichte," 14–15.

83. Pieper, *Hope and History,* 40 [*Werke,* Vol. 6, 394]. Lopez-Mendez (*Die Hoffnung im theologischen Denken Teilhard de Chardin,* 179ff.) seeks by all possible means to save Teilhard's position by insisting that he has not confused evolution and history. While admitting that Teilhard is not always sufficiently precise in his writings, and that on occasion he gives too radical an emphasis to his positions, such that it may appear that he confuses evolution and history, Lopez tries in spite of everything, by appealing to Teilhard's theology and by offering various, and not very convincing, arguments, to show that he is right. See Bravo, *La vision de l'histoire chez Teilhard de Chardin,* 365ff., 390ff. and Baudry, *Les grands axes de l'eschatologie teilhardienne,* 10–16.

84. Teilhard de Chardin, *The Human Phenomenon,* 221 [341].

85. We find this thesis, which states that evil will grow over the course of history in tandem with the good, also in the work of Maritain (*On the Philosophy of History,* 10, 42ff. [X, 621, 649ff.]), with his law of contrasting, two-sided progress.

86. Teilhard de Chardin, *The Human Phenomenon,* 207 [321]; see also *The Appearance of Man,* 168ff. [231ff.], and *The Future of Man,* 301f. [393f.].

87. Teilhard de Chardin, *The Human Phenomenon,* 207 [322].

88. Teilhard de Chardin, *The Activation of Energy,* 321 [335].

89. Teilhard de Chardin, *The Human Phenomenon,* 221 [341].

90. Ibid., 197, 195ff. [307, 304ff.].

91. Ibid., 161 [255].

92. Ibid., 196 [306].

93. Teilhard de Chardin, *The Future of Man,* 232 [299].

94. Ibid.

95. Teilhard de Chardin, *The Human Energy,* 153 [190], cited in Rideau, *La pensée du Père Teilhard de Chardin,* 146, fn. 52.

96. Lorenz, "Die Hoffnung auf Einsicht in das Wirken der Natur," 159.

97. Lorenz, *On Aggression,* 299 [258–59]. Pieper discusses Lorenz's position in *Hope and History,* 17, 40, 63f. [*Werke,* Vol. 6, 379, 394, 408f.].

98. It is worth keeping in mind the fact that Bloch nevertheless considers the real possibility that the dialectical process will not attain its end in the second version of *The Spirit of Utopia* (1923).

99. Nietzsche, *Ecce homo,* 327 [VI, 366]. Kopf (*Der Weg des Nihilismus von Friedrich Nietzsche bis zum Atombombe,* 13) claims that nihilism has been the dominant theme of the past century, a nihilism that is "about to actualize itself universally. It has now indeed become the epoch-defining event, as Nietzsche said it would be." See Leist, *Existenz im Nichts,* 166. Rauschning, *Masken und Metamorphosen des Nihilismus,* 129. Jannoud, *Au rendez-vous du nihilisme,* 25. Anders (*Die Antiquierheit des Menschen,* Vol. I, 304ff.) observes that the apocalyptic symbols of annihilation–the atomic bomb and philosophical nihilism–come together in a symbiosis that he calls a "syndrome."

100. Nietzsche, *Will to Power* [*Gesammelte Werke,* Vol. XVIII, 48], cited in Pieper, *In Tune with the World,* 61 [*Werke,* Vol. 6, 279]. Nietzsche also maintains "the belief that everything deserves to perish" (*The Will to Power,* vol. I, 22, cited in Pieper, *The End of Time,* 60 [*Werke,* Vol. 6, 317]).

101. Nietzsche, *Ecce homo,* 309 [VI, 349].

102. "That the destruction of the world . . . in a global war of annihilation, is not feared as an unspeakable calamity, but anticipated as something to be desired, even 'celebrated' as ordinarily only affirmations can be. Thus destruction becomes 'antifestival,'" Pieper, *In Tune with the World,* 62 [*Werke,* Vol. 6, 281–82].

103. See Pieper, *The End of Time*, 60 [*Werke*, Vol. 6, 317].

104. See Klima, *Le monde comme conscience et comme rien.*

105. "On the practical means of carrying out this euthanasia, Wolfson is particularly eloquent: we could, for example, program an explosion for a particular date. That would, of course, have to be carried out under international surveillance. The population would be witnesses of their own annihilation, watching it on huge screens: for once, even drugged out or doped up, we would be the authors of our own destiny. And even this damned planet, this cadaver-factory would be wiped out, after having finally been freed from its parasites. Then something wonderful would happen, something that is described in the Bible: 'There will be no more death, no more suffering, no more lamenting, no more pain, for everything that has existed until now will exist no more' (Rev 21:4)," Jaccard, *La tentation nihiliste*, 107–8.

106. "Let all form become formless . . . in a gigantic maelstrom. Let there be tremendous commotion and noise, terror, and explosion, and then let there be eternal silence and total and total forgetfulness," Cioran, *On the Heights of Despair*, 52f. [103–4]; see also 20, 54 [40, 106].

107. Jaccard, *La tentation nihiliste*, 9.

108. Ibid., 60.

109. On the relationship between boredom and despair, see chapter four.

110. See Pieper, *The End of Time*, 59f. [*Werke*, Vol. 6, 316].

111. See Pieper, *About Love*, 47ff. [*Werke*, Vol. 4, 342ff.].

112. See Anders, *Die atomare Drohung*, 93.

113. See Aquinas, *Quaestiones disputatae de Potentia Dei*, 5, 4, ad6. *Commentary on the Sentences*, 4, d.46, I, 3 ad6.

114. See Arendt, "Der Nihilismus-Ursprung und Geschichte im Spiegel der Forschungs-Literatur seit 1945," and *Der Nihilismus als Phänomen der Geistesgeschichte in der wissenschaftliche Diskussion unseres Jahrunderts.* Kopf, *Der Weg des Nihilismus von Friedrich Nietzsche bis zur Atombombe.* Hawoll, *Nihilismus und Metaphysik.* Leist, *Existenz im Nichts.* Penzo, *Il nihilismo da Nietzsche a Sartre.* Rauschning, *Masken und Metamorphosen des Nihilismus.* Vattimo, *The End of Modernity.*

115. "Creavit enim Deus ut essent omnia . . . , non ut in nihilum cederunt," in Aquinas, *Questiones quodlibetales*, 4, 3, 4 (and Wisdom 1:14), cited in Pieper, *The End of Time*, 63 [*Werke*, Vol. 6, 319]. Pieper already refers to this citation in 1935 (*On Hope*, 19 [*Werke*, Vol. 4, 261]) in order to counter the nihilist position.

116. Pieper, *The End of Time*, 67 [*Werke*, Vol. 6, 321]. A few lines above, he explains that "The proposition that 'there is no End in the absolute sense' can be legitimately laid down only on the basis of the concept of *creatio,* or rather on the basis of the belief that everything which is, is either *Creator* or *creatura,* and the human reality a creaturely reality. And all the dimensions of

the concept *creatura* must be held in view. If one were to see only the *vertibilitas ad nihilim*, the proximity to nothingness, one would be more likely to come, on the contrary, to the conclusion that there may very well be, indeed there must be, a total annihilation of this 'decaying existence'; this is the natural end of the creature. This strange notion of 'creatureliness,' from which the idea of the Creator is excluded, is, as we know, characteristic of one sector of existential philosophy. The full concept of creatureliness includes the provenance from the being-creating power of the Creator, who holds the *creatura* above nothingness with such an absolute strength of realization that this urge, to be, becomes simply identical with the inmost nature of the created entity. On the other hand, therefore, it must be seen, no, believed, that God has created things 'that they might be,'" 66–67 [321].

117. See Aquinas, *Summa theologiae,* I, 106, 6. *Quaestiones disputatae de potentia,* 5, 4.

118. Ibid., 5, 1, obj.16 (*On the Power of God,* vol. 2, 79) cited in Pieper, *On Hope,* 19 [*Werke,* Vol. 4, 261–62]. See Aquinas, *Summa contra gentiles,* II, 30.

119. Cortès, 4 May 1849, cited in Pieper, *The End of Time,* 75 [*Werke,* Vol. 6, 327].

120. See Nietzsche, *Gesammelte Werke,* Musarion-Ausgabe (Munich, 1922) Vol. XVI, 401, cited in Pieper, *Hope and History,* 104 [*Werke,* Vol. 6, 434].

121. Nietzsche, *Beyond Good and Evil,* part 8: "Peoples and Fatherlands," fr. 242, 176–77 [Vol. V, 182–83].

122. Häcker, *Vergil: Vater des Abendlandes,* epigraph (cited in Pieper, *The End of Time,* 76 [*Werke,* Vol. 6, 327]).

123. Rauschning, *Time of Delirium,* 47 [63].

124. Pieper draws a connection between a global totalitarianism and the "reign of the Antichrist," a typical and traditional designation in Western historical thought, which is based on a revelation, namely, of the final end of history. While this notion may be disorienting, the image it contains has, for Pieper, something familiar to the contemporary human being, who never refers to it. I am not going to enter into Pieper's presentation and discussion of this notion (which in any event is theological), which draws primarily on Thomas Aquinas and Soloviev. On this subject, see Pieper, *The End of Time* [*Werke,* Vol. 6, 352–68, 312, 315]; *Hope and History,* 104f. [*Werke,* Vol. 6, 434–35]; "Die Verborgenheit von Hoffnung und Verzweiflung," 174; "Über die Kunst, nicht zu verzweifeln," 206; "Sur l'Espérance des Martyrs," 78ff. For Cioran (*History and Utopia,* 41 [73]), it seems that the moment has come for humanity, which has been dispersed, to gather together "under the guardianship of one pitiless shepherd, a kind of planetary monster before whom the nations will prostrate themselves." There is certain to come a "grand-scale despot who will succeed in unifying the world" (42 [74–75]), a despot of whom Stalin and Hitler were

merely precursors. "[Our world] which is heading straight for a much more considerable tyranny than the one rampant in the first centuries of our era, which will be considerably different from that which raged in the first centuries of our era. . . . [The] vision . . . of the coming tyranny strikes me as so decisively apparent that it seems unworthy to attempt to demonstrate its well-foundedness. . . . No, I am not extravagant," 54–55 [93–94].

125. See also Huntington, *The clash of civilizations and the remaking of world order,* and his thesis of multi-polar hegemonies.

126. Huxley, *Brave New World Revisited,* 3.

127. Ibid., 4.

128. See Pieper, *The End of Time,* 78, 82, 117, 152 [*Werke,* Vol. 6, 329, 332, 352, 373]; "Die Verborgenheit von Hoffnung und Verzweiflung," 173; "Hoffnung und Geschichte," 21; "Sur l'Espérance des Martyrs," 82f.; "Über die Kunst, nicht zu verzweifeln," 184, 209. Maritain (*On the Philosophy of History,* 138, 162 [X, 728, 749]) also alludes to the theory of the transposition of time into the nontemporal.

129. This idea is also defended by Callot, Cottier, Maritain, Scherer, and Bovis.

130. Pieper, *The End of Time,* 152 [*Werke,* Vol. 6, 373]; see "Sur l'Espérance des Martyrs," 84. Pieper explains, by referring to the true story of two Tibetans that were found after the Second World War in a German prisoner camp in the United States, who were forced to fight with the Russian army, that these two human beings, who did not know what was happening during the war, did not despair, because they entrusted themselves to a meaning of history that was hidden and mysterious to their understanding, a meaning that was founded on their ancestral religious tradition. Pieper thus explains that "This is as indubitable as that the most extensive knowledge of concrete history, the most brilliant cultural-sociological analysis of Roman law, of the Dutch group portrait, or even of the contemporary constellation of world politics, *without* this conviction of an, in some way, absolutely guaranteed meaning of history as a whole, is *not* capable of affording this inner sense of position and direction. This comparison does not concern pious generalities. Rather can the superiority of the man who believes (even if he does not know) over the unbeliever (even if he knows) be very precisely identified, for instance in those extreme situations which history again and again holds ready for man: a superiority expressed as inner inviolability, as the capacity, above all, not to despair," *The End of Time,* 45 [*Werke,* Vol. 6, 307–8].

CONCLUSION

The philosophical analysis of human hope—in both its forms, as *espoir* and as fundamental *espérance*—presupposes an anthropology and an ontology. In contrast to the understanding conveyed by various philosophical traditions, which assume that human nature has to be *either* static *or* dynamic, Pieper conceives of human Dasein as a dialectic between a human nature that is given, namely, one that implies a *minimal-being*, and this nature's (both free and determined) ordering to its completion and fulfillment, that is, to its *full-being*. The German philosopher thus distinguishes his position from that of Sartre, insofar as he affirms a notion of human nature endowed with specific determinations at the first instant of existence (essence precedes existence), which is ordered toward the final goal that forms the object of fundamental hope. For Sartre, the object of fundamental hope is determined by freedom, while for Pieper it is determined by the inclination of human nature. Nevertheless, the two philosophers agree in viewing hope as the principle of a free action undertaken for the realization or the possession of a freely chosen good.

Pieper also distinguishes his position from that of Bloch by denying that the nature of human Dasein lies in the future. Indeed, according to Pieper, essence is not that which does not yet exist; in other words, the essence does not await its coming into being. Instead, the essence already exists from the very first moment of the existence of a *res*. For Pieper, this *minimal-being* that constitutes human Dasein is nevertheless characterized by an openness to what is to come, a future in which it realizes its possibilities. The human being is not immobile, but he is compelled to move continually forward into the future. Such a coming-to-be, which a philosophy of hope must necessarily take into account, presupposes the dimension of time, within which the human being is projected. Without temporality, the human being would no longer be "en route," and thus would no longer hope.

Homo viator, by virtue of his freedom and/or external events, is at the same time an *animal insecurum* with respect to the actual fulfillment of his being and/or his chosen projects. A philosophical analysis of hope thus lies at the heart of an ontological dynamism of the *not-yet-being*. In connection to the person, this dynamism is characterized by the categories of both determination (insofar as it concerns the *ontological* hope that expresses the human being's or animal's innate inclination toward the possible future) and freedom (insofar as it concerns a *metaphysical* hope). Hope constitutes the mainspring of human existence en route. It is the virtue of the *not-yet*; its motive force is the natural desire for the full actualization and fulfillment of the person and the community, and it has its roots in an anthropology in which the subject is a creature that suffers from a lack, a creature that hungers, as Bloch has so clearly shown. Hope is the human being's response to the potential reality of its existence, a response that is constituted by an openness to the actualization of its possibilities, be they free or determined. Hope is the entelechy of the ongoing development of the person, of history, and of the community. To cease to move ahead would mean to become static, to shrivel up and no longer live fully.

Although Pieper devotes considerable attention to the anthropological and ontological foundations of a philosophy of hope, he spends surprisingly little time studying the characteristics of hope. He focuses his analysis of the nature of hope more on the important distinction between ordinary and fundamental hope, making allusion to Landsberg, Marcel, and Plügge, and on hope's status as a virtue (that is, whether it is a natural or a theological virtue). The difference between the two forms of human hope and their corresponding objects strikes me as crucial; it finds support in the great majority of philosophers of hope. However, I distance myself to some extent from Pieper's thesis that the virtue of hope exists only as a theological virtue. I contend that it is reasonable to speak of a natural virtue of hope, which stands alongside the passion of hope described by Hume, Bloch, and Pieper.

Human hope (both ordinary and fundamental) is an intentional movement that presupposes an act of (perceptual and cognitional) consciousness of a good, in which the subject has an interest, but that is difficult to attain. Being "difficult" means that it lies beyond the facile exercise or the natural playing out of an activity, and thus demands of the individual a particular, and even exceptional, effort. It is always accompanied by *at least some degree of certainty* and *confidence* in the real possibility of attaining its object. We do not hope for something we are absolutely certain a priori we will never be able to possess. This being said, human hope also implies a leap, since it is the case that we do not know with total certainty (insofar as total certainty would transform hope into knowledge) whether we will truly attain the good in question; this uncertainty is due as much to external factors as to factors internal to the subject, the ultimate roots of which are existential uncertainty and human freedom. Hope draws its "certainty" either from a confidence in natural human faculties (a trust that they are capable through their own natural movement of attaining the good toward which the individual strives), or from a calculation of the more or less reliable probabilities of the future contingency, probabilities that can be assessed just as well by the virtue of prudence. The certainty of fundamental hope is rooted in the natural inclination of the human will toward the possession of the *summum bonum* (variously understood); it is also rooted in a metaphysics of being and of the good, which implies a fundamental trust in being, an assent to the whole of reality, in which love, gift, and fidelity play a primordial role. In addition, human hope presupposes a *desire* that is capable of finding fulfillment, that is, of attaining its object. It is also accompanied by an expectant *waiting* that is focused on a good, on something pleasurable or useful, which thus stands in contrast, on the one hand, to a longing for something bad or indifferent, and on the other hand, to *fear*, that is, the representation of a harmful or threatening evil that lies in the future. Hope implies, moreover, at least some degree of *love*, understood as concupiscence or friendship; this latter, with its attendant notions of gift, trust, openness, receptivity, and fidelity, is the basis of an interpersonal relation between an I and a thou, which are synthesized in a we: human hope is "choral," as Marcel put it.

Trust in contingent objects and events, in humanity as it marches toward its fatherland, in oneself and in another, and more fundamentally the *basic trust* inscribed in the depths of the person, without which existence would be impossible, has the function of providing the dynamic impulse for human hope, even if it does not constitute its essence. Trust entails a certain risk; it expresses itself by a bold leap, by a trusting attitude that abandons itself to things or events as they pass, or into the hands of someone who has the power to bring about the difficult good and the hoped-for possibility. Fundamental hope (which is linked to freedom) does not lie within the order of a prospect possessing a degree of reliability calculable by reason, concerning what is empirically possible or probable; rather, it involves a "superrational" moment, which eludes all planning, mastery, or attempts to possess the future; it constitutes a *response* to being, an absolute, trusting surrender that places no condition or limit on itself, a surrender that draws its strength from an ontology of interpersonality.

The analysis of the characteristics of human hope and of the distinction between hope and fundamental hope in turn raises the question of their opposites, namely, *common despair (les désespoirs)* and *despair (le désespoir)*. On the one hand, as the negative correlate to ordinary hope, there is the *despair of common or daily life*. This has many quite variegated and at times superficial objects, which are determined and constituted by Dasein's temporality; these frustrations may occur at the thwarting of a hope (which yields to a disappointment that affects the subject to varying degrees), or they may arise when an individual gives up the pursuit of a desired good. On the other hand, there is *despair*, which is the negative correlate of fundamental hope, and has a single object, one that deals a "fatal blow" to the very foundations of existence. It comes about as the result of a free and rational choice, occurring within a determinate moment of time. Despair is choosing to reject possibilities that are in principle realizable, and to do so a priori, before they are experienced; it insists that everything will turn out poorly, that what waits at the end is an absurd nothingness and that it is impossible for any individual and/or humanity as a whole one day to find fulfillment. Like a living death, it rejects the ontology of becoming, which implies an openness and a trust with respect to the future and which projects possibilities that can be brought about through *praxis* and through gift. Despair replaces the ontology of becoming with an ontology of *no-longer-being*, which is static, closed, and without a future, an ontology that has been emptied of the category of possibility. One can have fundamental hope and at the same time a multitude of common despairs, which affect existence only superficially; but fundamental hope is directly opposed to fundamental despair. As for this latter, it may coexist with many hopes, hiding itself either consciously or unconsciously behind a certain optimism.

A philosophy of hope thus eventually runs up against the question of death, which remains, according to Bloch, "the anti-utopia *par excellence*" confronting the human being, since the human being is a rational animal who projects himself and is projected toward the future of possibilities, and death constitutes, as Sartre grasped so well, the brutal cessation of this projection. If death were the final end of the existence of the person, it would undermine the hope principle, as both Pieper and Bloch saw, reducing it to a natural striving that fails to keep its promises, to a beautiful, but groundless, idea. Pieper does not discuss hope only at the level of personal death, as Bloch does. Rather, opening a whole new dimension, he deepens his analysis to the level of the death of humanity. Pieper seeks to think through a way to bring together personal hope and collective or historical hope. Doing so, he provides a contrast both to optimism and the philosophy of progress and to the mind-set that proclaims a despair principle at the heart of existence and history.

Although Bloch has made significant contributions to our understanding of the act of hope by drawing on the notions of hunger, possibility, obscure consciousness, the *not-yet*, and utopia, he nevertheless refuses to deal with the real possibility of the death of humanity. And although he tries to found a philosophy of hope on the transcendence of death by means of the subject's full identification with the collective consciousness, the latter cannot be transcended if what is at issue is the possible self-destruction of humanity. The "crossing over" that characterizes all thought ("Thinking means venturing beyond,"[1] Bloch insists) does not become actual in Bloch's own thought, except within the confines of temporality and thus of history.

One may wonder, given the possibility of the death of both the person and the species, whether there is a reason for hope: What reason would justify the conviction that the fundamentally hoped-for object, for both the person and the community, will be attained in spite of death? Conversely, one could also ask what reason exists for fundamental despair, or for the optimism of the philosophers of progress; one may wonder what justification *these* have. Pieper seeks to give a constructive response to the metaphysics of despair and of the nothing, which we find, he maintains, not only in nihilism and atheistic existentialism, but also disguised within the philosophy of progress. To do so, he proposes an answer that is neither rationalistic nor fideistic, but which forces the philosopher, when faced with the enigma of reality, to choose between two attitudes: he may either respect and admire it, or deny and reject it.

A philosophy of hope must choose between two metaphysics: a metaphysics of the nothing, in which being is an evil that is condemned to return to the nothing that is prior to being, or a metaphysics of being. Moreover, it entails a choice between a metaphysics of transcendence without transcendence, in which the whole of reality is imprisoned within mere temporality and in which the future is conceived solely in historical terms, and a metaphysics in which the immanent and historical dimension of reality is open to a transcendence with transcendence, that is, to the transhistorical and atemporal dimension of reality.

Reason for hope can be based either on a faith in human beings and their moral sense, that is, on a trust that the moral strength of humanity will prevent people from projecting the human species into suicide (though contemporary history has taught us that progress in science is not necessarily accompanied by moral progress), or it can be based on trust in the wholly Other, who, in spite of the bad choices that human beings may make that could end in catastrophe, will keep watch to ensure that humanity reaches its final destiny through a transfiguration of temporality into atemporality. Pieper's philosophy of hope rests upon an ontology that presupposes the subject-object relation, it rests upon an ontology of interpersonality and upon a metaphysics of being and of the gift, which implies on the part of the human being a loving assent to the whole of reality, an openness and a disponibility—in short, the free and trusting affirmation of the existence of an absolute Thou.

NOTE

1. Bloch, *The Principle of Hope*, 4 [2].

BIBLIOGRAPHY

I. JOSEF PIEPER

1. Books

About Love. Translated by Richard and Clara Winston. Chicago: Franciscan Herald Press, 1974. [*Über die Liebe.* München: Kösel, 1987. In vol. 4 of *Werke,* edited by Bertold Wald, 296–414. Hamburg: Felix Meiner Verlag, 1996.]

Abuse of Language, Abuse of Power. Translated by Lothar Krauth. San Francisco: Ignatius Press, 1988. [*Missbrauch der Sprache, Missbrauch der Macht.* Ostfildern bei Stuttgart: Schwabenverlag, 1988. In vol. 6 of *Werke,* edited by Bertold Wald, 132–51. Hamburg: Felix Meiner Verlag, 1999.]

Alles Glück ist Liebesglück. Selbstlosigkeit und/oder Glücksverlangen in der Liebe. Hamburg: Katholische Akademie Hamburg, 1992.

Arbeit, Freizeit, Musse–Was ist eine Universität? Akademische Reden und Beiträge (4). Schriftenreihe der Westfälischen Wilhelms–Universität Münster. Münster: Regensburg und Biermann Verlag, 1989.

Arbeit–Freizeit–Musse. Münster: Schriftenreihe der Industrie und Handelskammer Münster, 1983.

Auskunft über die Tugenden. Zürich: Verlag der Arche, 1970.

Belief and Faith: A Philosophical Tract. Translated by Richard and Clara Winston. New York: Pantheon Books, 1963. [*Über den Glauben. Ein philosophischer Traktat.* München: Kösel, 1967. In vol. 4 of *Werke,* edited by Bertold Wald, 198–255. Hamburg: Felix Meiner Verlag, 1996.]

Buchstabier-Übungen. Aufsätze, Reden, Notizen. München: Kösel, 1980.

Christenfibel. München: Kösel, 1979.

The Concept of Sin. Translated by Edward T. Oakes. South Bend: St. Augustine, 2001. [*Über den Begriff der Sünde.* München: Kösel, 1977. In vol. 5 of *Werke,* edited by Bertold Wald, 207–79. Hamburg: Felix Meiner Verlag, 1997.]

Das Viergespann. Klugheit–Gerechtigkeit–Tapferkeit–Mass. München: Kösel, 1977. In vol. 4 of *Werke,* edited by Bertold Wald, 1–197. Hamburg: Felix Meiner Verlag, 1996.

Death and Immortality. Translated by Richard and Clara Winston. South Bend, Ind.: St. Augustine, 2000. [*Tod und Unsterblichkeit.* München: Kösel, 1979. In vol. 5 of *Werke,* edited by Bertold Wald, 280–392. Hamburg: Felix Meiner Verlag, 1997.]

Eine Geschichte wie ein Strahl. Autobiographische Aufzeichnungen seit 1964. München: Kösel, 1988.

Enthusiasm and Divine Madness: On the Platonic Dialogue Phaedrus. Translated by Richard and Clara Winston. New York: Harcourt, 1964. [*Begeisterung und göttlicher Wahnsinn. Über den platonischen Dialog 'Phaidros.'* München: Kösel, 1962.]

Erkenntnis und Freiheit. Essays. München: Deutscher Taschenbuch Verlag, 1964.

Faith Hope Love. Translated by Richard and Clara Winston and Sr. Mary Frances McCarthy. San Francisco: Ignatius Press, 1997. [*Lieben, hoffen, glauben. Sonderausgabe der Titel Über die Liebe, Über die Hoffung und Über den Glauben.* München: Kösel, 1986. In vol. 4 of *Werke,* edited by Bertold Wald, 198–414. Hamburg: Felix Meiner Verlag, 1996.]

Fortitude and Temperance. Translated by Daniel F. Coogan. New York: Pantheon Books, 1954. [*Zucht und Mass. Über die vierte Kardinaltugend.* München: Kösel, 1964. In vol. 4 of *Werke,* edited by Bertold Wald, 137–57. Hamburg: Felix Meiner Verlag, 1999.]

Glauben, Hoffen, Lieben. Freiburg: Informationszentrum Berufe der Kirche, 1981.

Göttlicher Wahnsinn. Eine Platon-Interpretation. Ostfildern bei Stuttgart: Schwabenverlag, 1989.

Guide to Thomas Aquinas. Translated by Richard and Clara Winston. San Francisco: Ignatius Press, 1986. [*Hinführung zu Thomas von Aquin. Zwölf Vorlesungen.* München: Kösel, 1963.]

Happiness and Contemplation. Translated by Richard and Clara Winston. South Bend, Ind.: St. Augustine, 1998. [*Glück und Kontemplation.* München: Kösel, 1979. In vol. 6 of *Werke,* edited by Bertold Wald, 156–216. Hamburg: Felix Meiner Verlag, 1999.]

Hinführung zum Glauben. Köln: Adamas, 1978.

Hoffnung und Geschichte. Fünf Salzburger Vorlesungen. München: Kösel, 1967. In vol. 6 of *Werke,* edited by Bertold Wald, 375–440. Hamburg: Felix Meiner Verlag, 1999.

In Defense of Philosophy. Translated by Lothar Krauth. San Francisco: Ignatius Press, 1992. [*Verteidigungsrede für die Philosophie.* München: Kösel, 1966. In vol. 3 of *Werke,* edited by Bertold Wald, 76–155. Hamburg: Felix Meiner Verlag, 1995.]

In Tune with the World. A Theory of Festivity. Translated by Richard and Clara Winston. Chicago: Franciscan Herald Press, 1973. [*Zustimmung zur Welt. Eine Theorie des Festes.* München: Kösel, 1964. In vol. 6 of *Werke,* edited by Bertold Wald, 217–85. Hamburg: Felix Meiner Verlag, 1999.]

Interpretation. Begriff und Anspruch. München: Kösel, 1970. In vol. 3 of *Werke,* edited by Bertold Wald, 236–99. Hamburg: Felix Meiner Verlag, 1995.

Kleines Lesebuch von den Tugenden des menschlichen Herzens. Ostfildern bei Stuttgart: Schwabenverlag, 1988.

Kulturphilosophische Schriften. Vol. 6 of *Werke,* edited by Bertold Wald. Hamburg: Felix Meiner Verlag, 1999.

Kümmert euch nicht um Sokrates. Drei Fernsehspiele. Freiburg/Einsiedeln: Johannes Verlag, 1993.

Leisure: The Basis of Culture. Translated by Alexander Dru, with an introduction by T. S. Eliot. London: Faber and Faber, 1963. [*Musse und Kult.* München: Kösel, 1965. In vol. 6 of *Werke,* edited by Bertold Wald, 1–44. Hamburg: Felix Meiner Verlag, 1999.]

Lesebuch. With a foreword by Hans Urs von Balthasar. München: Kösel, 1984.

Menschliches Richtigsein. Die Kardinaltugenden–neu bedacht. Freiburg in Breisgau: Informationszentrum Berufe der Kirche, 1980.

Noch nicht aller Tage Abend. Autobiographische Aufzeichnungen 1945–1964. München: Kösel, 1979.

Noch wusste est niemand. Autobiographische Aufzeichnungen 1904–1945. München: Kösel, 1979.

On Hope. Translated by Mary Frances McCarthy. San Francisco: Ignatius Press, 1986. [*Über die Hoffnung.* München: Kösel, 1977. In vol. 4 of *Werke,* edited by Bertold Wald, 256–95. Hamburg: Felix Meiner Verlag, 1996.]

Philosophie, Kontemplation, Weisheit. Freiburg/Einsiedeln: Johannes Verlag, 1991.

Prudence. Translated by Richard and Clara Winston. New York: Pantheon Books, 1959. [*Traktat über die Klugheit.* München: Kösel, 1965. In vol. 4 of *Werke,* edited by Bertold Wald, 1–42. Hamburg: Felix Meiner Verlag, 1996.]

"Reality and the Good." In *Living the Truth.* Translated by Lothar Krauth and Stella Lange. San Francisco: Ignatius Press, 1989. [*Die Wirklichkeit und das Gute nach Thomas von Aquin.* Münster: Kösel, 1964. In vol. 5 of *Werke,* edited by Bertold Wald, 48–98. Hamburg: Felix Meiner Verlag, 1997.]

Schriften zum Philosophiebegriff. Vol. 3 of *Werke,* edited by Bertold Wald. Hamburg: Felix Meiner Verlag, 1995.

Schriften zur Philosophischen Anthropologie und Ethik: Das Menschenbild der Tugendlehre. Vol. 4 of *Werke,* edited by Bertold Wald. Hamburg: Felix Meiner Verlag, 1996.

Schriften zur Philosophischen Anthropologie und Ethik: Grundstrukturen menschlicher Existenz. Vol. 5 of *Werke,* edited by Bertold Wald. Hamburg: Felix Meiner Verlag, 1997.

Sehen und Schauen. Das Experiment mit der Blindheit. Irdische Kontemplation. Freiburg: Informationszentrum Berufe der Kirche, 1983.

Sprache, Terminologie, Jargon. Ostfildern bei Stuttgart: Schwabenverlag, 1989.

Sünde–eine Fehlleistung? Steinfeld: Salvator, 1985.

Tradition als Herausforderung. Aufsätze und Reden. München: Kösel, 1963.

Über das christliche Menschenbild. München: Kösel, 1964.

Über das Phänomen des Festes. Köln: Opladen, Westdeutscher Verlag (Arbeitsgemeinschaft für Forschung des Landes Nordrhein-Westfalen, 113th cahier), 1963.

Über das Schweigen Goethes. München: Kösel, 1962. In vol. 6 of *Werke,* edited by Bertold Wald, 45–71. Hamburg: Felix Meiner Verlag, 1999.

Über den Begriff der Tradition. Köln und Opladen: Westdeutscher Verlag, 1958.

Über die platonischen Mythen. München: Kösel, 1965.

Über die Schwierigkeit, heute zu glauben. Reden und Aufsätze. München: Kösel, 1974.

Überlieferung. Begriff und Anspruch. München: Kösel, 1970.

Unaustrinkbares Licht. Über das negative Element in der Weltansicht des Thomas von Aquin. München: Kösel, 1963.

Vom Sinn der Tapferkeit. München: Kösel, 1963. In vol. 3 of *Werke,* edited by Bertold Wald, 113–36. Hamburg: Felix Meiner Verlag, 1995.

Wahrheit der Dinge. Eine Untersuchung zur Anthropologie des Hochmittelalters. München: Kösel, 1966. In vol. 5 of *Werke,* edited by Bertold Wald, 95–179. Hamburg: Felix Meiner Verlag, 1997.

Was heisst Akademisch? Zwei Versuche über die Chance der Universität heute. München: Kösel, 1964. In vol. 6 of *Werke,* edited by Bertold Wald, 71–131. Hamburg: Felix Meiner Verlag, 1999.

Was heisst Glauben? Vierundzwanzig Rundfunk-Ansprachen. Köln: Adamas, 1974.

Was heisst Interpretation? Rheinisch–Westfälische Akademie der Wissenschaften, Sektion Geisteswissenschaften. Opladen: Westdeutscher Verlag, 1979. In vol. 3 of *Werke,* edited by Bertold Wald, 212–35. Hamburg: Felix Meiner Verlag, 1995.

Was heisst Philosophieren? München: Kösel, 1988. In vol. 3 of *Werke,* edited by Bertold Wald, 15–75. Hamburg: Felix Meiner Verlag, 1995. [In *Leisure: The Basis of Culture.* Translated by Alexander Dru, with an introduction by T. S. Eliot. London: Faber and Faber, 1963.]

Weistum, Dichtung, Sakrament. Aufsätze und Notizen. München: Kösel, 1954.

Welt und Umwelt. In vol. 5 of *Werke,* edited by Bertold Wald, 180–206. Hamburg: Felix Meiner Verlag, 1997.

2. *Articles*

"Actualité de la scolastique." *La Table Ronde* 166 (November 1961): 19–37.

"Anmerkungen über die mögliche Zukunft der Philosophie." In *Gegenwart und Tradition, Strukturen des Denkens. Eine Festschrift für Bernhard Lakebrink,* edited by C. Fabro, 235–43. Freiburg: Verlag Rombach, 1969.

"Arbeit–Freizeit–Musse." In *Weistum, Dichtung, Sakrament. Aufsätze und Notizen,* 201–12. München: Kösel, 1954.

"Auf dem Wege sein." In *Wo stehen wir heute,* edited by H. W. Baehr, 67–72. Gütersloh, 1960.

"Bemerkungen über den 'status viatoris.'" *Catholica* 4 (1935): 15–20.

"Ce que signifie la théologie du point de vue philosophique." *La Table Ronde* 213 (October 1965): 55–67.

"Christliche Philosophie?" *Hochland* 40 (1947/48): 501–12.

"Das Geheimnis und die Philosophie." In vol. 3 of *Werke,* edited by Bertold Wald, 304–14. Hamburg: Felix Meiner Verlag, 1995.

"Das Phänomen Liebe." In *Das lebendige Wort.* Feldkirch: Katholisches Bildungswerk Voralberg, 1977.

"Der gerechtfertigte Praktiker." *Neue Deutsche Hefte* 28 (1956): 260–66.

"Der Mensch ohne Wahrheitsverhältnis." In *Tradition als Herausforderung,* 256–68. München: Kösel, 1963.

"Der Philosophierende und die Sprache. Aphoristische Bemerkungen eines Thomas-Lesers." In vol. 3 of *Werke,* edited by Bertold Wald, 199–211. Hamburg: Felix Meiner Verlag, 1995.

"Der Verderb des Wortes und die Macht. Platons Kampf gegen die Sophistik." *Mitteilungen der Deutschen Forschungsgemeinschaft* 3 (1964): 22–38.

"Dialog über das Ende der Zeit." In *Josef Pieper Archiv, Deutsches Literaturarchiv.* Marbach am Neckar, Germany.

"Die Aktualität der Kardinaltugenden: Klugheit, Gerechtigkeit, Tapferkeit, Mass." In *Altes Ethos–Neues Tabu,* 11–38. Köln: Adamas, 1974; and J. Pieper, *Buchstabier-Übungen. Aufsätze, Reden, Notizen,* 109–30. München: Kösel, 1980.

"Die mögliche Zukunft der Philosophie." In vol. 3 of *Werke,* edited by Bertold Wald, 315–23. Hamburg: Felix Meiner Verlag, 1995.

"Die Verborgenheit von Hoffnung und Verzweiflung." In *Tradition als Herausforderung.* München: Kösel, 1963.

"Diskussion." In *Sprachenrecht und europaïsche Einheit,* edited by L. Weisgerber, 131–32. Köln and Opladen: Westdeutscher Verlag (Arbeitsgemeinschaft für Forschung des Landes Nordrhein-Westfalen, 81st cahier), 1959.

"Erkenntnis und Freiheit." In *Weistum, Dichtung, Sakrament. Aufsätze und Notizen,* 27–40. München: Kösel, 1954.

"Glück im Schauen." *Internationale katholische Zeitschrift. Communio* 4 (November/December 1975): 528–41.

"Heideggers Wahrheitsbegriff." In vol. 3 of *Werke,* edited by Bertold Wald, 186–98. Hamburg: Felix Meiner Verlag, 1995.

"Herkunftlose Zukunft und Hoffnung ohne Grund?" In *Über die Schwierigkeit, heute zu glauben. Reden und Aufsätze,* 178–95. München: Kösel, 1974.

"Hoffnung." In *Was heisst Glauben? Vierundzwanzig Rundfunk-Ansprachen,* 20–30. Köln: Adamas, 1974.

"Hoffnung." In *Handbuch theologischer Grundbegriffe,* edited by H. Fries, 698–706. München: Kösel, 1962.

"Hoffnung—auf was?" In *Tradition als Herausforderung,* 160–64. München: Kösel, 1963.

"Hoffnung der Kranken." *Heilen* 1 (1981): 15–21.

"Hoffnung und Geschichte." Cartell Rupert Mayer. *Mitteilungsblatt* (August 1975): 7–26.

"Irdische Kontemplation." In *Über die Schwierigkeit heute zu glauben. Reden und Aufsätze,* 171–77. München: Kösel, 1974.

"Josef Pieper." In vol. 1 of *Philosophie in Selbstdarstellung,* edited by J. Pongratz, 241–67. Hamburg: Felix Meiner Verlag, 1975.

"Kann der Zeitgenosse ein Kontemplativer Mensch sein? Ein Gespräch mit Professor Josef Pieper." *Herder Korrespondenz* 31 (August 1977), 8th cahier, 401–5.

"Kreatürliche Metaphysik. Ein Hinweis auf E. Przywara: Analogia entis." *Münsterischer Anzeige* (8 December 1932).

"Kreatürlichkeit. Bemerkungen über die Elemente eines Grundbegriffs." In *Buchstabier-Übungen. Aufsätze, Reden, Notizen,* 39–65. München: Kösel, 1980.

"'Kreatürlichkeit' und 'menschliche Natur.' Anmerkungen zum philosophischen Ansatz von Jean-Paul Sartre." In *Über die Schwierigkeit heute zu glauben. Reden und Aufsätze,* 304–21. München: Kösel, 1974; and vol. 3 of *Werke,* edited by Bertold Wald, 173–85. Hamburg: Felix Meiner Verlag, 1995.

"Meditation über das Mirandum." *Merkur* 23 (1950): 32–37.

"Musse und menschliche Existenz." In *Tradition als Herausforderung,* 193–203. München: Kösel, 1963.

"Musse und menschliche Existenz." In *Mensch und Freizeit,* 18–39. Österreichischer Bundesverlag, 1961.

"Nachdenkliches über die Klugheit." In *Weistum. Dichtung. Sakrament. Aufsätze und Notizen*, 92–99. München: Kösel, 1954.

"Philosophie heute. Die Situation des Philosophierenden heute." In *Verantwortung und Freiheit. Vocation spirituelle de l'Université*, edited by A. Schifferle, 229–49. Fribourg: Editions Universitaires Fribourg Suisse, 1990.

"Philosophie und Gemeinwohl." In *Weistum. Dichtung. Sakrament. Aufsätze und Notizen*, 70–83. München: Kösel, 1954.

"Philosophie und Weisheit." In *Philosophie–Kontemplation–Weisheit*, 87–91.

"Philosophieren heute." In *Veröffentlichungen der Katholischen Akademie Trier*, trierer scripte 10, 1975, 10th cahier, 5–28.

"Philosophische Bildung und geistige Arbeit." In vol. 3 of *Werke*, edited by Bertold Wald, 1–14. Hamburg: Felix Meiner Verlag, 1995.

"Platons eschatologische Mythen." *Neue Deutsche Hefte* 102 (November/December 1964): 54–60.

"Sachlichkeit und Klugheit. Über das Verhältnis von moderner Charakterologie und thomistischer Ethik." *Der katholische Gedanke* 5 (1932): 68–81.

"Selbstgespräch über die Hoffnung," Radio broadcast for Easter 1951 (NWDR). In *Weistum. Dichtung. Sakrament. Aufsätze und Notizen*, 84–91. München: Kösel, 1954.

"Speranza teologale e speranze umane." In *Atti del Quarto convegno internazionale per la pace e la civiltà cristiana*, Florenz 19.–25.6.1955. Florence: L'impronta 1956.

"Sur l'Espérance des Martyrs." In *Espoir Humain et Espérance Chrétienne*, 76–84. Paris: Horay, 1951.

"Thomas a Creatore." *Hochland* 35 (1938): 89–105.

"Tod und Unsterblichkeit." *Catholica* 13/2 (1959): 81–100.

"Tod und Unsterblichkeit." *Universitas* 16 (1961), 12th cahier, 1265–80.

"Tod und Unsterblichkeit." In *Tradition als Herausforderung*. München: Kösel, 1963.

"Tugendlehre als Aussage über den Menschen." In *Tradition als Herausforderung*, 151–59. München: Kösel, 1963.

"Über das Dilemma einer nicht-christlichen Philosophie." In vol. 3 of *Werke*, edited by Bertold Wald, 300–307. Hamburg: Felix Meiner Verlag, 1995.

"Über den Begriff der Tradition." *Tijdschrift voor filosofie* 19/1 (1957): 22–52.

"Über den Philosophie-Begriff Platons." In *Tradition als Herausforderung*. München: Kösel, 1963.

"Über die Hoffnung." In *Westdeutscher Rundfunk*, by J. Besch, 8–13, 1971.

"Über die Hoffnung der Kranken." In *Von der Hoffnung der Kranken*, edited by M.-P. Engelmeier, 13–34. St. Augustin: Verlag Wort und Werk, 1977.

"Über die Kunst, nicht zu verzweifeln." In *Über die Schwierigkeit heute zu glauben. Reden und Aufsätze*, 196–213. München: Kösel, 1974.

"Über die Schlichtheit der Sprache in der Philosophie." In *Tradition als Herausforderung*, 286–94. München: Kösel, 1963.

"Über die Wahrheit der platonischen Mythen." *Einsichten* (Gerhard Krüger zum 60. Geburtstag), 289–96. Frankfurt am Main: Klostermann, 1962.

"Unsterblichkeit—eine nicht-christliche Vorstellung?" In *Tradition als Herausforderung*, 92–122. München: Kösel, 1963.

"Verteidigung der Musse. Über philosophische Bildung und geistige Arbeit." *Hochland* 39/40 (1947): 289–302.

"Vie humaine et loisirs." *Way Forum*, Paris, 12.1957.

"Wahrheit der Dinge—ein verschollener Begriff." In *Festschrift für Leo Brandt*, 417–29. Köln-Opladen: Westdeutscher Verlag, 1969.

"Was heisst 'Christliches Abendland'?" In *Tradition als Herausforderung*, 36–47. München: Kösel, 1963.

"Was heisst 'dürftige Zeit'? Über das Fest im Ganzen des Daseins." *Universitas* 19 (1964): 521–27.

"Was heisst Glück? Erfüllung im Schauen." In *Buchstabier-Übungen. Aufsätze, Reden, Notizen*, 131–49. München: Kösel, 1980.

"Was heisst 'Gott spricht'? Vorüberlegungen zu einer kontroverstheologischen Diskussion." *Catholica* 19 (1965): 171–91.

"Was ist Glück?" *Hochland* 49/3 (February 1957): 217–24.

"Was man im Denken und Reden über die Hoffnung nicht vergessen darf. . . ." In *Engagement im Geiste der Hoffnung*, Matura-Festschrift der 8A-Klasse des Bundes-Aufbaugymnasiamus, 34. Horn, Austria, 1977.

"Wurzel der Verzweiflung." In *Wirklichkeit und Wahrheit. Einblick in die Arbeit des Verlags Jakob Hegner*, 76–81. Leipzig, 1937.

II. Other Authors

Adam, D. "Aquinas on Aristoteles on Happiness." *Medieval Philosophy and Theology* 1 (1991): 98–118.

Adorno, Theodor W. "Fortschritt." In *Die Philosophie und die Frage nach dem Fortschritt,* edited by H. Kuhn and Fr. Wiedemann, 30–48. München: Anton Pustet, 1964.

Aertsen, Jan A. *Nature and Creature: Thomas Aquinas's Way of Thought.* Leiden: E. J. Brill, 1988.

Agazzi, Evandro. "Mind and Body: A Philosophical Delineation of the Problem." *Epistemologia* 4, Special Issue (1981): 3–20.

Ahlbrecht, Ansgar. *Tod und Unsterblichkeit in der neueren protestantischen Theologie der Gegenwart.* Paderborn: Bonifacius-Druckerei, 1964.

Akwali Okafor, Simon. *Pieper's Theory of Festivity: Toward a Philosophy of Nigerian Education.* New York: Columbia University Press, 1982.

Alain. *Propos sur le bonheur.* Paris: Gallimard, 1975.

Alfaro, Juan. *Fides, spes, caritas,* pars tertia. Rome: Gregorian University Press, 1968, 511–61.

_____. *De la cuestion del hombre a la cuestion de dios.* Salamanca: Sigueme, 1989.

Alvira, Tomas. *Naturaleza y libertad. Estudio de los conceptos tomistas de voluntas ut natura y voluntas ut ratio.* Pamplona: Ediciones Universidad de Navarra, 1985.

Anders, Günther. *Die Antiquiertheit des Menschen.* 2 vols. München: Beck (Vol. 1, 1956, 1992; Vol. 2, 1980, 1992).

_____. *Die atomare Drohung. Radikale Überlegungen.* München: Beck, 1972, 1986.

_____. *Hiroshima ist überall.* München: Beck, 1982.

Anscombe, Gertrud Elizabeth Margaret. "Modern Moral Philosophy." *Philosophy* 33 (1958): 1–19.

Aquinas, Thomas. *On the Power of God.* 2 vols. London: Oates & Washbourne, 1933.

_____. *Summa Contra Gentes. Book Two: Creation.* Translated by James F. Anderson. Notre Dame: University of Notre Dame Press, repr. s.a.

_____. *Summa Contra Gentes. Book Four: Salvation.* Translated by Charles J. O'Neil. Notre Dame: University of Notre Dame Press, repr. s.a.

_____. *Summa Theologiae.* Vol. 16 of *Purpose and Happiness (1–2, q. 1–5).* Translated by Thomas Gilby. London and New York: Blackfriars, 1969.

_____. *Summa Theologiae.* Vol. 31of *Faith (2–2 q. 1–7).* Tranlsated by T. C. O'Brien. London and New York: Blackfriars, 1974.

Arendt, Dieter. "Der Nihilismus-Ursprung und Geschichte im Spiegel der Forschungs-Literatur seit 1945. Ein Erforschungsbericht, I–II." *Deutsche Vierteljahresschrift für Literaturwissenschaft und Geistesgeschichte* 43 (1969): 346–69, 544–66.

_____. *Der Nihilismus als Phänomen der Geistesgeschichte in der wissenschaftliche Diskussion unseres Jahrhunderts.* Darmstadt: Wissenschaftliche Buchgesellschaft, 1974.

Arendt, Hannah. *The Human Condition.* Translated by Margaret Canovan. Chicago: University of Chicago Press, 1998.

Aristotle. *The Basic Works of Aristotle.* Translated by Richard McKeon. New York: Random House, 1941.

_____. *The Complete Works of Aristotle.* 2 vols. Edited by J. Barnes. Princeton: Princeton University Press, 1985.

Aron, Raymond. *Dimensions de la conscience historique.* Paris: Plon, 1961.

Augustin. *De fide, spe et charitate.* In *Opera Omnia,* Patrologia Latina vol. XL. Paris, 1841.

_____. *The City of God.* Translated by Marcus Dods. New York: Modern Library, 1950.

_____. *On Christian Doctrine.* Translated by D. W. Robertson, Jr. New York: The Liberal Arts, 1958.

_____. *Exposition of the Psalms.* In vol. 3/16 of *The Works of Saint Augustine: A Translation for the 21st Century.* Edited by John E. Rotelle. Translated by Maria Boulding. New York: New City Press, 1990.

Bacon, Francis. *Novum Organum.* In vol. 1 of *The Works of Francis Bacon.* Stuttgart-Bad Cannstatt: Friedrich Frommann, 1989.

Bakunin, Michail. *Philosophie der Tat.* Edited by R. Beer. Köln: Jakob Hegner, 1968.

Ballay, Ladislaus. *Der Hoffnungsbegriff bei Augustinus, untersucht in seinen Werken: De doctrina christiana; Enchiridion sive de fide, spe et caritate ad Laurentium and Enarrationes in psalmos I–91.* München: Hüber, 1964.

Balthasar, Hans Urs von. "Die drei Gestalten der heutigen Hoffnung." *Theologische Quartalschrift* 152 (1972): 101–11.

Battisti, Siegfried. "Josef Pieper (geb. 1904)." In *Christliche Philosophie im katholischen Denken des 19. und 20. Jahrhunderts,* vol. 2, edited by E. Coreth, 667–72. Graz: Styria, 1988.

Baudry, Gérard-Henri. *Les grands axes de l'eschatologie teilhardienne.* Cahiers Teilhardiens, Lille, nr.8. Reprint of an article published in *Mélanges de Science Religieuse* 34 (1977): 213–35 and 35 (1978): 47–71.

Bäumer, Franz-Josef. *Fortschritt und Theologie. Philosophische und theologische Überlegungen zum Fortschrittsgedanken.* Bern: Peter Lang, 1985.

Baumgartern, Armin. *Was darf ich hoffen? Besinnung auf die Fragwürdige unserer Zeit.* Bern: Peter Lang, 1986.

Baumgartern, Hans Michael. "Die Idee des Fortschritts." *Philosophisches Jahrbuch* 70 (1962): 157–68.

Beck, Heinrich. "Materialistische Dialektik und thomasischer Seinsakt. Dialektischer Materialismus und Evolutionnismus als Problem im Horizont thomasischer Metaphysik." *Philosophisches Jahrbuch* 82 (1975): 54–71.

Benoit, Pierre. "Resurrection: At the End of Time or Immediately After Death?" In *Immortality and Resurrection,* edited by P. Benoit and R. Murphy, 103–14. New York, Herder and Herder, 1970.

Berdyaev, Nicolas. *The Destiny of Man.* London: The Centenary Press, 1937.

Berger, Peter. *Facing Up to Modernity.* New York: Basic Books, 1977.

Bernard, Charles-André. *Théologie de l'espérance selon saint Thomas d'Aquin.* Paris: Vrin, 1961.

Bernard, Claude. *La science expérimentale.* Paris: J. B. Ballière, 1878.

―――. *An Introduction to the Study of Experimental Medicine.* Translated by Henry Copley Greene. New York: Dover, 1957. [*Introduction à l'étude de la médecine expérimentale.* Paris: Delagrave, 1920.]

―――. *Cahier de notes. 1850–1860.* Paris: Gallimard, 1965.

―――. *The* Cahier rouge *of Claude Bernard.* Translated by Hebbel H. Hoff, Lucienne Guillemin, and Roger Guillemin. Cambridge: Schenkman, 1967. [*Le cahier rouge.* Paris: Gallimard, 1942.]

―――. *De la physiologie générale.* Paris: Hachette, 1972.

_____. *Lectures on the Phenomena of Life Common to Animals and Plants.* Translated by Hebbel H. Hoff, Roger Guillemin, and Lucienne Guillemin. Springfield, Ill.: Charles C. Thomas, 1974. [*Leçons sur les phénomènes de la vie communs aux animaux et aux végétaux.* Paris: Vrin, 1966.]

Bernath, Klaus. *Anima forma corporis. Eine Untersuchung über die ontologischen Grundlagen der Anthropologie des Thomas von Aquin.* Bonn: Bouvier, 1969.

Bernstein, John Andrew. *Progress and the Quest for Meaning: A Philosophical and Historical Inquiry.* London: Fairleigh Dickinson University Press, 1993.

Binoche, Bertrand. *Les trois sources des philosophies de l'histoire (1764–1798).* Paris: Presses Universitaires de France, 1994.

Blain, Lionel. "Deux philosophies centrées sur l'espérance: celle de Gabriel Marcel et celle d'Ernst Bloch." *Concilium* 59 (1970): 83–92.

Bloch, Ernst. *Philosophische Grundfragen I.* Frankfurt am Main: Suhrkamp, 1961.

_____. "Der Mensch als Möglichkeit." *Forum* 12 (1965), 140/141ème cahier, 357–61.

_____. *Ernst Bloch Werkausgabe.* 16 vols. Frankfurt am Main: Suhrkamp, 1969ff.

_____. *Atheismus im Christentum. Zur Religion des Exodus und des Reichs.* Vol. 14 of *Ernst Bloch Werkausgabe.* [*Atheism in Christianity: the Religion of the Exodus and the Kingdom.* Translated by J. T. Swann. New York: Herder and Herder, 1972.]

_____. *Experimentum Mundi. Frage, Kategorien des Herausbringens, Praxis.* Vol. 15 of *Ernst Bloch Werkausgabe.*

_____. *Das Materialismusproblem, seine Geschichte und seine Substanz.* Vol. 7 of *Ernst Bloch Werkausgabe.*

_____. *Subjekt–Objekt. Erläuterung zu Hegel.* Vol. 8 of *Ernst Bloch Werkausgabe.*

_____. *Tendenz–Latenz–Utopie.* Supplementary volume of *Ernst Bloch Werkausgabe.*

_____. *Tübinger Einleitung in die Philosophie.* In *Ernst Bloch Werkausgabe,* vol. 13.

_____. "Dialogue sur l'espérance. Gabriel Marcel et Ernst Bloch." In *Présence de Gabriel Marcel,* 1979, 1er cahier, 39–74.

——. *The Principle of Hope*. 3 vols. Translated by Neville Plaice, Stephen Plaice, and Paul Knight. Cambridge: MIT, 1986. [*Das Prinzip Hoffnung*. Vol. 5 of *Ernst Bloch Werkausgabe.*]

——. *Heritage of Our Times*. Translated by Neville and Stephen Plaice. Berkeley: University of California Press, 1991. [*Erbschaft dieser Zeit*. Vol. 4 of *Ernst Bloch Werkausgabe.*]

——. *The Spirit of Utopia*. Translated by Anthony A. Nassar. Stanford: Stanford University Press, 2000. [*Geist der Utopie*. Bearbeitete neuauflage der zweiten Fassung von 1923. In *Ernst Bloch Werkausgabe*, vol. 3]

Blondel, Maurice. *Exigences philosophiques du Christiannisme*. Paris: Presses Universitaires de France, 1950.

Blumenberg, Hans. *Säkularisierung und Selbstbehauptung*. Frankfurt am Main: Suhrkamp, 1974.

——. *The Legitimacy of the Modern Age*. Translated by Robert M. Wallace. Cambridge: MIT, 1991.

Boia, Lucian. *La fin du monde. Une histoire sans fin*. Paris: Éditions la Découverte, 1990.

Bollnow, Otto Friedrich. *Neue Geborgenheit. Das Problem einer Überwindung des Existentialismus*. Stuttgart: Kohlhammer, 1955.

——. *Vom Wesen der Stimmungen*. Frankfurt am Main: Klostermann, 1956.

Born, Max. "Die Hoffnung auf Einsicht aller Menschen in die Grösse der atomaren Gefährdung." In *Die Hoffnungen unserer Zeit*, 127–40. München: Piper, 1963.

Boros, Ladislas, "Has Life a Meaning?" In *Immortality and Resurrection*, edited by P. Benoit and R. Murphy, 11–20. New York: Herder and Herder, 1970.

Bougerol, Jacques-Guy. *La théologie de l'espérance aux XIIème et XIIIème siècle*. 2 vols. Paris: Études augustiniennes, 1985.

Boven, Luc. "The Value of Hope." *Philosophical and Phenomenological Research* 54/3 (1999): 667–81.

Bovis, André de. "Philosophie ou théologie de l'histoire?" *Nouvelle Revue Théologique* 91 (1959): no. 4, 355–75 and no. 5, 449–57.

Braine, David. *The Human Person: Animal and Spirit*. Notre Dame: University of Notre Dame Press, 1992.

Brandt, Reinhard. "Zum 'Streit der Fakultäten.'" In *Neue Autographen und Dokumente zu Kants Leben, Schriften und Vorlesungen, (Kant-Forschungen,* vol. 1), edited by R. Brandt and W. Stark, 31–78. Hamburg: Felix Meiner Verlag, 1987.

Brantschen, Johannes Baptist. *Hoffnung für Zeit und Ewigkeit. Der Traum von wachen Christenmenschen.* Freiburg: Herder, 1992.

Braun, Eberhard. "Possibilité et non-encore-être: l'ontologie traditionnelle et l'ontologie du non-encore-être." In *Utopie–Marxisme selon E. Bloch. Un système de l'inconstructible hommages à Ernst Bloch pour son 90ème anniversaire,* edited by G. Raulet, 155–70. Paris: Payot, 1976.

Bravo, Francisco. *La vision de l'histoire chez Teilhard de Chardin.* Paris: Cerf, 1970.

Brednow, Walter. "Der Mensch und die Hoffnung" *Die Sammlung* 9 (1954): 529–39 and 596–608.

Breitholz, Paul, and Markus van der Giet, eds. *Josef Pieper. Schriftenverzeichnis 1929–1989.* München: Kösel, 1979.

Breton, Stanislas. "Le thème de l'espérance et la réflexion philosophique." In *Savoir, faire, espérer: les limites de la raison,* 43–62. Bruxelles: Facultés Universitaires St. Louis, 1979.

Bruch, Jean-Louis. *La philosophie religieuse de Kant.* Paris: Aubier, Montaigne, 1968.

Brunner, Emil. *Das Ewige als Zukunft und Gegenwart.* Munich: Hamburg, 1965.

Buckley, Michael J. *At the Origins of Modern Atheism.* New Haven: Yale University Press, 1987.

Bultmann, Rudolf. *Theology of the New Testament.* Translated by Kendrick Grobel. New York: Scribner, 1951. [Mohr, J. C. B. *Theologie des Neuen Testaments.* Tübingen, 1965.]

Burg, Peter. "Kants Deutung der Französischen Revolution im 'Streit der Fakultäten.'" In *Akten des 4. Internationalen Kant-Kongresses,* edited by G. Funke, 656–67. Berlin: W. de Gruyter, 1974.

Buri, Fritz. "Zur gegenwärtigen Diskussion über das Problem Hoffnung." *Theologische Zeitschrift* 22 (1966): 196–211.

———. *Hoffnung–Wesen und Bewährung.* Hamburg: Evangelischer Verlag, 1967.

Burns, Norman T. *Christian Mortalism from Tyndale to Milton.* Cambridge, Mass.: Harvard University Press, 1972.

Bury, John Bagnell. *The Idea of Progress. An Inquiry into its Origin and Growth.* New York: The Macmillan Company, 1932.

Calderon Bouchet, Ruben. *Esperanza, historia y utopia.* Buenos Aires: Ediciones Dictio, 1980.

Callot, Emile. *Les trois moments de la philosophie théologique de l'histoire. Augustin Vico Herder. Situation actuelle.* Paris: La Pensée Universelle, 1974.

Campagnolo, Umberto. "La crise de notre temps et son utopie." *Comprendre* 24 (1974): no. 39–40, 9–20.

Camus, Albert. *Théatre, récits, nouvelles.* Paris: Gallimard (Pléiade), 1962.

———. *The Myth of Sisyphus and Other Essays.* Translated by Justin O'Brien. New York: Knopf, 1967. [*Le Mythe de Sisyphe* in *Essais.* Paris: Gallimard (Pléiade), 1965, 89–211.]

———. *Nuptials.* In *Lyrical and Critical Essays.* Translated by Ellen Conroy Kennedy. New York: Knopf, 1968, 63–105. [*Les Noces* in *Essais.* Paris: Gallimard (Pléiade), 1965, 51–88.]

———. *The Rebel: An Essay on Man in Revolt.* Translated by Anthony Bower. New York: Knopf, 1978. [*L'homme révolté* in *Essais.* Paris: Gallimard (Pléiade), 1965, 407–709.]

———. *Notebooks. 1935–1942.* Translated by Philip Thody. In *Notebooks. 1935–1951.* New York: Marlowe, 1998. [*Carnets (5.1935–2.1942).* Paris: Gallimard, 1962.]

———. *Notebooks. 1942–1951.* Translated by Justin O'Brien. In *Notebooks. 1935–1951.* New York: Marlowe, 1998. [*Carnets (1.1942–3.1951).* Paris: Gallimard, 1964.]

Canguilhem, Georges. "La décadence de l'idée de Progrès." *Revue de Métaphysique et de Morale* 92/4 (1987): 437–54.

Capps, Walter H., ed. *The Future of Hope.* Philadelphia: Fortress Press, 1970.

Carré, Ambroise-Marie. *Espérance et désespoir.* Paris: Cerf, 1953.

Caturelli, Alberto. *Metafisica del Trabajo.* Buenos Aires: Libraria Huemul, 1982.

Cauchy, Venant. *Désir naturel et béatitude chez St. Thomas.* Montréal/Paris: St. Boniface/Fides, 1958.

Cesana, Andreas. *Geschichte als Entwicklung? Zur Kritik des geschichtsphilosophischen Entwicklungsdenkens.* Berlin: Walter de Gruyter, 1988.

Cessario, Romanus. *The Moral Virtues and Theological Ethics.* Notre Dame: University of Notre Dame Press, 1990.

Charlesworth, Max. "Hope: An Ontological Foundation?" In *The Sources of Hope,* edited by R. Fitzgerald, 167–75. Rushcutters Bay, Australia: Pergamon Press, 1979.

Cioran, Emile. *History and Utopia.* Translated by Richard Howard. New York: Seaver, 1987. [*Histoire et utopie.* Paris: Gallimard, 1960.]

———. *On the Heights of Despair.* Translated by Ilinca Zarifopol-Johnston. Chicago and London: University of Chicago Press, 1992. [*Sur les cimes du désespoir.* Paris: L'Herne, 1934, 1990.]

Cléro, Jean-Pierre. *La philosophie des passions chez David Hume.* Paris: Klincksieck, 1985.

Cohen, Hermann. *Religion of Reason Out of the Sources of Judaism.* Translated by Simon Kaplan. Atlanta: Scholars, 1995. [*Die Religion der Vernunft aus den Quellen des Judentums.* Leipzig, 1919].

Comte-Sponville, André. *Le mythe d'Icare. Traité du désespoir et de la béatitude.* 2 vols. Paris: Presses Universitaires de France, 1988.

———. *A Short Treatise on the Great Virtues: The Uses of Philosophy in Everyday Life.* Translated by Catherine Temerson. London: Heinemann, 1996. [*Petit traité des grandes vertus.* Paris: Presses Universitaires de France, 1995].

Conlon, Walter M. "The Certitude of Hope." *The Thomist* (1947): 75–119 and 226–52.

Coreth, Emerich. *Metaphysik. Eine methodisch-systematische Grundlegung.* Innsbruck/Wien: Tyrolia, 1963, 1980.

Cottier, Georges. "Sur la philosophie de l'Histoire. A propos d'un livre de Josef Pieper." *Nova et Vetera,* 4./6., 30, no. 2 (1955): 117–26.

———. *Horizons de l'athéisme.* Paris: Cerf, 1969.

———. *Le conflit des espérances.* Paris: Desclée de Brouwer, 1977.

———. "L'inversion du progrès." *Nova et Vetera* 58/4 (1983): 286–99.

———. "Le vrai sens du progrès." *Rivista Internazionale di Filosofia del Diritto* 62 (1985): 399–420.

———. "Intellectus et ratio." *Revue Thomiste* 88 (1988): 215–28.

———. *Histoire et connaissance de Dieu.* Fribourg: Editions Universitaires Fribourg Suisse, 1993.

Cousins, Ernest H., ed. *Hope and the Future of Man.* London: Garnstone Press, 1973.

Cuénot, Claude. *Pierre Teilhard de Chardin. Les grandes étapes de son évolution.* Paris: Plon, 1958.

Cullmann, Oscar. *Immortality of the Soul or Resurrection of the Dead: The Witness of the New Testament.* London: Epworth, 1958. [*Unsterblichkeit der Seele oder Auferstehung der Toten? Antwort des Neuen Testaments.* Stuttgart: Kreuz, 1963.]

Daniélou, Jean. *The Lord of History: Reflections on the Inner Meaning of History.* Translated by Nigel Abercrombie. London and Chicago: Longmans and Regnery, 1964. [*Essai sur le mystère de l'histoire.* Paris: Seuil, 1953].

D'Arc, Jeanne. *Mort, immortalité, résurrection.* Paris: Desclée de Brouwer, 1992.

Dauenhauer, Bernard P. *Silence: The Phenomenon and its Ontological Significance.* Bloomington: Indiana University Press, 1980.

_____. "Hope and its Ramifications for Politics." *Man World* 17/3–4 (1986): 453–76.

_____. *The Politics of Hope.* New York/London: Routledge and Kegan Paul, 1986.

Day, John Patrick. "Hope." *American Philosophical Quarterly* 6/2 (1969): 89–102.

_____. "The Anatomy of Hope and Fear." *Mind* 79 (1970): 369–84.

_____. *Hope: A Philosophical Inquiry.* Helsinki: Acta Philosophica Fennica, 1991 (51).

Delesalle, Jacques. "Le plaisir, le bonheur et la joie." *Mélanges de science religieuse* 60/1 (1983): 3–29, 60/2 (1983): 92–107.

Delfgauuw, Bernard. *Geschichte als Fortschritt.* 3 vols. Köln: J. P. Bachem, 1962–1966.

Delvaille, Jules. *Essai sur l'histoire de l'idée de progrès jusqu'à la fin du XVIIIème siècle.* Paris: Alcan, 1910; Hildesheim/New York: G. Olms, 1977.

Demandt, Alexander. *Endzeit? Die Zukunft der Geschichte.* Berlin: Siedler, 1993.

Descartes, René. *Discourse on the Method.* In *The Philosophical Works of Descartes,* vol. 1, translated by Elizabeth S. Haldane and G. R. T. Ross, 79–130. New York: Dover, 1955.

_____. *Oeuvres de Descartes.* Edited by Ch. Adam and P. Tannery. 11 vols. Paris: Vrin, 1974–86.

Descoqs, Pedro. "L'athéisme est un humanisme." *Revue de Philosophie* (1946): 39–89.

Desroches, Henri. *Sociologie de l'espérance*. Paris: Calmann-Lévy, 1973.

Dessauer, Philipp. "Was ist der Mensch." *Hochland* 37 (1940): 289–92.

Disse, Jörg. "Le fondement de l'espérance chez Ernst Bloch." *Freiburger Zeitschrift für Philosophie und Theologie* 34 (1987): 185–203.

Djuric, Mihailo. "Die Frage nach dem Ende der Geschichte." *Perspektiven der Philosophie* 5 (1979): 171–88.

Dominici, Caterina. *La filosofia di Josef Pieper in relazione alle correnti filosofiche e culturali contemporare*. Bologna: Patron, 1980.

Downie, Robert S. "Hope." *Philosophical and Phenomenological Research* 24/2 (1963): 248–51.

Dupré, Louis. *Passage to Modernity: An Essay in the Hermeneutics of Nature and Culture*. New Haven: Yale University Press, 1993.

Edmaier, Alois. *Horizonte der Hoffnung. Eine philosophische Studie*. Regensburg: Fr. Pustet, 1968.

Eickelschulte, Dietmar. "Beatitudo als Prozess. Zur Frage nach dem Ort der theologischen Ethik bei Thomas von Aquin." In *Sein und Ethos. Untersuchung zur Grundlegung des Ethik*, edited by P. Engelhardt, 158–85. Mainz: Matthias Grünenwald Verlag, 1963.

Eliade, Mircea. *The Myth of the Eternal Return, or Cosmos and History*. Translated by Willard R. Trask. Princeton: Princeton University Press, 1971. [*Le mythe de l'éternel retour. Archétypes et répétition*. Paris: Gallimard, 1949].

Eliot, Thomas Stearns. *Four Quartets*. London: Faber and Faber, 1945, 1948.

Ellul, Jacques. *L'espérance oubliée*. Paris: Gallimard, 1972.

Evans, C. Stephan. *Existentialism: The Philosophy of Despair and the Quest for Hope*. Dallas: Probe Ministries International, 1984.

Fahrenbach, Helmut. *Wesen und Sinn der Hoffnung. Versuch über ein Grenzphänomen zwischen philosophischer und theologischer Daseinsauslegung*. Ph.D. diss. Ruprecht-Karl-Universität Heidelberg, 1956.

Fancelli, Manlio. "Il tema della speranza nella cultura contemporanea." *Giornale Critico della Filosofia Italiana* 21 (1969): 422–50.

Fechtrupp, Hermann, Friedbert Schulze, and Thomas Sternberg, eds. *Aufklärung durch Tradition. Symposium aus Anlass des 90. Geburtstags von Josef Pieper im Mai 1994 in Münster* (Dokumentationen der Josef Pieper Stiftung, vol. 1). Münster: Lit Verlag, 1995.

_____. *Nachdenken über Tugenden* (Dokumentationen der Josef Pieper Stiftung, vol. 3). Münster: Lit Verlag, 1996.

_____. *Sprache und Philosophie* (Dokumentationen der Josef Pieper Stiftung, vol. 2). Münster: Lit Verlag, 1996.

_____. *Die Wahrheit und das Gute* (Dokumentationen der Josef Pieper Stiftung, vol. 4). Münster: Lit Verlag, 1999.

Fendt, Gene. *For What May I Hope? Thinking with Kant and Kierkegaard.* Bern: Peter Lang, 1990.

Fetscher, Iring. "Der Tod im Lichte des Marxismus." In *Grenz-Erfahrung Tod,* edited by A. Paus, 283–317. Graz: Styria, 1976.

_____. "Immanuel Kant und die Französische Revolution." In *Materialien zu Kants Rechtsphilosophie,* edited by Z. Batscha, 269–90. Frankfurt am Main: Suhrkamp, 1976.

Finkielkraut, Alain. *Le mécontemporain.* Paris: Gallimard, 1991.

Fitzgerald, Ross, ed. *The Sources of Hope.* Rushcutters Bay, Australia: Pergamon Press, 1979.

_____. "Hope, Meaning and Transcendence of the 'Self.'" In *The Sources of Hope,* 244–54. Rushcutters Bay, Australia: Pergamon Press, 1971.

Flasch, Kurt. "Ars imitatur naturam: Platonischer Naturbegriff und mittelalterliche Philosophie der Kunst." In *Parusia. Studien zur Philosophie Platons und zur Problemgeschichte des Platonismus* (Festgabe für J. Hirschberger), 265–306. Frankfurt am Main: Minerva, 1965.

Foot, Philippa. *Virtues and Vices.* Berkeley: University of California Press, 1978.

Forest, Aimé. *Consentement et création.* Paris: Aubier, Montaigne, 1943.

Frankl, Viktor E. *The Will to Meaning: Foundations and Applications of Logotherapy.* New York and Cleveland: The World Publishing Company, 1969. [*Der Wille zum Sinn. Ausgewählte Vorträge über Logotherapie.* Bern: Hans Huber, 1972].

_____. *La psychothérapie et son image de l'homme.* Paris: Resma, 1970.

_____. *Die Sinnfrage in der Psychotherapie.* Munich: Piper Verlag, 1985.

Frentz, Emmerich Raitz von. "Analyse der Hoffnung." *Scholastik* 9 (1934): 555–63.

Freud, Sigmund. "Das Unbehagen in der Kultur." In *Fragen der Gesellschaft. Ursprünge der Religion.* Bd. IX der *Sigmund Freud Studienausgabe.* Frankfurt am Main: Fischer, 1974, 191–270.

──────. *Der Mann Moses und die monotheistische Religion im Fragen der Gesellschaft. Ursprünge der Religion.* Bd. IX der *Sigmund Freud Studienausgabe.* Frankfurt am Main: Fischer, 1974, 455–581.

Fries, Albert. "Hoffnung und Heilsgewissheit bei Thomas von Aquin." In *Studia Moralia,* vol. 8 (Contributiones ad problema spei) (7), 131–236. Paris: Desclée de Brouwer, 1969.

Fromm, Erich. *The Revolution of Hope: Toward a Humanized Technology.* New York: Harper and Row, 1968.

Gauthier, René-Antoine. *Magnanimité. L'idéal de la grandeur dans la philosophie païenne et dans la théologie chrétienne.* Paris: Vrin, 1951.

Geach, Peter. *The Virtues. The Stanton Lectures 1973–74.* Cambridge: Cambridge University Press, 1977.

Gehlen, Arnold. *Man: His Nature and Place in the World.* Translated by Clare McMillan and Karl Pillemer. New York: Columbia University Press, 1988. [*Der Mensch. Seine Natur und seine Stellung in der Welt.* Bonn: Athenäum, 1950.]

Geiger, Louis. *La participation dans la philosophie de saint Thomas.* Paris: Vrin, 1942.

──────. "L'homme, image de Dieu. A propos de *Summa theologiae,* I, 93, 4." *Rivista di Filosofia Neo-Scolastica* 66 (1974): 511–32.

Gide, André. *Journals.* 4 vols. Translated by Justin O'Brien. Chicago: University of Illinois Press, 2000. [*Journal 1889–1939.* Paris: Gallimard, 1939].

Gillon, L. B. "Certitude de notre espérance." *Revue thomiste* 47/2 (1939): 232–48.

Giovanni, Alberto di. "Speranza e storia." *Rivista di filosofia Neo-Scolastica* 63 (1971): 623–45.

──────. *Escatologia, speranza e storia.* Firenze: La Nuova Italia, 1972.

Girardi, Jules, and Jean-François Six, eds. *L'athéisme dans la philosophie contemporaine* or *Des chrétiens interrogent l'athéisme.* Paris, Desclée, 1967ff.

Glenn, Marie Michael. *A Comparison of the Thomistic and the Scotistic Concepts of Hope.* Notre Dame: University of Notre Dame Press, 1956.

Godfrey, Joseph J. *A Philosophy of Human Hope*. Dordrecht: Martinus Nijhoff Publishers, 1987.

Goethe, Johann Wolfgang. "Die Natur." In *Sämtliche Werke,* vol. 16, part one. *Naturwissenschaftliche Schriften.* Zürich: Artemis, 1977.

Gouhier, Henri. *L'Histoire et sa philosophie*. Paris: Vrin, 1952.

Grazia, Diego. "Pensar la esperanza en el horizonte de la postmodernidad I e II." *Rivesta de filosofia* 8 (1985): 113–48 and 391–415.

Grentrup, Theodor. *Hoffen und Vertrauen.* Würzburg: Echter Verlag, 1948.

Greshake, Gisbert, and Gerhard Lohfink. *Naherwartung-Auferstehung-Unsterblichkeit. Untersuchungen zur christlichen eschatologie.* Freiburg: Herder, 1982.

Grimaldi, Nicolas. *Le désir et le temps*. Paris: Vrin, 1992.

――――. *Ontologie du temps. L'attente et la rupture.* Paris: Presses Universitaires de France, 1993.

Gueroult, Martial. "Les postulats de la philosophie de l'histoire. Le sens de l'histoire." *Revue de Métaphysique et de Morale* 91/4 (1986): 435–44.

――――. *L'histoire de l'histoire de la philosophie.* 3 vols. Paris: Aubier, 1988.

Guindon, Roger. *Béatitude et théologie morale chez saint Thomas d'Aquin. Origines–Interprétation.* Ottawa: Editions de l'Université d'Ottawa, 1956.

Guise, René. "Les romans de 'fin du monde': le problème de la mort collective dans la littérature de l'imaginaire au XIXème siècle." In *La mort en toutes lettres,* 171–81. France: Presses Universitaires de Nancy, 1983.

Günther, Joachim. "Josef Pieper 75 Jahre." *Neue Deutsche Hefte* 25, cahier 2, no. 162 (1979): 443–49.

Gusdorf, Georges. *La vertu de force.* Paris: Presses Universitaires de France, 1967.

Haas, John M. *The Holy and the Good. The Relationship between Religion and Morality in the Thought of Rudolf Otto and Josef Pieper.* Washington D.C.: The Catholic University of America, 1988.

――――. "Come Pieper ripensa Tommaso d'Aquino." In *La Filosofia cristiana del novecento (I). Josef Pieper,* edited by B. Schumacher, 51–66. Rome: Edizioni Romane di Cultura, 1997.

Habichler, Alfred. *Reich Gottes als Thema des Denkens bei Kant. Entwicklungsgeschichtliche und systematische Studie zur kantischen Reich-Gottes-Idee.* Mainz: Matthias Grünewald Verlag, 1989.

Hacks, Peter. "Das Poetische." In *Das Poetische. Ansätze zu einer postrevolutionären Dramaturgie,* 118–37. Frankfurt am Main: Suhrkamp, 1972.

Hamain, L. "Morale chrétienne et réalités terrestres. Une réponse de saint Thomas d'Aquin: la 'béatitude imparfaite.'" *Recherches de théologie ancienne et médiévale* 34 (1967): 134–76 and 35 (1968): 260–90.

Hamonic, Thierry-Marie. "Dieu peut-il être légitimement convoité?" *Revue Thomiste* 100 (1992): 239–64.

Harent, S. "Espérance." In *Dictionnaire de Théologie Catholique,* vol. 5, part 1, 605–76. Paris: Librairie Letouzey et Ané, 1939.

Harrison, Jonathan. "Christian Virtues." In *Ethical Essays,* vol. 2. Aldershot: Avebury, 1993.

Hartmann, Nicolai. *Möglichkeit und Wirklichkeit.* Berlin: Walter de Gruyter, 1938.

Hawoll, Hans-Jürgen. *Nihilismus und Metaphysik. Entwicklungsgeschichtliche Untersuchung vom deutschen Idealismus bis zu Heidegger.* Stuttgart: Frommann-Holzboog, 1989.

Hegel, Georg Wilhelm Friedrich. *Lectures on the Philosophy of World History. Introduction: Reason in History.* Translated by H. B. Nisbet. Cambridge: Cambridge University Press, 1975. [*Die Vernunft in der Geschichte.* Hamburg: Felix Meiner Verlag, 1955].

Heidegger, Martin. *Platons Lehre von der Wahrheit. Mit einem Brief über den 'Humanismus.'* Bern: Francke, 1947.

———. *Being and Time.* Translated by John Macquarrie and Edward Robinson. San Francisco: Harper and Row, 1962. [Original title: *Sein und Zeit.* Tübingen: Max Niemeyer, 1986.]

Hempel, Hans-Peter. "Das Sein-und-Zeit-Verständnis Ernst Blochs." In *Bloch-Almanach,* edited by Ernst Bloch. Ludwigshafen: Archiv der Stadtbibliothek, 6, 11–29, 1986.

Hersch, Jeanne. "'Was kann ich wissen? Was soll ich tun? Was darf ich hoffen?' Essai de paraphrase anachronique et inactuelle." In *Savoir, faire, espérer: les limites de la raison,* 345–67. Bruxelles: Faculté Universitaires St. Louis, 1976.

Hirsch, Eike Christian. *Höchstes Gut und Reich Gottes in Kants kritischen Hauptwerken als Beispiel für die Säkularisierung seiner Metaphysik.* Heidelberg, 1969.

Hofmeier, Johann. "Espérance: instinct, passion, compréhension." *Concilium* 59 (1970): 29–37.

Hollenbach, Johannes Michael. *Sein und Gewissen. Über den Ursprung der Gewissensregung. Eine Begegnung zwischen Martin Heidegger und thomistischer Philosophie.* Baden-Baden: Bruno Grimm, Verlag für Kunst und Wissenschaft, 1954.

Holte, Ragnar. *Béatitude et sagesse. Saint Augustin et le problème de la fin de l'homme dans la philosophie ancienne.* Paris: Études Augustiniennes, 1962.

Holz, Hans Heinz. "Kategorie Möglichkeit und Moduslehre." In *Ernst Bloch zu ehren. Beiträge zu seinem Werk,* edited by S. Unseld, 99–120. Frankfurt am Main: Suhrkamp, 1965.

Horkheimer, Max. *Die Sehnsucht nach dem ganz Anderen. Ein Interview mit Kommentar von H. Gumnior.* Hamburg: Fuche-Verlag, 1970.

Hufnagel, Alfons. *Intuition und Erkenntnis nach Thomas von Aquin.* Münster in Westfalen: Verlag der Aschendorffschen Verlagsbuchhandlung, 1932.

Humboldt, Wilhelm von. *Wilhelm und Caroline von Humboldt in ihren Briefen.* vol. 4. Reprint of the 1907–1918 edition. Osnabrück: Otto Zeller, 1968.

Hume, David. *A Treatise of Human Nature.* Edited by D. F. Norton and M. J. Norton. Oxford: Oxford University Press, 2001.

Huntington, Samuel. *The Clash of Civilizations and the Remaking of World Order.* New York: Simon and Schuster, 1996.

Hutschnecker, M. D., and Arnold A. *Hope: The Dynamics of Self-Fulfillment.* New York: G. P. Putnam's Sons, 1981.

Huxley, Aldous. *Brave New World Revisited.* New York: Harper and Brothers, 1958.

Inagaki, B. T. "Pieper's Philosophy of Culture." *Century* (Tokyo) 11 (1959): 45–51.

Inge, William Ralph. *The Idea of Progress.* Oxford: The Clarendon Press, 1920.

Jaccard, Roland. *La tentation nihiliste.* Paris: Presses Universitaires de France, 1989, 1991.

Jankélévitch, Vladimir. *L'aventure, l'ennui, le sérieux.* Paris: Aubier, Montaigne, 1963.

_____. *Traité des vertus.* 3 vols. Paris: Bordas/Mouton, 1968ff.

Jannoud, Claude. *Au rendez-vous du nihilisme. Symptômes.* Paris: Arléa, 1989.

Jaspers, Karl. *Die Atombombe und die Zukunft des Menschen–Politisches Bewusstsein in unserer Zeit.* München: Piper, 1958.

_____. "Wo stehen wir heute?" In *Wo stehen wir heute?,* various authors, 33–46. Gütersloh: Bertelsmann, 1960.

_____. "Die Kraft der Hoffnung." *Merkur* 17, no. 181 (1963): 213–22.

_____. *Philosophy.* 3 vols. Translated by E. B. Ashton. Chicago & London: University of Chicago Press, 1970. [*Philosophie.* Berlin, Göttingen, Heidelberg: Springer, 1948].

_____. *Vom Ursprung und Ziel der Geschichte.* München: Piper, 1988.

Jauss, Hans Robert. "Ursprung und Bedeutung der Fortschrittsidee in der 'Querelle des Anciens et des Modernes?'" In *Die Philosophie und die Frage nach dem Fortschritt,* edited by H. Kuhn and Fr. Wiedemann, 51–72. München: Anton Pustet, 1964.

Jolivet, Régis. *L'intuition intellectuelle et le problème de la métaphysique.* Paris: Beauchesne, 1934.

_____. *Le problème de la mort chez M. Heidegger et J. P. Sartre.* Abbaye Saint Wandrille: Éditions de Fontenelle, 1950.

Jonas, Hans. *The Phenomenon of Life: Toward a Philosophical Biology.* Chicago: The University of Chicago Press, 1966.

Jüngel, Eberhard. *Tod.* Stuttgart: Kreuz, 1971.

Kaltenbrunner, Gerd-Klaus, ed. *Das Geschäft der Tröster. Hoffnung zum halben Preis.* Freiburg: Herder, 1980.

Kant, Immanuel. *Kants Werke.* Berlin, G. Reimer, (A.B.), 1902–38.

_____. *Religion Within the Limits of Reason Alone.* Translated by Theodore M. Greene and Hoyt H. Hudson. New York: Harper and Row, 1960.

_____. "Speculative Beginning of Human History." In *Perpetual Peace and Other Essays on Politics, History, and Morals.* Translated by Ted Humphrey, 49–60. Indianapolis: Hackett, 1983.

_____. "To Perpetual Peace: A Philosophical Sketch" In *Perpetual Peace and Other Essays on Politics, History, and* Morals. Translated by Ted Humphrey, 107–43. Indianapolis: Hackett, 1983.

_____. "The Contest of the Faculties." In *Kant's Political Writings.* 2nd ed. Translated by H. B. Nisbett. Cambridge: Cambridge University Press, 1990.

_____. "The End of All Things." In *Essays and Treatises.* 2 vols. Translated by Giuseppe Micheli, II, 423–44. Bristol, England: Theommes, 1993.

_____. "Of a Gentle Tone Lately Assumed in Philosophy (1796)." In *Essays and Treatises.* 2 vols. Translated by Giuseppe Micheli, II, 159–87. Bristol, England: Theommes, 1993.

_____. "What Means, to Orient Oneself in Thinking?" In *Essays and Treatises.* 2 vols. Translated by Giuseppe Micheli, II, 385–407. Bristol, England: Theommes, 1993.

Kast, Verena. *Freude. Inspiration. Hoffnung.* Olten: Walter Verlag, 1991.

Kierkegaard, Søren. *The Sickness Unto Death.* Translated by Howard V. and Edna H. Hong. Princeton: Princeton University Press, 1980.

Kijm, J. M. "L'expérience du vide." In *Situation I. Beiträge zur phäno-menologischen Psychologie und Psychopathologie,* 150–71. Utrecht: Antwerpen, 1954.

Kleber, Hermann. *Glück als Lebensziel. Untersuchungen zur Philosophie des Glücks bei Thomas von Aquin.* Münster: Aschendorff, 1988.

Klima, Ladislav. *Le monde comme conscience et comme rien.* Translated by E. Abrams. Paris: Edition de la Différence, 1995.

Kluxen, Wolfgang. "Anima separata und Personsein bei Thomas von Aquin." In *Thomas von Aquin. Interpretation und Rezeption,* edited by W. P. Eckert, 96–116. Mainz: Matthias Grünewald, 1974.

_____. *Philosophische Ethik bei Thomas von Aquin.* Hamburg: Félix Meiner Verlag, 1980.

Kopf, Albert. *Der Weg des Nihilismus von Friedrich Nietzsche bis zur Atombombe.* München: Minerva-Publikation, 1988.

Kranz, Gisbert. "Der Philosoph und der Dichter. Zum Werk von Josef Pieper." *Salzburger Jahrbuch für Philosophie* 20 (1975): 131–51.

Kuhn, Helmut. "Die Weisheit der Alten in unsere Zeit. Zum 70. Geburtstag von Josef Pieper." *Philosophisches Jahrbuch* 81 (1974): 350–61.

_____. "'Veritas filia temporis.' Über die Glaubwürdigkeit der Geschichtsphilosophie." *Philosophisches Jahrbuch* 84 (1977): 13–34.

Kuhn, Hermann, and Fr. Wiedemann, eds. *Die Philosophie und die Frage nach dem Fortschritt.* München: Anton Pustet, 1964.

Kunisch, Hermann. "Sapientis est ordinare. Josef Pieper zum 85. Geburtstag." *Communio* (1989): 267–75.

Labourdette, Marie-Michel. *Cours de théologie morale. L'espérance (Thomas d'Aquin: Somme théologique, II–II, q.17–22).* Photocopied lecture from 1959–60, 1959.

Lachelier, Jules. *Oeuvres de Jules Lachelier.* 2 vols. Paris: Félix Alcan, 1933.

Lachenmann, Hans. *Hoffnung oder Illusion? Die Frage nach der Zukunft im Werk Teilhard de Chardins.* Konstanz: Friedrich Bahn Verlag, 1965.

Lacoste, Jean-Yves. *Notes sur le temps. Essai sur les raisons de la mémoire et de l'espérance.* Paris: Presses Universitaires de France, 1990.

Ladrière, Jean. "Raison et eschatologie." *Revue de l'Université d'Ottawa.* LV, no. 4 (1985): 173–92.

Lain Entralgo, Pedro. *L'attente et l'espérance. Histoire et théorie de l'espérance humaine.* Paris: Desclée de Brouwer, 1966.

_____. *Anthropologia de la esperanza.* Barcelona: Labor, 1978.

Lalande, André. *Vocabulaire technique et critique de la philosophie.* Paris: Presses Universitaires de France, 1926, 1986.

Landgrebe, Ludwig. "Das philosophische Problem des Endes der Geschichte." In *Phänomenologie und Geschichte,* 182–201. Gütersloh: G. Mohn, 1967.

Landsberg, Paul-Louis. *The Experience of Death: The Moral Problem of Suicide.* Translated by Cynthia Rowland. New York: Arno, 1977. [*Essai sur l'expérience de la mort et Le problème moral du suicide.* Paris, Seuil: 1951, 1993].

Laporta, Jorge. *La destinée de la nature humaine selon Thomas d'Aquin.* Paris: Vrin, 1965.

_____. "Pour trouver le sens exact des termes *appetitus naturalis, desiderium naturale, amor naturalis,* etc. chez Thomas d'Aquin." *Archives d'histoire doctrinale et littéraire du moyen-âge* 48 (1973): 37–95.

Lasch, Christopher. *The True and Only Heaven: Progress and Its Critics.* New York: W. W. Norton, 1991.

Lash, Nicholas. *A Matter of Hope: A Theologian's Reflection on the Thought of Karl Marx.* Notre Dame: University of Notre Dame Press, 1981.

Lauand, Luiz Jean. *O que e una universidade? Introdução a filosofia da educacão de Josef Pieper.* São Paulo: Universidade de São Paulo, 1987.

Leeuw, Gerardus van der. *La religion dans son essence et ses manifestations. Phénoménologie de la religion.* Paris: Payot, 1970.

Leist, Fritz. *Existenz im Nichts. Versuch einer Analyse des Nihilismus.* München: Manz Verlag, 1961.

Lemaire, Benoit. *L'espérance sans illusion. L'espérance chrétienne dans la perspective de Gustave Thibon.* Montréal: Paulines, 1980.

Leopardi, Giacomo. *Opere.* Milan/Rome: Zibaldone, 1937.

Lersch, Philippe. *Aufbau der Person.* München: J. A. Barth, 1956.

Le Senne, René. *La découverte de Dieu.* Paris: Aubier, Montaigne (in particular the chapter "Introduction à la description de l'espérance" [revised between 1939 and 1942] published in *Giornale di Metafisica* 10 (1955): 361–83).

Levy, Benny and Jean-Paul Sartre. *Hope Now: The 1980 Interviews.* Translated by Adrian van den Hoven. Chicago and London: University of Chicago Press, 1996. [*L'espoir maintenant. Les entretiens de 1980.* Lagrasse: Verdier, 1991.]

Link, H. G. "Hoffnung." In *Historisches Wörterbuch der Philosophie,* vol. 3, 1157–66. Darmstadt: Schwabe, 1974.

Lohfink, Gerhard, and Gisbert Greshake. *Naherwartung– Auferstehung–Unsterblichkeit. Untersuchungen zur christlichen eschatologie.* Freiburg: Herder, 1982.

Lopez-Mendez, Antonio. *Die Hoffnung im theologischen Denken Teilhard de Chardins. Hoffnung als Synthese: Versuch einer systematischen Darstellung.* Bern: Peter Lang, 1976.

Lorenz, Konrad. "Die Hoffnung auf Einsicht in das Wirken der Natur." In *Die Hoffnungen unserer Zeit,* 141–59. München: Piper, 1963.

———. *On Aggression.* Translated by Marjorie Kerr Wilson. New York: Harcourt, Brace and World, 1966. [*Das sogennante Böse. Zur Naturgeschichte der Agression.* München: Deutscher Taschenbuch Verlag, 1963, 1992].

Löw, Reinhard, and Robert Spämann. *Die Frage wozu? Geschichte und Wiederentdeckung des teleologischen Denkens.* München: Piper, 1991.

Löwith, Karl. "The Theological Background of the Philosophy of History." *Social Research* (1946): 51–80.

———. *Weltgeschichte und Heilsgeschehen. Die theologischen Voraussetzungen der Geschichtsphilosophie.* Stuttgart/Berlin: Kohlhammer, 1949, 1990. [*Meaning in History. The Theological Implications of the Philosophy of History.* Chicago: University of Chicago Press, 1949].

———. "Vom Sinn der Geschichte." In *Der Sinn der Geschichte,* edited by L. Reinisch, 31–49. München: Beck, 1961.

———. "Besprechung des Buches *Die Legitimität der Neuzeit* von Hans Blumenberg." In *Sämtliche Schriften* vol. 2, 452–59. Stuttgart: J. B. Metzlersche Verlagsbuchhandlung, 1983.

Lubac, Henri de. *Le drame de l'humanisme athée.* Paris: Cerf, 1983.

Lübbe, Hermann. *Säkularisierung. Geschichte eines ideenpolitischen Begriffs.* Freiburg: Karl Alber Verlag, 1965.

———. *Fortschritt als Orientierungsproblem. Aufklärung in der Gegenwart.* Freiburg: Rombach, 1975.

Luyten, Norbert. *Mensch-Sein als Aufgabe.* Freiburg: Universitätsverlag Freiburg Schweiz, 1985.

Lynch, William F. *Images of Hope. Imagination as Healer of the Hopeless.* New York/Toronto: The New American Library, 1966.

———. "The Absolute Enemy of Hope." In *The Source of Hope,* edited by R. Fitzgerald, 36–43. Rushcutters Bay, Australia: Pergamon Press, 1979.

MacInerny, Ralph. *Aquinas on Human Action: A Theory of Practice.* Washington, D.C.: The Catholic University of America Press, 1992.

MacIntyre, Alasdair. *After Virtue: A Study in Moral Theory.* Notre Dame, Ind.: University of Notre Dame Press, 1981, 1984.

Mackenzie, Robert. *The Nineteenth Century: A History.* London: T. Nelson and Sons, Paternoster Row, 1885.

Madaule, Jacques. "Est-il encore possible de donner un sens à l'histoire?" *Comprendre* 43/44 (1978): 82–90.

Maier, Hans. "Das Heilige Denken. Zum Werk Josef Pieper." In *Aufklärung durch Tradition. Symposium aus Anlass des 90. Geburtstags von Josef Pieper im Mai 1994 in Münster,* (Dokumentationen der Josef Pieper Stiftung, Band 1), edited by H. Fechtrupp, Fr. Schulze, and Th. Sternberg, 27–40. Münster: Lit Verlag, 1995.

Malvezzi, Piero, and Giovanni Pirelli. *Lettere di condannati a morte della Resistenza italiana (8 settembre 1943–25 aprile 1945)*. Torino: Einaudi, 1994.

Marcel, Gabriel. *Homo viator: Introduction to a Metaphysic of Hope*. Translated by Emma Craufurd. Chicago: Henry Regnery, 1951. [*Homo viator. Prolégomènes à une métaphysique de l'espérance*. Paris: Aubier, 1944.]

———. *The Mystery of Being*. Translated by René Hague. Chicago: Henry Regnery, 1951, 2 vols. [*Le mystère de l'être*, 2 tomes, Paris, Aubier, 1951.]

———. "Structure de l'espérance." *Dieu Vivant* 19 (1951): 73–80.

———. *Man Against Mass Society*. Translated by G. S. Fraser. Chicago: Regnery, 1952. [*Les hommes contre l'humain*. Paris: Editions Universitaires, 1991.]

———. *Le déclin de la sagesse*. Paris: Plon, 1954.

———. *The Existential Background of Human Dignity*. Cambridge: Harvard University Press, 1963. [*La dignité humaine et ses assises existentielles*. Paris: Aubier, Montaigne, 1964.]

———. *Being and Having: An Existential Diary*. Translated by Katherine Farrer. New York: Harper & Row, 1965. [*Être et Avoir*. Paris: Aubie, Montaigne, 1935.]

———. *Presence and Immortality*. Translated by Michael A. Machado. Pittsburgh: Duquesne, 1967. [*Présence et immortalité*. Paris: Flammarion, 1969.]

———. *Problematic Man*. Translated by Brian Thompson. New York: Herder and Herder, 1967. [*L'homme problématique*. Paris: Aubier, Montaigne, 1955.]

———. *Tragic Wisdom and Beyond*. Translated by Stephen Jolin and Peter McCormick. Evanston: Northwestern University Press, 1973. [*Pour une Sagesse tragique et son au-delà*. Paris: Plon, 1968.]

———. "Extraits des Entretiens qui eurent lieu à Dijon les 17 et 18 mars 1973 sur la pensée de Gabriel Marcel." *Revue de métaphysique et de morale* 79 (1974): 328–410.

———. "Dialogue sur l'espérance. Gabriel Marcel et Ernst Bloch." In *Présence de Gabriel Marcel*, cahier 1, 39–74, 1979.

_____. "Concrete Approaches to Investigating the Ontological Mystery." In *Gabriel Marcel's Perspectives on the Broken World*, translated by Katherine Rose Hanley, 172–209. Milwaukee: Marquette, 1998. [*Positions et approches concrètes du mystère ontologique*. Paris/Louvain: Vrin/Nauwelaerts, 1949.]

_____. *Creative Fidelity*. Translated by Robert Rosthal. New York: Fordham University Press, 2002. [*Du refus à l'invocation*. Paris: Gallimard, 1940.]

Maritain, Jacques. *An Essay on Christian Philosophy*. Translated by Edward H. Flannery. New York: Philosophical Library, 1955. [*De la philosophie chrétienne*, In *Oeuvres complètes*. 15 volumes, Fribourg/Paris: Editions Universitaires Fribourg Suisse/ Editions Saint-Paul, 1982ff., vol. V.]

_____. *On the Philosophy of History*. Edited by Joseph Evans. New York: Scribner, 1957. [*Pour une philosophie de l'histoire*. In *Oeuvres complètes*. 15 tomes. Fribourg/Paris: Editions Universitaires Fribourg Suisse/ Editions Saint-Paul, 1982 ff., vol. X, 1985.]

Marquard, Odo. *Schwierigkeiten mit der Geschichtsphilosophie. Aufsätze*. Frankfurt am Main: Suhrkamp, 1973.

Marsch, Wolf-Dieter. *Zukunft*. Stuttgart: Kreuz-Verlag, 1969.

Martelet, Gustave. *Victoire sur la mort*. Paris: Chronique Sociale de France, 1962.

Martin, Mike W. *Self-Deception and Morality*. Lawrence, Kans.: University Press of Kansas, 1986.

Matsuda, Yoshiyuki, ed. *On 'Yutori'–Symposium on Joseph Pieper's of Leisure*. Tokyo: Sebundo-Shinkosha, 1987.

Matz, Ulrich. "Zur Problematik der heute wirksamen Staatszielvorstellungen." In *Regierbarkeit. Studien zu ihrer Problematisierung*, edited by W. Hennis, P. Graf Kielmansegg, and U. Matz, vol. 1, 82–102. Stuttgart: Klett-Cotta, 1977.

Meilaender, Gilbert. "Josef Pieper: Explorations in the Thought of a Philosopher of Virtue." *The Journal of Religious Ethics* 7 (1983): vol. 11/1 114–34. Reprinted in Meilander, *The Theory and Practice of Virtue*. Notre Dame: University of Notre Dame Press, 1984, 18–44.

_____. *The Theory and Practice of Virtue*. Notre Dame: University of Notre Dame Press, 1984.

Menninger, Karl. "Hope." *American Journal of Psychiatry,* 12, no. 6 (116) (1959): 481–91.

Menxel, François von. *Elpis. Espoir. Espérance. Études sématiques et théologiques du vocabulaire de l'espérance dans l'Hellénisme et le Judaisme avant le Nouveau Testament.* Bern: Peter Lang, 1983.

Meyer, H. *Natur und Kunst bei Aristoteles.* In *Studien zur Geschichte und Kultur des Altertums.* Vol. 10, 2nd cahier. Paderborn: Schöningh, 1919.

Middendorf, Heinrich. *Über die Hoffnung.* Würzburg: K. Triltsch, 1937. (Republished Amsterdam: Rodopi, 1985.)

Millan Puelles, Antonio. *La sintesis humana de naturaleza y libertad.* Madrid: Ateneo, 1961.

Minkowski, Eugène. "L'espérance." *Tijdschrift voor filosofie* 21/1 (1959): 96–107.

Mollard, Georges. "Le problème de l'unité de l'espérance." *Revue Thomiste* 18 (1935): 196–210.

Möller, Charles. *Littérature du XXème siècle et Christianisme.* Vol. 3. Paris and Tournai: Casterman, 1957; *Espoir des hommes.* Vol. 4 of *L'espérance en Dieu notre Père,* (1960).

Moltmann, Jürgen. *Theologie der Hoffnung.* Gütersloh: Kaiser TB, 1964, 1997.

———. *Umkehr zur Zukunft.* München: 1970, 1992.

Montanari, G. "La distinzione tra 'voluntas ut natura' e 'voluntas ut ratio' nella doctrina tomista della libertà." *Aquinas* 5 (1962): 58–100.

Morin, Edgar. *L'homme et la mort.* Paris: Seuil, 1970.

Mounier, Emmanuel. *L'espoir des désespérés.* Paris: Seuil, 1953.

Müller, Klaus. "Über das rechte Verhältnis von Philosophie und Theologie. Josef Pieper im Kontext einer neu entfachten Debatte." In *Die Wahrheit und das Gute* (Dokumentationen der Josef Pieper Stiftung, Band 4), edited by H. Fechtrupp, Fr. Schulze, and Th. Sternberg, 75–93. Münster: Lit Verlag, 1999.

Mundhenk, Johannes. *Die Seele im System des Thomas von Aquin. Ein Beitrag zur Beurteilung der Grundbegriffe der thomistischen Psychologie.* Hamburg: Felix Meiner Verlag, 1980.

Munos-Alonso, A. "Las esperanzas humanas y su fundamento." In *Speranza Teologale e speranza umane* (acte du colloque de Florence sur l'espérance en juin 1955), 152–57. Firenze: Tipografia 'L'impronta,' 1955.

Münster, Arno. *Ernst Bloch, messianisme et utopie. Introduction à une 'phénoménologie' de la conscience anticipante,* with Ernst Bloch's final interview as an appendix. Paris: Presses Universitaires de France, 1989.

Mury, Gilbert. "Le marxiste devant la mort." *La Vie Spirituelle. Supplément* 77 (May 1966): 230–54.

Muyskens, James Leroy. *The Sufficiency of Hope: The Conceptual Foundations of Religions.* Philadelphia: Temple University Press, 1979.

Napoli, Giovanni di. "Storia e speranza." *Rassegna di Scienze filosofiche* 30 (1977): 43–84.

Nédoncelle, Maurice. *Vers une philosophie de l'amour et de la personne.* Paris: Aubier, Montaigne, 1957.

Nevent, E. "La vertu d'espérance. Son caractère surnaturel." *Divus Thomas* 39 (1936): 97–112.

Newman, John Henry. *An Essay in Aid of a Grammar of Assent.* London: Longmans, Green and Co., 1924.

Nietzsche, Friedrich. *Human, All-Too Human: A Book for Free Spirits.* 2 vols. Translated by Helen Zimmern. New York: Russell and Russell, 1964.

―――. *The Will to Power.* 2 vols. Translated by Anthony M. Ludovici. New York: Russell and Russell, 1964.

―――. *Beyond Good and Evil.* Translated by Walter Kaufmann. New York: Vintage Books, 1966.

―――. *Thus Spoke Zarathustra.* In *The Portable Nietzsche.* Translated by Walter Kaufmann. Middlesex: Penguin, 1979.

―――. *Sämtliche Werke. Kritische Studienausgabe.* 15 vols. Berlin and New York: Walter de Gruyter, 1980.

―――. *On the Genealogy of Morals and Ecce Homo.* Translated by Walter Kaufmann. New York: Vintage Books, 1989.

Nink, Caspar. *Metaphysik des sittlich Guten.* Freiburg: Herder, 1955.

Nisbert, Robert. *History of the Idea of Progress.* New York: Basic Books, 1980.

Nowotny, Joan. "Despair and the Object of Hope." In *The Sources of Hope,* edited by R. Fitzgerald, 44–66. Rushcutters Bay, Australia: Pergamon Press, 1979.

O'Riordan, Sean. "The Psychology of Hope." *Studia Moralia* 7 (1969): 33–55.

Olivier, Harold H. "Relational Metaphysics and the Human Future." In *The Sources of Hope,* edited by R. Fitzgerald, 176–97. Rushcutters Bay, Australia: Pergamon Press, 1979.

Oppenheimer, J. Robert. *The Flying Trapeze: Three Crises for Physicists.* London: Oxford University Press, 1964.

Ormea, Ferdinando. "Marxisten angesichts des Todes." *Internationale Dialog Zeitschrift 3,* 2nd cahier (1970): 98–114.

Pannenberg, Wolfhart. *What is Man? Contemporary Anthropology in Theological Perspective.* Translated by Duane A. Priebe. Philadelphia: Fortress, 1970. [*Was ist der Mensch?* Göttingen: Vandenhoeck and Ruprecht, 1964.]

Pascal. *Pensées.* Translated by A. J. Krailsheimer. London: Penguin, 1966.

_____. *Oeuvres complètes.* Paris: Gallimard (Pléiade), 1969.

Pasqua, Hervé. *Bas-fonds et profondeur. Critique de l'idolâtrie et métaphysique de l'espérance. Essai sur la philosophie de Gustave Thibon.* Paris: Klincksieck, 1985.

Paul, Jean-Marie. *Dieu est mort en Allemagne. Des Lumières à Nietzsche.* Paris: Payot, 1994.

Peghaire, Julien. *Intellectus et ratio selon S. Thomas d'Aquin.* Paris/Ottawa: Vrin/Institut d'Études Médiévales, 1936.

Pellegrino, Ubaldo. "Crisi dell'uomo e metafisica in Josef Pieper." In *S. Tommaso e il pensiero moderno,* 316–30. Rome: Città Nuova Editrice, 1974.

_____. "Antropologia naturale e suprannaturale in Josef Pieper." In *S. Tommaso d'Aquino nel suo settimo centenario.* Vol. 7, 126–35. Napoli: Edizioni domenicane italiane, 1978.

_____. "Verità e antropologia in Josef Pieper." Introduction to *Verità delle cose. Un'indagine sull'antropologia del Medio Evo,* by J. Pieper, 5–28. Milano: Massimo, 1981.

_____. "Crisi dell'uomo e metafisica in Josef Pieper." In *La Filosofia cristiana del novecento (I). Josef Pieper,* edited by B. Schumacher, 31–40. Rome: Edizioni Romane di Cultura, 1997.

Pelletier, Lucien. "Libération et salut d'après Ernst Bloch." Vol. 1 of *Laval théologique et philosophique* 41 (June 1985): 171–93 and Vol. 2 (October 1985): 417–31.

Penzo, Giorgio. *Il nichilismo da Nietzsche a Sartre.* Rome: Città Nuova, 1976.

Pestieau, Joseph. *L'espoir incertain. Essai sur le pouvoir.* Louvain-la-Neuve: Éditions de l'Institut Supérieur de Philosophie, 1984.

Peters, Curtis Harold. *Immanuel Kant on Hope.* Ph.D. diss., Washington University, 1975.

Philonenko, Alexis. *La théorie kantienne de l'histoire.* Paris: Vrin, 1982.

――――. "L'idée de progrès chez Kant." In *Études kantiennes* by Alexis Philonenko, 52–75. Paris: Vrin, 1982.

Pinckaers, Servais. "La nature vertueuse de l'espérance." In *Le renouveau de la morale*, by Servais Pinckaers, 178–240. Tournai: Castermann, 1964. (Reprint of a part of his doctoral dissertation, with the same title, Angelicum, 1959.)

Pirelli, Giovanni, and Piero Malvezzi. *Lettere di condannati a morte della Resistenza italiana (8 settembre 1943–25 aprile 1945.* Torino: Einaudi, 1994.

Plato. *Complete Works.* Edited by John M. Cooper. Indianapolis: Hackett, 1997.

Plourde, Simone. *Gabriel Marcel. Philosophe et témoin de l'espérance.* Montréal: Les Presses de l'Université du Québec, 1975.

Plügge, Herbert. "Über suizidale Kranke." *Psyche,* 7th cahier 5 (1951): 433–50.

――――. "Über die Hoffnung." In *Situation I. Beiträge zur phänomenologischen Psychologie und Psychopathologie,* 54–67. Utrecht: Antwerpen, 1954.

Pluta, Olaf. *Kritiker der Unsterblichkeitsdoktrin in Mittelalter und Renaissance.* Amsterdam: Grüner, 1986.

Pohier, J. M. "Psychology and Virtue." *New Blackfriars* 50 (1969).

Pohlenz, Max. *Die Stoa. Geschichte einer geistigen Bewegung.* 2 vols. Göttingen: Vandenhoeck, Ruprecht, 1948.

Pojman, Louis P. *Religious Belief and the Will.* London: Routledge and Kegan Paul, 1986.

Pollard, Sidney. *The Idea of Progress.* London: C. A. Watts, 1968.

Popper, Karl R. *The Open Society and Its Enemies.* 2 vols. London: Routledge and Kegan Paul, 1957.

Post, Werner. "Hoffnung." In *Handbuch philosophicher Grundbegriffe.* Vol. 2, 692–700. München: Kösel, 1973.

Price, Henry Habberley. *Belief.* London and New York: George Allen and Unwin Ltd, Humanities Press, 1969.

Proust, Françoise. *Kant et le ton de l'histoire.* Paris: Payot, 1991.

Quinn, Michael Sean. "Hoping." *The Southwestern Journal of Philosophy* 7/1 (1976): 53–65.

Ramirez, Santiago. "De certitudine spei christianae." *La ciencia thomista* 57 (1938): 184–206 and 353–83.

_____. *La esencia de la esperanza cristiana.* Madrid: Punta Europa, 1960.

Rapp, Friedrich. *Fortschritt. Entwicklung und Sinngehalt einer philosophischer Idee.* Darmstadt: Wissenschaftliche Buchgesellschaft, 1992.

Rassam, Joseph. "Le silence." *Revue de l'Enseignement Philosophique* 22/5 (1972): 11–31.

_____. *Le silence comme introduction à la métaphysique.* Toulouse: Association des Publications de l'Université de Toulouse-Le-Mirail, 1980.

Rauchfleisch, Udo. *Leiden-verzweifeln-hoffen.* Freiburg: Paulusverlag Freiburg Schweiz, 1991.

Raulet, Gérard. *Humanisation de la nature. Naturalisation de l'homme. Ernst Bloch ou le projet d'une autre rationalité.* Paris: Klincksieck, 1982.

Rauschning, Hermann. *Gespräche mit Hitler.* New York: Europa Verlag, 1940.

_____. *Time of Delirium.* Translated by Richard and Clara Winston. New York and London: Appleton-Century, 1946. [*Die Zeit des Deliriums.* Zürich: Amstutz, Herdeg and Co, 1948].

_____. *Masken und Metamorphosen des Nihilismus. Der Nihilismus des XX. Jahrhunderts.* Frankfurt am Main: Humboldt-Verlag, 1954.

Reeves, Hubert. *The Hour of Our Delight: Cosmic Evolution, Order and Complexity.* New York: W. H. Freeman and Company, 1991. [*L'heure de s'enivrer. L'univers a-t-il un sens?* Paris: Seuil, 1986, 1992.]

Reisinger, Ferdinand. *Der Tod im marxistischen Denken heute. Schaff, Kolakowski, Machovec, Prucha.* München: Kaiser Grünewald, 1977.

Revers, William Josef. *Die Psychologie der Langeweile.* Meisenheim am Glan: Anton Hain, 1949.

————. *Über die Hoffnung. Die anthropologische Bedeutung der Zukunft.* Salzburg: Anton Pustet, 1967.

Rhonheimer, Martin. *Natural Law and Practical Reason: A Thomistic View of Moral Autonomy.* Translated by Gerald Malsbary. New York: Fordham University Press, 2000. [*Natur als Grundlage der Moral. Die personale Struktur des Naturgesetzes bei Thomas von Aquin. Eine Auseinandersetzung mit autonomer und teleologischer Ethik.* Innsbruck: Tyrolia-Verlag, 1987.]

Ricoeur, Paul. *History and Truth.* Translated by Charles A. Kelbley. Evanston: Northwestern University Press, 1965. [*Histoire et vérité.* Paris: Seuil, 1955, 1964].

————. "Hope and the Structure of Philosophical Systems." *Proceedings of the American Catholic Philosophical Association* 44 (1970): 55–69.

Rideau, Emile. *La pensée du Père Teilhard de Chardin.* Paris: Seuil, 1965.

Riedel, Manfred. "Geschichtstheologie, Geschichtsideologie, Geschichtsphilosophie. Untersuchungen zum Ursprung und zur Systematik einer kritischen Theorie der Geschichte bei Kant." In *Philosophische Perspektiven,* (1973) 200–226.

Riet, George von. "Liberté et espérance chez Kant." *Revue philosophique de Louvain* 78, no. 38 (1980): 185–224.

Rodheudt, Guido. *Die Anwesenheit des Verborgenen. Zugänge zur Philosophie Josef Piepers.* Münster: Lit Verlag, 1997.

Rolfes, Helmuth. *Der Sinn des Lebens im marxistischen Denken. Eine kritische Darstellung.* Düsseldorf: Patmos, 1971.

Ronze, Bernard. *L'homme de quantité.* Paris: Gallimard, 1977.

Rotermundt, Rainer. *Jedes Ende ist ein Anfang. Auffassungen vom Ende der Geschichte.* Darmstadt: Wissenschaftliche Buchgesellschaft, 1994.

Rousselot, Pierre. *The Intellectualism of Saint Thomas.* New York: Sheed and Ward, 1935. [*L'intellectualisme de Saint Thomas.* Paris: Beauchesne, 1924.]

Ruiz de la Pena, Juan Luis. *Muerte y marxismo humanista.* Salamanca: Sigueme, 1978.

Sakharov, Anatoly M. "L'humanité a la possibilité d'éviter son anéantissement." *Comprendre* 43/44 (1978): 130–36.

Salomon, Albert. "The Religion of Progress." *Social Research: An International Quarterly of Political and Social Science* (1946): 441–62.

Sampson, R. V. *Progress in the Age of Reason: The Seventeenth Century to the Present Day.* Cambridge, Mass.: Harvard University Press, 1956.

Sartre, Jean-Paul. "Notes. A propos de l'existentialisme. Mise au point par J.-P. Sartre. Extraits du journal *Action.*" In *Lettres* 3, no. 1 (1945): 82–88.

_____. "Introduction." In *Descartes,* 9–52. Paris and Geneva: Trois Collines, 1946.

_____. *Situations.* 10 tomes. Paris: Gallimard, 1947.

_____. *Existentialism and Human Emotions.* Translated by Bernard Frechtman and Hazel E. Barnes. New York: Philosophical Library, 1957. [*L'existentialisme est un humanisme.* Paris: Nagel, 1946.]

_____. *The Devil and the Good Lord.* In *The Devil and the Good Lord and Two Other Plays,* translated by Kitty Black, 3–149. New York: Vintage Books, 1962. [*Le diable et le bon Dieu.* Paris: Gallimard, 1951.]

_____. *The Flies.* In *No Exit and The Flies,* translated by Stuart Gilbert. New York: Knopf, 1963. [*Les mouches.* Paris: Gallimard, 1943.]

_____. *Nausea.* Translated by Lloyd Alexander. New York: New Directions, 1964. [*La Nausée.* Paris: Gallimard, 1938.]

_____. *The Words.* Translated by Bernard Frechtman. New York: Braziller, 1964. [*Les Mots.* Paris: Gallimard, 1964.]

_____. *Anti-Semite and Jew.* Translated by George J. Becker. New York: Schocken, 1965. [*Réflexions sur la question juive.* Paris: P. Morihien, 1946.]

_____. *Situations.* Translated by Benita Eisler. New York: Braziller, 1965.

_____. *Being and Nothingness.* Translated by Hazel E. Barnes. New York: Washington Square, 1992. [*L'Être et le Néant. Essai d'ontologie phénoménologique.* Paris: Gallimard, 1943.]

Sartre, Jean-Paul, and Benny Lévy. *Hope Now: The 1980 Interviews.* Translated by Adrian van den Hoven. Chicago and London: University of Chicago Press, 1996.

Sauter, Gerhard. *Zukunft und Verheissung. Das Problem der Zukunft in der gegenwärtigen theologische und philosophische Diskussion.* Zürich: Zwingli Verlag, 1965.

Schäffler, Richard. *Was dürfen wir hoffen?* Darmstadt: Wissenschaftliche Buchgesellschaft, 1979.

_____. "Philosophie der Hoffnung als Skolastik der praktischen Vernunft." *Philosophisches Jahrbuch* 88/2 (1981): 242–56.

Scheffczyk, Leo. *'Unsterblichkeit' bei Thomas von Aquin auf dem Hintergrund der neueren Diskussion.* München: Verlag der Bayerischen Akademie der Wissenschaft, 1989.

Scheler, Max. *Tod und Fortleben.* In *Schriften aus dem Nachlass.* Vol. 1. Bern: Francke Verlag, 1957, 11–64.

_____. "Zur Rehabilitierung der Tugend (1913)." In *Vom Umsturz der Werte. Abhandlungen und Werte* in *Gesammelte Werk,* 15–31. Bern: Francke Verlag, 1972·

_____. *Ressentiment.* Translated by Lewis B. Coser and William W. Holdheim. Milwaukee: Marquette, 1984. ["Das Ressentiment im Aufbau der Moralen." In *Vom Umsturz der Werte. Abhandlungen und Werte.* In *Gesammelte Werke.* Bern, München: Francke Verlag, 1972, 33–147.]

Scherer, Georg. *Der Tod als Frage an die Freiheit.* Essen: Fredebeul and Koenen, 1971.

_____. *Das Problem des Todes in der Philosophie.* Darmstadt: Wissenschaftliche Buchgesellschaft, 1979, 1988.

_____. *Sinnerfahrung und Unsterblichkeit.* Darmstadt: Wissenschaftliche Buchgesellschaft, 1985.

Schiller, Friedrich. *Schiller's Works.* Edited by J. G. Fischer. Philadelphia: George Barrie, 1883ff. [*Werke.* P. Brandt (Hrsg.), Leipzig: Verlag Albrecht Seemann.]

Schiller, Hans-Ernst. *Metaphysik und Gesellschaftskritik. Zur Konkretisierung der Utopie im Werk Ernst Blochs.* Königstein: Forum Academicum, 1982.

Schlegel, Friedrich. *The Philosophy of History.* London: Bell and Daldy, 1873. [*Die Philosophie der Geschichte, Vorlesungen I und X,* Kritische Friedrich-Schlegel Ausgabe. München, Paderborn, Wien: Schöningh, 1971.]

Schlicht. *Das Wesen der christlichen Hoffnung.* Trier, 1906.

Schmitz, Kennith. *The Gift: Creation.* Milwaukee: Marquette University Press, 1982.

Schnoor, Heike. *Psychoanalyse der Hoffnung. Die psychische und psychosomatische Bedeutung von Hoffnung und Hoffnungslosigkeit.* Heidelberg: Roland Asanger Verlag, 1988.

Schockenhoff, Eberhard. *Bonum hominis. Die anthropologischen und theologischen Grundlagen der Tugendethik des Thomas von Aquin.* Mainz: Matthias Grünenwald, 1987.

Schottländer, Rudolf. *Theorie der Vertrauens.* Berlin: Walter de Gruyter, 1957.

Schulz, Walter. "Der Tod, die stärkste Nicht-Utopie." In *'Denken heisst Überschreiten.' In memoriam Ernst Bloch 1885–1977,* edited by K. Bloch and A. Reif, 67–69. Köln: Europäische Verlagsanstalt, 1978.

Schumacher, Bernard N. "Espérance." In *Dictionnaire d'éthique et de philosophie morale,* edited by M. Canto-Sperber, 524–28. Paris: Presses Universitaires de France, 1996.

————. *Auseinandersetzung mit dem Tod. Über das Wissen vom Tode und das Übel des Todes dargestellt im Kontext der zeitgenössischen Philosophie,* Darmstadt: Wissenschaftliche Buchgesellschaft, 2003.

————. "'Quelle ressemblance y a-t-il entre un disciple de la Grèce et un disciple du ciel?' Le rapport entre philosophie et théologie chez Josef Pieper." *Revue Philosophique de Louvain* 95/3 (1997): 457–83.

————. "Deux philosophes allemands contemporains de l'espérance: Ernst Bloch et Josef Pieper." *Revue de Métaphysique et de Morale* 1 (1999): 105–32.

————. "Esperanza e historia." *Communio,* Argentina, 6/4 (1999): 51–64.

————. "La mort comme la possibilité de l'impossibilité. Une analyse critique de Heidegger." *Archives de Philosophie* 62 (1999): 71–94.

————. ed. *La filosofia cristiana del novecento (I). Josef Pieper.* Rome: Edizioni Romane di Cultura, 1997.

————. ed. *Jean-Paul Sartre. Das Sein und das Nichts.* Berlin: Akademie Verlag, 2003.

Simon, Yves R. *Freedom of Choice.* Translated by Peter Wolff. New York: Fordham University Press, 1969. [*Traité du libre arbitre.* Fribourg: Éditions Universitaires Fribourg Suisse, 1951, 1989.]

————. *The Definition of Moral Virtue.* New York: Fordham University Press, 1986.

Six, Jean-François, and Jules Girardi, eds. *L'athéisme dans la philosophie contemporaine—Des chrétiens interrogent l'athéisme.* Paris: Desclée, 1967ff.

Smith, Morton. *Hope and History: An Exploration.* New York: Harper and Row, 1980.

Sokolowski, Robert. *The God of Faith and Reason*. Notre Dame, Ind.: University of Notre Dame, 1982.

Soloviev, Vladimir. *Trois entretiens sur la guerre, la morale et la religion*. Translated by B. Marchadier and F. Rouleau. Paris: O.E.I.L. (collection chrétienne, 2), 1984.

Sonnemans, Heino. *Hoffnung ohne Gott? In Konfrontation mit Ernst Bloch*. Freiburg: Herder, 1973.

_____. *Seele. Unsterblichkeit–Auferstehung. Zur griechischen und christlichen Anthropologie und Eschatologie*. Freiburg: Herder, 1984.

Spaemann, Robert. *Basic Moral Concepts*. Translated by T. J. Armstrong. London and New York: Routledge, 1989. [*Moralische Grundbegriffe*. München: Beck, 1982.]

Spaemann, Robert, and Reinhard Löw. *Die Frage wozu? Geschichte und Wiederentdeckung des teleologischen Denkens*. München: Piper, 1991.

Spinoza, Baruch. *Oeuvres complètes*. Paris: Gallimard, 1988.

_____. *Ethics*. Translated by G. H. R. Parkinson. Oxford: Oxford University Press, 2000.

Splett, Jörg. "'Gentleman und Christ.' Ein Bild geglückten Menschseins bei Josef Pieper." In *Die Wahrheit und das Gute* (Dokumentationen der Josef Pieper Stiftung, Band 4), edited by H. Fechtrupp, Fr. Schulze, and Th. Sternberg, 51–74. Münster: Lit Verlag, 1999.

Staehelin, Balthasar. *Haben und Sein. Ein medizinpsychologischen Vorschlag als Ergänzung zum Materialismus der heutigen Wissenschaft. Fünf Beiträge zur Wirklichkeitsanalyse*. Zürich: Theologischer Verlag, 1969, 1986.

_____. *Die Welt als Du*. Zürich: Editio Academia, 1970, 1973.

_____. *Urvertrauen und zweite Wirklichkeit. Das Ftan ist nie krank*. Zürich: Editio Academia, 1973.

_____. *Der finale Mensch. Therapie für Materialisten*. Zürich: Theologischer Verlag, 1976.

_____. *Der psychosomatische Christus*. Schaffausen: Novalis Verlag AG, 1980, 1982.

Staehelin, Balthasar, Silvio Jenny, and Stephanos Geroulanos, eds. *Hoffnung*. Engadiner Kollegium. Zürich: Editio Academica, 1979.

Stotland, Ezra. *The Psychology of Hope: An Integration of Experimental, Clinical, and Social Approaches*. San Francisco: Jossey-Bass, 1969.

Sturm, Vilma. "Das Menschenbild. Zum Werk Josef Piepers." *Schweizer Rundschau* 49, 10th cahier (1950): 673–84.

Sutherland, Stewart. "Hope." In *The Philosophy in Christianity,* edited by G. Vesey, 193–206. Cambridge: Cambridge University Press, 1989.

Teilhard de Chardin, Pierre. *The Future of Man.* Translated by Norman Denny. New York: Harper and Row, 1964. [*L'avenir de l'homme.* Vol. 5 of *Oeuvres de Teilhard de Chardin.* Paris: Seuil, 1955–76, 1959.]

———. *The Appearance of Man.* Translated by J. M. Cohen. New York: Harper and Row, 1965. [*L'apparition de l'homme.* Vol. 2 of *Oeuvres.* 1956.]

———. *The Activation of Energy.* Translated by René Hague. New York: Harcourt Brace Jovanovich, 1969. [*L'activation de l'énergie.* Vol. 7 of *Oeuvres.* 1963.]

———. *The Human Phenomenon.* Translated by Sarah Appleton-Weber. Brighton: Sussex, 1999. [*Le phénomène humain.* Vol. 1 of *Oeuvres.* 1955.]

Theunissen, Michael. *Der Begriff Verzweiflung. Korrekturen an Kierkegaard.* Frankfurt am Main: Suhrkamp, 1993.

Thibon, Gustave. *Notre regard qui manque à la lumière.* Paris: Amiot et Dumont, 1955.

Thielicke, Helmut. *Tod und Leben. Studien zur christlichen Anthropologie.* Tübingen: Möhr, 1946.

Tillich, Paul. *The Courage To Be.* New Haven: Yale University Press, 1952.

Toynbee, Arnold J. "Sinn oder Sinnlosigkeit." In *Der Sinn der Geschichte,* edited by L. Reinisch, 83–99. München: Beck, 1961.

———. "Un 'Etat mondial' est-il réalisable?" *La Table Ronde.* 234/235 (1967): 5–28.

Tugendhat, Ernst. "Antike und moderne Ethik." In *Probleme der Ethik,* 33–56. Stuttgart: Reclam, 1984.

Unamuno, Miguel de. *The Tragic Sense of Life.* Translated by J. E. Crawford Flitch. New York: Dover, 1954. [*Del sentimiento trágico de la vida. La agonía del Cristianismo.* Madrid: Ramón Akal González, 1983.]

Urdanoz, Teofilo. "Para una Filosofia y Teologia de la esperanza." *La Ciencia Tomista* 63, vol. 84, no. 264 (1957): 549–612.

Üxküll, Jakob. *Streifzüge durch die Umwelten von Tieren und Menschen. Ein Bilderbuch unsichtbarer Welten. Bedeutungslehre.* Hamburg: Rowohlt, 1956.

Vachon, Louis-Albert. *La vertu d'espérance et le péché de présomption. Leur nature et leur opposition naturelle.* Québec: Presses de l'Université Laval, 1958.

Vattimo, Gianni. *The End of Modernity: Nihilism and Hermeneutics in Postmodern Culture.* Translated by Jon R. Snyder. Baltimore: John Hopkins University Press, 1988.

Vaughn, Stanley Bruce. *Intersubjectivity as the Ground of Hope: Psychoanalytic and Theological Perspectives.* Ph.D. diss., University of Vanderbilt, 1991.

Verneaux, Roger. *Leçons sur l'athéisme contemporain.* Paris: Téqui, 1964.

Vernekohl, Wilhelm. "Deuter des christlichen Menschenbildes." In *Begegnungen,* 217–30. Regensberg: Verlag Regensberg, 1959.

Versins, Pierre. "Fins du monde." In *Encyclopédie de l'utopie des voyages extraordinaires et de la science fiction,* 325–36. Lausanne: L'Age d'homme, 1972.

Vieillard-Baron, Jean-Louis. *L'illusion historique et l'espérance céleste.* Paris: Berg International, L'Île verte, 1981.

Viviano, Benedict T. *The Kingdom of God in History.* Wilmington, Del.: Michael Glazier, 1988.

Vlachos, Georges. *La pensée politique de Kant. Métaphysique de l'ordre et dialectique du progrès.* Paris: Presses Universitaires de France, 1962.

Waffelaert, G. J. "Analysis actus spei." *Jahrbuch für Philosophie und spekulative Theologie* 4 (1890): 1–10, 210–16, 285–311.

Wald, Berthold. "Wahrheit und Sinn. Über die Konvergenz von analytischer und hermeneutischer Perspektive im Philosophiebegriff Josef Piepers." *Salzburger Jahrbuch für Philosophie* 40 (1995): 131–39.

———. "'Was ich für meine Sache halte.' Zum 90. Geburtstag von Josef Pieper." *Philosophisches Jahrbuch* 102 (1995): 113–18.

———. "Wende zum Menschen." In *Nachwort zu Josef Pieper. Werke,* vol. 5, *Schriften zur philosophischen Anthropologie und Ethik. Grundstrukturen menschlicher Existenz,* 399–410. Hamburg: Felix Meiner, 1996.

———. "Aktualität durch Enthistorisierung. Zu einem Brief von Josef Pieper an Gustav Gundlach aus der Zeit der NS-Diktatur." *Philosophisches Jarhbuch* 104 (1997): 175–81.

———. "Moralische Verbindlichkeit und menschliches Richtigsein. Zur Rehabilitierung der Tugend." *Theologie und Philosophie* 72 (1997): 553–64.

———. "Vollendete Negativität oder theologisch gegründete Weltlichkeit? Die Kulturphilosophie Josef Piepers als eine Antwort auf das Nein zur Welt." *Theologie und Glaube* 89 (1999): 219–35.

Walgrave, Jan-Hendrik. "Quelques remarques sur le désir naturel chez Saint Thomas." In *San Tommaso e l'odierna problematica teologica*, 221–30. Rome: Pontificia Accademia di San Tommaso, Città Nuova Editrice, 1974.

Welte, Bernhard. "Das Gute als Einheit des Unterschiedenen. Eine thomistische Betrachtung." In *Sein und Ethos. Untersuchung zur Grundlegung der Ethik*, edited by P. Engelhardt, 129–43. Mainz: Matthias Grünewald, 1964.

———. *Der Ernstfall der Hoffnung. Gedanken über den Tod.* Freiburg: Herder, 1980.

Weyand, Klaus. *Kants Geschichtsphilosophie. Ihre Entwicklung und ihr Verhältnis zur Aufklärung.* Köln: Kölneruniversitäts-Verlag, 1963.

Wheatley, J. M. O. "Wishing and Hoping." *Analysis,* 18/6 (June 1958): 121–31.

Widmer, Hans. *Anthropologie der Hoffnung. Einführung in Denken und Werk Pedro Lain Entralgos und kritische Darlegung von 'La espera y la esperanza.'* Ph.D. diss., Institutum philosophicum Innsbruck, 1968.

Wisser, Richard. "Philosophieren und Philosophie. Das Denken Josef Piepers und Helmut Kuhns." *Hochland* 59 (1966): 153–60.

Wittmann, Michael. *Die Ethik des Hl. Thomas von Aquin.* Frankfurt am Main: Minerva, 1962.

Wohlgschaft, Hermann. *Hoffnung angesichts des Todes. Das Todesproblem bei Karl Barth und in der zeitgenössischen Theologie des deutschen Sprachraums.* München: Schöningh, 1977.

Woschitz, Karl Matthäus. *Elpis. Hoffnung. Geschichte, Philosophie, Exegese, Theologie eines Schlüsselbegriffs.* Freiburg: Herder, 1979.

Wucherer-Huldenfeld, Augustinus. "Beiträge zur Theologie der Hoffnung." In *Personalisation. Studien zur Tiefenpsychologie und Psychotherapie,* 124–53. Freiburg: Herder, 1964.

Wust, Peter. *Peter Wust. Gesammelte Werke.* 10 vols. Edited by W. Vernekohl. Münster: Regensberg, 1963ff.

————. *Ungewissheit und Wagnis.* Vol. 4 of *Peter Wust Gesammelte Werke.* Edited by W. Vernekohl. Münster: Verlag Regensberg Münster, 1964, 25–293.

Yovel, Yirmiyahu. *Kant and the Philosophy of History.* Princeton: Princeton University Press, 1980.

Zavalloni, Roberto. *Psicologia della speranza. Per sentirsi realizzati.* Milano: Paoline, 1991.

Zimara, Coelestin. *Das Wesen der Hoffnung in Natur und Übernatur.* Paderborn: Ferdinand Schöningh, 1933.

UNIDENTIFIED AUTHORS

Filosofia e teologia della speranza. Atti del XVII convegno di assistenti universitaria di filosofia (Padova 1972). Padova: Editrice Gregoriana, 1973.

La speranza. Atti del Congresso promosso dal Pontificio Ateneo 'Antonianum' 30.V–2.VI.1982. Brescia/Rome: La Scuola Editrice/Ed. Antonianum, 1984.

"Les écrivains de la fin du monde de l'Apocalypse à la bombe atomique." *Magazine littéraire* 232 (1986): 14–46.

Speranza teologale e speranze humane. Atti del Quarto convegno internazionale per la pace et la civiltà cristiana, Firenze, 19–25 June 1955. Firenze: Tipografia 'L'impronta,' 1955.

INDEX

Page numbers in italic refer to end-of-chapter notes.